TRAINING & REFERENCE

murach's
Oracle SQL
and PL/SQL

works with all versions through 11g

Joel Murach

 MIKE MURACH & ASSOCIATES, INC.
1-800-221-5528 • (559) 440-9071 • Fax: (559) 440-0963
murachbooks@murach.com • www.murach.com

Authors:	Joel Murach
Editor:	Mike Murach
Cover Design:	Zylka Design
Production:	Tom Murach
	Cynthia Vasquez

Books for Java developers

Murach's Java SE 6

Murach's Java Servlets and JSP, Second Edition

Books for .NET developers

Murach's C# 2008

Murach's ASP.NET 3.5 Web Programming with C# 2008

Murach's Visual Basic 2008

Murach's ASP.NET 3.5 Web Programming with VB 2008

Murach's ADO.NET 2.0 Database Programming with VB 2005

Murach's SQL Server 2005 for Developers

Books for IBM mainframe programmers

Murach's OS/390 and z/OS JCL

Murach's Mainframe COBOL

Murach's CICS for the COBOL Programmer

DB2 for the COBOL Programmer, Part 1

For more on Murach books, please visit us at www.murach.com

Printed in the United States of America

10 9 8 7 6 5 4 3 2 1
ISBN: 978-1-890774-50-9

murach's
Oracle SQL
and PL/SQL

Contents

Expanded contents

Section 1 An introduction to SQL

Section 2   The essential SQL skills

Section 3 Database design and implementation

Section 4 The essential PL/SQL skills

Introduction

Since its release in 1979, Oracle Database has become the leading relational database management system in the world. Today, Oracle has a huge base of customers and continues to dominate the database market, especially for mission-critical enterprise systems. In short, Oracle Database and Oracle database programmers are here to stay.

Over the years, Oracle Database has gained a reputation for being expensive and difficult to use. Today, however, Oracle offers the Express Edition of Oracle Database as a free download. Oracle also offers a free product called SQL Developer that makes it easier to work with an Oracle database. And now, this book takes advantage of these products to make it easier than ever to master the SQL and PL/SQL skills that you need to work with an Oracle database.

Who this book is for

This book is designed for application developers who need to work with an Oracle database. It shows how to code all the SQL statements that developers need for their applications. It shows how to code these statements so they run efficiently. And it works for users of any release of Oracle Database through 10g and 11g.

This book is also a good choice for anyone who wants to learn standard SQL. Since SQL is a standard language for accessing database data, most of the SQL code in this book will work with any database management system. As a result, once you use this book to learn how to use SQL to work with an Oracle database, you can transfer most of what you have learned to another database management system such as SQL Server or DB2.

This book is also the right *first* book for anyone who wants to become a database administrator. Although this book doesn't present the advanced skills that are needed by a DBA, it will get you started in that direction. Then, when you complete this book, you'll be prepared for more advanced books on the subject.

5 reasons why you'll learn faster with this book

- Unlike most Oracle books, this one starts by showing you how to query an existing database rather than how to create a new database. Why? Because that's what you're most likely to need to do first on the job. Once you master those skills, you can learn how to design and implement a database if you need to do that. Or, you can learn how to work with other database features like transactions or stored procedures if you need to do that.

- Unlike most Oracle books, this one shows how to use Oracle SQL Developer to enter and run your SQL statements. SQL Developer is a graphical tool that's an intuitive and user-friendly replacement for SQL*Plus, an arcane command prompt tool that has been around since the early days of Oracle. As a result, using SQL Developer instead of SQL*Plus will help you learn more quickly.

- Like all our books, this one includes hundreds of examples that range from the simple to the complex. That way, you can quickly get the idea of how a feature works from the simple examples, but you'll also see how the feature is used in the real world from the complex examples.

- Like most of our books, this one has exercises at the end of each chapter that give you hands-on experience by letting you practice what you've learned. These exercises also encourage you to experiment and to apply what you've learned in new ways.

- If you page through this book, you'll see that all of the information is presented in "paired pages," with the essential syntax, examples, and guidelines on the right page and the perspective and extra explanation on the left page. This helps you learn more with less reading, and it is the ideal reference format when you need to refresh your memory about how to do something.

What you'll learn in this book

- In section 1, you'll learn the concepts and terms you need for working with any database. You'll also learn how to use Oracle Database and Oracle SQL Developer to run SQL statements on your own computer.

- In section 2, you'll learn all the SQL skills for retrieving data from a database and for adding, updating, and deleting that data. These skills move from the simple to the complex so you won't have any trouble if you're new to SQL. But these skills are also sure to raise your expertise even if you already have SQL experience.

- In section 3, you'll learn how to design a database and how to implement that design by using the DDL (Data Definition Language) statements that are a part of SQL. When you're done, you'll be able to design and implement your own database. In addition, you'll gain valuable perspective that will make you a better SQL programmer, even if you never have to design a database.

- In section 4, you'll learn how to use Oracle's procedure language, PL/SQL, to create stored procedures, functions, and triggers. In addition, you'll learn how to manage transactions and locking. Once you master these features, you'll have a powerful set of PL/SQL skills.

- In section 5, you'll learn how to work with the timestamp, interval, and large object data types. These data types became available with releases 9i and 8, and they provide features that are critical for storing data in today's global and digital world.

What software you need for this book

To run SQL statements with an Oracle database using the techniques in this book, we recommend that you use:

- The Express Edition of Oracle Database 10g or 11g

- Oracle SQL Developer

Both of these products can be downloaded for free from Oracle's web site. And appendix A of this book provides complete instructions for installing them.

If you want to use another edition of Oracle Database, you can still use the techniques described in this book. However, you may need to install that edition, and you may need to use a different procedure to connect SQL Developer to it. That's why appendix B shows you how to do both.

Unfortunately, you can't use SQL Developer to connect to versions of Oracle Database that are prior to version 9.2.0.1. So if your company is using an earlier version, one alternative is to use SQL*Plus to work with it as described in chapter 2. A better training alternative, though, is to download and install the Express Edition of Oracle Database and SQL Developer as described in appendix A. Then, when you're through training, you can use SQL*Plus or a commercial product like Toad to work with the version of Oracle Database that your company uses.

What you can download from our web site

You can download all the source code for this book from our web site. That includes:

- The script files that create and populate the database tables for the three schemas used by this book.

- The SQL, PL/SQL, and Java source code for all of the examples in this book

Here again, appendix A provides complete instructions for downloading and installing these items on your computer.

Support materials for trainers and instructors

If you're a corporate trainer or a college instructor who would like to use this book for a course, we offer an Instructor's CD that includes: (1) instructional objectives that describe the skills a student should have upon completion of each chapter; (2) the solutions to the book exercises; (3) completion and multiple-choice tests that measure mastery of the skills described in the objectives; and (4) PowerPoint slides that you can use to review and reinforce the content that's presented in the figures of the book.

To learn more about this Instructor's CD and to find out how to get it, please go to our web site at www.murach.com and click on the Trainers link or the Instructors link. Or, if you prefer, you can call Kelly at 1-800-221-5528 or send an email to kelly@murach.com.

Please let us know how this book works for you

My goals when I started this book were (1) to provide an Oracle book for application developers that will help them work more effectively; (2) to cover the database design and implementation skills that application developers are most likely to use; and (3) to do both in a way that helps you learn faster and better than you can with any other book. Now, I sincerely hope that I have succeeded.

If you have any comments about this book, I would appreciate hearing from you. Good luck with your Oracle projects!

Joel Murach, Author
joelmurach@yahoo.com

Section 1

An introduction to SQL

Before you begin to learn the fundamentals of programming in SQL, you need to understand some concepts and terms related to SQL and relational databases. That's what you'll learn in chapter 1. Then, in chapter 2, you'll learn about some of the tools you can use to work with an Oracle database. At that point, you'll have all of the background and skills that you need to work with the rest of this book.

1

An introduction to relational databases and SQL

This chapter presents the concepts and terms that you should understand before you begin learning how to use SQL to work with an Oracle database. Although this chapter doesn't present the coding details, it does present an overview of the most important types of SQL statements that are presented in this book.

An introduction to client/server systems

In case you aren't familiar with client/server systems, the topics that follow introduce you to their essential hardware and software components. When you use SQL to access an Oracle database, that system is often a client/server system.

The hardware components of a client/server system

Figure 1-1 presents the three hardware components of a client/server system: the clients, the network, and the server. The *clients* are usually the PCs that are already available on the desktops throughout a company. And the *network* is the cabling, communication lines, network interface cards, hubs, routers, and other components that connect the clients and the server.

The *server*, commonly referred to as a *database server*, is a computer that has enough processor speed, internal memory (RAM), and disk storage to store the files and databases of the system and provide services to the clients of the system. This computer can be a high-powered PC, a midrange system like an AS/400 or Unix system, or even a mainframe system. When a system consists of networks, midrange systems, and mainframe systems, often spread throughout the country or world, it is commonly referred to as an *enterprise system*.

To back up the files of a client/server system, a server usually has a tape drive or some other form of offline storage. It often has one or more printers or specialized devices that can be shared by the users of the system. And it can provide programs or services like e-mail that can be accessed by all the users of the system.

In a simple client/server system, the clients and the server are part of a *local area network* (*LAN*). However, two or more LANs that reside at separate geographical locations can be connected as part of a larger network such as a *wide area network* (*WAN*). In addition, individual systems or networks can be connected over the Internet.

A simple client/server system

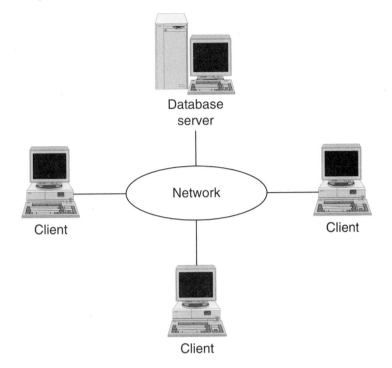

The three hardware components of a client/server system

- The *clients* are the PCs, Macintoshes, or workstations of the system.
- The *server* is a computer that stores the files and databases of the system and provides services to the clients. When it stores databases, it's often referred to as a *database server*.
- The *network* consists of the cabling, communication lines, and other components that connect the clients and the servers of the system.

Client/server system implementations

- In a simple *client/server system* like the one above, the server is typically a high-powered PC that communicates with the clients over a *local area network* (*LAN*).
- The server can also be a midrange system, like an AS/400 or a Unix system, or it can be a mainframe system. Then, special hardware and software components are required to make it possible for the clients to communicate with the midrange and mainframe systems.
- A client/server system can also consist of one or more PC-based systems, one or more midrange systems, and a mainframe system in dispersed geographical locations. This type of system is commonly referred to as an *enterprise system*.
- Individual systems and LANs can be connected and share data over larger private networks, such as a *wide area network* (*WAN*), or a public network like the Internet.

Figure 1-1   The hardware components of a client/server system

The software components of a client/server system

Figure 1-2 presents the software components of a typical client/server application. Here, the server requires a *database management system* (*DBMS*) like Oracle or Microsoft SQL Server. This DBMS manages the databases that are stored on the server.

In contrast to a server, each client requires *application software* to perform useful work. This can be a purchased software package like a financial accounting package, or it can be custom software that's developed for a specific application.

Although the application software is run on the client, it uses data that's stored on the server. To do that, it uses a *data access API* (*application programming interface*) such as JDBC. Since the technique you use to work with an API depends on the programming language and API you're using, you won't learn those techniques in this book. Instead, you'll learn about a standard language called *SQL* (*Structured Query Language*) that lets any application communicate with any DBMS. (In conversation, SQL is pronounced as either *S-Q-L* or *sequel*.)

Once the software for both client and server is installed, the client communicates with the server via *SQL queries* (or just *queries*) that are passed to the DBMS through the API. After the client sends a query to the DBMS, the DBMS interprets the query and sends the results back to the client.

In a client/server system, the processing is divided between the clients and the server. In this figure, for example, the DBMS on the server processes the requests that are made by the application running on the client. Theoretically, at least, this balances the workload between the clients and the server so the system works more efficiently.

Client software, server software, and the SQL interface

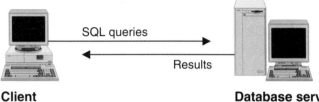

Client
Application software
Data access API

Database server
Database management system
Database

Server software

- To store and manage the databases of the client/server system, each server requires a *database management system* (*DBMS*) like Oracle.

- The processing that's done by the DBMS is typically referred to as *back-end processing*, and the database server is referred to as the *back end*.

Client software

- The *application software* does the work that the user wants to do. This type of software can be purchased or developed.

- The *data access API* (*application programming interface*) provides the interface between the application program and the DBMS. The most common data access API for Oracle is *JDBC* (*Java Database Connectivity*).

- The processing that's done by the client software is typically referred to as *front-end processing*, and the client is typically referred to as the *front end*.

The SQL interface

- The application software communicates with the DBMS by sending *SQL queries* through the data access API. When the DBMS receives a query, it provides a service like returning the requested data (the *query results*) to the client.

- *SQL* stands for *Structured Query Language*, which is the standard language for working with a relational database.

Client/server versus file-handling systems

- In a client/server system, the processing done by an application is typically divided between the client and the server.

- In a file-handling system, all of the processing is done on the clients. Although the clients may access data that's stored in files on the server, none of the processing is done by the server. As a result, a file-handling system isn't a client/server system.

Figure 1-2   The software components of a client/server system

Other client/server architectures

In its simplest form, a client/server system consists of a single database server and one or more clients. Many client/server systems today, though, include additional servers. For example, figure 1-3 shows two client/server systems that include an additional server between the clients and the database server.

The first illustration is for a simple Windows-based system. With this system, only the user interface for an application runs on the client. The rest of the processing that's done by the application is stored in one or more *business components* on the *application server*. Then, the client sends requests to the application server for processing. If the request involves accessing data in a database, the application server formulates the appropriate query and passes it on to the database server. The results of the query are then sent back to the application server, which processes the results and sends the appropriate response back to the client.

Similar processing is done by a web-based system, as illustrated by the second example in this figure. In this case, though, a *web browser* running on the client is used to send requests to a *web application* running on a *web server* somewhere on the Internet. The web application, in turn, can use *web services* to perform some of its processing. Then, the web application or web service can pass requests for data on to the database server.

Although this figure should give you an idea of how client/server systems can be configured, you should realize that they can be much more complicated than what's shown here. For example, business components can be distributed over any number of application servers, and those components can communicate with databases on any number of database servers. Similarly, the web applications and services in a web-based system can be distributed over numerous web servers that access numerous database servers. In most cases, though, you don't need to know how a system is configured to use SQL.

Before I go on, you should know that client/server systems aren't the only systems that support SQL. For example, traditional mainframe systems and newer *thin client* systems also use SQL. Unlike client/server systems, though, most of the processing for these types of systems is done by a mainframe or another high-powered machine. The terminals or PCs that are connected to the system do little or no work.

An application that uses an application server

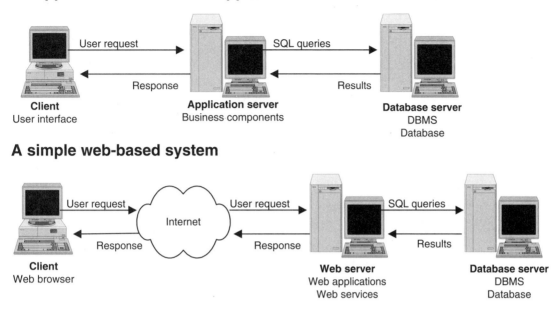

A simple web-based system

Description

- In addition to a database server and clients, a client-server system can include additional servers, such as *application servers* and *web servers*.

- Application servers are typically used to store *business components* that do part of the processing of the application. In particular, these components are used to process database requests from the user interface running on the client.

- Web servers are typically used to store *web applications* and *web services*. Web applications are applications that are designed to run on a web server. Web services are like business components, except that, like web applications, they are designed to run on a web server.

- In a web-based system, a *web browser* running on a client sends a request to a web server over the Internet. Then, the web server processes the request and passes any requests for data on to the database server.

- More complex system architectures can include two or more application servers, web servers, and database servers.

Figure 1-3   Other client/server architectures

An introduction to the relational database model

In 1970, Dr. E. F. Codd developed a model for a new type of database called a *relational database.* This type of database eliminated some of the problems that were associated with standard files and other database designs. By using the relational model, you can reduce data redundancy, which saves disk storage and leads to efficient data retrieval. You can also view and manipulate data in a way that is both intuitive and efficient. Today, relational databases are the de facto standard for database applications.

How a table is organized

The model for a relational database states that data is stored in one or more *tables.* It also states that each table can be viewed as a two-dimensional matrix consisting of *rows* and *columns.* This is illustrated by the relational table in figure 1-4. Each row in this table contains information about a single vendor.

In practice, the rows and columns of a relational database table are often referred to by the more traditional terms, *records* and *fields.* In fact, some software packages use one set of terms, some use the other, and some use a combination. In this book, I use the terms *rows* and *columns* because those are the terms used by Oracle.

In general, each table is modeled after a real-world entity such as a vendor or an invoice. Then, the columns of the table represent the attributes of the entity such as name, address, and phone number. And each row of the table represents one instance of the entity. A *value* is stored at the intersection of each row and column, sometimes called a *cell.*

If a table contains one or more columns that uniquely identify each row in the table, you can define these columns as the *primary key* of the table. For instance, the primary key of the Vendors table in this figure is the vendor_id column. In this example, the primary key consists of a single column. However, a primary key can also consist of two or more columns, in which case it's called a *composite primary key.*

In addition to primary keys, some database management systems let you define additional keys that uniquely identify each row in a table. If, for example, the vendor_name column in the Vendors table contains unique data, it can be defined as a *non-primary key.* In Oracle, this is called a *unique key.*

Indexes provide an efficient way of accessing the rows in a table based on the values in one or more columns. Because applications typically access the rows in a table by referring to their key values, an index is automatically created for each key you define. However, you can define indexes for other columns as well. If, for example, you frequently need to sort the Vendor rows by zip code, you can set up an index for that column. Like a key, an index can include one or more columns.

The Vendors table in an Accounts Payable database

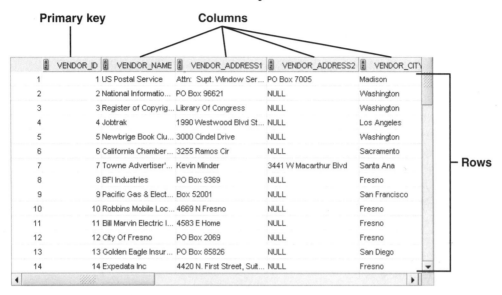

Concepts

- A *relational database* consists of *tables*. Tables consist of *rows* and *columns*, which can also be referred to as *records* and *fields*.

- A table is typically modeled after a real-world entity, such as an invoice or a vendor.

- A column represents some attribute of the entity, such as the amount of an invoice or a vendor's address.

- A row contains a set of values for a single instance of the entity, such as one invoice or one vendor.

- The intersection of a row and a column is sometimes called a *cell*. A cell stores a single *value*.

- Most tables have a *primary key* that uniquely identifies each row in the table. The primary key is usually a single column, but it can also consist of two or more columns. If a primary key uses two or more columns, it's called a *composite primary key*.

- In addition to primary keys, some database management systems let you define one or more *non-primary keys*. In Oracle, these keys are called *unique keys*. Like a primary key, a non-primary key uniquely identifies each row in the table.

- A table can also be defined with one or more *indexes*. An index provides an efficient way to access data from a table based on the values in specific columns. An index is automatically created for a table's primary and non-primary keys.

Figure 1-4   How a database table is organized

How tables are related

The tables in a database can be related to other tables by values in specific columns. The two tables shown in figure 1-5 illustrate this concept. Here, each row in the Vendors table is related to one or more rows in the Invoices table. This is called a *one-to-many relationship*.

Typically, relationships exist between the primary key in one table and the *foreign key* in another table. The foreign key is simply one or more columns in a table that refer to a primary key in another table. In this figure, for example, the vendor_id column is the foreign key in the Invoices table and is used to create the relationship between the Vendors table and the Invoices table.

When you define a foreign key for a table in Oracle, you can't add rows to the table with the foreign key unless there's a matching primary key in the related table. For example, if you try to add a row to the Invoices table with a vendor_id value that doesn't exist in the Vendors table, Oracle won't add the row and will display an error. This helps to maintain the integrity of the data that's stored in the database.

Although one-to-many relationships are the most common, two tables can also have a one-to-one or many-to-many relationship. If a table has a *one-to-one relationship* with another table, the data in the two tables could be stored in a single table. Because of that, one-to-one relationships are used infrequently.

In contrast, a *many-to-many relationship* is usually implemented by using an intermediate table that has a one-to-many relationship with the two tables in the many-to-many relationship. In other words, a many-to-many relationship can usually be broken down into two one-to-many relationships.

The relationship between the Vendors and Invoices tables in the database

Primary key

VENDOR_ID	VENDOR_NAME	VENDOR_ADDRESS1	VENDOR_ADDRESS2	VENDOR_CITY
113	114 Postmaster	Postage Due Technician	1900 E Street	Fresno
114	115 Roadway Package...	Dept La 21095	NULL	Pasadena
115	116 State of California	Employment Developmen...	PO Box 826276	Sacramento
116	117 Suburban Propane	2874 S Cherry Ave	NULL	Fresno
117	118 Unocal	P.O. Box 860070	NULL	Pasadena
118	119 Yesmed, Inc	PO Box 2061	NULL	Fresno
119	120 Dataforms/West	1617 W. Shaw Avenue	Suite F	Fresno
120	121 Zylka Design	3467 W Shaw Ave #103	NULL	Fresno
121	122 United Parcel Servi...	P.O. Box 505820	NULL	Reno
122	123 Federal Express C...	P.O. Box 1140	Dept A	Memphis

INVOICE_ID	VENDOR_ID	INVOICE_NUMBER	INVOICE_DATE	INVOICE_TOTAL
29	29	123 4-314-3057	02-MAY-08	13.75
30	30	94 203339-13	02-MAY-08	17.5
31	31	123 2-000-2993	03-MAY-08	144.7
32	32	89 125520-1	05-MAY-08	95
33	33	123 1-202-2978	06-MAY-08	33
34	34	110 0-2436	07-MAY-08	10976.06
35	35	123 1-200-5164	07-MAY-08	63.4
36	36	110 0-2060	08-MAY-08	23517.58
37	37	110 0-2058	08-MAY-08	37966.19
38	38	123 963253272	09-MAY-08	61.5

Foreign key

Concepts

- The vendor_id column in the Invoices table is called a *foreign key* because it identifies a related row in the Vendors table. A table may contain one or more foreign keys.
- When you define a foreign key for a table in Oracle, you can't add rows to the table with the foreign key unless there's a matching primary key in the related table.
- The most common type of relationship is a *one-to-many relationship* as illustrated by the Vendors and Invoices tables. A table can also have a *one-to-one relationship* or a *many-to-many relationship* with another table.

Figure 1-5   How the tables in a relational database are related

How columns in a table are defined

When you define a column in a table, you assign properties to it as indicated by the design of the Invoices table in figure 1-6. The most critical property for a column is its data type, which determines the type of information that can be stored in the column. With Oracle, you can choose from the *data types* listed in this figure as well as several other data types that are described in chapter 8. As you define each column in a table, you generally try to assign the data type that will minimize the use of disk storage because that will improve the performance of the queries later.

In addition to a data type, you must identify whether the column can store a *null value* (or just *null*). A null represents a value that's unknown, unavailable, or not applicable. If you don't allow null values for a column, you must provide a value for that column when you store a new row in the table.

You can also assign a *default value* to each column. Then, that value is assigned to the column if another value isn't provided. You'll learn more about how to work with nulls and default values later in this book.

The columns of the Invoices table

Common Oracle data types

Type	Description
CHAR, VARCHAR2	A string of letters, symbols, and numbers in the ASCII character set.
NUMBER	Integer and decimal numbers that contain an exact value.
FLOAT	Floating-point numbers that contain an approximate value.
DATE	Dates and times.

Description

- The *data type* that's assigned to a column determines the type of information that can be stored in the column.

- Each column definition also indicates whether or not it can contain *null values*. A null value indicates that the value of the column is unknown.

- A column can also be defined with a *default value*. Then, that value is used if another value isn't provided when a row is added to the table.

Figure 1-6   How the columns in a table are defined

An introduction to SQL and SQL-based systems

In the topics that follow, you'll learn how SQL and SQL-based database management systems evolved. In addition, you'll learn how some of the most popular SQL-based systems compare.

A brief history of SQL

Prior to the release of the first relational database management system, each database had a unique physical structure and a unique programming language that the programmer had to understand. That all changed with the advent of SQL and the relational database management system.

Figure 1-7 lists the important events in the history of SQL. In 1970, Dr. E. F. Codd published an article that described the relational database model he had been working on with a research team at IBM. By 1978, the IBM team had developed a database system based on this model, called System/R, along with a query language called *SEQUEL* (*Structured English Query Language*). Although the database and query language were never officially released, IBM remained committed to the relational model.

The following year, Relational Software, Inc. released the first relational database management system, called *Oracle*. This RDBMS ran on a minicomputer and used SQL as its query language. This product was widely successful, and the company later changed its name to Oracle to reflect that success.

In 1982, IBM released its first commercial SQL-based RDBMS, called *SQL/DS* (*SQL/Data System*). This was followed in 1985 by *DB2* (*Database 2*). Both systems ran only on IBM mainframe computers. Later, DB2 was ported to other operating systems, including Unix and Windows. Today, it continues to be IBM's premier database system.

During the 1980s, other SQL-based database systems, including SQL Server, were developed. Although each of these systems used SQL as its query language, each implementation was unique. That began to change in 1989, when the *American National Standards Institute* (*ANSI*) published its first set of standards for a database query language. These standards have been revised a few times since then, most recently in 2003. As each database manufacturer has attempted to comply with these standards, their implementations of SQL have become more similar. However, each still has its own *dialect* of SQL that includes additions, or *extensions*, to the standards.

Although you should be aware of the SQL standards, they will have little effect on your job as a SQL programmer. The main benefit of the standards is that the basic SQL statements are the same in each dialect. As a result, once you've learned one dialect, it's relatively easy to learn another. On the other hand, porting applications that use SQL from one type of database to another often requires substantial changes.

Important events in the history of SQL

Year	Event
1970	Dr. E. F. Codd developed the relational database model.
1978	IBM developed the predecessor to SQL, called *Structured English Query Language* (*SEQUEL*). This language was used on a database system called System/R, but neither the system nor the query language was ever released.
1979	Relational Software, Inc. (later renamed Oracle) released the first relational DBMS, Oracle.
1982	IBM released their first relational database system, SQL/DS (SQL/Data System).
1985	IBM released DB2 (Database 2).
1987	Microsoft released SQL Server.
1989	The American National Standards Institute (ANSI) published the first set of standards for a database query language, called ANSI/ISO SQL-89, or SQL1. These standards were similar to IBM's DB2 SQL dialect. Because they were not stringent standards, most commercial products could claim adherence.
1992	ANSI published revised standards (ANSI/ISO SQL-92, or SQL2) that were more stringent than SQL1 and incorporated many new features. These standards introduced *levels of compliance*, or *levels of conformance*, that indicated the extent to which a dialect met the standards.
1999	ANSI published SQL3 (ANSI/ISO SQL:1999). These standards incorporated new features, including support for objects. Levels of compliance were dropped and were replaced by a *core specification* that defined the essential elements for compliance, plus nine *packages*. Each package is designed to serve a specific market niche.
2003	ANSI published SQL4 (ANSI/ISO SQL:2003). These standards introduced XML-related features, standardized sequences, and identity columns.

Description

- Although SQL is a standard language, each vendor has its own *SQL dialect*, or *variant*, that may include extensions to the standards.

How knowing "standard SQL" helps you

- The most basic SQL statements are the same for all SQL dialects.
- Once you have learned one SQL dialect, you can easily learn other dialects.

How knowing "standard SQL" does not help you

- Any non-trivial application will require modification when moved from one SQL database to another.

Figure 1-7   A brief history of SQL

A comparison of Oracle, DB2, and Microsoft SQL Server

Although this book is about Oracle, you may want to know about some of the other SQL-based relational database management systems. Figure 1-8 compares two of the most popular, DB2 and Microsoft (MS) SQL Server, with Oracle.

One of the main differences between the Oracle and SQL Server is that Oracle runs under most operating systems, including z/OS, Unix, and Windows. In contrast, SQL Server only runs under the Windows operating system. Since many developers consider z/OS and Unix to be more stable and secure than Windows, most large companies use z/OS or Unix as the operating system for the servers that store the databases for mission-critical applications. As a result, they can't use SQL Server and must use Oracle or DB2.

Oracle has a huge installed base of customers and continues to dominate the marketplace, especially for servers running the Unix operating system. Oracle works well for large systems and has a reputation for being extremely reliable, but also has a reputation for being expensive and difficult to use.

DB2 was originally designed to run on IBM mainframe systems and continues to be the premier database for those systems. It also dominates in hybrid environments where IBM mainframes and newer servers must coexist. Although it has a reputation for being expensive, it also has a reputation for being reliable and easy to use.

SQL Server is widely used for small- to medium-sized departmental systems. It has a reputation for being inexpensive and easy to use. However, it also has a reputation for not scaling well for systems with a large number of users.

Of course, all three of these databases are constantly evolving and competing for different segments of the database market. For example, some developers say that the latest versions of Oracle and DB2 are easier to use. In addition, Oracle and DB2 have both introduced editions of their databases that are less expensive. As a result, Oracle and DB2 may begin to take some market share away from SQL Server for medium-sized departmental systems. Conversely, other developers say that the latest version of SQL Server has improved security, reliability, performance, and scalability. As a result, they claim that SQL Server is ready to be used for mission-critical systems with a large number of users.

MySQL and other SQL-based systems

If you search the Internet, you'll find that dozens of other relational database products are also available. These include proprietary systems like Informix, Sybase, and Teradata. They also include *open source systems* like MySQL and PostgreSQL, which can be run on most operating systems including Unix and Linux. The source code for open source systems is available to the public and can usually be used and redistributed for free.

A comparison of Oracle, DB2, and Microsoft SQL Server

	Oracle	DB2	MS SQL Server
Release Year	1979	1985	1987
Platforms	Unix	OS/390, z/OS	Windows
	OS/390, z/OS	Unix	
	Windows	Windows	

Description

- Oracle is typically used for large, mission-critical, systems that run on one or more Unix servers.

- DB2 is typically used for large, mission-critical systems that run on legacy IBM mainframe systems using the z/OS or OS/390 operating system.

- Microsoft (MS) SQL Server is typically used for small- to medium-sized systems that run on one or more Windows servers.

- MySQL is a popular *open-source database* that runs on all major operating systems and is commonly used for web applications.

Figure 1-8   A comparison of Oracle, DB2, and Microsoft SQL Server

The SQL statements

In the topics that follow, you'll learn about some of the SQL statements provided by Oracle. As you'll see, you can use some of these statements to manipulate the data in a database, and you can use others to work with database objects. Although you may not be able to code these statements after reading these topics, you should have a good idea of how they work. Then, you'll be better prepared to learn the details of coding these statements when they're presented in the rest of this book.

An introduction to the SQL statements

Figure 1-9 summarizes some of the most common SQL statements. As you can see, these statements can be divided into two categories. The statements that work with the data in a database are called the *data manipulation language* (*DML*). These statements are presented in the first group in this figure, and these are the statements that application programmers use the most.

The statements that work with the objects in a database are called the *data definition language* (*DDL*). On large systems, these statements are used exclusively by *database administrators*, or *DBAs*. It's the DBA's job to maintain existing databases, tune them for faster performance, and create new databases. On smaller systems, though, the SQL programmer may fill the role of the DBA.

SQL statements used to work with data (DML)

Statement	Description
SELECT	Retrieves data from one or more tables.
INSERT	Adds new rows to a table.
UPDATE	Changes existing rows in a table.
DELETE	Deletes existing rows from a table.

SQL statements used to work with database objects (DDL)

Statement	Description
CREATE USER	Creates a new user for a database.
CREATE TABLE	Creates a new table in a database.
CREATE SEQUENCE	Creates a new sequence that automatically generates numbers.
CREATE INDEX	Creates a new index for a table.
ALTER USER	Changes the definition of an existing user.
ALTER TABLE	Changes the definition of an existing table.
ALTER SEQUENCE	Changes the definition of an existing sequence.
ALTER INDEX	Changes the structure of an existing index.
DROP USER	Deletes an existing user.
DROP TABLE	Deletes an existing table.
DROP SEQUENCE	Deletes an existing sequence.
DROP INDEX	Deletes an existing index.
GRANT	Grants privileges to a user.
REVOKE	Revokes privileges from a user.

Description

- The SQL statements can be divided into two categories: the *data manipulation language (DML)* that lets you work with the data in the database and the *data definition language (DDL)* that lets you work with the objects in the database.

- SQL programmers typically work with the DML statements, while *database administrators (DBAs)* use the DDL statements.

Figure 1-9   An introduction to the SQL statements

How to work with database objects

To give you an idea of how you use the DDL statements shown in the previous figure, figure 1-10 presents some examples. Here, the first statement creates a user named AP. Then, the second statement grants all privileges to this user. As a result, this user can create and delete the tables and other database objects for the AP database that's used in many of the examples throughout this book. In addition, this user can select, insert, update, and delete data that's stored in these tables.

The third example creates the Invoices table that's used throughout this chapter. If you don't understand all of this code right now, don't worry. You'll learn how to code statements like this in chapter 10. For now, just realize that this statement defines each column in the table, including its data type, whether or not it allows null values, and its default value if it has one.

In addition, the third example defines the primary and foreign key columns for the table. These definitions are one type of *constraint*. Since the Invoices table includes foreign keys to the Vendors and Terms tables, these tables must be created before the Invoices table. Conversely, before you can delete the Vendors and Terms tables, you must delete the Invoices table.

The fourth statement in this figure changes the Invoices table by adding a column to it. Like the statement that created the table, this statement specifies all the attributes of the new column. Then, the fifth statement deletes the column that was just added.

The sixth statement creates an index on the Invoices table. In this case, the index is for the vendor_id column, which is used frequently to access the table. Then, the seventh statement deletes the index that was just added.

The last statement creates a *sequence* that can be used to automatically generate a value for the invoice_id column of the Invoices table. In particular, this sequence begins with a value of 115 and increments the sequence by 1 each time the sequence is used. In figure 1-13, you can see how a sequence can be used when inserting a row into the Invoices table.

A statement that creates a new user for a database

```
CREATE USER ap IDENTIFIED BY ap
```

A statement that grants privileges to a user

```
GRANT ALL PRIVILEGES TO ap
```

A statement that creates a new table

```
CREATE TABLE invoices
(
  invoice_id              NUMBER          NOT NULL,
  vendor_id               NUMBER          NOT NULL,
  invoice_number          VARCHAR2(50)    NOT NULL,
  invoice_date            DATE            NOT NULL,
  invoice_total           NUMBER(9,2)     NOT NULL,
  payment_total           NUMBER(9,2)                     DEFAULT 0,
  credit_total            NUMBER(9,2)                     DEFAULT 0,
  terms_id                NUMBER          NOT NULL,
  invoice_due_date        DATE            NOT NULL,
  payment_date            DATE,
  CONSTRAINT invoices_pk
    PRIMARY KEY (invoice_id),
  CONSTRAINT invoices_fk_vendors
    FOREIGN KEY (vendor_id)
    REFERENCES vendors (vendor_id),
  CONSTRAINT invoices_fk_terms
    FOREIGN KEY (terms_id)
    REFERENCES terms (terms_id)
)
```

A statement that adds a new column to a table

```
ALTER TABLE invoices
ADD balance_due NUMBER(9,2)
```

A statement that deletes the new column

```
ALTER TABLE invoices
DROP COLUMN balance_due
```

A statement that creates an index on the table

```
CREATE INDEX invoices_vendor_id_index
  ON invoices (vendor_id)
```

A statement that deletes the new index

```
DROP INDEX invoices_vendor_id_index
```

A statement that creates a sequence for generating invoice_id values

```
CREATE SEQUENCE invoice_id_seq
START WITH 115
INCREMENT BY 1
```

Figure 1-10   Typical statements for working with database objects

How to query a single table

Figure 1-11 shows how to use a SELECT statement to query a single table in a database. To start, this figure shows some of the columns and rows of the Invoices table. Then, in the SELECT statement that follows, the SELECT clause names the columns to be retrieved, and the FROM clause names the table that contains the columns, called the *base table*. In this case, six columns will be retrieved from the Invoices table.

Note that the last column, balance_due, is calculated from three other columns in the table. In other words, a column by the name of balance_due doesn't actually exist in the database. This type of column is called a *calculated value*, and it exists only in the results of the query.

In addition to the SELECT and FROM clauses, this SELECT statement includes a WHERE clause and an ORDER BY clause. The WHERE clause gives the criteria for the rows to be selected. In this case, a row is selected only if it has a balance due that's greater than zero. Finally, the returned rows are sorted by the invoice_date column.

This figure also shows the *result set* (or *result table*) that's returned by the SELECT statement. A result set is a logical table that's created temporarily within the database. When an application requests data from a database, it receives a result set.

The Invoices base table

	INVOICE_ID	VENDOR_ID	INVOICE_NUMBER	INVOICE_DATE	INVOICE_TOTAL	PAYMENT_TOTAL	CREDIT_TOTAL	TERMS_ID
1	1	34	QP58872	25-FEB-08	116.54	116.54	0	4
2	2	34	Q545443	14-MAR-08	1083.58	1083.58	0	4
3	3	110	P-0608	11-APR-08	20551.18	0	1200	5
4	4	110	P-0259	16-APR-08	26881.4	26881.4	0	3
5	5	81	MABO1489	16-APR-08	936.93	936.93	0	3
6	6	122	989319-497	17-APR-08	2312.2	0	0	4
7	7	82	C73-24	17-APR-08	600	600	0	2
8	8	122	989319-487	18-APR-08	1927.54	0	0	4
9	9	122	989319-477	19-APR-08	2184.11	2184.11	0	4
10	10	122	989319-467	24-APR-08	2318.03	2318.03	0	4
11	11	122	989319-457	24-APR-08	3813.33	3813.33	0	3
12	12	122	989319-447	24-APR-08	3689.99	3689.99	0	3
13	13	122	989319-437	24-APR-08	2765.36	2765.36	0	2
14	14	122	989319-427	25-APR-08	2115.81	2115.81	0	1
15	15	121	97/553B	26-APR-08	313.55	0	0	4

A SELECT statement that retrieves and sorts selected columns and rows from the Invoices table

```
SELECT invoice_number, invoice_date, invoice_total,
    payment_total, credit_total,
    invoice_total - payment_total - credit_total AS balance_due
FROM invoices
WHERE invoice_total - payment_total - credit_total > 0
ORDER BY invoice_date
```

The result set defined by the SELECT statement

	INVOICE_NUMBER	INVOICE_DATE	INVOICE_TOTAL	PAYMENT_TOTAL	CREDIT_TOTAL	BALANCE_DUE
1	P-0608	11-APR-08	20551.18	0	1200	19351.18
2	989319-497	17-APR-08	2312.2	0	0	2312.2
3	989319-487	18-APR-08	1927.54	0	0	1927.54
4	97/553B	26-APR-08	313.55	0	0	313.55
5	97/553	27-APR-08	904.14	0	0	904.14
6	97/522	30-APR-08	1962.13	0	200	1762.13

Concepts

- You use the SELECT statement to retrieve selected columns and rows from a *base table*. The result of a SELECT statement is a *result table*, or *result set*, like the one shown above.

- A result set can include *calculated values* that are calculated from columns in the table.

- A SELECT statement is commonly referred to as a *query*.

Figure 1-11   How to query a single table

How to join data from two or more tables

Figure 1-12 presents a SELECT statement that retrieves data from two tables. This type of operation is called a *join* because the data from the two tables is joined together into a single result set. For example, the SELECT statement in this figure joins data from the Invoices and Vendors tables.

An *inner join* is the most common type of join. When you use an inner join, rows from the two tables in the join are included in the result table only if their related columns match. These matching columns are specified in the FROM clause of the SELECT statement. In the SELECT statement in this figure, for example, rows from the Invoices and Vendors tables are included only if the value of the vendor_id column in the Vendors table matches the value of the vendor_id column in one or more rows in the Invoices table. If there aren't any invoices for a particular vendor, that vendor won't be included in the result set.

Although this figure shows only how to join data from two tables, you can extend this syntax to join data from three or more tables. If, for example, you want to include line item data from a table named Invoice_Line_Items in the results shown in this figure, you can code the FROM clause of the SELECT statement like this:

```
FROM vendors
    INNER JOIN invoices
        ON vendors.vendor_id = invoices.vendor_id
    INNER JOIN invoice_line_items
        ON invoices.invoice_id = invoice_line_items.invoice_id
```

Then, in the SELECT clause, you can include any of the columns in the Invoice_Line_Items table.

In addition to inner joins, most relational databases including Oracle support other types of joins such as *outer joins*. An outer join lets you include all rows from a table even if the other table doesn't have a matching row. You'll learn more about the different types of joins in chapter 4.

A SELECT statement that joins data from the Vendors and Invoices tables

```
SELECT vendor_name, invoice_number, invoice_date, invoice_total
FROM vendors INNER JOIN invoices
    ON vendors.vendor_id = invoices.vendor_id
WHERE invoice_total >= 500
ORDER BY vendor_name, invoice_total DESC
```

The result set defined by the SELECT statement

	VENDOR_NAME	INVOICE_NUMBER	INVOICE_DATE	INVOICE_TOTAL
7	Federal Express Corporation	963253230	15-MAY-08	739.2
8	Ford Motor Credit Company	9982771	03-JUN-08	503.2
9	Franchise Tax Board	RTR-72-3662-X	04-JUN-08	1600
10	Fresno County Tax Collector	P02-88D77S7	06-JUN-08	856.92
11	IBM	Q545443	14-MAR-08	1083.58
12	Ingram	31359783	23-MAY-08	1575
13	Ingram	31361833	23-MAY-08	579.42
14	Malloy Lithographing Inc	0-2058	08-MAY-08	37966.19
15	Malloy Lithographing Inc	P-0259	16-APR-08	26881.4
16	Malloy Lithographing Inc	0-2060	08-MAY-08	23517.58
17	Malloy Lithographing Inc	P-0608	11-APR-08	20551.18
18	Malloy Lithographing Inc	0-2436	07-MAY-08	10976.06
19	Pollstar	77290	04-JUN-08	1750

Concepts

- A *join* lets you combine data from two or more tables into a single result set.
- The most common type of join is an *inner join*. This type of join returns rows from both tables only if their related columns match.
- An *outer join* returns rows from one table in the join even if the other table doesn't contain a matching row.

Figure 1-12   How to join data from two or more tables

How to add, update, and delete data in a table

Figure 1-13 shows how you can use the INSERT, UPDATE, and DELETE statements to modify the data in a table. In this figure, for example, the first statement uses the INSERT statement to add a row to the Invoices table. To do that, the INSERT clause names the columns whose values are supplied in the VALUES clause.

In chapter 7, you'll learn more about specifying column names and values. For now, just note that you have to specify a value for a column unless it's a column that allows null values or a column that's defined with a default value.

When working with primary keys, you often use the NEXTVAL pseudo column of a sequence to get the next value in a sequence of numbers that are automatically generated. In this figure, for example, the NEXTVAL pseudo column of the sequence named invoice_id_seq is used to get the value for the invoice_id column. To review how this sequence is defined, you can refer back to figure 1-10.

The two UPDATE statements in this figure show how to change the data in one or more rows of a table. The first statement, for example, assigns a value of 35.89 to the credit_total column of the invoice in the Invoices table with invoice number 367447. The second statement adds 30 days to the invoice due date for each row in the Invoices table whose terms_id column has a value of 4.

To delete rows from a table, you use the DELETE statement. For example, the first DELETE statement in this figure deletes the invoice with invoice number 4-342-8069 from the Invoices table. The second DELETE statement deletes all invoices with a balance due of zero. However, since the Invoices table has a foreign key that references the Invoice_Line_Items table, these DELETE statements won't work unless the invoice doesn't contain any line items. As a result, to get these delete statements to work, you would need to delete the corresponding rows from the Invoice_Line_Items table first.

A statement that adds a row to the Invoices table

```
INSERT INTO invoices
   (invoice_id, vendor_id, invoice_number, invoice_date,
    invoice_total, terms_id, invoice_due_date)
VALUES
   (invoice_id_seq.NEXTVAL, 12, '3289175', '18-JUL-08',
    165, 3, '17-AUG-08')
```

A statement that changes the value of the credit_total column for a selected row in the Invoices table

```
UPDATE invoices
SET credit_total = 35.89
WHERE invoice_number = '367447'
```

A statement that changes the values in invoice_due_date column for all invoices with the specified terms_id

```
UPDATE invoices
SET invoice_due_date = invoice_due_date + 30
WHERE terms_id = 4
```

A statement that deletes a selected invoice from the Invoices table

```
DELETE FROM invoices
WHERE invoice_number = '4-342-8069'
```

A statement that deletes all paid invoices from the Invoices table

```
DELETE FROM invoices
WHERE invoice_total - payment_total - credit_total = 0
```

Concepts

- You use the INSERT statement to add rows to a table.
- You use the UPDATE statement to change the values in one or more rows of a table based on the condition you specify.
- You use the DELETE statement to delete one or more rows from a table based on the condition you specify.
- An INSERT, UPDATE, or DELETE statement can be referred to as an *action query*.

Warning

- If you're new to SQL statements, please don't execute the statements above until you read chapter 7 and understand the effect that these statements can have on the database.

Figure 1-13   How to add, update, and delete data in a table

How to work with views

A *view* is a database object that's similar to a table. However, a view is a predefined query that provides another way of viewing the data that's stored in a table. To create a view, you use the CREATE VIEW statement as shown in figure 1-14. This statement causes the SELECT statement you specify to be stored with the database. In this case, the CREATE VIEW statement creates a view named vendors_min that retrieves three columns from the Vendors table.

To access the view, you issue a SELECT statement that refers to the view. This causes a *virtual table* to be created from the SELECT statement in the view. Then, the SELECT statement that referred to the view is executed on this virtual table to create the result set.

You can use views to restrict the data that a user is allowed to access or to present data in a form that's easier for the user to understand. In some databases, users may be allowed to access data only through views.

A CREATE VIEW statement for a view

```
CREATE VIEW vendors_min AS
    SELECT vendor_name, vendor_state, vendor_phone
    FROM vendors
```

The virtual table for the view

	VENDOR_NAME	VENDOR_STATE	VENDOR_PHONE
1	US Postal Service	WI	(800) 555-1205
2	National Information Data Ctr	DC	(301) 555-8950
3	Register of Copyrights	DC	NULL
4	Jobtrak	CA	(800) 555-8725
5	Newbrige Book Clubs	NJ	(800) 555-9980
6	California Chamber Of Commerce	CA	(916) 555-6670
7	Towne Advertiser's Mailing Svcs	CA	NULL

A SELECT statement that uses the view

```
SELECT *
FROM vendors_min
WHERE vendor_state = 'CA'
ORDER BY vendor_name
```

The result set

	VENDOR_NAME	VENDOR_STATE	VENDOR_PHONE
1	ASC Signs	CA	NULL
2	Abbey Office Furnishings	CA	(559) 555-8300
3	American Express	CA	(800) 555-3344
4	Aztek Label	CA	(714) 555-9000
5	BFI Industries	CA	(559) 555-1551
6	Bertelsmann Industry Svcs. Inc	CA	(805) 555-0584
7	Bill Jones	CA	NULL

Description

- A *view* consists of a SELECT statement that's stored with the database.
- When you use a view, a *virtual table* is created on the server that represents the view.

Figure 1-14   How to work with views

SQL coding guidelines

SQL is a freeform language. That means that you can include line breaks, spaces, and indentation without affecting the way the database interprets the code. In addition, SQL isn't case-sensitive like some languages. That means that you can use uppercase or lowercase letters or a combination of the two without affecting the way the database interprets the code.

Although you can code SQL statements with a freeform style, we suggest that you follow the coding recommendations presented in figure 1-15. The examples in this figure illustrate the value of these coding recommendations. The first example presents an unformatted SELECT statement that's difficult to read. In contrast, this statement is much easier to read after our coding recommendations are applied as shown in the second example.

The third example illustrates how to code a *block comment*. This type of comment is typically coded at the beginning of a group of statements and is used to document the entire group. Block comments can also be used within a statement to describe blocks of code, but that's not common.

The fourth example in this figure includes a *single-line comment*. This type of comment is typically used to document a single line of code. A single-line comment can be coded on a separate line as shown in this example, or it can be coded at the end of a line of code. In either case, the comment is delimited by the end of the line.

Although many programmers sprinkle their code with comments, that shouldn't be necessary if you write your code so it's easy to read and understand. Instead, you should use comments only to clarify sections of code that are difficult to understand. Then, if you change the code, you should be sure to change the comments too. Otherwise, the comments won't accurately represent what the code does, which will make the code even more difficult to understand.

A SELECT statement that's difficult to read

```
select invoice_number, invoice_date, invoice_total, payment_total,
credit_total, invoice_total - payment_total - credit_total as balance_due
from invoices where invoice_total - payment_total - credit_total > 0 order
by invoice_date
```

A SELECT statement that's coded with a readable style

```
SELECT invoice_number, invoice_date, invoice_total,
    payment_total, credit_total,
    invoice_total - payment_total - credit_total AS balance_due
FROM invoices
WHERE invoice_total - payment_total - credit_total > 0
ORDER BY invoice_date
```

SELECT statement with a block comment

```
/*
Author: Joel Murach
Date: 8/22/2008
*/
SELECT invoice_number, invoice_date, invoice_total,
    invoice_total - payment_total - credit_total AS balance_due
FROM invoices
```

A SELECT statement with a single-line comment

```
-- The fourth column calculates the balance due
SELECT invoice_number, invoice_date, invoice_total,
    invoice_total - payment_total - credit_total AS balance_due
FROM invoices
```

Coding recommendations

- Capitalize all keywords, and use lowercase for the other code in a SQL statement.
- Separate the words in names with underscores, as in invoice_number.
- Start each clause on a new line.
- Break long clauses into multiple lines and indent continued lines.
- Use *comments* only for portions of code that are difficult to understand. Then, make sure that the comments are correct and up-to-date.

How to code a comment

- To code a *block comment*, type /* at the start of the block and */ at the end.
- To code a *single-line comment*, type -- followed by the comment.

Description

- Line breaks, white space, indentation, and capitalization have no effect on the operation of a statement.
- Comments can be used to document what a statement does or what specific parts of a statement do. They are not executed by the system.

Figure 1-15   SQL coding guidelines

An introduction to PL/SQL

SQL isn't a procedural language like Java or other procedural languages. However, Oracle provides an extension to standard SQL known as *PL/SQL* (*Procedural Language/SQL*) that allows you to write procedural code that includes if/else statements, loops, and error handling. This topic gives you a quick overview of how PL/SQL works. Then, you can learn the details of working with PL/SQL in section 4 of this book.

How to work with stored procedures

A *stored procedure* is a set of one or more SQL or PL/SQL statements that are stored together in a database. To create a stored procedure, you use the CREATE PROCEDURE statement as shown in figure 1-16. In this figure, the stored procedure begins by defining two *parameters*. The first is named invoice_number_param and is of the VARCHAR2 type. The second is named credit_total_param and is of the NUMBER data type. Note that these data types correspond with the data types that are used for the invoice_number and credit_total columns of the Invoices table.

The body of this stored procedure contains two statements. The first statement is an UPDATE statement that updates the credit_total column of the Invoices table. The second statement is a COMMIT statement that makes the update permanent.

If the body of the stored procedure encounters an error, the EXCEPTION block is executed. In that case, the ROLLBACK statement rolls back any changes that the stored procedure has made to the database so far.

When you code the statements in a stored procedure, you must code a semicolon at the end of each statement. In this figure, for example, a semicolon is coded after the UPDATE statement, the COMMIT statement, and the ROLL-BACK statement. A semicolon is also coded after the END statement that ends the stored procedure. Finally, you must code a front slash (/) at the end of a stored procedure.

To use the stored procedure, you send a request for it to be executed. One way to do that is to use the CALL statement shown in this figure. You can also execute a stored procedure from an application program by issuing an appropriate statement. How you do that depends on the programming language and the API you're using to access the database. Either way, when the server receives the request, it executes the stored procedure.

A CREATE PROCEDURE statement

```
CREATE OR REPLACE PROCEDURE update_invoices_credit_total
(
  invoice_number_param VARCHAR2,
  credit_total_param NUMBER
)
AS
BEGIN
  UPDATE invoices
  SET credit_total = credit_total_param
  WHERE invoice_number = invoice_number_param;

  COMMIT;
EXCEPTION
  WHEN OTHERS THEN
    ROLLBACK;
END;
/
```

A statement that executes the stored procedure

```
CALL update_invoices_credit_total('367447', 35.89)
```

Concepts

- *PL/SQL (Procedural Language/SQL)* is an Oracle extension to standard SQL that allows you to write procedural code that includes if/else statements, loops, and error handling.

- A *stored procedure* is a type of subprogram that contains one or more SQL or PL/SQL statements that have been compiled and stored with the database.

Figure 1-16   How to work with stored procedures

How to work with user-defined functions

A *user-defined function* (*UDF*) is similar to a stored procedure in many ways. To start, the syntax for creating a user-defined function is similar to the syntax for creating a stored procedure. Like a stored procedure, a user-defined function can accept several parameters. In addition, a function returns a value.

However, unlike a stored procedure, a UDF can't modify the data that's stored in a table. Instead, it performs some processing and returns a value. User-defined functions work similarly to the built-in functions provided by Oracle that are described in chapter 8, but they allow programmers to create custom functions for a specific database.

To create a function, you use the CREATE FUNCTION statement as shown in figure 1-17. This function begins by defining an input parameter named vendor_id_param of the INTEGER type. Then, it defines a variable named avg_invoice_total_var of the NUMBER type with nine digits and two decimal positions.

Within the body of the user-defined function, the SELECT statement uses the built-in AVG function to find the average of all invoice totals for each vendor and store it in the variable. Then the RETURN statement returns the variable.

To use a function, you can code the name of the function in a SELECT statement followed by a set of parentheses. Within the parentheses, you can code the parameters accepted by the function, separating multiple parameters with a comma. In this figure, the avg_invoice_total function only accepts a single parameter, the vendor's ID. As a result, you can code the vendor_id column within the parentheses that come after the function's name. Then, this column will return the average invoice amount for each vendor.

How to work with triggers

A *trigger* is a special type of stored procedure that's executed automatically when an insert, update, or delete operation is executed on a table. Triggers are used most often to validate data before a row is added or updated, but they can also be used to maintain the relationships between tables.

A CREATE FUNCTION statement

```
CREATE OR REPLACE FUNCTION avg_invoice_total
(
    vendor_id_param INTEGER
)
RETURN NUMBER
AS
    avg_invoice_total_var NUMBER(9,2);
BEGIN
  SELECT AVG(invoice_total)
  INTO avg_invoice_total_var
  FROM invoices
  WHERE vendor_id = vendor_id_param;

  RETURN avg_invoice_total_var;
END;
/
```

A statement that uses the function

```
SELECT vendor_id, invoice_total, avg_invoice_total(vendor_id)
FROM invoices
ORDER BY vendor_id
```

The result set

	VENDOR_ID	INVOICE_TOTAL	AVG_INVOICE_TOTAL(VENDOR_ID)
1	34	1083.58	600.06
2	34	116.54	600.06
3	37	224	188
4	37	224	188
5	37	116	188
6	48	856.92	856.92
7	72	85.31	10963.66

Concepts

- A *user-defined function* (*UDF*) is a type of subprogram that contains one or more SQL or PL/SQL statements that have been compiled and stored with the database.

Figure 1-17   How to work with user-defined functions

How to use SQL from an application program

This book teaches you how to use SQL from within the Oracle environment. As you learned in the last chapter, however, SQL is commonly used from application programs too. So in the topics that follow, you'll get a general idea of how that works. And you'll see, it's easy to recognize the SQL statements in an application program because they're coded just as they would be if they were running on their own.

Common data access models

Figure 1-18 shows three common ways for an application to access an Oracle database. To access an Oracle database from a Java application, for example, you can use *JDBC (Java Database Connectivity)*. This *data access model* requires a *driver* to communicate with Oracle.

Since Java is commonly used to work with Oracle databases, this figure lists two JDBC drivers that are provided by a default installation of Oracle and are commonly used by Java applications. To start, the thin driver is commonly used by Java applications that run on a client. These types of applications include standalone Java applications and applets. On the other hand, the OCI driver is commonly used for applications that run on a server such as Java web applications that use servlets and JSP. Although the OCI driver requires more system resources than the thin driver, it usually runs faster, and it provides for additional features such as connection pooling.

To access an Oracle database from an application written in a .NET language such as Visual Basic or C#, you can use Microsoft's newest data access model, *ADO.NET*. Like JDBC, this data access model requires a driver to communicate with Oracle.

To access Oracle from a Visual Basic 6 or Access application, you can use a data access model called *ADO*. This data access model was the predecessor to ADO.NET, and it used a protocol known as OLE DB to communicate with the database.

Common options for accessing Oracle data

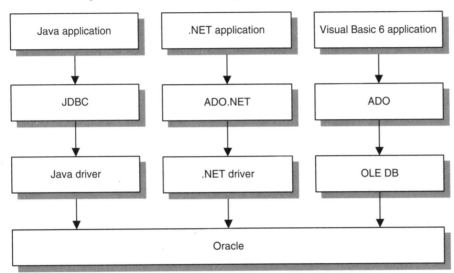

Two commonly used Oracle JDBC drivers

Name	Description
Thin driver	Requires fewer system resources than the OCI driver. This driver is written entirely in Java and is commonly used for applications that run on a client.
OCI driver	Requires more system resources than the thin driver. However, it runs faster and is commonly used for applications that run on a server.

Description

- To work with the data in an Oracle database, an application uses a *data access model*. For a Java application, that model is typically *JDBC* (*Java Database Connectivity*). For a .NET application written in Visual Basic or C#, that model is typically *ADO.NET*. For an Access or Visual Basic 6 application, that model is typically *ADO* (*ActiveX Data Objects*).

- Each data access model defines a set of objects you can use to connect to and work with an Oracle database. For example, each of the three models shown above includes a Connection object that you can use to specify the information for connecting to a database.

- The data access models require additional software, called *drivers*, to communicate with an Oracle database. For example, JDBC requires one of the drivers described above.

Figure 1-18   Common data access models

Java code that retrieves data from an Oracle database

Figure 1-19 presents Java code that uses the JDBC to execute a SQL statement against an Oracle database. This code is from a simple application that retrieves and displays information from the Vendors and Invoices tables. It creates the JDBC objects used by the application and then uses them to display the data that's retrieved.

If you have some Java programming experience, you shouldn't have much trouble understanding this code. If you don't have Java experience, that's fine too. In that case, focus on how this code uses a data access API to execute SQL against an Oracle database. If you want to learn more about using Java to work with a database, we recommend *Murach's Java SE 6* and *Murach's Java Servlets and JSP*.

Before you attempt to execute this code, you need to add a JAR file that contains the Oracle JDBC driver to your classpath. That way, Java will be able to find the files for the driver. The easiest way to do that is to copy the JAR file that contains the drivers into the JDK's jre/lib/ext directory. For example, the ojdbc14.jar file contains classes for working with JDK 1.4 and 1.5. By default, this JAR file is installed in the directory shown in this figure when you install Oracle 10g Express Edition.

For more information about Oracle's JDBC drivers, you can open the readme.txt file that's shown in this figure. This file contains information about the drivers that are specific to the version of Oracle that's installed on your system.

The code in this figure begins by importing all classes in the java.sql package. These classes define JDBC objects like the Connection object that are used to access an Oracle database.

Within the main method, the first block of code uses the forName method of the Class class to load the Oracle JDBC driver. This block of code is needed if you're using Oracle 10g because its database driver uses JDBC 3.0 (which is part of JDK 1.5). If you're using Oracle 11g, though, you will usually want to omit this block of code because the 11g driver supports JDBC 4.0 (which is part of JDK 1.6), and JDBC 4.0 can automatically find the driver.

After the driver has been loaded, this code defines the Connection, Command, and ResultSet objects that are used by the application and sets them equal to null values. Within the try block, the first four statements create a Connection object. To do that, the first statement specifies a database URL that uses the thin driver to connect to the Express Edition (XE) of Oracle that's running on port 1521 on the same computer as the Java application. Then, the second and third statements specify the username and password for the AP user. Finally, the fourth statement uses the getConnection method of the DriverManager class to return a Connection object.

Once the Connection object has been created, the next three statements execute a SELECT statement. Here, the first statement creates a Statement object. Then, the second statement defines the SELECT statement. Finally, the third statement executes the query and stores the result in the ResultSet object.

The readme file that describes the JDBC drivers for Oracle

```
C:\oraclexe\app\oracle\product\10.2.0\server\jdbc\readme.txt
```

The JAR file that contains the JDBC driver for Oracle 10g Express

```
C:\oraclexe\app\oracle\product\10.2.0\server\jdbc\lib\ojdbc14.jar
```

Java code that retrieves data from an Oracle database

```java
import java.sql.*;
import java.text.NumberFormat;

public class DBTestApp
{
    public static void main(String args[])
    {
        // Load the database driver
        // NOTE: This block is necessary for Oracle 10g (JDBC 3.0),
        // but not for Oracle 11g (JDBC 4.0)
        try
        {
            Class.forName("oracle.jdbc.OracleDriver");
        }
        catch(ClassNotFoundException e)
        {
            e.printStackTrace();
        }

        // define common JDBC objects
        Connection connection = null;
        Statement statement = null;
        ResultSet rs = null;
        try
        {
            // Connect to the database
            String dbUrl = "jdbc:oracle:thin:@localhost:1521:XE";
            String username = "ap";
            String password = "ap";
            connection = DriverManager.getConnection(
                dbUrl, username, password);

            // Execute a SELECT statement
            statement = connection.createStatement();
            String query =
                "SELECT vendor_name, invoice_number, invoice_total " +
                "FROM vendors INNER JOIN invoices " +
                "    ON vendors.vendor_id = invoices.vendor_id " +
                "WHERE invoice_total >= 500 " +
                "ORDER BY vendor_name, invoice_total DESC";
            rs = statement.executeQuery(query);
```

Figure 1-19   Java code that retrieves data from an Oracle database (part 1 of 2)

After the result of the SELECT statement has been stored in the ResultSet object, a while loop is used to process the values that are stored in the ResultSet object. To do that, the getXxxx methods of the ResultSet object are used to retrieve the values that are stored in the vendor_name, invoice_number, and invoice_total columns. Here, the getString method is used to get the VARCHAR2 type and the getDouble method is used to get the NUMBER type. Finally, the NumberFormat class is used to apply currency formatting to the invoice_total column, and the values are printed to the console.

If this code encounters an error, the catch block will be executed. In this figure, that block of code prints information about the error to the console. But whether or not this code executes successfully, the finally block will close all of the resources that were used to execute the SELECT statement and process its results.

Now that you've reviewed this code, you can also see that only one statement in this figure uses SQL. That's the statement that specifies the SELECT statement to be executed. Of course, if an application updates data, it can execute INSERT, UPDATE, and DELETE statements as well. With the skills that you'll learn in this book, though, you won't have any trouble coding the SQL statements you need.

However, you can also see that there's a lot involved in accessing an Oracle database from an application program. That's why most application programmers use a framework that makes it easier to execute SQL statements against a database. In some cases, application programmers write their own utility classes or data access classes. In other cases, application programmers use an existing framework such as Hibernate.

Java code that retrieves data from an Oracle database   **Page 2**

```java
            // Display the results of a SELECT statement
            System.out.println("Invoices with totals over 500:\n");
            while(rs.next())
            {
                String vendorName = rs.getString("vendor_name");
                String invoiceNumber = rs.getString("invoice_number");
                double invoiceTotal = rs.getDouble("invoice_total");

                NumberFormat currency = NumberFormat.getCurrencyInstance();
                String invoiceTotalString = currency.format(invoiceTotal);

                System.out.println(
                    "Vendor:      " + vendorName + "\n" +
                    "Invoice No: " + invoiceNumber + "\n" +
                    "Total:       " + invoiceTotalString + "\n");
            }
        }
        catch(SQLException e)
        {
            e.printStackTrace();
        }
        finally
        {
            try
            {
                if (rs != null)
                    rs.close();
                if (statement != null)
                    statement.close();
                if (connection != null)
                    connection.close();
            }
            catch(SQLException e)
            {
                e.printStackTrace();
            }
        }
    }
}
```

Description

*   Before you can use Java to work with Oracle, you must make a JAR file that contains a JDBC driver available to your system. The easiest way to do that is to copy the JAR into the JDK's jre/lib/ext directory.

*   The ojdbc14.jar file contains classes for use with JDK 1.4 and 1.5 including the JDBC driver classes.

*   To execute a SQL statement from a Java application, you can use JDBC objects like the Connection, Statement, and ResultSet objects.

Figure 1-19   Java code that retrieves data from an Oracle database (part 2 of 2)

Perspective

To help you understand how SQL is used from an application program, this chapter has introduced you to the hardware and software components of a client/ server system. It has also described how relational databases are organized and how you use some of the SQL statements to work with the data in a relational database. With that as background, you're now ready to start using Oracle. In the next chapter, then, you'll learn how to use some of the tools for working with an Oracle database.

Although this book shows how to work with a relational database, another type of database that has come into use recently is the *object database*. This type of database is designed to store and retrieve the objects that are used by applications written in an object-oriented programming language such as Java or C++. Although object databases have some advantages over relational databases, they also have some disadvantages. In general, object databases haven't yet become widely used, but they have acquired a niche in some areas such as engineering, telecommunications, financial services, high energy physics, and molecular biology.

If you read more about Oracle's advanced features, you'll see that Oracle provides some capabilities for working with objects that allow it to work like an object database. For example, Oracle allows you to define custom data types such as an Invoice data type. Then, you can store an Invoice object within a database without having to parse the object so you can store its values within multiple columns of a row. However, since these features haven't yet come into widespread use, they aren't covered in this book.

Terms

client	unique key
server	index
database server	foreign key
network	one-to-many relationship
client/server system	one-to-one relationship
local area network (LAN)	many-to-many relationship
enterprise system	data type
wide area network (WAN)	null value
database management system (DBMS)	null
back end	default value
application software	SQL dialect
application programming interface (API)	SQL extension
data access API	open source system
JDBC (Java Database Connectivity)	data manipulation language (DML)
front end	data definition language (DDL)
SQL (Structured Query Language)	database administrator (DBA)
query	constraint
query results	sequence
application server	base table
web server	result table
business component	result set
web application	calculated value
web service	join
web browser	inner join
relational database	outer join
table	action query
row	view
column	virtual table
record	comment
field	block comment
cell	single-line comment
value	PL/SQL (Procedural Language/SQL)
primary key	stored procedure
composite primary key	user-defined function (UDF)
non-primary key	trigger

2

How to use Oracle SQL Developer and other tools

In the last chapter, you learned about some of the SQL statements that you can use to work with the data in a relational database. Before you learn the details of coding these statements, however, you need to learn how to work with an Oracle database, how to use Oracle SQL Developer to enter and execute SQL statements, and how to use the SQL Reference manual.

How to work with an Oracle database

Since Oracle Database 11g Express Edition has not been released as of press time for this book, this topic uses Oracle Database 10g Express Edition to illustrate the skills for working with the Oracle Database. However, when the Express Edition of 11g becomes available, you should be able to use similar techniques to work with that version of the Oracle Database.

How to start and stop the database service

If you installed the Express Edition of the Oracle Database on your computer as described in appendix A, the *database service* starts automatically when you start your computer. This piece of software is often referred to as the *database server*, or the *database engine*. It receives SQL statements that are passed to it, processes them, and returns the results.

The *database listener* also starts automatically when you start your computer. This piece of software listens for requests from remote clients and returns the results to them.

From time to time, however, you may want to stop the database. If, for example, you aren't going to be using the database and you want to free the resources on your computer, you can stop the database. Or, if the port that is being used by the Oracle Database conflicts with another program, you can stop the database. Then, when you want to work with the database again, you can start it.

The easiest way to stop the database service is to use the Stop Database command that's available from the Windows Start menu as described in figure 2-1. When you select this item on a Windows system, a DOS window will be displayed that indicates that the Oracle service is stopping. Then, the DOS window will display a message when the Oracle service has successfully stopped. Although this doesn't stop the database listener, the database listener won't be able to return any results unless the database service is running.

When you're running the Oracle Database on your own computer for training purposes, you can stop the database whenever you want. However, if a database is running in a production environment, you should make sure that all users are logged off and that no applications are using the database before you stop the database.

The easiest way to start the database service and listener is to use the Start Database command that's available from the Windows Start menu. When you select this command on a Windows system, a DOS window will be displayed that indicates the status of the Oracle listener and service.

How to stop the database

- Start→All Programs→Oracle Database 10g Express Edition→Stop Database

The DOS window that's displayed when the database is being stopped

How to start the database

- Start→All Programs→Oracle Database 10g Express Edition→Start Database

The DOS window that's displayed when the database is started

Description

- After you install the Oracle Database, the *database service* and *database listener* will start automatically each time you start your computer. The database service can also be referred to as the *database server* or the *database engine*.
- To stop or start the database server and listener, you can use the commands that are available from the Windows Start menu.
- When Oracle Database 11g Express Edition becomes available, you should be able to use a similar technique to stop and start that version of the Oracle Database.

Figure 2-1   How to start and stop the database service

How to use the Database Home Page

Figure 2-2 shows how to use a web-based tool known as the Database Home Page to work with an Oracle database. This tool is installed when you install the Oracle Database as described in appendix A, and it's useful for handling some tasks. In particular, it provides a way to create a new user for the database.

To begin, you can start the Database Home Page by selecting the Go To Database Home Page command from the Windows Start menu. Then, you can log in as the system user. If you followed the advice of appendix A, that means you'll use "system" as the username and "system" as the password.

After you've logged in, you can use the Create User command and the resulting web page to create a new user. When you create a new user, you provide a username and a password. You can also limit the types of tasks that the user will be able to do. In chapter 12, you can learn more about this. But for now, you don't need to restrict any of the user's privileges when you create a new user.

You can get a feel for the functionality that's available from the Database Home Page by browsing through its Administration, Browser, SQL, and Utilities menus. If you do that, you'll see that you can use this tool to accomplish a wide range of tasks. For most tasks, though, it's easier to use the SQL Developer tool that's described later in this chapter.

The Database Home Page

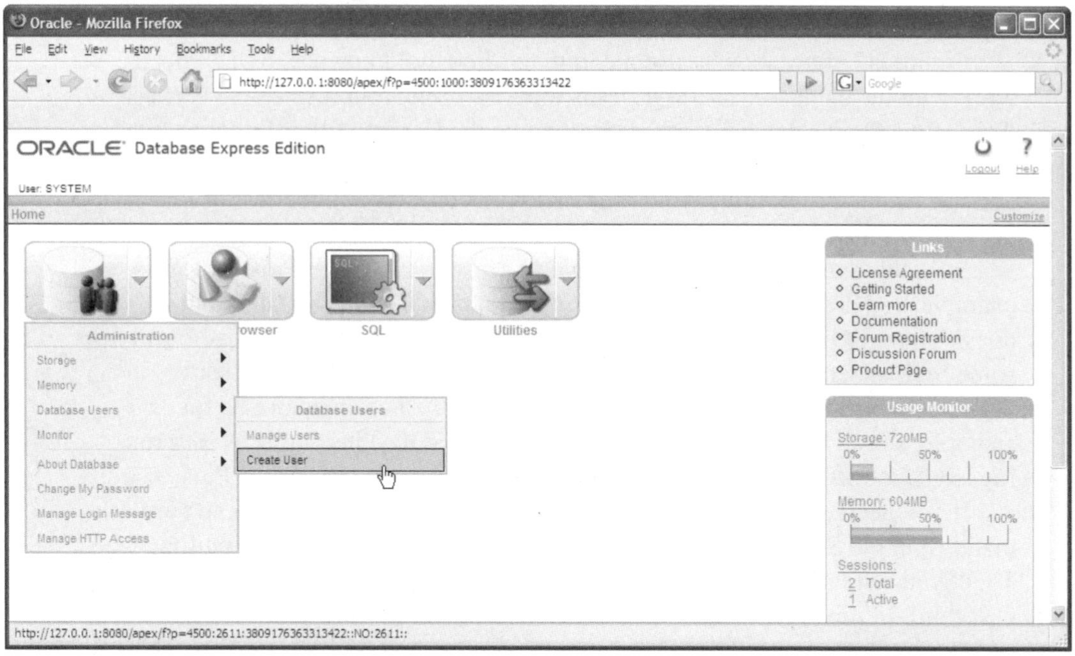

How to start the Database Home Page

- From the Windows Start menu, select All Programs→Oracle Database 10g Express Edition→Go To Database Home Page. Then, use the Database Login page to log in.

How to use the Database Home Page to create a user for a database

- Log in as the system user, select the Administration→Database Users→Create User command, and use the resulting web page to create the user.

Description

- The Database Home Page is a web-based tool that's installed with the Oracle Database. You can use it to work with an Oracle Database.

- After you log in, you can use the Administration, Browser, SQL, and Utilities menus to work with the database.

- For most tasks, it's easier to use the SQL Developer tool that's described later in this chapter.

Figure 2-2   How to use the Database Home Page

How to use SQL*Plus

Figure 2-3 shows how to use a command-line tool known as SQL*Plus to work with the database. The SQL*Plus tool has been around since the earliest days of the Oracle database, and many Oracle developers still use it. However, the newer SQL Developer tool described later in this chapter is easier to learn and use than the SQL*Plus tool. That's why this chapter and the rest of this book shows how to work with the SQL Developer tool.

Still, there may be times when it makes sense to use SQL*Plus. If, for example, you are working on a computer that has SQL*Plus installed but doesn't have SQL Developer installed, you may need to use SQL*Plus to run some SQL statements. Or, you may need to develop a batch file that uses SQL*Plus to run one or more SQL scripts. Figure A-5 of appendix A, for example, shows how to run a batch file that starts SQL*Plus and uses it to run four SQL scripts. In that case, of course, it makes sense to use SQL*Plus.

If you need to start SQL*Plus, you can do that by selecting the Run command from the Start menu, entering "sqlplus", and selecting the OK button. Then, you can connect to the database as a user by entering the username and password. In this figure, for example, I started by connecting as the AP user.

Once you're connected to the database, you can run SQL statements. To do that, you type the SQL statement followed by a semicolon and press the Enter key. Then, if the statement selects data, SQL*Plus will display the data. In this figure, for example, I entered a SQL statement that displays the vendor_name for the vendor with an id of 11.

At any time, you can connect to the database as a different user by entering the CONNECT command. When you enter this command, SQL*Plus prompts you for a username and password. In this figure, for example, I entered the CONNECT command to connect as the OM user.

The SQL*Plus tool

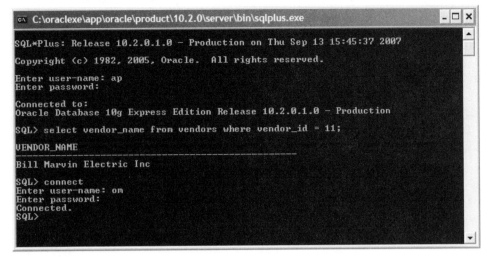

Description

- SQL*Plus is a command-line tool that's installed with the Oracle Database. You can use it to work with an Oracle Database.

- To start SQL*Plus, select the Run command from the Start menu, enter "sqlplus", and select the OK button.

- To connect to a database, enter the username and password. If necessary, you can enter the CONNECT command to have SQL*Plus prompt you for a username and password.

- To run a SQL statement, type it, type a semicolon, and press the Enter key.

- For most tasks, it's easier to use the SQL Developer tool that's described later in this chapter.

Figure 2-3   How to use SQL*Plus

How to use SQL Developer to work with a database

Oracle SQL Developer is a free graphical tool that makes it easy to work with Oracle databases, and it's the tool that we recommend for working with an Oracle database. As you will see, this tool makes it easy for you to review or modify the design of a database.

As of press time for this book, the current version of SQL Developer is version 1.5, so that's the version presented in this chapter. However, with some minor variations, the skills presented in this chapter should work for later versions as well.

When you use SQL Developer, you can connect to any Oracle Database version 9.2.0.1 or later. To connect to earlier versions, you need to use another tool such as the SQL*Plus tool described in the previous figure.

How to create a database connection

Before you can work with a database, you need to create a connection to the database. When you start SQL Developer, the Connections window displays all available database connections. To create a new connection, you can use the procedure described in figure 2-4.

If you have installed the software for this book as described in figure A-5 of appendix A, the AP, OM, and EX users with passwords of AP, OM, and EX will be available on your system. As a result, you will be able to create connections for these three users. Specifically, we suggest that you use the AP user to work with the tables in the AP schema, the OM user to work with the tables in the OM schema, and the EX user to work with the tables in the EX schema.

When you create a database connection, you should note that the usernames and passwords are not case-sensitive. As a result, it doesn't matter if you enter the usernames and passwords in uppercase or lowercase. In this figure, for example, I entered the usernames and passwords in lowercase because it's easier to type in lowercase.

How to export or import database connections

If you want to copy several database connections from one computer to another, you can export the database connections to an XML file as described in this figure. Then, you can use this XML file to import those database connections on another computer. For example, I exported the database connections for the AP, OM, and EX users to this file:

```
c:\murach\oracle_sql\db_setup\connections.xml
```

As a result, if you want, you can use the technique shown in this figure to import the connections that are stored in this file.

The dialog box for creating database connections

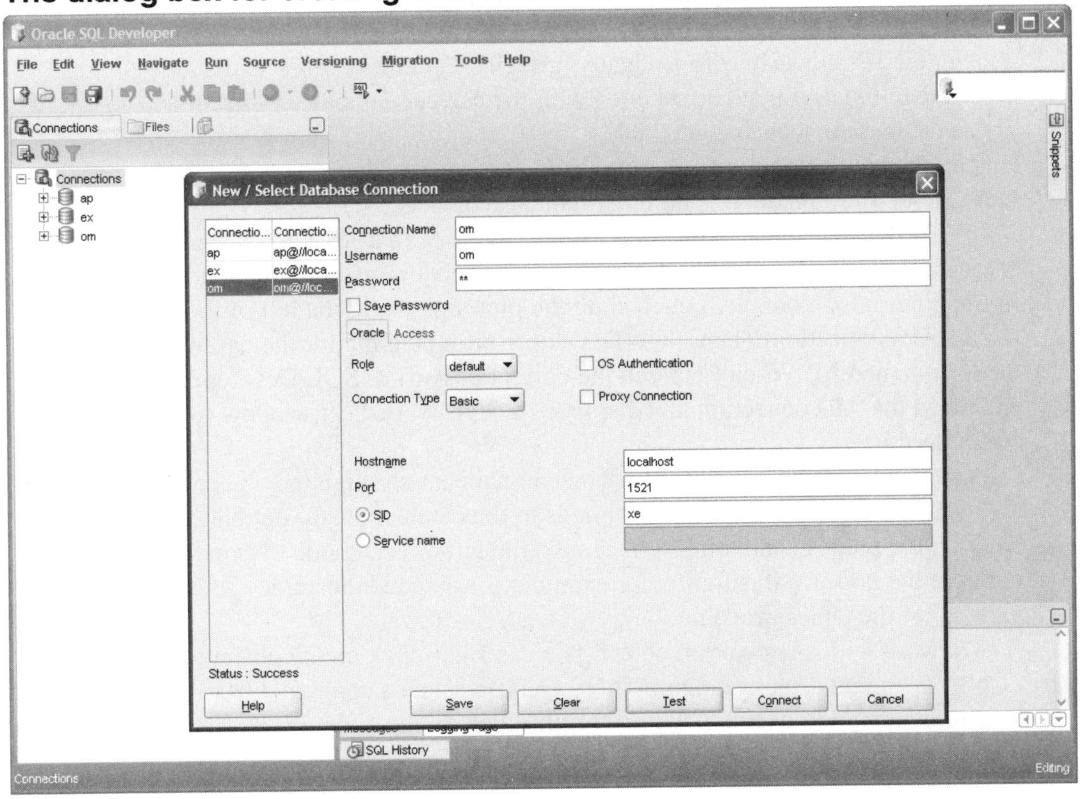

How to create a database connection

1. Right-click on the Connections node in the Connections window and select the New Connection command to display the dialog box for creating database connections.

2. Enter a connection name, username, and password for the connection.

3. Click the Test button to test the connection. If the connection works, a success message is displayed above the Help button.

4. Click the Save button to save the connection. When you do, the connection will be added to the dialog box and to the Connections window.

How to export or import database connections

- To export database connections, right-click the Connections node, select the Export Connections command, and use the resulting dialog box to select the connections that you want to export and to specify the path and filename for the XML file for the connections.

- To import connections, right-click the Connections node, select the Import Connections command, and use the resulting dialog box to navigate to the XML file for the connections. Then, select the connections that you want to import.

Figure 2-4   How to create, export, or import a database connection

How to navigate through the database objects

Figure 2-5 shows how to navigate through the *database objects* that are available to the user that corresponds with the current database connection. These database objects include tables, views, indexes, and so on. For this chapter, however, you can focus on the tables. Later in this book, you'll learn more about views, indexes, and other database objects.

When you expand a connection for the first time in a session, you must enter the password for the username in the Connection Information dialog box. In this figure, for example, I clicked on the plus sign (+) to the left of the node for the AP connection. Then, SQL Developer prompted me for the password for the user named AP. When I entered the correct password, SQL Developer expanded the AP connection and displayed a SQL Worksheet window for the AP connection.

Once you expand a connection, you can navigate through the objects that are available for the user that corresponds to the connection. To do that, you can click on the plus (+) and minus (-) signs to the left of each node to expand or collapse the node. In this figure, for example, I expanded the Tables node to view all of the tables available to the AP user.

To work with a node or an object, you can right-click on the object to display a context-sensitive menu. Then, you can select a command from the resulting menu. For example, you can right-click on the node for the AP connection to display a list of commands for working with that connection.

The Connection Information dialog box

The tables available to the AP user

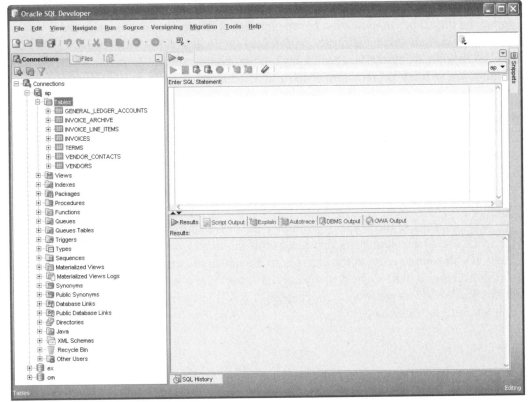

Description

- Each connection provides access to the *database objects* that are available to the user that corresponds with the connection. These database objects include tables, views, and so on.

- Before you can expand a connection for the first time in a session, you must enter the correct password for the connection. Once you enter a password for a connection, you can navigate through the nodes for the database objects. You can also use the SQL Worksheet window to enter and run SQL statements.

- To navigate through the database objects for a connection, click on the plus (+) and minus (-) signs to the left of each node to expand or collapse the node.

- To work with a node or an object, right-click on the node or object and select a command from the resulting menu.

Figure 2-5   How to navigate through the database objects

How to view the column definitions for a table

To view the column names for a table, you can expand the node for the table. In figure 2-6, for example, I expanded the node for the Vendors table so the names for all of columns in the table are displayed below the table.

To view the column definitions for a table, you can click on the table name to display a table that contains the definition of each column. In this figure, for example, the right-hand window shows a table that contains the definitions for each column in the Vendors table. For each column, this table shows the column name, the data type, an indication of whether or not the column can contain null values, the default value, the position of the column within the table, whether or not the column is a primary key, and any column comments. By default, the columns are displayed in the sequence in which they were created.

How to view the data for a table

To view the data for a table, you just click on the Data tab after you display the column definitions for the table. By switching back and forth between the Column and Data tabs, you can quickly see how the data corresponds to the data definitions.

You can also use the Data tab to modify the data in a row, and you can use the Insert and Delete buttons at the start of this tab to add rows or delete rows. Then, if you want to commit the changes to the table, you can click on the Commit Changes button. Or, if you want to rollback the changes, you can click on the Rollback Changes button. In chapter 7, you'll learn more about committing and rolling back changes.

How to view the column definitions for a table

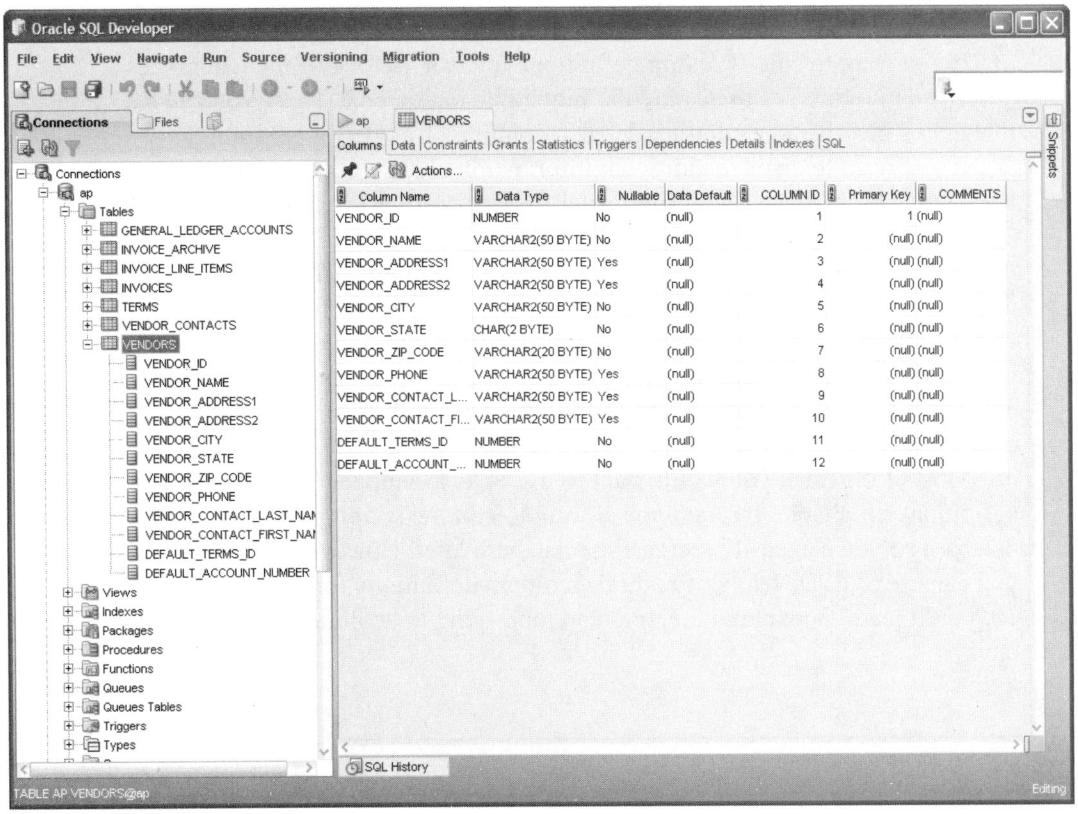

How to view the column definitions for a table

- To view the column names for a table, expand the Tables node and then expand the node for the table you wish to view. This displays the columns in the Connections window.

- To view the column definitions for a table, click on the name of the table in the Connections window. This displays detailed information about the columns of the table in the window to the right of the Connections window.

- By default, the columns are displayed in the sequence in which they were created.

How to view the data for a table

- Click on the Data tab in the window that's displaying the column definitions for the table.

Figure 2-6   How to view the column definitions and data for a table

How to edit the column definitions

If you want to edit a column definition, you can use one of the techniques described in figure 2-7 to display the Edit Table dialog box. Then, you can use this dialog box to add a column, delete a column, or modify a column.

If you want to display additional information about a column, you can select the column by clicking on it. Then, additional properties are displayed in the Column Properties group that's displayed on the right side of the dialog box. In this figure, for example, the properties for the DefaultTermsID column are displayed. In addition, a default value of 3 has been entered for this column. Note that the properties that are available change depending on the data type of the column. For a column with the VARCHAR2 data type, for example, the properties also indicate the length of the column. You'll learn more about that in chapter 8.

Most of the time, you won't want to use SQL Developer to edit the column definitions for a table. Instead, you'll want to edit the scripts that create the database so you can easily recreate the database later. However, if necessary, you can use SQL Developer to edit the column definitions for a table. In chapter 10, you'll learn more about creating and modifying the column definitions for a table.

How to edit the column definition of a table

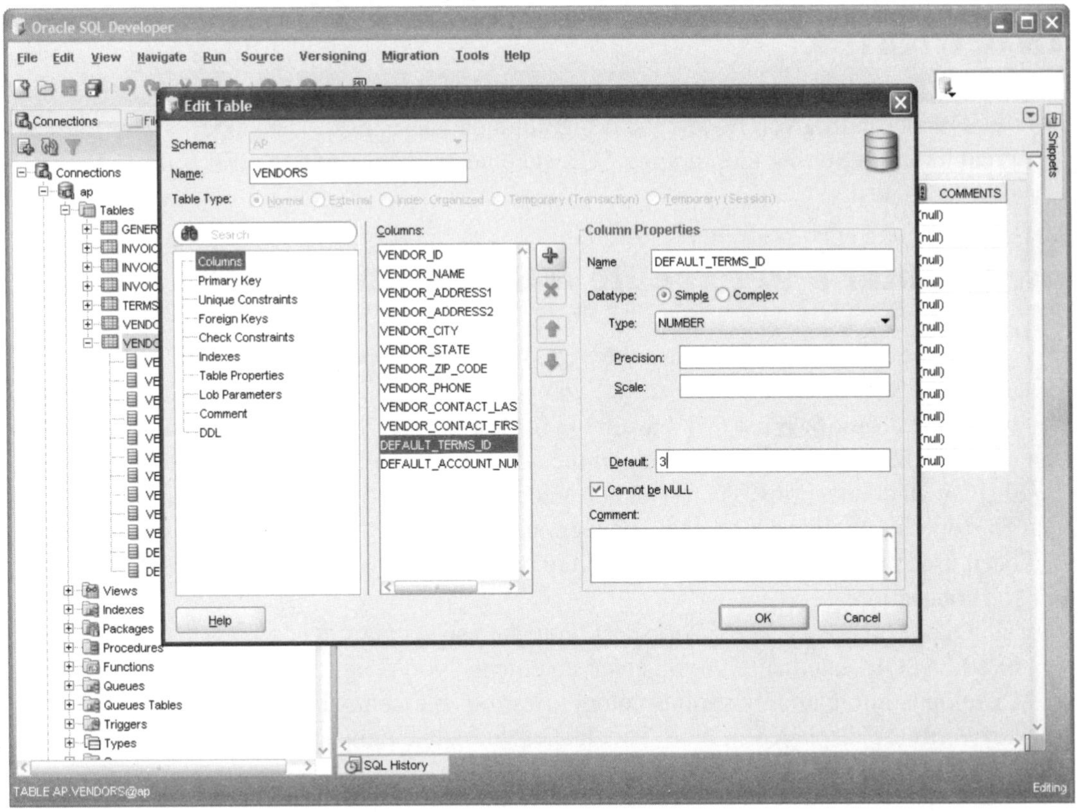

Description

- To edit the definition of a table, right-click on the table name, select the Edit command, and use the Edit Table dialog box to modify the table.

- You can use the Edit Table dialog box to add a column, delete a column, or change the properties of an existing column such as the name, data type, default value, and so on.

- You can also use the Edit Table dialog box to add, delete, or modify a table-level constraint, an index, or a table-level comment.

- For more information about creating tables, see chapter 10.

Figure 2-7   How to edit the column definitions

How to use SQL Developer to run SQL statements

Besides letting you review the design of a database, SQL Developer is a great tool for entering and running SQL statements. That's what you'll learn how to do next.

How to enter and execute a SQL statement

Figure 2-8 shows how to use the SQL Worksheet window to enter and execute a SQL statement. The easiest way to open a SQL Worksheet window is to use the drop-down list that's available from the Open SQL Worksheet button on the toolbar. First, you can click on the arrow to the right of this button to display all connections. Then, you can select the connection you want to use. This opens a Worksheet for that connection. But first, if the connection hasn't been used in the current session, you may be prompted to enter the password for the connection.

Once you open a SQL Worksheet, you can use standard techniques to enter or edit a SQL statement. As you enter statements, you'll notice that SQL Developer automatically applies colors to various elements. For example, keywords are displayed in blue. This makes your statements easier to read and understand and can help you identify coding errors.

When you enter SQL statements, you'll notice that SQL Developer automatically displays a drop-down list that helps you enter SQL statements. This feature often provides help for entering SQL keywords, table names, column names, and so on. In this figure, for example, SQL Developer displayed a drop-down list after I entered the ORDER BY keywords and pressed the spacebar. At this point, you can easily select a column name from the drop-down list.

If you experiment with this code completion feature, you'll find that SQL Developer doesn't display column names automatically until you enter the name of the table that's used by the statement. As a result, if you want to use the code completion feature, you may want to enter the table name before you enter the column names.

Most of the time, SQL Developer automatically displays the drop-down list after you enter some code followed by a space. Usually, that's what you want. However, there are times when you may want to manually prompt SQL Developer to display the drop-down list. To do that, you can press the Ctrl key and the spacebar at the same time (Ctrl+spacebar).

In addition, you can use SQL Developer to automatically comment or uncomment a line. To do that, you can move the insertion point into the line. Then, you can press Ctrl key and the front slash at the same time (Ctrl+/).

To execute a single SQL statement like the one in this figure, you can press F9 or click the Execute Statement button in the toolbar for the SQL Worksheet window. If the statement returns data, that data is displayed in the Results tab. In

A SELECT statement and its results

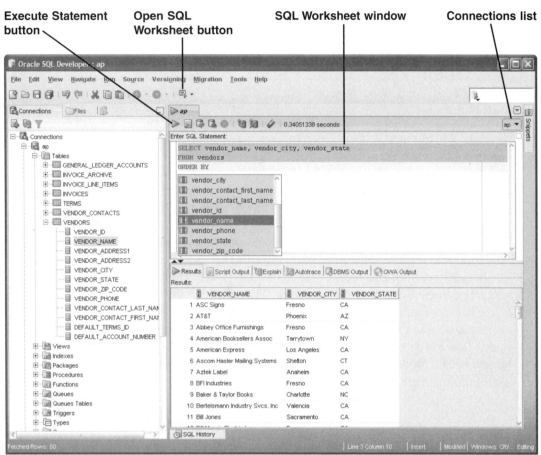

Description

- To open a new SQL Worksheet window, drop down the list from the Open SQL Worksheet button. Then, select the connection you want to use.
- To change the connection for the worksheet, use the Connections list.
- To enter a SQL statement, type it into the SQL Worksheet window.
- As you enter the text for a statement, the SQL Worksheet window applies color to various elements, such as SQL keywords, to make them easy to identify.
- As you enter the text for a statement, you can use the code completion feature to select SQL keywords, table names, column names, and so on.
- To manually display the code completion list, press Ctrl+spacebar.
- To comment out a line or to uncomment a line, press Ctrl+/.
- To execute a SQL statement, press the F9 key or click the Execute Statement button in the toolbar. If the statement retrieves data, the data is displayed in the Results tab of the SQL Worksheet window.

Figure 2-8   How to enter and execute a SQL statement

this figure, for example, the result set returned by the SELECT statement is displayed. If necessary, you can adjust the height of the Results pane by dragging the bar that separates the SQL Worksheet window from the Results tab.

How to work with the Snippets window

Figure 2-9 shows how to use the Snippets window to enter a *snippet* of code into the SQL Worksheet window. To start, if the Snippets tab isn't displayed on the right side of the SQL Developer window, you can select the Snippets command from the View menu to display the Snippets window. Otherwise, you can display the Snippets window by clicking on the Snippets tab that's displayed on the right side of the SQL Developer window. Then, you can use the drop-down list at the top of the Snippets window to select a category of snippets, and you can drag a snippet from the Snippets window into the SQL Worksheet window. At that point, you can edit the snippet code so it's appropriate for your SQL statement.

In this figure, for example, I dragged the COUNT(*) and SUM(expr) snippets into the SQL Worksheet window. Then, I edited the SUM(expr) snippet to replace the expr placeholder with a valid expression.

For now, don't worry if you don't understand the SQL statement presented in this figure. The main point is that you can use the Snippets window to enter a variety of SQL code. As you learn more about SQL statements, you'll see how useful this can be.

How to use the Snippets window

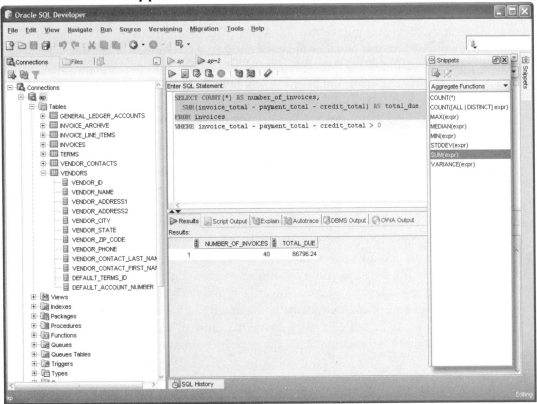

Description

- If the Snippets tab isn't displayed on the right side of the SQL Developer window, you can display it by selecting the Snippets command from the View menu.

- To display the Snippets window, click on the Snippets tab that's displayed on the right side of the SQL Developer window.

- To display another category of *snippets*, select the category from the drop-down list at the top of the Snippets window. The snippets are organized in 10 categories including: Date Formats, Number Formats, Date/Time Functions, Number Functions, Character Functions, Conversion Functions, and Pseudocolumns.

- To enter a snippet into your code, drag the snippet from the Snippets window into the SQL Worksheet window. Then, if necessary, edit the snippet code so it's appropriate for your SQL statement.

- The Snippets window will become more useful as you learn more about formats and functions.

Figure 2-9   How to use the Snippets window

How to handle syntax errors

If an error occurs during the execution of a SQL statement, SQL Developer displays a dialog box that includes the error number, a brief description of the error, and the location of the error in your code. In figure 2-10, for example, the dialog box displays an error number of "ORA-00942" and a brief description that says "table or view does not exist." This dialog box also indicates that the error occurred at line 2, column 5, where a table or view named Vendor is referenced.

In this example, the problem is that the Vendor table doesn't exist in the database. To fix the problem, you need to edit the SQL statement so the table is Vendors instead of Vendor. Then, you should be able to successfully run the SQL statement.

This figure also lists some other common causes of errors. As you can see, most errors are caused by incorrect syntax. However, it's also possible that you will get an error if you are connected as the wrong user. If, for example, you are connected as the EX user and you try to run a statement that references tables in the AP schema, you may get an error. Regardless of what's causing the problem, you can usually identify and correct the problem without much trouble. In some cases, though, it may be difficult to figure out the cause of an error. Then, you can usually get more information about the error by searching the Internet.

How to handle syntax errors

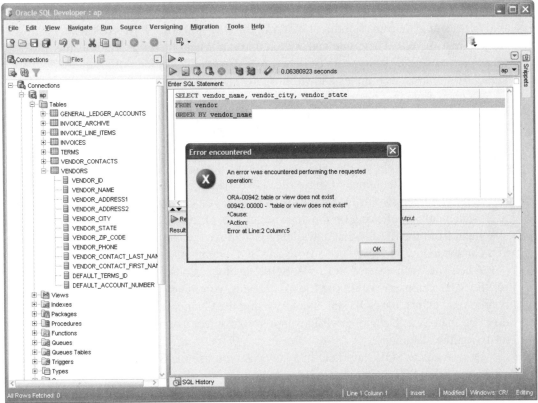

Common causes of errors

- Misspelling the name of a table or column
- Misspelling a keyword
- Omitting the closing quotation mark for a character string
- Being connected as the wrong user

Description

- If an error occurs during the execution of a SQL statement, SQL Developer displays a dialog box that includes an error code, a brief description of the error, and the location of the error in the code.
- Most errors are caused by incorrect syntax and can be corrected without any additional assistance. Otherwise, you can usually get more information about an error by searching for the error code or description on the Internet.

Figure 2-10   How to handle syntax errors

How to open and save SQL statements

After you get a SQL statement working the way you want it to work, you may want to save it. Then, you can open it and run it again later or use it as the basis for a new SQL statement. To save a SQL statement, you can use the standard Windows techniques shown in figure 2-11.

To open a file that has been saved, you use the Open command. In this figure, for example, the Open dialog box shows the SQL statements that have been saved for chapter 3. They are saved in the scripts\ch03 directory that is created when you download and install the source code for this book. The screen in this figure shows the tabs for three files that have been opened for that chapter. Note that the names of these files have the sql extension.

After you open two or more SQL worksheets, you can switch between the SQL statements by clicking on the appropriate tab. Or, you can select the SQL statement from the file list that's available just above the Connections list. Then, you can cut, copy, and paste code from one SQL statement to another.

When you open a saved SQL file, SQL Developer doesn't set a connection for the SQL statement within the file. As a result, you must specify a connection before you can run the SQL statement by using the Connections list. If you don't do that, SQL Developer will prompt you to select a connection when you try to run the statement.

To save a new SQL statement in a new file, you use the Save command. To save a modified SQL statement in its original file, you also use the Save command. And to save a modified SQL statement in a new file, you use the Save As command.

To set the default directory that you want to use for saving new SQL statements, you can use the Tools→Preferences command that's described in this figure. Note, however, that there's no way to set the default directory for opening files.

For both the Open and Save dialog boxes, you can specify a recently used directory by clicking on its icon. In this figure, for example, the Open dialog box shows that the ch02, ch03, and db_setup directories have all been used recently. As a result, you can easily specify one of these directories by clicking on it.

The Open File dialog box

Description

- To open a SQL file, click the Open button in the toolbar, press Ctrl+O, or select the File→Open command. Then, use the Open dialog box to locate and open the SQL file.

- To specify a connection for a SQL statement that you open, select a connection from the Connections list (see figure 2-8). Otherwise, when you try to run the statement, SQL Developer will display a dialog box that prompts you to select a connection.

- To switch between open statements, select the appropriate tab. Or, click on the drop-down arrow that's displayed to the right of the SQL Worksheet tabs, and select the file name from the file list.

- To cut, copy, and paste code from one SQL statement to another, use the standard Windows techniques.

- To save a SQL statement, click the Save button in the toolbar, press Ctrl+S, or select the File→Save command. Then, if necessary, use the Save dialog box to specify a file name for the SQL statement.

- To change the default directory for new statements that you want to save, use the Tools→Preferences command. Then, expand the Database node, click on the Worksheet Parameters node, and change the default path for scripts.

- To specify a recently used directory in an Open or Save dialog box, click on the icon for the recently used directory.

Figure 2-11   How to open and save SQL statements

How to enter and execute a SQL script

A *SQL script* is a file that contains one or more SQL statements. So far in this chapter, each of the SQL files that has been presented has been a SQL script that contains just one SQL statement. However, a SQL script typically contains multiple statements.

When you code multiple SQL statements within a script, you must code a semicolon at the end of each SQL statement. For example, figure 2-12 shows a script that contains two SQL statements. Then, you can press F5 or click the Run Script button to execute all of the SQL statements that are stored in the script. When you do, the results of the script will be displayed in the Script Output tab.

However, if you want to execute a single SQL statement that's stored within a script, you can do that by moving the insertion point into the statement and pressing the F9 key or clicking the Execute Statement button in the toolbar. Then, if the statement retrieves data, the data is displayed in a Results tab like the one in figure 2-8. In this figure, for example, the insertion point is in the first SQL statement, and this statement is a SELECT statement that retrieves data. As a result, if you press the F9 key, the result set is displayed in the Results tab.

A SQL script and its results

Run Script button

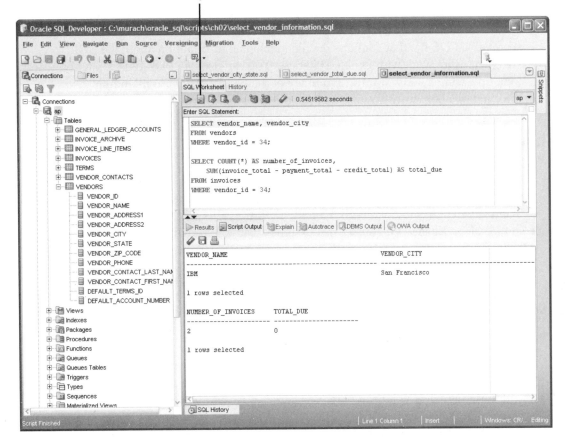

Description

- A *SQL script* is a file that contains one or more SQL statements. When you code a script that contains more than one statement, you must code a semicolon at the end of each statement.

- To run the entire SQL script, press the F5 key or click the Run Script button that's located just to the right of the Execute Statement button. The results are displayed in the Script Output tab.

- To execute one SQL statement within a script, move the insertion point into the statement. Then, press the F9 key or click the Execute Statement button in the toolbar. If the statement retrieves data, the data is displayed in the Results tab.

Figure 2-12   How to enter and execute a SQL script

How to use the SQL Reference manual

Figure 2-13 shows how to use another useful tool for working with the Oracle Database: the SQL Reference manual. This manual is available as a searchable PDF file that contains detailed technical information about the SQL statements that work with Oracle Database. You can use this PDF file to quickly look up a wide variety of information about the Oracle Database including information about its SQL statements and functions.

How to view the manual

If you have the PDF file for the SQL Reference manual installed on your computer as described in appendix A, you can open the manual by using the Windows Explorer to double-click on the PDF file. This will open the PDF file in the Adobe Reader. Of course, this assumes that you have the Adobe Reader installed on your system. If you don't, you can download it for free from Adobe's web site.

How to look up information

Once you've opened the PDF file for the SQL Reference manual in the Adobe Reader, there are several ways that you can look up information. In short, you can use any standard techniques for working with a PDF file to work with this manual. If you need help, you can use the Adobe Reader's Help menu to learn more about using Adobe Reader.

One easy way to look up information is to scroll through the table of contents. To do that, click on the plus (+) and minus (-) signs in the left column to expand or collapse the topics. Then, when you find the topic you want, click on it to display the topic in the right pane. Once you do that, you can scroll up or down to view the entire topic. In this figure, for example, I expanded the topic named "SQL Statements: SAVEPOINT to UPDATE," and I clicked on the SELECT topic to display information about the SQL SELECT statement.

Another easy to way to look up information is to search for a specific word or phrase. To do that, type the word or phrase in the Find text box and press the Enter key. Then, you can click on the Find Next or Find Previous button to find the next or previous occurrence of the word or phrase. In this figure, for example, I entered "select statement" into the Find text box and pressed the Enter key.

How to use the Oracle Database SQL Reference manual

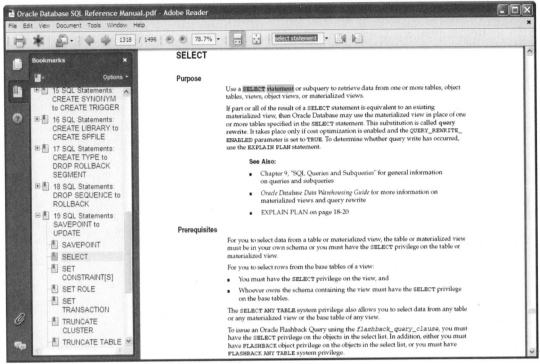

Description

- The Oracle Database SQL Reference manual is available as a searchable PDF file that contains detailed technical information about the SQL statements that work with the Oracle Database.

- If you have the PDF file for the SQL Reference manual installed on your computer, you can start it by using the Windows Explorer to double-click on the file.

- To scroll through the table of contents, click on the plus (+) and minus (-) signs to expand or collapse the topics. When you find the topic you want, click on it to display the topic in the right pane. Then, you can scroll up or down to view the entire topic.

- To search for a particular word or phrase, type the word or phrase in the Find text box in the toolbar and press the Enter key. Then, you can click on the Find Next or Find Previous button to find the next or previous occurrence of the word or phrase.

Note

- The name of the Oracle Database SQL Reference manual varies slightly from one release to another.

Figure 2-13   How to use the Oracle Database SQL Reference manual

Perspective

In this chapter, you learned how to use the tools that you need to work with an Oracle database and to enter and execute SQL statements. With that as background, you're ready to go on to the next chapter, where you'll start learning the details of coding your own SQL statements. To start, you'll learn the details for coding a SELECT statement that retrieves data from a single table.

Before you go on to the next chapter, though, we recommend that you install all of the software for this book on your computer as described in Appendix A. You should also do the exercises that follow. That will get you off to a good start with Oracle Database and the Oracle Database tools.

Terms

Oracle Database
database service
database server
database engine
database listener
Database Home Page
SQL*Plus
database object
Oracle SQL Developer
snippet
SQL script
Oracle Database SQL Reference manual

Before you start the exercises...

Before you start the exercises for this chapter, you need to install Oracle Database Express Edition and Oracle SQL Developer. You also need to download and install the source files for this book, and you need to create the users and tables for this book. The procedures for doing all of these tasks are provided in appendix A.

Exercises

In these exercises, you'll use SQL Developer to review the tables in the AP schema that's used throughout this book. In addition, you'll use SQL developer to enter SQL statements and run them against these tables.

Make sure Oracle Database is running

1.   Use the procedure in figure 2-1 to start the database service for Oracle Database. If it is already running, you'll get a message that confirms that. Otherwise, the database service will be started. Either way, you can close the DOS window that's opened.

Use SQL Developer to review the Accounts Payable database

2. Start Oracle SQL Developer. If you created a menu or desktop shortcut when you installed SQL Developer, you can use that shortcut now. Otherwise, you can use the Windows Explorer to find and double-click on the sqldeveloper.exe file.

3. Create the AP, EX, and OM connections as described in figure 2-4. When you're done, the Connections window should display three connections: AP, EX, and OM.

4. In the Connections window, click on the AP connection to expand it. When you're prompted for a password, enter "ap". That will expand the connection so you can see all of the database objects in the AP schema.

5. Use the techniques in figures 2-5 and 2-6 to navigate through the database objects and view the column definitions for at least the Vendors and Invoices tables.

6. Use the technique in figure 2-6 to view the data for the Vendors and Invoices tables.

Use SQL Developer to enter and run SQL statements

7. Use the technique in figure 2-8 to open a SQL Worksheet window for the AP connection. Then, enter and run this SQL statement:

```
SELECT vendor_name FROM vendors
```

8. Use the code completion feature described in figure 2-8 to enhance this SQL statement so it includes an ORDER BY clause and some additional columns like this:

```
SELECT vendor_name, vendor_address1, vendor_city, vendor_state,
    vendor_zip_code
FROM vendors
ORDER BY vendor_name
```

Then, run the statement.

9. Move the cursor into the ORDER BY clause and press Ctrl+/ to comment out the line. Then, press Ctrl+/ again to uncomment the line.

10. Delete the *e* at the end of vendor_zip_code and run the statement again. Note that this syntax error is handled as in figure 2-10.

11. Open another Worksheet window, and use the COUNT and SUM snippets as shown in figure 2-9 as you enter this statement:

```
SELECT COUNT(*) AS number_of_invoices,
    SUM(invoice_total) AS grand_invoice_total
FROM invoices
```

Then, run the statement.

12. Use the Tools→Preferences command to set the default path for scripts as described in figure 2-11. Then, click on the tab for the Worksheet window of exercise 8, click the Save button to save this statement, and note the directory in the Save dialog box. Next, click the Cancel button in the Save dialog box to cancel the command.

Use SQL Developer to open and run scripts

13. Use the technique in figure 2-11 to open the select_vendor_city_state script that's in the c:\murach\oracle_sql\scripts\ch02 directory. Notice that this script contains just one SQL statement. Then, run the statement. Because you didn't specify a connection for this statement, SQL Developer will ask you to select one before it runs the statement.

14. Click on the Open button. Note that the recently used directories including the ch02 directory are shown on the left side of the Open dialog box. Then, click on the ch02 directory to display the files that are stored in this directory. Next, click the Cancel button to close this dialog box.

15. Open the select_vendor_total_due script that's in the ch02 directory. Note that this opens another tab. Next, select the AP connection from the connection list and run this script.

16. Open the select_vendor_information script that's in the ch02 directory. Notice that this script contains two SQL statements that end with semicolons (scroll down if you need to). Then, move the insertion point to the first statement and press F9 to run that statement. Next, move the insertion point to the second statement and press F9 to run that statement. Last, press F5 or click the Run Script button to run both of the statements that are stored in this script. If you scroll through the Script Output window, you will see the results of the two SELECT statements that were run.

Close and restart SQL Developer

17. Continue to experiment on your own. Make sure to leave at least one saved script open. When you're ready to end this session, use the File→Exit command or click on the Close button in the upper right corner of the SQL Developer window.

18. Restart SQL Developer. When it starts, notice that all of the saved scripts that you left open are automatically opened. However, any unsaved scripts that you entered are lost.

19. Run one of the open scripts. Note that you have to select a connection and provide a password for the connection before the script will run.

20. Exit from SQL Developer.

Section 2

The essential SQL skills

This section teaches you the essential SQL coding skills for working with the data in an Oracle database. The first four chapters show you how to retrieve data from a database using the SELECT statement. In chapter 3, you'll learn how to code the basic clauses of the SELECT statement to retrieve data from a single table. In chapter 4, you'll learn how to retrieve data from two or more tables. In chapter 5, you'll learn how to summarize the data that you retrieve. And in chapter 6, you'll learn how to code subqueries, which are SELECT statements that are coded within other statements.

Next, chapter 7 shows you how to use the INSERT, UPDATE, and DELETE statements to add new rows to a table, to modify rows in a table, and to remove rows from a table. Then, chapter 8 shows you how to work with the various types of data that Oracle supports and how to use some of the built-in functions that Oracle provides for working with these data types. When you complete the six chapters in this section, you'll have all the skills you need to code SELECT, INSERT, UPDATE, and DELETE statements.

3

How to retrieve data from a single table

In this chapter, you'll learn how to code SELECT statements that retrieve data from a single table. You should realize, though, that the skills covered here are the essential ones that apply to any SELECT statement, no matter how many tables it operates on and no matter how complex the retrieval. So you'll want to have a good understanding of the material in this chapter before you go on to the chapters that follow.

An introduction to the SELECT statement

To help you learn to code the SELECT statement, this chapter starts by presenting its basic syntax. Next, it presents several examples that will give you an idea of what you can do with this statement. Then, the rest of this chapter will teach you the details of coding this statement.

The basic syntax of the SELECT statement

Figure 3-1 presents the basic syntax of the SELECT statement. The syntax summary at the top of this figure uses some conventions that are used throughout this book. First, capitalized words are called *keywords*, and you must spell them exactly as shown, though you can use whatever capitalization you prefer. For example, the following are equivalent: "SELECT", "Select", "select" and "sELeCt". Second, you must provide replacements for words in lowercase. For example, you must enter a list of columns in place of *select_list*, and you must enter a table name in place of *table_source*.

Beyond that, you can choose between the items in a syntax summary that are separated by pipes (|) and enclosed in braces ({}) or brackets ([]). And you can omit items enclosed in brackets. If you have a choice between two or more optional items, the default item is underlined. And if an element can be coded multiple times in a statement, it's followed by an ellipsis (…). You'll see examples of pipes, braces, default values, and ellipses in syntax summaries later in this chapter. For now, compare the syntax in this figure with the coding examples in figure 3-2 to see how the two are related.

The syntax summary in this figure has been simplified so that you can focus on the four main clauses of the SELECT statement: the SELECT clause, the FROM clause, the WHERE clause, and the ORDER BY clause. Most of the SELECT statements you code will contain all four clauses. However, only the SELECT and FROM clauses are required.

The SELECT clause is always the first clause in a SELECT statement. It identifies the columns you want to include in the result set. These columns are retrieved from the *base tables* named in the FROM clause. Since this chapter focuses on retrieving data from a single table, the FROM clauses in all of the statements in this chapter name a single base table. In the next chapter, though, you'll learn how to retrieve data from two or more tables. And as you progress through this book, you'll learn how to select data from other sources such as views and expressions.

The WHERE and ORDER BY clauses are optional. The ORDER BY clause determines how the rows in the result set are to be sorted, and the WHERE clause determines which rows in the base table are to be included in the result set. The WHERE clause specifies a search condition that's used to *filter* the rows in the base table. This search condition can consist of one or more *Boolean expressions*, or *predicates*. A Boolean expression is an expression that evaluates

The simplified syntax of the SELECT statement

```
SELECT select_list
FROM table_source
[WHERE search_condition]
[ORDER BY order_by_list]
```

The four clauses of the SELECT statement

Clause	Description
SELECT	Describes the columns that will be included in the result set.
FROM	Names the table from which the query will retrieve the data.
WHERE	Specifies the conditions that must be met for a row to be included in the result set. This clause is optional.
ORDER BY	Specifies how the rows in the result set will be sorted. This clause is optional.

Description

- You use the basic SELECT statement shown above to retrieve the columns specified in the SELECT clause from the *base table* specified in the FROM clause and store them in a result set.

- The WHERE clause is used to *filter* the rows in the base table so that only those rows that match the search condition are included in the result set. If you omit the WHERE clause, all of the rows in the base table are included.

- The search condition of a WHERE clause consists of one or more *Boolean expressions*, or *predicates*, that result in a value of True, False, or Unknown. If the combination of all the expressions is True, the row being tested is included in the result set. Otherwise, it's not.

- If you include the ORDER BY clause, the rows in the result set are sorted in the specified sequence. Otherwise, the sequence of the rows is not guaranteed by Oracle.

Note

- The syntax shown above does not include all of the clauses of the SELECT statement. You'll learn about the other clauses later in this book.

Figure 3-1   The basic syntax of the SELECT statement

to True or False. When the search condition evaluates to True, the row is included in the result set.

In this book, we won't use the terms "Boolean expression" or "predicate" because they don't clearly describe the content of the WHERE clause. Instead, we'll just use the term "search condition" to refer to an expression that evaluates to True or False.

SELECT statement examples

Figure 3-2 presents five SELECT statement examples. All of these statements retrieve data from the Invoices table.

The first statement in this figure retrieves all of the rows and columns from the Invoices table. This statement uses an asterisk (*) as a shorthand to indicate that all of the columns should be retrieved, and the WHERE clause is omitted so there are no conditions on the rows that are retrieved. You can see the results after this statement as they're displayed by SQL Developer. Here, both horizontal and vertical scroll bars are displayed, indicating that the result set contains more rows and columns than can be displayed on the screen at one time.

Notice that this statement doesn't include an ORDER BY clause. Without an ORDER BY clause, Oracle doesn't guarantee the sequence in which the rows are presented. They might be in the sequence you expect, or they might not. As a result, if the sequence matters to you, you should include an ORDER BY clause.

The second statement retrieves selected columns from the Invoices table. As you can see, the columns to be retrieved are listed in the SELECT clause. Like the first statement, this statement doesn't include a WHERE clause, so all the rows are retrieved. Then, the ORDER BY clause causes the rows to be sorted by the invoice_total column in ascending sequence. Later in this chapter, you'll learn how to sort rows in descending sequence.

The third statement also lists the columns to be retrieved. In this case, though, the last column is calculated from two columns in the base table (credit_total and payment_total), and the resulting column is given the name total_credits. In addition, the WHERE clause specifies that only the invoice with an invoice_id of 17 should be retrieved.

The fourth SELECT statement includes a WHERE clause whose condition specifies a range of values. In this case, only invoices with invoice dates between May 1, 2008 and May 31, 2008 are retrieved. In addition, the rows in the result set are sorted by invoice date.

The last statement in this figure shows another variation of the WHERE clause. In this case, only those rows with an invoice_total greater than 50,000 are retrieved. Since none of the rows in the Invoices table satisfies this condition, the result set is empty.

A SELECT statement that retrieves all the data from the Invoices table

```
SELECT *
FROM invoices
```

	INVOICE_ID	VENDOR_ID	INVOICE_NUMBER	INVOICE_DATE	INVOICE_TOTAL	PAYMENT_TOTAL	CREDIT_TOTAL
1	1	34	QP58872	25-FEB-08	116.54	116.54	0
2	2	34	Q545443	14-MAR-08	1083.58	1083.58	0
3	3	110	P-0608	11-APR-08	20551.18	0	1200
4	4	110	P-0259	16-APR-08	26881.4	26881.4	0

```
(114 rows selected)
```

A SELECT statement that retrieves three columns from each row, sorted in ascending sequence by invoice_total

```
SELECT invoice_number, invoice_date, invoice_total
FROM invoices
ORDER BY invoice_total
```

	INVOICE_NUMBER	INVOICE_DATE	INVOICE_TOTAL
1	25022117	24-MAY-08	6
2	24863706	27-MAY-08	6
3	24780512	29-MAY-08	6
4	21-4748363	09-MAY-08	9.95

```
(114 rows selected)
```

A SELECT statement that retrieves two columns and a calculated value for a specific invoice

```
SELECT invoice_id, invoice_total,
       (credit_total + payment_total) AS total_credits
FROM invoices
WHERE invoice_id = 17
```

	INVOICE_ID	INVOICE_TOTAL	TOTAL_CREDITS
1	17	356.48	356.48

A SELECT statement that retrieves all invoices between given dates

```
SELECT invoice_number, invoice_date, invoice_total
FROM invoices
WHERE invoice_date BETWEEN '01-MAY-2008' AND '31-MAY-2008'
ORDER BY invoice_date
```

	INVOICE_NUMBER	INVOICE_DATE	INVOICE_TOTAL
1	7548906-20	01-MAY-08	27
2	4-321-2596	01-MAY-08	10
3	4-327-7357	01-MAY-08	162.75
4	4-342-8069	01-MAY-08	10

```
(70 rows selected)
```

A SELECT statement that returns an empty result set

```
SELECT invoice_number, invoice_date, invoice_total
FROM invoices
WHERE invoice_total > 50000
```

	INVOICE_NUMBER	INVOICE_DATE	INVOICE_TOTAL

Figure 3-2   SELECT statement examples

How to code the SELECT clause

Figure 3-3 presents an expanded syntax for the SELECT clause. The keywords shown in the first line allow you to restrict the rows that are returned by a query. You'll learn how to code them in a moment. But first, you'll learn various techniques for identifying which columns are to be included in a result set.

How to code column specifications

Figure 3-3 summarizes the techniques you can use to code column specifications. You saw how to use some of these techniques in the previous figure. For example, you can code an asterisk in the SELECT clause to retrieve all of the columns in the base table, and you can code a list of column names separated by commas. Note that when you code an asterisk, the columns are returned in the order that they occur in the base table.

You can also code a column specification as an *expression*. For example, you can use an arithmetic expression to perform a calculation on two or more columns in the base table, and you can use a string expression to combine two or more string values. An expression can also include one or more functions. You'll learn more about each of these techniques in the topics that follow.

The expanded syntax of the SELECT clause

```
SELECT [ALL|DISTINCT]
    column_specification [[AS] result_column]
    [, column_specification [[AS] result_column]] ...
```

Five ways to code column specifications

Source	Option	Syntax
Base table value	All columns	*
	Column name	column_name
Calculated value	Result of a concatenation	String expression (see figure 3-5)
	Result of a calculation	Arithmetic expression (see figure 3-6)
	Result of a scalar function	Scalar function (see figure 3-7)

Column specifications that use base table values

The * is used to retrieve all columns

```
SELECT *
```

Column names are used to retrieve specific columns

```
SELECT vendor_name, vendor_city, vendor_state
```

Column specifications that use calculated values

An arithmetic expression is used to calculate balance_due

```
SELECT invoice_number,
    invoice_total - payment_total - credit_total AS balance_due
```

A string expression is used to derive full_name

```
SELECT first_name || ' ' || last_name AS full_name
```

Description

- Use SELECT * only when you need to retrieve all columns from a table. Otherwise, list the names of the columns you need.
- An *expression* is a combination of column names and operators that evaluate to a single value. In the SELECT clause, you can code arithmetic expressions, string expressions, and expressions that include one or more functions.
- After each column specification, you can code an AS clause to specify the name for the column in the result set. See figure 3-4 for details.

Note

- The other elements shown in the syntax summary above let you control the number of rows that are returned by a query. You can use the DISTINCT keyword to eliminate duplicate rows. See figure 3-9 for details.

Figure 3-3   How to code column specifications

How to name the columns in a result set

By default, a column in a result set is given the same name as the column in the base table. You can specify a different name, however, if you need to. You can also name a column that contains a calculated value. When you do that, the new column name is called a *column alias*. Figure 3-4 presents two techniques for creating column aliases.

The first technique is to code the column specification followed by the AS keyword and the column alias. This is the coding technique specified by the American National Standards Institute (ANSI, pronounced 'ann-see'), and it's illustrated by the first example in this figure.

The second technique is to code the column specification followed by a space and the column alias. This coding technique is illustrated by the second example. Whenever possible, though, you should use the first technique since the AS keyword makes it easier to identify the alias for the column, which makes your SQL statement easier to read and maintain.

When you code an alias, you must enclose the alias in double quotes if the alias contains a space or is a keyword that's reserved by Oracle. In this figure, the first two examples specify an alias for the invoice_number column that uses two words with a space between them.

In addition, these two examples specify an alias for the invoice_date column that uses a keyword that's reserved by Oracle: the DATE keyword. If you don't enclose this keyword in double quotes, you will get an error when you attempt to execute either of these SQL statements. When you enter a statement into SQL Developer, it boldfaces keywords that are reserved by Oracle. This makes it easy to identify Oracle keywords when you're writing SQL statements.

When you enclose an alias in double quotes, the result set uses the capitalization specified by the alias. Otherwise, the result set capitalizes all letters in the column name. In this figure, for instance, the first two columns in the first result set use the capitalization specified by the aliases. However, since no alias is specified for the third column, all letters in the name of this column are capitalized.

When you code a column that contains a calculated value, it's a good practice to specify an alias for the calculated column. If you don't, Oracle will assign the entire calculation as the name, which can be unwieldy, as shown in the third example. As a result, you usually assign a name to any column that's calculated from other columns in the base table.

Two SELECT statements that name the columns in the result set

A SELECT statement that uses the AS keyword

```
-- DATE is a reserved keyword.
-- As a result, it must be enclosed in quotations.
SELECT invoice_number AS "Invoice Number", invoice_date AS "Date",
    invoice_total AS total
FROM invoices
```

A SELECT statement that omits the AS keyword

```
SELECT invoice_number "Invoice Number", invoice_date "Date",
    invoice_total total
FROM invoices
```

The result set for both SELECT statements

	Invoice Number	Date	TOTAL
1	QP58872	25-FEB-08	116.54
2	Q545443	14-MAR-08	1083.58
3	P-0608	11-APR-08	20551.18
4	P-0259	16-APR-08	26881.4
5	MABO1489	16-APR-08	936.93

A SELECT statement that doesn't provide a name for a calculated column

```
SELECT invoice_number, invoice_date, invoice_total,
    invoice_total - payment_total - credit_total
FROM invoices
```

	INVOICE_NUMBER	INVOICE_DATE	INVOICE_TOTAL	INVOICE_TOTAL-PAYMENT_TOTAL-CREDIT_TOTAL
1	QP58872	25-FEB-08	116.54	0
2	Q545443	14-MAR-08	1083.58	0
3	P-0608	11-APR-08	20551.18	19351.18
4	P-0259	16-APR-08	26881.4	0
5	MABO1489	16-APR-08	936.93	0

Description

- By default, a column in the result set is given the same name as the column in the base table. If that's not what you want, you can specify a *column alias* for the column.

- One way to name a column is to use the AS keyword as shown in the first example above. Although the AS keyword is optional, it enhances readability.

- If an alias includes spaces or an Oracle reserved keyword, you must enclose it in double quotes.

- When you enclose an alias in quotes, the result set uses the capitalization specified by the alias. Otherwise, the result set capitalizes all letters in the column name.

Figure 3-4   How to name the columns in a result set

How to code string expressions

A *string expression* consists of a combination of one or more character columns and *literal values*. To combine, or *concatenate*, the columns and values, you use the *concatenation operator* (||). This is illustrated by the examples in figure 3-5.

The first example shows how to concatenate the vendor_city and vendor_state columns in the Vendors table. Notice that because no alias is assigned to this column, Oracle assigns a name, which is the entire expression. Also notice that the data in the vendor_state column appears immediately after the data in the vendor_city column in the results. That's because of the way vendor_city is defined in the database. Because it's defined as a variable-length column (the VARCHAR2 data type), only the actual data in the column is included in the result. In contrast, if the column had been defined with a fixed length, any spaces after the name would have been included in the result. You'll learn about data types and how they affect the data in your result set in chapter 8.

The second example shows how to format a string expression by adding spaces and punctuation. Here, the vendor_city column is concatenated with a *string literal*, or *string constant*, that contains a comma and a space. Then, the vendor_state column is concatenated with that result, followed by a string literal that contains a single space and the vendor_zip_code column.

Occasionally, you may need to include a single quotation mark or an apostrophe within a literal string. If you simply type a single quote, however, the system will misinterpret it as the end of the literal string. As a result, you must code two single quotation marks in a row. This is illustrated by the third example in this figure.

How to concatenate string data

```
SELECT vendor_city, vendor_state, vendor_city || vendor_state
FROM vendors
```

	VENDOR_CITY	VENDOR_STATE		VENDOR_CITY||VENDOR_STATE
1	Auburn Hills	MI		Auburn HillsMI
2	Fresno	CA		FresnoCA
3	Olathe	KS		OlatheKS
4	Fresno	CA		FresnoCA
5	East Brunswick	NJ		East BrunswickNJ

How to format string data using literal values

```
SELECT vendor_name,
    vendor_city || ', ' || vendor_state || ' ' ||
    vendor_zip_code AS address
FROM vendors
```

	VENDOR_NAME		ADDRESS
1	Data Reproductions Corp		Auburn Hills, MI 48326
2	Executive Office Products		Fresno, CA 93710
3	Leslie Company		Olathe, KS 66061
4	Retirement Plan Consultants		Fresno, CA 93704
5	Simon Direct Inc		East Brunswick, NJ 08816

How to include apostrophes in literal values

```
SELECT vendor_name || '''s address: ',
    vendor_city || ', ' || vendor_state || ' ' || vendor_zip_code
FROM vendors
```

	VENDOR_NAME||'''SADDRESS:'		VENDOR_CITY||','||VENDOR_STATE||''||VENDOR_ZIP_CODE
1	Data Reproductions Corp's address:		Auburn Hills, MI 48326
2	Executive Office Products's address:		Fresno, CA 93710
3	Leslie Company's address:		Olathe, KS 66061
4	Retirement Plan Consultants's address:		Fresno, CA 93704
5	Simon Direct Inc's address:		East Brunswick, NJ 08816

Description

- A *string expression* can consist of one or more character columns, one or more *literal values*, or a combination of character columns and literal values.

- The columns specified in a string expression must contain string data (that means they're defined with the CHAR or VARCHAR2 data type).

- The literal values in a string expression also contain string data, so they can be called *string literals* or *string constants*. To create a literal value, enclose one or more characters within single quotation marks (').

- You can use the *concatenation operator* (||) to combine columns and literals in a string expression.

- You can include a single quote within a literal value by coding two single quotation marks, as shown in the third example above.

Figure 3-5   How to code string expressions

How to code arithmetic expressions

Figure 3-6 shows how to code *arithmetic expressions*. To start, it summarizes the four *arithmetic operators* you can use in this type of expression. Then, it presents two examples that show how to use these operators.

The SELECT statement in the first example includes an arithmetic expression that calculates the balance due for an invoice. This expression subtracts the payment_total and credit_total columns from the invoice_total column. The resulting column is given the name balance_due.

When Oracle evaluates an arithmetic expression, it performs the operations from left to right based on the *order of precedence*. This order says that multiplication and division are done first, followed by addition and subtraction. If that's not what you want, you can use parentheses to specify how you want an expression evaluated. Then, the expressions in the innermost sets of parentheses are evaluated first, followed by the expressions in outer sets of parentheses. Within each set of parentheses, the expression is evaluated from left to right in the order of precedence.

To illustrate how parentheses and the order of precedence affect the evaluation of an expression, consider the second example in this figure. Here, the expressions in the second and third columns both use the same operators. However, when Oracle evaluates the expression in the second column, it performs the multiplication operation before the addition operation because multiplication comes before addition in the order of precedence. In contrast, when Oracle evaluates the expression in the third column, it performs the addition operation first because it's enclosed in parentheses. As you can see in the result set, these two expressions result in different values.

Unlike some other databases, Oracle doesn't provide a modulo operator that can be used to return the remainder of a division operation. Instead, you must use the MOD function as described in the next figure.

The arithmetic operators in order of precedence

*	Multiplication
/	Division
+	Addition
-	Subtraction

A SELECT statement that calculates the balance due

```
SELECT invoice_total, payment_total, credit_total,
    invoice_total - payment_total - credit_total AS balance_due
FROM invoices
```

	INVOICE_TOTAL	PAYMENT_TO...	CREDIT_TOTAL	BALANCE_DUE
1	116.54	116.54	0	0
2	1083.58	1083.58	0	0
3	20551.18	0	1200	19351.18
4	26881.4	26881.4	0	0
5	936.93	936.93	0	0

A SELECT statement that uses parentheses to control the sequence of operations

```
SELECT invoice_id,
    invoice_id + 7 * 3 AS order_of_precedence,
    (invoice_id + 7) * 3 AS add_first
FROM invoices
ORDER BY invoice_id
```

	INVOICE_ID	ORDER_OF_PRECEDENCE	ADD_FIRST
1	1	22	24
2	2	23	27
3	3	24	30
4	4	25	33
5	5	26	36

Description

- Unless parentheses are used, the operations in an expression take place from left to right in the *order of precedence*. For arithmetic expressions, multiplication and division are done first, followed by addition and subtraction.

- Whenever necessary, you can use parentheses to clarify or override the sequence of operations. Then, the operations in the innermost sets of parentheses are done first, followed by the operations in the next sets, and so on.

Figure 3-6   How to code arithmetic expressions

How to use scalar functions

Figure 3-7 introduces you to *scalar functions*, which operate on a single value and return a single value. These functions work differently than the *aggregate functions* described in chapter 5 that are used to summarize data. For now, don't worry about the details of how these functions work, because you'll learn more about them in chapter 8. Instead, just focus on how they're used in column specifications.

To code a function, you begin by entering its name followed by a set of parentheses. If the function requires one or more *parameters*, you enter them within the parentheses and separate them with commas. When you enter a parameter, you need to be sure it has the correct data type.

The first example in this figure shows how to use the SUBSTR function to extract the first character of the vendor_contact_first_name and vendor_contact_last_name columns. The first parameter of this function specifies the column name; the second parameter specifies the starting position; and the third parameter specifies the number of characters to return. The results of the two functions are then concatenated to form initials, as shown in the result set for this statement.

The second example shows how to use the TO_CHAR function. This function converts a column with a DATE or NUMBER data type to a character string. A common use for it is in concatenation operations, where all the data being concatenated *must* be string data. This function has two parameters. The first parameter, which specifies the column name, is required. The second parameter, which specifies a format mask for the column, is optional. In this example, a format mask of 'MM/DD/YYYY' is used to convert the payment_date column from a DATE type to a CHAR type. This format mask specifies that the date should be displayed with a two-digit month, followed by a forward slash, followed by a two-digit day, followed by another forward slash, followed by a four-digit year.

In the second example, the payment_date column for Invoice # P-0608 is NULL. Note that this causes the TO_CHAR function to return an empty string for the payment date.

The third example uses the SYSDATE function to return the current date. Since this function doesn't accept any parameters, you don't need to code any parentheses after the name of the function. In fact, if you do code parentheses after the name of the function, you will get an error when you execute the statement. In this example, the second column uses the SYSDATE function to return the current date, and the third column uses the SYSDATE function to calculate the number of days between the two dates. Here, the third column also uses the ROUND function to round the decimal value that's returned by the calculation to an integer.

The fourth example shows how to use the MOD function to return the remainder of a division of two integers. Here, the second column contains an expression that returns the remainder of the division operation when the invoice-id column is divided by 10. In the result set, you can see the results for IDs 9 through 11 (the remainders are 9, 0, and 1).

A SELECT statement that uses the SUBSTR function

```
SELECT vendor_contact_first_name, vendor_contact_last_name,
    SUBSTR(vendor_contact_first_name, 1, 1) ||
    SUBSTR(vendor_contact_last_name, 1, 1) AS initials
FROM vendors
```

	VENDOR_CONTACT_FIRST_NAME	VENDOR_CONTACT_LAST_NAME	INITIALS
1	Cesar	Arodondo	CA
2	Rachael	Danielson	RD
3	Zev	Alondra	ZA
4	Salina	Edgardo	SE
5	Daniel	Bradlee	DB

A SELECT statement that uses the TO_CHAR function

```
SELECT 'Invoice: # ' || invoice_number || ', dated ' ||
    TO_CHAR(payment_date, 'MM/DD/YYYY') ||
    ' for $' || TO_CHAR(payment_total) AS "Invoice Text"
FROM invoices
```

	Invoice Text
1	Invoice: # QP58872, dated 04/11/2006 for $116.54
2	Invoice: # Q545443, dated 05/14/2006 for $1083.58
3	Invoice: # P-0608, dated for $0
4	Invoice: # P-0259, dated 05/12/2006 for $26881.4
5	Invoice: # MABO1489, dated 05/13/2006 for $936.93

A SELECT statement that uses the SYSDATE and ROUND functions

```
SELECT invoice_date,
    SYSDATE AS today,
    ROUND(SYSDATE - invoice_date)  AS invoice_age_in_days
FROM invoices
```

	INVOICE_DATE	TODAY	INVOICE_AGE_IN_DAYS
1	18-JUL-08	01-AUG-08	15
2	20-JUN-08	01-AUG-08	43
3	14-JUN-08	01-AUG-08	49

A SELECT statement that uses the MOD function

```
SELECT invoice_id,
    MOD(invoice_id, 10) AS Remainder
FROM invoices
ORDER BY invoice_id
```

	INVOICE_ID	REMAINDER
9	9	9
10	10	0
11	11	1

Description

- A SQL statement can include a *function*. A function performs an operation and returns a value.

- For more information on using functions, see chapter 8.

Figure 3-7   How to use scalar functions

How to use the Dual table

The Dual table is automatically available to all users. This table is useful for testing expressions that use literal values, arithmetic calculations, and functions as shown in figure 3-8. In particular, the Dual table is often used in the documentation that shows how Oracle's built-in scalar functions work.

In the example in this figure, the second column in the result set shows the value of the calculation 10 minus 7, and the third column shows the date that's returned by the SYSDATE function. This shows that you can perform test calculations in more than one column of the Dual table.

A SELECT statement that uses the Dual table

```
SELECT 'test'  AS test_string,
       10-7    AS test_calculation,
       SYSDATE AS test_date
FROM Dual
```

	TEST_STRING		TEST_CALCULATION		TEST_DATE
1	test			3	01-AUG-08

Description

- The Dual table is automatically created and made available to users.
- The Dual table is useful for testing expressions that use literal values, arithmetic, operators, and functions.

Figure 3-8   How to use the Dual table

How to use the DISTINCT keyword to eliminate duplicate rows

By default, all of the rows in the base table that satisfy the search condition in the WHERE clause are included in the result set. In some cases, though, that means that the result set will contain duplicate rows, or rows whose column values are identical. If that's not what you want, you can include the DISTINCT keyword in the SELECT clause to eliminate the duplicate rows.

Figure 3-9 illustrates how this works. Here, both SELECT statements retrieve the vendor_city and vendor_state columns from the Vendors table. The first statement, however, doesn't include the DISTINCT keyword. Because of that, the same city and state can appear in the result set multiple times. In the results shown in this figure, for example, you can see that "Anaheim CA" occurs twice. In contrast, the second statement includes the DISTINCT keyword, so each city/state combination is included only once.

A SELECT statement that returns all rows

```
SELECT vendor_city, vendor_state
FROM vendors
ORDER BY vendor_city
```

	VENDOR_CITY	VENDOR_STATE
1	Anaheim	CA
2	Anaheim	CA
3	Ann Arbor	MI
4	Auburn Hills	MI
5	Boston	MA

(122 rows selected)

A SELECT statement that eliminates duplicate rows

```
SELECT DISTINCT vendor_city, vendor_state
FROM vendors
ORDER BY vendor_city
```

	VENDOR_CITY	VENDOR_STATE
1	Anaheim	CA
2	Ann Arbor	MI
3	Auburn Hills	MI
4	Boston	MA
5	Brea	CA

(53 rows selected)

Description

- The DISTINCT keyword prevents duplicate (identical) rows from being included in the result set.

- The ALL keyword causes all rows matching the search condition to be included in the result set, regardless of whether rows are duplicated. Since this is the default, it's a common practice to omit the ALL keyword.

- To use the DISTINCT or ALL keyword, code it immediately after the SELECT keyword.

Figure 3-9   How to use the DISTINCT keyword to eliminate duplicate rows

How to use the ROWNUM pseudo column to limit the number of rows

In addition to eliminating duplicate rows, you can limit the number of rows that are retrieved by a SELECT statement. To do that, you can use the ROWNUM pseudo column as shown in figure 3-10. A *pseudo column* works similarly to a column in a table. However, you can only use a pseudo column to select data. In other words, you can't insert, update, or delete the values stored in a pseudo column.

If you want to learn more about how pseudo columns work, you can search the Oracle Database SQL Reference manual for *pseudocolumn*. Note that the Oracle documentation doesn't include a space between the words pseudo and column.

The first example shows how to limit the number of rows in the result set to the first five rows. Here, the ROWNUM pseudo column is used in the WHERE clause to return the first five rows in the Invoices table.

The second example shows how to add an ORDER BY clause to sort the first five rows of the table so the largest invoice total is displayed first. Since the sort operation is applied after the first five rows are retrieved, this doesn't retrieve the five largest invoice totals in the Invoices table. Instead, it returns the first five rows of the table and then sorts them.

If you want to return the five largest invoice totals for the entire Invoices table, you need to sort the result set before you use the ROWNUM pseudo column to limit the number of rows included in the result set. To do that, you can use a *subquery* as shown in the third example. In the FROM clause, this example supplies a SELECT statement that sorts the Invoices table instead of supplying the name of the Invoices table. As a result, the table is sorted before the WHERE clause is applied.

For more information about working with subqueries, see chapter 6. In addition, if the ROWNUM pseudo column isn't adequate for your needs, you might want to use the ROW_NUMBER function described in chapter 8.

A SELECT statement that uses the ROWNUM pseudo column to limit the number of rows in the result set

```
SELECT vendor_id, invoice_total
FROM invoices
WHERE ROWNUM <= 5
```

	VENDOR_ID	INVOICE_TOTAL
1	34	116.54
2	34	1083.58
3	110	20551.18
4	110	26881.4
5	81	936.93

A SELECT statement that sorts the result set after the WHERE clause

```
SELECT vendor_id, invoice_total
FROM invoices
WHERE ROWNUM <= 5
ORDER BY invoice_total DESC
```

	VENDOR_ID	INVOICE_TOTAL
1	110	26881.4
2	110	20551.18
3	34	1083.58
4	81	936.93
5	34	116.54

A SELECT statement that sorts the result set before the WHERE clause

```
SELECT vendor_id, invoice_total
FROM (SELECT * FROM invoices
      ORDER BY invoice_total DESC)
WHERE ROWNUM <= 5
```

	VENDOR_ID	INVOICE_TOTAL
1	110	37966.19
2	110	26881.4
3	110	23517.58
4	72	21842
5	110	20551.18

Description

- You can use the ROWNUM pseudo column to limit the number of rows included in the result set.

- If you want to sort the result set before you use the ROWNUM pseudo column to limit the number of rows included in the result set, you can use a *subquery* as shown in the third example. For more information about working with subqueries, see chapter 6.

Figure 3-10   How to use the ROWNUM pseudo column

How to code the WHERE clause

The WHERE clause in a SELECT statement filters the rows in the base table so that only the rows you need are retrieved. In the topics that follow, you'll learn a variety of ways to code this clause.

How to use the comparison operators

Figure 3-11 shows you how to use the *comparison operators* in the search condition of a WHERE clause. As you can see in the syntax summary at the top of this figure, you use a comparison operator to compare two expressions. If the result of the comparison is True, the row being tested is included in the query results.

The examples in this figure show how to use some of the comparison operators. The first WHERE clause, for example, uses the equal operator (=) to retrieve only those rows whose vendor_state column have a value of IA. Since the state code is a string literal, it must be enclosed in single quotes.

In contrast, a numeric literal like the one in the second WHERE clause isn't enclosed in quotes. This clause uses the greater than (>) operator to retrieve only those rows that have a balance due greater than zero.

The third WHERE clause illustrates another way to retrieve all the invoices with a balance due. Like the second clause, it uses the greater than operator. Instead of comparing the balance due to a value of zero, however, it compares the invoice total to the total of the payments and credits that have been applied to the invoice.

The fourth WHERE clause illustrates how you can use comparison operators other than the equal operator with string data. In this example, the less than operator (<) is used to compare the value of the vendor_name column to a literal string that has the letter M in the first position. That will cause the query to return all vendors with names that begin with the letters A through L.

You can also use the comparison operators with *date literals*, as illustrated by the fifth and sixth WHERE clauses. The fifth clause will retrieve rows with invoice dates on or before May 31, 2008, and the sixth clause will retrieve rows with invoice dates on or after May 1, 2008. Like string literals, date literals must be enclosed in single quotes. In addition, you can use different formats to specify dates, as shown by the two date literals shown in this figure. You'll learn more about the acceptable date formats and date comparisons in chapter 8.

The last WHERE clause shows how you can test for a *not equal* condition. To do that, you code a *less than* sign followed by a *greater than* sign. In this case, only rows with a credit total that's not equal to zero will be retrieved.

Whenever possible, you should compare expressions that have similar data types. If you attempt to compare expressions that have different data types, Oracle may implicitly convert the data types for you. Although implicit conversions are often acceptable, they will occasionally yield unexpected results. In chapter 8, you'll learn how to explicitly convert data types so your comparisons will always yield the results that you want.

The syntax of the WHERE clause with comparison operators

```
WHERE expression_1 operator expression_2
```

The comparison operators

=	Equal
>	Greater than
<	Less than
<=	Less than or equal to
>=	Greater than or equal to
<>	Not equal

Examples of WHERE clauses that retrieve...

Vendors located in Iowa

```
WHERE vendor_state = 'IA'
```

Invoices with a balance due (two variations)

```
WHERE invoice_total - payment_total - credit_total > 0
WHERE invoice_total > payment_total + credit_total
```

Vendors with names from A to L

```
WHERE vendor_name < 'M'
```

Invoices on or before a specified date

```
WHERE invoice_date <= '31-MAY-08'
```

Invoices on or after a specified date

```
WHERE invoice_date >= '01-MAY-08'
```

Invoices with credits that don't equal zero

```
WHERE credit_total <> 0
```

Description

- You can use a comparison operator to compare any two expressions that result in like data types. Although unlike data types may be converted to data types that can be compared, the comparison may produce unexpected results.
- If the result of a comparison results in a True value, the row being tested is included in the result set. If it's False or Unknown, the row isn't included.
- To use a string literal or a *date literal* in a comparison, enclose it in quotes. To use a numeric literal, enter the number without quotes.
- Character comparisons are case-sensitive. 'CA' and 'Ca', for example, are not equivalent.

Figure 3-11   How to use the comparison operators

How to use the AND, OR, and NOT logical operators

Figure 3-12 shows how to use *logical operators* in a WHERE clause. You can use the AND and OR operators to combine two or more search conditions into a *compound condition*. And you can use the NOT operator to negate a search condition. The examples in this figure illustrate how these operators work.

The first two examples illustrate the difference between the AND and OR operators. When you use the AND operator, both conditions must be true. So in the first example, only those vendors located in Springfield, New Jersey, are retrieved from the Vendors table. When you use the OR operator, though, only one of the conditions must be true. So in the second example, all vendors located in New Jersey *and* all the vendors located in Pittsburgh are retrieved.

The third example shows a compound condition that uses two NOT operators. As you can see, this expression is difficult to understand. Because of that, you should avoid using this operator. The fourth example in this figure, for instance, shows how the search condition in the third example can be rephrased to eliminate the NOT operator. As a result, the condition in the fourth example is much easier to understand.

The last two examples in this figure show how the order of precedence for the logical operators and the use of parentheses affect the result of a search condition. By default, the NOT operator is evaluated first, followed by AND and then OR. However, you can use parentheses to override the order of precedence or to clarify a logical expression, just as you can with arithmetic expressions. In the next to last example, for instance, no parentheses are used, so the two conditions connected by the AND operator are evaluated first. In the last example, though, parentheses are used so the two conditions connected by the OR operator are evaluated first.

The syntax of the WHERE clause with logical operators

```
WHERE [NOT] search_condition_1 {AND|OR} [NOT] search_condition_2 ...
```

Examples of queries using logical operators

A search condition that uses the AND operator

```
WHERE vendor_state = 'NJ' AND vendor_city = 'Springfield'
```

A search condition that uses the OR operator

```
WHERE vendor_state = 'NJ' OR vendor_city = 'Pittsburgh'
```

A search condition that uses the NOT operator

```
WHERE NOT (invoice_total >= 5000 OR NOT invoice_date <= '01-JUL-2008')
```

The same condition rephrased to eliminate the NOT operator

```
WHERE invoice_total < 5000 AND invoice_date <= '01-JUL-2008'
```

A compound condition without parentheses

```
SELECT invoice_number, invoice_date, invoice_total
FROM invoices
WHERE invoice_date > '01-MAY-2008' OR invoice_total > 500
AND invoice_total - payment_total - credit_total > 0
ORDER BY invoice_number
```

	INVOICE_NUMBER	INVOICE_DATE	INVOICE_TOTAL
1	0-2058	08-MAY-08	37966.19
2	0-2060	08-MAY-08	23517.58
3	0-2436	07-MAY-08	10976.06

```
(91 rows selected)
```

The same compound condition with parentheses

```
WHERE (invoice_date > '01-MAY-2008' OR invoice_total > 500)
AND invoice_total - payment_total - credit_total > 0
ORDER BY invoice_number
```

	INVOICE_NUMBER	INVOICE_DATE	INVOICE_TOTAL
1	0-2436	07-MAY-08	10976.06
2	109596	14-JUN-08	41.8
3	111-92R-10092	04-JUN-08	46.21

```
(39 rows selected)
```

Description

- You can use the AND and OR *logical operators* to create *compound conditions* that consist of two or more conditions. You use the AND operator to specify that the search must satisfy both of the conditions, and you use the OR operator to specify that the search must satisfy at least one of the conditions.

- You can use the NOT operator to negate a condition, but that can make the search condition difficult to understand. If it does, you should rephrase the condition to eliminate NOT.

- When Oracle evaluates a compound condition, it evaluates the operators in this sequence: (1) NOT, (2) AND, and (3) OR. You can use parentheses to override this order of precedence or to clarify the sequence in which the operations will be evaluated.

Figure 3-12   How to use the AND, OR, and NOT logical operators

How to use the IN operator

Figure 3-13 shows how to code a WHERE clause that uses the IN operator. When you use this operator, the value of the test expression is compared with the list of expressions in the IN phrase. If the test expression is equal to one of the expressions in the list, the row is included in the query results. This is illustrated by the first example in this figure, which will return all rows whose terms_id column is equal to 1, 3, or 4.

You can also use the NOT operator with the IN phrase to test for a value that's not in a list of expressions. This is illustrated by the second example in this figure. In this case, only those vendors who are not in California, Nevada, or Oregon are retrieved.

If you look at the syntax of the IN phrase shown at the top of this figure, you'll see that you can code a *subquery* in place of a list of expressions. Subqueries are a powerful tool that you'll learn about in chapter 6. For now, though, you should know that a subquery is simply a SELECT statement within another statement. In the third example in this figure, for instance, a subquery is used to return a list of vendor_id values for vendors who have invoices dated May 1, 2008. Then, the WHERE clause retrieves a vendor row only if the vendor is in that list. Note that for this to work, the subquery must return a single column, in this case, vendor_id.

The syntax of the WHERE clause with the IN operator

```
WHERE test_expression [NOT] IN ({subquery|expression_1 [, expression_2]...})
```

Examples of the IN operator

The IN operator with a list of numeric literals

```
WHERE terms_id IN (1, 3, 4)
```

The IN operator preceded by NOT

```
WHERE vendor_state NOT IN ('CA', 'NV', 'OR')
```

The IN operator with a subquery

```
WHERE vendor_id IN
    (SELECT vendor_id
     FROM invoices
     WHERE invoice_date = '01-MAY-2008')
```

Description

- You can use the IN operator to test whether an expression is equal to a value in a list of expressions. Each of the expressions in the list must evaluate to the same type of data as the test expression.

- The list of expressions can be coded in any order without affecting the order of the rows in the result set.

- You can use the NOT operator to test for an expression that's not in the list of expressions.

- You can also compare the test expression to the items in a list returned by a *subquery* as illustrated by the third example above. You'll learn more about coding subqueries in chapter 6.

Figure 3-13   How to use the IN operator

How to use the BETWEEN operator

Figure 3-14 shows how to use the BETWEEN operator in a WHERE clause. When you use this operator, the value of a test expression is compared to the range of values specified in the BETWEEN phrase. If the value falls within this range, the row is included in the query results.

The first example in this figure shows a simple WHERE clause that uses the BETWEEN operator. It retrieves invoices with invoice dates between May 1, 2008 and May 31, 2008. Note that the range is inclusive, so invoices with invoice dates of May 1 and May 31 are included in the results.

The second example shows how to use the NOT operator to select rows that are not within a given range. In this case, vendors with zip codes that aren't between 93600 and 93799 are included in the results.

The third example shows how you can use a calculated value in the test expression. Here, the payment_total and credit_total columns are subtracted from the invoice_total column to give the balance due. Then, this value is compared to the range specified in the BETWEEN phrase.

The last example shows how you can use calculated values in the BE-TWEEN phrase. Here, the first value selects the function SYSDATE (which represents the current date), and the second value is SYSDATE plus 30 days. So the query results will include all those invoices that are due between the current date and 30 days from the current date.

However, please note the warning about date comparisons in this figure. In particular, an invoice-date of May 31, 2008 at 2:00 PM isn't less than or equal to "31-May-2008", and it isn't between "01-May-2008" and "31-May-2008". To learn more about date comparisons, please read chapter 8.

The syntax of the WHERE clause with the BETWEEN operator

```
WHERE test_expression [NOT] BETWEEN begin_expression AND end_expression
```

Examples of the BETWEEN operator

The BETWEEN operator with literal values

```
WHERE invoice_date BETWEEN '01-MAY-2008' AND '31-MAY-2008'
```

The BETWEEN operator preceded by NOT

```
WHERE vendor_zip_code NOT BETWEEN 93600 AND 93799
```

The BETWEEN operator with a test expression coded as a calculated value

```
WHERE invoice_total - payment_total - credit_total BETWEEN 200 AND 500
```

The BETWEEN operator with the upper and lower limits coded as calculated values

```
WHERE invoice_due_date BETWEEN SYSDATE AND (SYSDATE + 30)
```

Description

- You can use the BETWEEN operator to test whether an expression falls within a range of values. The lower limit must be coded as the first expression, and the upper limit must be coded as the second expression. Otherwise, the result set will be empty.

- The two expressions used in the BETWEEN operator for the range of values are inclusive. That is, the result set will include values that are equal to the upper or lower limit.

- You can use the NOT operator to test for an expression that's not within the given range.

Warning about date comparisons

- All columns that have the DATE data type include both a date and time, and so does the value returned by the SYSDATE function. But when you code a date literal like "31-May-2008", the time defaults to 00:00:00 on a 24-hour clock, or 12:00 AM (midnight). As a result, a date comparison may not yield the results you expect. For instance, May 31, 2008 at 2:00 PM isn't between "01-May-2008" and "31-May-2008".

- To learn more about date comparisons, please see chapter 8.

Figure 3-14   How to use the BETWEEN operator

How to use the LIKE operator

One final operator you can use in a search condition is the LIKE operator, shown in figure 3-15. You use this operator along with the *wildcards* shown at the top of this figure to specify the *string pattern*, or *mask*, that you want to match. The examples in this figure show how this works.

In the first example, the LIKE phrase specifies that all vendors in cities that start with the letters SAN should be included in the query results. Here, the percent sign (%) indicates that any characters can follow these three letters. So San Diego and Santa Ana are both included in the results.

The second example selects all vendors whose vendor name starts with the letters COMPU, followed by any one character, the letters ER, and any characters after that. Two vendor names that match that pattern are Compuserve and Computerworld.

The LIKE operator provides a powerful technique for finding information in a database that can't be found using any other technique.

The syntax of the WHERE clause with the LIKE operator

```
WHERE match_expression [NOT] LIKE pattern
```

Wildcard symbols

Symbol	Description
%	Matches any string of zero or more characters.
_	Matches any single character.

WHERE clauses that use the LIKE operator

Example	Results that match the mask
WHERE vendor_city LIKE 'SAN%'	"San Diego" and "Santa Ana"
WHERE vendor_name LIKE 'COMPU_ER%'	"Compuserve" and "Computerworld"

Description

- You use the LIKE operator to retrieve rows that match a *string pattern*, called a *mask*. Within the mask, you can use special characters, called *wildcard* characters, that determine which values in the column satisfy the condition.

- You can use the NOT operator before the LIKE operator. Then, only those rows with values that don't match the string pattern will be included in the result set.

Figure 3-15   How to use the LIKE operator

How to use the IS NULL condition

In chapter 1, you learned that a column can contain a *null value*. A null isn't the same as zero, a blank string that contains one or more spaces (' '), or an empty string that doesn't contain any spaces (''). Instead, a null value indicates that the data is not applicable, not available, or unknown. When you allow null values in one or more columns, you need to know how to test for them in search conditions. To do that, you can use the IS NULL condition, as shown in figure 3-16.

This figure uses a table named null_sample to illustrate how to search for null values. This table contains two columns. The first column, invoice_id, is an identification column. The second column, invoice_total, contains the total for the invoice, which can be a null value. As you can see in the first example, the invoice with an invoice_id of 3 contains a null value.

The second example in this figure shows what happens when you retrieve all the invoices with invoice totals equal to zero. Notice that the row with a null invoice total isn't included in the result set. Likewise, it isn't included in the result set that contains all the invoices with invoices totals that aren't equal to zero, as illustrated by the third example. Instead, you have to use the IS NULL condition to retrieve rows with null values, as shown in the fourth example.

You can also use the NOT operator with the IS NULL condition as illustrated in the last example in this figure. When you use this operator, all of the rows that don't contain null values are included in the query results.

The syntax of the WHERE clause with the IS NULL condition

```
WHERE expression IS [NOT] NULL
```

The contents of the Null_Sample table

```
SELECT *
FROM null_sample
```

	INVOICE_ID	INVOICE_TOTAL
1	1	125
2	2	0
3	3	(null)
4	4	2199.99
5	5	0

A SELECT statement that retrieves rows with zero values

```
SELECT *
FROM null_sample
WHERE invoice_total = 0
```

	INVOICE_ID	INVOICE_TOTAL
1	2	0
2	5	0

A SELECT statement that retrieves rows with non-zero values

```
SELECT *
FROM null_sample
WHERE invoice_total <> 0
```

	INVOICE_ID	INVOICE_TOTAL
1	1	125
2	4	2199.99

A SELECT statement that retrieves rows with null values

```
SELECT *
FROM null_sample
WHERE invoice_total IS NULL
```

	INVOICE_ID	INVOICE_TOTAL
1	3	(null)

A SELECT statement that retrieves rows without null values

```
SELECT *
FROM null_sample
WHERE invoice_total IS NOT NULL
```

	INVOICE_ID	INVOICE_TOTAL
1	1	125
2	2	0
3	4	2199.99
4	5	0

Figure 3-16   How to use the IS NULL condition

How to code the ORDER BY clause

The ORDER BY clause specifies the sort order for the rows in a result set. In most cases, you can use column names from the base table to specify the sort order as you saw in some of the examples earlier in this chapter. However, you can also use other techniques to sort the rows in a result set, as described in the topics that follow.

How to sort a result set by a column name

Figure 3-17 presents the expanded syntax of the ORDER BY clause. As you can see, you can sort by one or more expressions in either ascending or descending sequence. This is illustrated by the three examples in this figure.

The first two examples show how to sort the rows in a result set by a single column. In the first example, the rows in the vendors table are sorted in ascending sequence by the vendor_name column. Since ascending is the default sequence, the ASC keyword is omitted. In the second example, the rows are sorted by the vendor_name column in descending sequence.

To sort by more then one column, you simply list the names in the ORDER BY clause separated by commas as shown in the third example. Here, the rows in the Vendors table are first sorted by the vendor_state column in ascending sequence. Then, within each state, the rows are sorted by the vendor_city column in ascending sequence. Finally, within each city, the rows are sorted by the vendor_name column in ascending sequence. This can be referred to as a *nested sort* because one sort is nested within another.

Although all of the columns in this example are sorted in ascending sequence, you should know that doesn't have to be the case. For example, we could have sorted by the vendor_name column in descending sequence like this:

```
ORDER BY vendor_state, vendor_city, vendor_name DESC
```

Note that the DESC keyword in this example applies only to the vendor_name column. The vendor_state and vendor_city columns are still sorted in ascending sequence.

If you study the first example in this figure, you can see that capital letters come before lowercase letters in an ascending sort. As a result, "ASC Signs" comes before "Abbey Office Furnishings" in the result set. For some business applications, this is acceptable. But if it isn't, you can use the LOWER function to convert the column to lowercase letters in the ORDER BY clause like this:

```
ORDER BY LOWER(vendor_name)
```

Then, the rows will be sorted in the correct alphabetical sequence. In chapter 8, you can learn more about this function.

The expanded syntax of the ORDER BY clause

```
ORDER BY expression [ASC|DESC] [, expression [ASC|DESC]] ...
```

An ORDER BY clause that sorts by one column in ascending sequence

```
SELECT vendor_name,
    vendor_city || ', ' || vendor_state || ' ' || vendor_zip_code AS address
FROM vendors
ORDER BY vendor_name
```

	VENDOR_NAME		ADDRESS
1	ASC Signs		Fresno, CA 93703
2	AT&T		Phoenix, AZ 85062
3	Abbey Office Furnishings		Fresno, CA 93722

An ORDER BY clause that sorts by one column in descending sequence

```
SELECT vendor_name,
    vendor_city || ', ' || vendor_state || ' ' || vendor_zip_code AS address
FROM vendors
ORDER BY vendor_name DESC
```

	VENDOR_NAME		ADDRESS
1	Zylka Design		Fresno, CA 93711
2	Zip Print & Copy Center		Fresno, CA 93777
3	Zee Medical Service Co		Washington, IA 52353

An ORDER BY clause that sorts by three columns

```
SELECT vendor_name,
    vendor_city || ', ' || vendor_state || ' ' || vendor_zip_code AS address
FROM vendors
ORDER BY vendor_state, vendor_city, vendor_name
```

	VENDOR_NAME		ADDRESS
1	AT&T		Phoenix, AZ 85062
2	Computer Library		Phoenix, AZ 85023
3	Wells Fargo Bank		Phoenix, AZ 85038
4	Aztek Label		Anaheim, CA 92807
5	Blue Shield of California		Anaheim, CA 92850
6	Diversified Printing & Pub		Brea, CA 92621
7	ASC Signs		Fresno, CA 93703

Description

- The ORDER BY clause specifies how you want the rows in the result set sorted. You can sort by one or more columns, and you can sort each column in either ascending (ASC) or descending (DESC) sequence. ASC is the default.

- By default, in an ascending sort, special characters appear first in the sort sequence, followed by numbers, then by capital letters, then by lowercase letters, and then by null values. In a descending sort, this sequence is reversed.

- With one exception, you can sort by any column in the base table, regardless of whether it's included in the SELECT clause. The exception is if the query includes the DISTINCT keyword. Then, you can only sort by columns included in the SELECT clause.

Figure 3-17   How to sort a result set by a column name

How to sort a result set by an alias, an expression, or a column number

Figure 3-18 presents three more techniques that you can use to specify sort columns. First, you can use a column alias that's defined in the SELECT clause. The first SELECT statement in this figure, for example, sorts by a column named address, which is an alias for the concatenation of the vendor_city, vendor_state, and vendor_zip_code columns. Within the address column, the result set is sorted by the vendor_name column.

You can also use an arithmetic or string expression in the ORDER BY clause, as illustrated by the second example in this figure. Here, the expression consists of the vendor_contact_last_name column concatenated with the vendor_contact_first_name column. Here, neither of these columns is included in the SELECT clause.

The last example in this figure shows how you can use column numbers to specify a sort order. To use this technique, you code the number that corresponds to the column of the result set, where 1 is the first column, 2 is the second column, and so on. In this example, the ORDER BY clause sorts the result set by the second column, which contains the concatenated address, then by the first column, which contains the vendor name. The result set returned by this statement is the same as the result set returned by the first statement.

Notice, however, that the statement that uses column numbers is more difficult to read because you have to look at the SELECT clause to see what columns the numbers refer to. In addition, if you add or remove columns from the SELECT clause, you may also have to change the ORDER BY clause to reflect the new column positions. As a result, we don't recommend this coding technique.

An ORDER BY clause that uses an alias

```
SELECT vendor_name,
    vendor_city || ', ' || vendor_state || ' ' || vendor_zip_code AS address
FROM vendors
ORDER BY address, vendor_name
```

VENDOR_NAME	ADDRESS
1 Aztek Label	Anaheim, CA 92807
2 Blue Shield of California	Anaheim, CA 92850
3 Malloy Lithographing Inc	Ann Arbor, MI 48106
4 Data Reproductions Corp	Auburn Hills, MI 48326

An ORDER BY clause that uses an expression

```
SELECT vendor_name,
    vendor_city || ', ' || vendor_state || ' ' || vendor_zip_code AS address
FROM vendors
ORDER BY vendor_contact_last_name || vendor_contact_first_name
```

VENDOR_NAME	ADDRESS
1 Dristas Groom & McCormick	Fresno, CA 93720
2 Internal Revenue Service	Fresno, CA 93888
3 US Postal Service	Madison, WI 53707
4 Yale Industrial Trucks-Fresno	Fresno, CA 93706

An ORDER BY clause that uses column positions

```
SELECT vendor_name,
    vendor_city || ', ' || vendor_state || ' ' || vendor_zip_code AS address
FROM vendors
ORDER BY 2, 1
```

VENDOR_NAME	ADDRESS
1 Aztek Label	Anaheim, CA 92807
2 Blue Shield of California	Anaheim, CA 92850
3 Malloy Lithographing Inc	Ann Arbor, MI 48106
4 Data Reproductions Corp	Auburn Hills, MI 48326

Description

- The ORDER BY clause can include a column alias that's specified in the SELECT clause.

- The ORDER BY clause can include any valid expression. The expression can refer to any column in the base table, even if it isn't included in the result set.

- The ORDER BY clause can use numbers to specify the columns to use for sorting. In that case, 1 represents the first column in the result set, 2 represents the second column, and so on.

Figure 3-18 How to sort a result set by an alias, an expression, or a column number

Perspective

The goal of this chapter has been to teach you the basic skills for coding SELECT statements. You'll use these skills in almost every SELECT statement you code. As you'll see in the chapters that follow, however, there's a lot more to coding SELECT statements than what's presented here. In the next three chapters, then, you'll learn additional skills for coding SELECT statements.

Terms

base table	order of precedence
keyword	function
filter	parameter
Boolean expression	date literal
predicate	comparison operator
expression	logical operator
column alias	compound condition
string expression	pseudo column
concatenate	subquery
concatenation operator	string pattern
literal value	mask
string literal	wildcard
string constant	null value
arithmetic expression	nested sort
arithmetic operator	

Exercises

Run some of the examples in this chapter

In these exercises, you'll use Oracle SQL Developer to run some of the scripts for the examples in this chapter. This assumes that you already know how to use SQL Developer, as described in chapter 2.

1. Start Oracle SQL Developer.

2. Open the script for fig3-02a that you should find in this directory: c:\murach\oracle_sql\scripts\ch03. Then, press the F9 key or click on the Execute Statement button to run the script. This shows you the data that's in the Invoices table that you'll be working with in this chapter.

3. Open and run the script for fig3-02b.

4. Open and run the scripts for any of the other examples in this chapter that you're interested in reviewing.

Enter and run your own SELECT statements

In these exercises, you'll enter and run your own SELECT statements. To do that, you can open the script for an example that is similar to the statement you need to write, copy the statement into a new Worksheet window, and then modify the statement. That can save you both time and syntax errors.

5. Write a SELECT statement that returns three columns from the Vendors table: vendor_name, vendor_contact_last_name, and vendor_contact_first_name. Then, run this statement.

    Next, add code to this statement so it sorts the result set by last name and then first name. Then, run this statement again. This is a good way to build and test a statement, one clause at a time.

6. Write a SELECT statement that returns one column from the Vendors table named full_name. Create this column from the vendor_contact_first_name and vendor_contact_last_name columns, and format it like this: last name, comma, space, first name (for example, "Doe, John"). Next, sort the result set by last name and then first name. Then, filter the result set for contacts whose last name begins with the letter A, B, C, or E.

7. Write a SELECT statement that returns four columns from the Invoices table named Due Date, Invoice Total, 10%, and Plus 10%. These columns should contain this data:

Due Date	The invoice_due_date column
Invoice Total	The invoice_total column
10%	10% of the value of invoice_total
Plus 10%	The value of invoice_total plus 10%

    (For example, if invoice_total is 100, 10% is 10, and Plus 10% is 110.) Next, filter the result set so it returns only those rows with an invoice total that's greater than or equal to 500 and less than or equal to 1000. Then, sort the result set in descending sequence by invoice_due_date.

8. Write and run a SELECT statement that returns four columns from the Invoices table named Number, Total, Credits, and Balance Due. These columns should include this data:

Number	The invoice_number column
Total	The invoice_total column
Credits	Sum of the payment_total and credit_total columns
Balance Due	Invoice_total minus the sum of payment_total and credit_total

    Next, filter for invoices with a balance due that's greater than or equal to $500. Then, sort the result set by balance due in descending sequence. Last, use the ROWNUM pseudo column so the result set contains only the rows with the 10 largest balance dues.

Work with nulls and use the Dual table

9. Write a SELECT statement that returns the balance due and the payment date from the Invoices table, but only when the payment_date column contains a null value. Then, modify the WHERE clause so it returns any invalid rows (rows in which the balance due is zero and the payment date is null).

10. Use the Dual table to create a row with these columns:

Starting Principal	Starting principle which should be equal to $51,000
New Principal	Starting principal plus a 10% increase
Interest	6.5% of the new principal
Principal + Interest	The new principal plus the interest (add the expression you used for the new principal calculation to the expression you used for the interest calculation)

Now, add a column named "System Date" that uses the TO_CHAR function to show the results of the SYSDATE function when it's displayed with this format:

`'dd-mon-yyyy hh24:mi:ss'`

This format will display the day, month, year, hours, minutes, and seconds of the system date, and this will show that the system date also includes a time. (You should be able to figure out how to use the TO_CHAR and SYSDATE functions by studying figure 3-7.)

How to retrieve data from two or more tables

In the last chapter, you learned how to create result sets that contain data from a single table. Now, this chapter will show you how to create result sets that contain data from two or more tables. To do that, you can use either a join or a union.

How to work with inner joins

A *join* lets you combine columns from two or more tables into a single result set. In the topics that follow, you'll learn how to use the most common type of join, an *inner join*. You'll learn how to use other types of joins later in this chapter.

How to code an inner join

Figure 4-1 presents the *explicit syntax* for coding an inner join. This syntax was introduced in version 9i of Oracle. As you'll see later in this chapter, Oracle also provides an implicit syntax that you can use to code inner joins. However, the syntax shown in this figure is the one you'll use most often.

To join data from two tables, you code the names of the two tables in the FROM clause along with the JOIN keyword and an ON phrase that specifies the *join condition*. The join condition indicates how the two tables should be compared. In most cases, they're compared based on the relationship between the primary key of the first table and a foreign key of the second table.

The SELECT statement in this figure, for example, joins data from the Vendors and Invoices tables based on the vendor_id column in each table. Notice that because the equal operator is used in this condition, the value of the vendor_id column in a row in the Vendors table must match the vendor_id in a row in the Invoices table for that row to be included in the result set. In other words, only vendors with one or more invoices will be included. Although you'll code most inner joins using the equal operator, you should know that you can compare two tables based on other conditions too.

In this example, the Vendors table is joined with the Invoices table using a column that has the same name in both tables: vendor_id. Because of that, the columns must be qualified to indicate which table they come from. As you can see, you code a *qualified column name* by entering the table name and a period in front of the column name. Although this example uses qualified column names only in the join condition, you must qualify a column name anywhere it appears in the statement if the same name occurs in both tables. If you don't, Oracle will return an error indicating that the column name is ambiguous. Of course, you can also qualify column names that aren't ambiguous. However, we recommend you do that only if it clarifies your code.

The explicit syntax for an inner join

```
SELECT select_list
FROM table_1
    [INNER] JOIN table_2
        ON join_condition_1
    [[INNER] JOIN table_3
        ON join_condition_2]...
```

A SELECT statement that joins the Vendors and Invoices tables

```
SELECT invoice_number, vendor_name
FROM vendors INNER JOIN invoices
    ON vendors.vendor_id = invoices.vendor_id
ORDER BY invoice_number
```

The result set

	INVOICE_NUMBER		VENDOR_NAME
1	0-2058		Malloy Lithographing Inc
2	0-2060		Malloy Lithographing Inc
3	0-2436		Malloy Lithographing Inc
4	1-200-5164		Federal Express Corporation

```
(114 rows selected)
```

Description

- A *join* is used to combine columns from two or more tables into a result set based on the *join conditions* you specify. For an *inner join*, only those rows that satisfy the join condition are included in the result set.

- A join condition names a column in each of the two tables involved in the join and indicates how the two columns should be compared. In most cases, you use the equal operator to retrieve rows with matching columns. However, you can also use any of the other comparison operators in a join condition.

- In most cases, you'll join two tables based on the relationship between the primary key in one table and a foreign key in the other table. However, you can also join tables based on relationships not defined in the database. These are called *ad hoc relationships*.

- If the two columns in a join condition have the same name, you have to qualify them with the table name so Oracle can distinguish between them. To code a *qualified column name*, type the table name, followed by a period, followed by the column name.

Notes

- The INNER keyword is optional and is seldom used.

- This syntax for coding an inner join can be referred to as the *explicit syntax*. It is also called the *SQL-92 syntax* because it was introduced by the SQL-92 standards.

- You can also code an inner join using the *implicit syntax*. See figure 4-7 for more information.

Figure 4-1   How to code an inner join

When and how to use table aliases

When you name a table to be joined in the FROM clause, you can refer to the table by an *alias*. A *table alias* is similar to a column alias, except that you do not use the word AS, like you do when you assign a column alias. After you assign a table alias, you must use the alias in place of the original table name throughout the query. This is illustrated in figure 4-2.

The first SELECT statement in this figure joins data from the Vendors and Invoices tables. Here, both tables have been assigned aliases that consist of a single letter. Table aliases are used to reduce typing and to make a query more understandable, particularly when table names are lengthy.

The alias used in the second SELECT statement in this figure, for example, simplifies the name of the Invoice_Line_Items table to just Line_Items. That way, the shorter name can be used to refer to the invoice_id column of the table in the join condition. Although this doesn't improve the query in this example much, it can have a dramatic effect on a query that refers to the Invoice_Line_Items table several times.

The syntax for an inner join that uses table aliases

```
SELECT select_list
FROM table_1 n1
    [INNER] JOIN table_2 n2
        ON n1.column_name operator n2.column_name
    [[INNER] JOIN table_3 n3
        ON n2.column_name operator n3.column_name]...
```

An inner join with aliases for all tables

```
SELECT invoice_number, vendor_name, invoice_due_date,
    (invoice_total - payment_total - credit_total) AS balance_due
FROM vendors v JOIN invoices i
    ON v.vendor_id = i.vendor_id
WHERE (invoice_total - payment_total - credit_total) > 0
ORDER BY invoice_due_date DESC
```

The result set

	INVOICE_NUMBER	VENDOR_NAME	INVOICE_DUE_DATE	BALANCE_DUE
1	40318	Data Reproductions Corp	20-JUL-08	21842
2	39104	Data Reproductions Corp	20-JUL-08	85.31
3	0-2436	Malloy Lithographing Inc	17-JUL-08	10976.06

`(40 rows selected)`

An inner join with an alias for only one table

```
SELECT invoice_number, line_item_amt, line_item_description
FROM invoices JOIN invoice_line_items line_items
    ON invoices.invoice_id = line_items.invoice_id
WHERE account_number = 540
ORDER BY invoice_date
```

The result set

	INVOICE_NUMBER	LINE_ITEM_AMT	LINE_ITEM_DESCRIPTION
1	97/553B	313.55	Card revision
2	97/553	904.14	DB2 Card decks
3	97/522	765.13	SCMD Flyer

`(8 rows selected)`

Description

- A *table alias* is an alternative table name assigned in the FROM clause. You can use an alias when a long table name would make qualified column names long or confusing.

- If you assign an alias to a table, you must use that alias to refer to the table throughout your query. You can't use the original table name.

- You can use an alias for any table in a join without using an alias for any other table.

- Use table aliases whenever they simplify or clarify the query. Avoid using them when they make a query more confusing or difficult to read.

Figure 4-2   When and how to use table aliases

How to work with tables from different schemas

If you use the procedure in figure A-5 of appendix A to create the tables for this book, all of the tables will be organized into three *schemas*. First, all tables pertaining to accounts payable such as the Vendors and Invoices tables are stored in the schema named AP. Then, all tables pertaining to order management are stored in a schema named OM. Finally, all tables that are used by the smaller examples presented in this book are stored in a schema named EX.

In addition, the procedure in figure A-5 creates one *user* that is the *owner* for each schema. In particular, a user named AP is the owner of the AP schema, a user named OM is the owner of the OM schema, and a user named EX is the owner of the EM schema.

When you connect to Oracle as a user that's the owner of a schema, you do not need to qualify any table name with the schema name. This is the case most of the time. If, for example, you connect as the AP user, you can access any of the tables in the AP schema. However, you may occasionally need to join to a table that's in another schema. To do that, you must qualify the table name in the other schema by prefixing the table name with the schema name. This is shown in figure 4-3.

Before you can work with tables in another schema, you must log on as a user that has appropriate permissions to work with the tables in that schema. The first example in this figure shows a statement that can be used to grant permissions to the AP user that allows that user to select data from the Customers table in the OM schema. To run this statement, you must log on as the OM user, which has the appropriate permissions to grant this permission to the AP user.

For now, that's all you need to know about granting permissions. However, you'll learn more about users and permissions in chapter 12. Usually, though, you won't need to worry about this since your database administrator (DBA) will be responsible for granting the appropriate permissions to each user.

Once you have granted the appropriate permissions to the AP user, you can log on as the AP user and run the SELECT statement shown in the second example. This statement joins data from two tables (Vendors and Customers) in two different schemas (AP and OM). To do that, this statement qualifies the Customers table with the name of the OM schema. Since this example assumes that you're logged on as the AP user, it isn't necessary to qualify the Vendors table with the name of the AP schema. However, if you thought it improved the readability of the statement, you could qualify the Vendors table too, and the result of the query would be the same.

The syntax of a table name that's qualified with a schema name

```
schema_name.table_name
```

A SQL statement that grants the SELECT permission on the Customers table in the OM schema to the AP schema

```
GRANT SELECT ON customers TO ap
```

A SQL statement that joins to a table from another schema

```
SELECT vendor_name, customer_last_name, customer_first_name,
    vendor_state AS state, vendor_city AS city
FROM vendors v
    JOIN om.customers c
    ON v.vendor_zip_code = c.customer_zip
ORDER BY state, city
```

The result set

	VENDOR_NAME	CUSTOMER_LAST_NAME	CUSTOMER_FIRST_NAME	STATE	CITY
1	Wells Fargo Bank	Marissa	Kyle	AZ	Phoenix
2	Aztek Label	Irvin	Ania	CA	Anaheim
3	Lou Gentile's Flower Basket	Damien	Deborah	CA	Fresno
4	Shields Design	Damien	Deborah	CA	Fresno
5	Costco	Neftaly	Thalia	CA	Fresno
6	Costco	Holbrooke	Rashad	CA	Fresno
7	Gary McKeighan Insurance	Holbrooke	Rashad	CA	Fresno
8	Zylka Design	Neftaly	Thalia	CA	Fresno
9	Zylka Design	Holbrooke	Rashad	CA	Fresno

```
(37 rows)
```

Description

- Before you can access a table in another schema, you must log on as a user that has appropriate access permissions.

- To grant access permissions to a user, you can use a GRANT statement. For more information about using the GRANT statement, see chapter 12.

- To join to a table in another schema, you must prefix the table name with the schema name.

Figure 4-3   How to work with tables from different schemas

How to use compound join conditions

Although a join condition typically consists of a single comparison, you can include two or more comparisons in a join condition using the AND and OR operators. Figure 4-4 illustrates how this works.

In the first SELECT statement in this figure, you can see that the Invoices and Invoice_Line_Items tables are joined based on two comparisons. First, the primary key of the Invoices table, invoice_id, is compared with the foreign key of the Invoice_Line_Items table, also named invoice_id. As in previous examples, this comparison uses an equal condition. Then, the invoice_total column in the Invoices table is tested for a value greater than the value of the invoice_line_item_amt column in the Invoice_Line_Items table. That means that only those invoices that have two or more line items will be included in the result set. You can see part of this result set in this figure.

Another way to code these conditions is to code the primary join condition in the FROM clause and the other condition in the WHERE clause. This is illustrated by the second SELECT statement in this figure.

When you code separate compound join conditions like this, you may wonder which technique is most efficient. However, Oracle typically does a good job of optimizing queries so they run efficiently regardless of how you write the query. As a result, you can usually focus on writing a query so the code is easy to read and maintain. Then, if you encounter performance problems with your queries, you can work on optimizing the query later.

An inner join with two conditions

```
SELECT invoice_number, invoice_date,
    invoice_total, line_item_amt
FROM invoices i JOIN invoice_line_items li
    ON (i.invoice_id = li.invoice_id) AND
        (i.invoice_total > li.line_item_amt)
ORDER BY invoice_number
```

The same join with the second condition coded in a WHERE clause

```
SELECT invoice_number, invoice_date,
    invoice_total, line_item_amt
FROM invoices i JOIN invoice_line_items li
    ON i.invoice_id = li.invoice_id
WHERE i.invoice_total > li.line_item_amt
ORDER BY invoice_number
```

The result set

	INVOICE_NUMBER	INVOICE_DATE	INVOICE_TOTAL	LINE_ITEM_AMT
1	97/522	30-APR-08	1962.13	765.13
2	97/522	30-APR-08	1962.13	1197
3	I77271-001	05-JUN-08	662	75.6
4	I77271-001	05-JUN-08	662	58.4

```
(6 rows selected)
```

Description

- A join condition can include two or more conditions connected by AND or OR operators.

- In most cases, your code will be easier to read if you code the join condition in the ON expression and search conditions in the WHERE clause.

Figure 4-4   How to use compound join conditions

How to use a self-join

A *self-join* is a join where a table is joined with itself. Although self-joins are rare, there are some unique queries that are best solved using self-joins.

Figure 4-5 presents an example of a self-join that uses the Vendors table. Notice that since the same table is used twice, aliases are used to distinguish one occurrence of the table from the other. In addition, each column name used in the query is qualified by the alias since the columns occur in both tables.

The join condition in this example uses three comparisons. The first two match the vendor_city and vendor_state columns in the two tables. As a result, the query will return rows for vendors that reside in the same city and state as another vendor. Because a vendor resides in the same city and state as itself, however, a third comparison is included to exclude rows that match a vendor with itself. To do that, this condition uses the not equal operator to compare the vendor_id columns in the two tables.

Notice that the DISTINCT keyword is also included in this SELECT statement. That way, a vendor appears only once in the result set. Otherwise, it would appear once for each row with a matching city and state.

This example also shows how you can use columns other than key columns in a join condition. Keep in mind, however, that this is an unusual situation and you're not likely to code joins like this often.

A self-join that returns vendors from cities in common with other vendors

```
SELECT DISTINCT v1.vendor_name, v1.vendor_city,
    v1.vendor_state
FROM vendors v1 JOIN vendors v2
    ON (v1.vendor_city = v2.vendor_city) AND
        (v1.vendor_state = v2.vendor_state) AND
        (v1.vendor_id <> v2.vendor_id)
ORDER BY v1.vendor_state, v1.vendor_city
```

The result set

	VENDOR_NAME		VENDOR_CITY	VENDOR_STATE
1	AT&T		Phoenix	AZ
2	Computer Library		Phoenix	AZ
3	Wells Fargo Bank		Phoenix	AZ
4	Aztek Label		Anaheim	CA
5	Blue Shield of California		Anaheim	CA
6	ASC Signs		Fresno	CA
7	Abbey Office Furnishings		Fresno	CA
8	BFI Industries		Fresno	CA

`(84 rows selected)`

Description

- A *self-join* is a join that joins a table with itself.
- When you code a self-join, you must use aliases for the tables, and you must qualify each column name with the alias.

Figure 4-5   How to use a self-join

Inner joins that join more than two tables

So far in this chapter, you've seen how to join data from two tables. Depending on the requirement, however, you may have to join many more tables. For example, you sometimes need to join 10 or more tables.

The SELECT statement in figure 4-6 joins data from four tables: Vendors, Invoices, Invoice_Line_Items, and General_Ledger_Accounts. Each of the joins is based on the relationship between the primary key of one table and a foreign key of the other table. For example, the account_number column is the primary key of the General_Ledger_Accounts table and a foreign key of the Invoice_Line_Items table.

This SELECT statement also begins to show how table aliases make a statement easier to code and read. Here, the one-letter and two-letter aliases that are used by the tables allow you to code the ON clause more concisely.

A SELECT statement that joins four tables

```
SELECT vendor_name, invoice_number, invoice_date,
    line_item_amt, account_description
FROM vendors v
    JOIN invoices i
        ON v.vendor_id = i.vendor_id
    JOIN invoice_line_items li
        ON i.invoice_id = li.invoice_id
    JOIN general_ledger_accounts gl
        ON li.account_number = gl.account_number
WHERE (invoice_total - payment_total - credit_total) > 0
ORDER BY vendor_name, line_item_amt DESC
```

The result set

	VENDOR_NAME	INVOICE_NUMBER	INVOICE_DATE	LINE_ITEM_AMT	ACCOUNT_DESCRIPTION
1	Abbey Office Furnishings	203339-13	02-MAY-08	17.5	Office Supplies
2	Blue Cross	547481328	20-MAY-08	224	Group Insurance
3	Blue Cross	547480102	19-MAY-08	224	Group Insurance
4	Blue Cross	547479217	17-MAY-08	116	Group Insurance
5	Cardinal Business Media, Inc.	134116	01-JUN-08	90.36	Card Deck Advertising
6	Coffee Break Service	109596	14-JUN-08	41.8	Meals
7	Compuserve	21-4748363	09-MAY-08	9.95	Books, Dues, and Subscriptions
8	Computerworld	367447	31-MAY-08	2433	Card Deck Advertising

`(44 rows selected)`

Description

- You can think of a multi-table join as a series of two-table joins proceeding from left to right.

Figure 4-6   Inner joins that join more than two tables

How to use the implicit inner join syntax

Earlier in this chapter, we mentioned that Oracle provides an *implicit syntax* for joining tables. This syntax was used prior to Oracle 9i. Although we recommend that you use the explicit syntax when you're developing SQL statements for newer versions of Oracle, you should be familiar with the implicit syntax in case you ever need to maintain existing SQL statements that use it.

Figure 4-7 presents the implicit syntax for an inner join, along with two statements that use it. As you can see, the tables to be joined are simply listed in the FROM clause. Then, the join conditions are included in the WHERE clause.

The first SELECT statement joins data from the Vendors and Invoices tables. Like the SELECT statement you saw back in figure 4-1, these tables are joined based on an equal comparison between the vendor_id columns in the two tables. In this case, though, the comparison is coded as the search condition of the WHERE clause. If you compare the result set shown in this figure with the one in figure 4-1, you'll see that they're identical.

The second SELECT statement uses the implicit syntax to join data from four tables. This is the same join you saw in figure 4-6. Notice in this example that the three join conditions are combined in the WHERE clause using the AND operator. In addition, an AND operator is used to combine the join conditions with the search condition.

Because the explicit syntax for joins lets you separate join conditions from search conditions, statements that use the explicit syntax are typically easier to read than those that use the implicit syntax. In addition, the explicit syntax helps you avoid a common coding mistake with the implicit syntax: omitting the join condition. As you'll learn later in this chapter, an implicit join without a join condition results in a cross join, which can return a large number of rows. For these reasons, we recommend that you use the explicit syntax in all your new SQL code.

The implicit syntax for an inner join

```
SELECT select_list
FROM table_1, table_2 [, table_3]...
WHERE table_1.column_name operator table_2.column_name
    [AND table_2.column_name operator table_3.column_name]...
```

A SELECT statement that joins the Vendors and Invoices tables

```
SELECT invoice_number, vendor_name
FROM vendors v, invoices i
WHERE v.vendor_id = i.vendor_id
ORDER BY invoice_number
```

The result set

	INVOICE_NUMBER	VENDOR_NAME
1	0-2058	Malloy Lithographing Inc
2	0-2060	Malloy Lithographing Inc
3	0-2436	Malloy Lithographing Inc
4	1-200-5164	Federal Express Corporation
5	1-202-2978	Federal Express Corporation

```
(114 rows selected)
```

A statement that joins four tables

```
SELECT vendor_name, invoice_number, invoice_date,
    line_item_amt, account_description
FROM   vendors v, invoices i, invoice_line_items  li,
    general_ledger_accounts gl
WHERE v.vendor_id = i.vendor_id
  AND i.invoice_id = li.invoice_id
  AND li.account_number = gl.account_number
  AND (invoice_total - payment_total - credit_total) > 0
ORDER BY vendor_name, line_item_amt DESC
```

The result set

	VENDOR_NAME	INVOICE_NUMBER	INVOICE_DATE	LINE_ITEM_AMT	ACCOUNT_DESCRIPTION
1	Abbey Office Furnishings	203339-13	02-MAY-08	17.5	Office Supplies
2	Blue Cross	547480102	19-MAY-08	224	Group Insurance
3	Blue Cross	547481328	20-MAY-08	224	Group Insurance
4	Blue Cross	547479217	17-MAY-08	116	Group Insurance
5	Cardinal Business Media, Inc.	134116	01-JUN-08	90.36	Card Deck Advertising

```
(44 rows selected)
```

Description

- Instead of coding a join condition in the FROM clause, you can code it in the WHERE clause along with any search conditions. Then, you simply list the tables you want to join in the FROM clause separated by commas.

- This syntax for coding joins is referred to as the *implicit syntax*, or the *theta syntax*. It was used prior to the SQL-92 standards, which introduced the explicit syntax.

- If you omit the join condition from the WHERE clause, a cross join is performed. You'll learn about cross joins later in this chapter.

Figure 4-7   How to use the implicit inner join syntax

How to work with outer joins

Although inner joins are the type of join you'll use most often, Oracle also supports *outer joins*. Unlike an inner join, an outer join returns all of the rows from one or both tables involved in the join, regardless of whether the join condition is true. You'll see how this works in the topics that follow.

How to code an outer join

Figure 4-8 presents the explicit syntax for coding an outer join. Because this syntax is similar to the explicit syntax for inner joins, you shouldn't have any trouble understanding how it works. The main difference is that you include the LEFT, RIGHT, or FULL keyword to specify the type of outer join you want to perform. As you can see in the syntax, you can also include the OUTER keyword, but it's optional and is usually omitted.

The table in this figure summarizes the differences between left, right, and full outer joins. When you use a *left outer join*, the result set includes all the rows from the first, or left, table. Similarly, when you use a *right outer join*, the result set includes all the rows from the second, or right, table. And when you use a *full outer join*, the result set includes all the rows from both tables.

The example in this figure illustrates a left outer join. Here, the Vendors table is joined with the Invoices table. Notice that the result set includes vendor rows even if no matching invoices are found. In that case, null values are returned for the columns in the Invoices table.

When coding outer joins, it's a common practice to avoid using right joins. To do that, you can substitute a left outer join for a right outer join by reversing the order of the tables in the FROM clause and using the LEFT keyword instead of RIGHT. This often makes it easier to read statements that join more than two tables.

The explicit syntax for an outer join

```
SELECT select_list
FROM table_1
    {LEFT|RIGHT|FULL} [OUTER] JOIN table_2
        ON join_condition_1
    [{LEFT|RIGHT|FULL} [OUTER] JOIN table_3
        ON join_condition_2]...
```

What outer joins do

Joins of this type	Keep unmatched rows from
Left outer join	The first (left) table
Right outer join	The second (right) table
Full outer join	Both tables

A SELECT statement that uses a left outer join

```
SELECT vendor_name, invoice_number, invoice_total
FROM vendors LEFT JOIN invoices
    ON vendors.vendor_id = invoices.vendor_id
ORDER BY vendor_name
```

The result set

	VENDOR_NAME	INVOICE_NUMBER	INVOICE_TOTAL
1	ASC Signs	(null)	(null)
2	AT&T	(null)	(null)
3	Abbey Office Furnishings	203339-13	17.5
4	American Booksellers Assoc	(null)	(null)
5	American Express	(null)	(null)

```
(202 rows selected)
```

Description

- An *outer join* retrieves all rows that satisfy the join condition, plus unmatched rows in one or both tables.
- In most cases, you use the equal operator to retrieve rows with matching columns. However, you can also use any of the other comparison operators.
- When a row with unmatched columns is retrieved, any columns from the other table that are included in the result set are given null values.

Notes

- The OUTER keyword is optional and typically omitted.
- You can also code left outer joins and right outer joins using the implicit syntax. See figure 4-11 for more information.

Figure 4-8   How to code an outer join

Outer join examples

To give you a better understanding of how outer joins work, figure 4-9 presents three more examples. These examples use the Departments and Employees tables shown at the top of this figure. In each case, the join condition joins the tables based on the values in their department_number columns.

The first SELECT statement performs a left outer join on these two tables. In the result set produced by this statement, you can see that department number 3 (Operations) is included in the result set even though none of the employees in the Employees table work in that department. Because of that, a null value is assigned to the last_name column from that table.

The second SELECT statement uses a right outer join. In this case, all of the rows from the Employees table are included in the result set. Notice, however, that two of the employees, Locario and Watson, are assigned to a department that doesn't exist in the Departments table. Of course, if the department_number column in this table had been defined as a foreign key to the Departments table, this would not have been allowed. In this case, though, a foreign key wasn't defined, so null values are returned for the department_name column in these two rows.

The third SELECT statement in this figure illustrates a full outer join. If you compare the results of this query with the results of the queries that use a left and right outer join, you'll see that this is a combination of the two joins. In other words, each row in the Departments table is included in the result set, along with each row in the Employees table. Because the department_number column from both tables is included in this example, you can clearly identify the row in the Departments table that doesn't have a matching row in the Employees table and the two rows in the Employees table that don't have matching rows in the Departments table.

The Departments table

DEPARTMENT_NUMBER	DEPARTMENT_NAME
1	Accounting
2	Payroll
3	Operations
4	Personnel
5	Maintenance

The Employees table

EMPLOYEE_ID	FIRST_NAME	LAST_NAME	DEPARTMENT_NUMBER
1	Cindy	Smith	2
2	Elmer	Jones	4
3	Ralph	Simonian	2
4	Olivia	Hernandez	1
5	Robert	Aaronsen	2
6	Denise	Watson	6
7	Thomas	Hardy	5
8	Rhea	O'Leary	4
9	Paulo	Locario	6

A left outer join

```
SELECT department_name AS dept_name,
    d.department_number AS dept_no,
    last_name
FROM departments d
    LEFT JOIN employees e
    ON d.department_number =
        e.department_number
ORDER BY department_name
```

	DEPT_NAME	DEPT_NO	LAST_NAME
1	Accounting	1	Hernandez
2	Maintenance	5	Hardy
3	Operations	3	(null)
4	Payroll	2	Smith
5	Payroll	2	Simonian
6	Payroll	2	Aaronsen
7	Personnel	4	Jones
8	Personnel	4	O'Leary

A right outer join

```
SELECT department_name AS dept_name,
    e.department_number AS dept_no,
    last_name
FROM departments d
    RIGHT JOIN employees e
    ON d.department_number =
        e.department_number
ORDER BY department_name
```

	DEPT_NAME	DEPT_NO	LAST_NAME
1	Accounting	1	Hernandez
2	Maintenance	5	Hardy
3	Payroll	2	Aaronsen
4	Payroll	2	Simonian
5	Payroll	2	Smith
6	Personnel	4	Jones
7	Personnel	4	O'Leary
8	(null)	6	Locario
9	(null)	6	Watson

A full outer join

```
SELECT department_name
        AS dept_name,
    d.department_number
        AS d_dept_no,
    e.department_number
        AS e_dept_no,
    last_name
FROM departments d
    FULL JOIN employees e
    ON d.department_number =
        e.department_number
ORDER BY department_name
```

	DEPT_NAME	D_DEPT_NO	E_DEPT_NO	LAST_NAME
1	Accounting	1	1	Hernandez
2	Maintenance	5	5	Hardy
3	Operations	3	(null)	(null)
4	Payroll	2	2	Simonian
5	Payroll	2	2	Smith
6	Payroll	2	2	Aaronsen
7	Personnel	4	4	O'Leary
8	Personnel	4	4	Jones
9	(null)	(null)	6	Watson
10	(null)	(null)	6	Locario

Figure 4-9   Outer join examples

Outer joins that join more than two tables

Like inner joins, you can use outer joins to join data from more than two tables. The two examples in figure 4-10 illustrate how this works. These examples use the Departments and Employees tables you saw in the previous figure, along with a Projects table. All three tables are shown at the top of this figure.

The first example in this figure uses left outer joins to join the data in the three tables. Here, you can see once again that none of the employees in the Employees table are assigned to the Operations department. Because of that, null values are returned for the columns in both the Employees and Projects tables. In addition, you can see that two employees, Hardy and Jones, aren't assigned to a project.

The second example in this figure uses full outer joins to join the three tables. This result set includes unmatched rows from the Departments and Employees table, just like the result set you saw in figure 4-9 that was created using a full outer join. In addition, the result set in this example includes an unmatched row from the Projects table: the one for project number P1014. In other words, none of the employees are assigned to this project.

The Departments table

DEPARTMENT_NUMBER	DEPARTMENT_NAME
1	Accounting
2	Payroll
3	Operations
4	Personnel
5	Maintenance

The Employees table

EMPLOYEE_ID	FIRST_NAME	LAST_NAME	DEPARTMENT_NUMBER
1	Cindy	Smith	2
2	Elmer	Jones	4
3	Ralph	Simonian	2
4	Olivia	Hernandez	1
5	Robert	Aaronsen	2
6	Denise	Watson	6
7	Thomas	Hardy	5
8	Rhea	O'Leary	4
9	Paulo	Locario	6

The Projects table

PROJECT_NUMBER	EMPLOYEE_ID
P1011	8
P1011	4
P1012	3
P1012	1
P1012	5
P1013	6
P1013	9
P1014	10

A SELECT statement that joins the three tables using left outer joins

```
SELECT department_name,
    last_name,
    project_number AS proj_no
FROM departments d
    LEFT JOIN employees e
        ON d.department_number =
            e.department_number
    LEFT JOIN projects p
        ON e.employee_id =
            p.employee_id
ORDER BY department_name, last_name,
    project_number
```

DEPARTMENT_NAME	LAST_NAME	PROJ_NO
1 Accounting	Hernandez	P1011
2 Maintenance	Hardy	(null)
3 Operations	(null)	(null)
4 Payroll	Aaronsen	P1012
5 Payroll	Simonian	P1012
6 Payroll	Smith	P1012
7 Personnel	Jones	(null)
8 Personnel	O'Leary	P1011

A SELECT statement that joins the three tables using full outer joins

```
SELECT department_name, last_name,
    project_number AS proj_no
FROM departments dpt
    FULL JOIN employees emp
        ON dpt.department_number =
            emp.department_number
    FULL JOIN projects prj
        ON emp.employee_id =
            prj.employee_id
ORDER BY department_name
```

DEPARTMENT_NAME	LAST_NAME	PROJ_NO
1 Accounting	Hernandez	P1011
2 Maintenance	Hardy	(null)
3 Operations	(null)	(null)
4 Payroll	Simonian	P1012
5 Payroll	Smith	P1012
6 Payroll	Aaronsen	P1012
7 Personnel	Jones	(null)
8 Personnel	O'Leary	P1011
9 (null)	Locario	P1013
10 (null)	(null)	P1014
11 (null)	Watson	P1013

Figure 4-10   Outer joins that join more than two tables

How to use the implicit outer join syntax

When you're writing new queries that use outer joins, you may use either the explicit outer join syntax described in figure 4-8 or the implicit outer join syntax shown in figure 4-11. However, to make your code easier to read and maintain, you should try to be consistent with the syntax that's used elsewhere in the application you are working on.

Note, however, that you can't perform a full outer join using the implicit syntax. As a result, if you need to perform a full outer join, you'll have to use the explicit outer join syntax.

The implicit syntax for an outer join

```
SELECT select_list
FROM table_1, table_2 [, table 3]...
WHERE table_1.column_name [(+)] table_2.column_name [(+)]
    [table_2.column_name [(+)] table_3.column_name [(+)]]...
```

A SELECT statement that joins two tables using a left outer join

```
SELECT department_name AS dept_name,
    dpt.department_number AS dept_no,
    last_name
FROM departments dpt, employees emp
WHERE dpt.department_number = emp.department_number (+)
ORDER BY department_name
```

The result set

	DEPT_NAME	DEPT_NO	LAST_NAME
1	Accounting	1	Hernandez
2	Maintenance	5	Hardy
3	Operations	3	(null)
4	Payroll	2	Simonian
5	Payroll	2	Aaronsen
6	Payroll	2	Smith
7	Personnel	4	Jones
8	Personnel	4	O'Leary

```
(8 rows selected)
```

A SELECT statement that joins two tables using a right outer join

```
SELECT department_name AS dept_name,
    emp.department_number AS dept_no,
    last_name
FROM departments dpt, employees emp
WHERE dpt.department_number (+) = emp.department_number
ORDER BY department_name
```

The result set

	DEPT_NAME	DEPT_NO	LAST_NAME
1	Accounting	1	Hernandez
2	Maintenance	5	Hardy
3	Payroll	2	Aaronsen
4	Payroll	2	Simonian
5	Payroll	2	Smith
6	Personnel	4	Jones
7	Personnel	4	O'Leary
8	(null)	6	Locario
9	(null)	6	Watson

```
(9 rows selected)
```

Description

- The implicit syntax for outer joins is an alternative to the SQL-92 standards.

Figure 4-11   How to use the implicit outer join syntax

Other skills for working with joins

The topics that follow present other skills for working with joins. In the first topic, you'll learn how to use inner and outer joins in the same statement. Next, you'll learn how to join tables with the USING and NATURAL keywords. Then, you'll learn how to use another type of join, called a cross join.

How to combine inner and outer joins

Figure 4-12 shows how you can combine inner and outer joins. In this example, the Departments table is joined with the Employees table using an inner join and the Employees table is joined to the Projects table with a left outer join. The result is a table that includes all of the departments that have employees assigned to them, all of the employees assigned to those departments, and the projects those employees are assigned to. Here, you can clearly see that two employees, Hardy and Jones, haven't been assigned projects.

The Departments table

DEPARTMENT_NUMBER	DEPARTMENT_NAME
1	Accounting
2	Payroll
3	Operations
4	Personnel
5	Maintenance

The Employees table

EMPLOYEE_ID	FIRST_NAME	LAST_NAME	DEPARTMENT_NUMBER
1	Cindy	Smith	2
2	Elmer	Jones	4
3	Ralph	Simonian	2
4	Olivia	Hernandez	1
5	Robert	Aaronsen	2
6	Denise	Watson	6
7	Thomas	Hardy	5
8	Rhea	O'Leary	4
9	Paulo	Locario	6

The Projects table

PROJECT_NUMBER	EMPLOYEE_ID
P1011	8
P1011	4
P1012	3
P1012	1
P1012	5
P1013	6
P1013	9
P1014	10

A SELECT statement that combines an outer and an inner join

```
SELECT department_name AS dept_name, last_name, project_number
FROM departments dpt
    JOIN employees emp
        ON dpt.department_number = emp.department_number
    LEFT JOIN projects prj
        ON emp.employee_id = prj.employee_id
ORDER BY department_name
```

The result set

DEPT_NAME	LAST_NAME	PROJECT_NUMBER
1 Accounting	Hernandez	P1011
2 Maintenance	Hardy	(null)
3 Payroll	Simonian	P1012
4 Payroll	Smith	P1012
5 Payroll	Aaronsen	P1012
6 Personnel	Jones	(null)
7 Personnel	O'Leary	P1011

(7 rows selected)

Description

- You can combine inner and outer joins within a single SELECT statement using either the explicit or the implicit join syntax.

Figure 4-12 How to combine inner and outer joins

How to join tables with the USING keyword

When you use the equals operator to join two tables on a common column, the join can be referred to as an *equijoin* (or an *equi-join*). When you code an equijoin, it's common for the columns that are being compared to have the same name. For joins like these, you can simplify the query with the USING keyword that was introduced with Oracle 9i. In other words, you can code a USING clause instead of an ON clause to specify the join as shown in figure 4-13.

Here, the first example shows how to join the Vendors and Invoices tables on the vendor_id column with a USING clause. This returns the same results as the query shown in figure 4-1 that uses the ON clause. Note that the USING clause only works because the vendor_id column exists in both the Vendors and Invoices tables.

The second example shows how to join the Departments, Employees, and Projects tables with the USING keyword. Here, the first USING clause uses an inner join to join the Departments table to the Employees table on the department_number column. Then, the second USING clause uses a left join to join the Employees table to the Projects table on the employee_id column. This shows that you can use a USING clause for inner and outer joins, and it returns the same result as the query shown in figure 4-12.

In some rare cases, you may want to join a table by multiple columns. To do that with a USING clause, you can code multiple column names within the parentheses, separating each column name with a comma. This yields the same result as coding two equijoins connected with the AND operator.

Since the USING clause is more concise than the ON clause, it can make your code easier to read and maintain. As a result, it often makes sense to use the USING clause when you're developing new statements. However, if you can't get the USING clause to work correctly for a complex query, you can always use an ON clause instead.

The syntax for a join that uses the USING keyword

```
SELECT select_list
FROM table_1
    [{LEFT|RIGHT|FULL} [OUTER]] JOIN table_2
        USING(join_column_1[, join_column_2]...)
    [[{LEFT|RIGHT|FULL} [OUTER]] JOIN table_3
        USING (join_column_2[, join_column_2]...)]...
```

A SELECT statement that uses the USING keyword to join two tables

```
SELECT invoice_number, vendor_name
FROM vendors
    JOIN invoices USING (vendor_id)
ORDER BY invoice_number
```

The result set

	INVOICE_NUMBER	VENDOR_NAME
1	0-2058	Malloy Lithographing Inc
2	0-2060	Malloy Lithographing Inc
3	0-2436	Malloy Lithographing Inc
4	1-200-5164	Federal Express Corporation

(114 rows selected)

A SELECT statement that uses the USING keyword to join three tables

```
SELECT department_name AS dept_name, last_name, project_number
FROM departments
    JOIN employees USING (department_number)
    LEFT JOIN projects USING (employee_id)
ORDER BY department_name
```

The result set

	DEPT_NAME	LAST_NAME	PROJECT_NUMBER
1	Accounting	Hernandez	P1011
2	Maintenance	Hardy	(null)
3	Payroll	Simonian	P1012
4	Payroll	Smith	P1012
5	Payroll	Aaronsen	P1012
6	Personnel	Jones	(null)
7	Personnel	O'Leary	P1011

(7 rows selected)

Description

- You can use the USING keyword to simplify the syntax for joining tables.
- The join can be an inner join or an outer join.
- The tables must be joined by a column that has the same name in both tables.
- If you want to include multiple columns, you can separate each table with a comma.
- The join must be an *equijoin*, which means that the equals operator is used to compare the two columns.

Figure 4-13   How to join tables with the USING keyword

How to join tables with the NATURAL keyword

Figure 4-14 shows how to use NATURAL keyword that was introduced with Oracle 9i to code a *natural join*. When you code a natural join, you don't specify the column that's used to join the two tables. Instead, the database automatically joins the two tables based on all columns in the two tables that have the same name. As a result, this type of join only works correctly if the database is designed in a certain way.

For instance, if you use a natural join to join the Vendors and Invoices tables as shown in the first example, the join works correctly because these tables only have one column in common: the vendor_id column. As a result, the database joins these two tables on the vendor_id column. However, if these tables had another column in common, this query would attempt to join these tables on both columns and would yield unexpected results.

Although natural joins are easy to code, these joins don't explicitly specify the join column. As a result, they might not work correctly if the structure of the database changes later. Because of that, you'll usually want to avoid using natural joins for production code.

In addition, if you use natural joins, you may get unexpected results for more complex queries. In that case, you can use the USING or ON clauses to explicitly specify the join since these clauses give you more control over the join. If necessary, you can mix a natural join with the USING or ON clauses within a single SELECT statement. In this figure, for example, the second SELECT statement uses a natural join for the first join and uses a USING clause for the second join. The result is the same as the result for the second statement in figure 4-13.

The syntax for a join that uses the NATURAL keyword

```
SELECT select_list
FROM table_1
    NATURAL JOIN table_2
    [NATURAL JOIN table_3]...
```

A SELECT statement that uses the NATURAL keyword to join tables

```
SELECT invoice_number, vendor_name
FROM vendors
    NATURAL JOIN invoices
ORDER BY invoice_number
```

The result set

	INVOICE_NUMBER		VENDOR_NAME
1	0-2058		Malloy Lithographing Inc
2	0-2060		Malloy Lithographing Inc
3	0-2436		Malloy Lithographing Inc
4	1-200-5164		Federal Express Corporation

```
(114 rows selected)
```

A SELECT statement that uses the NATURAL keyword to join three tables

```
SELECT department_name AS dept_name, last_name, project_number
FROM departments
    NATURAL JOIN employees
    LEFT JOIN projects USING (employee_id)
ORDER BY department_name
```

The result set

	DEPT_NAME		LAST_NAME		PROJECT_NUMBER
1	Accounting		Hernandez		P1011
2	Maintenance		Hardy		(null)
3	Payroll		Simonian		P1012
4	Payroll		Smith		P1012
5	Payroll		Aaronsen		P1012
6	Personnel		Jones		(null)
7	Personnel		O'Leary		P1011

```
(7 rows selected)
```

Description

- You can use the NATURAL keyword to create a *natural join* that simplifies the syntax for joining tables. A natural join can be used to join two tables based on all columns in the two tables that have the same name.

- Although the code for a natural join is shorter than the code for joins that use the ON or USING clauses, a natural join only works correctly for certain types of database structures. In addition, a natural join often yields unexpected results for complex queries. As a result, it's more common to use the ON or USING clauses to join tables.

Figure 4-14   How to join tables with the NATURAL keyword

How to use cross joins

A *cross join* produces a result set that includes each row from the first table joined with each row from the second table. The result set is known as the *Cartesian product* of the tables. Figure 4-15 shows how to code a cross join using either the explicit or implicit syntax.

To use the explicit syntax, you include the CROSS JOIN keywords between the two tables in the FROM clause. Notice that because of the way a cross join works, you don't include a join condition. The same is true when you use the implicit syntax. In that case, you simply list the tables in the FROM clause and omit the join condition from the WHERE clause.

The two SELECT statements in this figure illustrate how cross joins work. Both of these statements combine data from the Departments and Employees tables. As you can see, the result is a table that includes 45 rows. That's each of the five rows in the Departments table combined with each of the nine rows in the Employees table. Although this result set is relatively small, you can imagine how large it would be if the tables included hundreds or thousands of rows.

As you study these examples, you should realize that cross joins have few practical uses. As a result, you'll rarely, if ever, need to use one. In fact, you're most likely to code a cross join by accident if you use the implicit join syntax and forget to code the join condition in the WHERE clause. That's one of the reasons why it's generally considered a good practice to use the explicit join syntax.

How to code a cross join using the explicit syntax

The explicit syntax for a cross join

```
SELECT select_list
FROM table_1 CROSS JOIN table_2
```

A cross join that uses the explicit syntax

```
SELECT departments.department_number, department_name, employee_id,
    last_name
FROM departments CROSS JOIN employees
ORDER BY departments.department_number
```

How to code a cross join using the implicit syntax

The implicit syntax for a cross join

```
SELECT select_list
FROM table_1, table_2
```

A cross join that uses the implicit syntax

```
SELECT departments.department_number, department_name, employee_id,
    last_name
FROM departments, employees
ORDER BY departments.department_number
```

The result set

	DEPARTMENT_NUMBER	DEPARTMENT_NAME	EMPLOYEE_ID	LAST_NAME
1	1	Accounting	4	Hernandez
2	1	Accounting	3	Simonian
3	1	Accounting	9	Locario
4	1	Accounting	8	O'Leary
5	1	Accounting	7	Hardy
6	1	Accounting	6	Watson
7	1	Accounting	5	Aaronsen

```
(45 rows selected)
```

Description

- A *cross join* joins each row from the first table with each row from the second table. The result set returned by a cross join is known as a *Cartesian product*.
- To code a cross join using the explicit syntax, use the CROSS JOIN keywords in the FROM clause.
- To code a cross join using the implicit syntax, list the tables in the FROM clause and omit the join condition from the WHERE clause.

Figure 4-15   How to use cross joins

How to work with unions

Like a join, a *union* combines data from two or more tables. Instead of combining columns from base tables, however, a union combines rows from two or more result sets. You'll see how that works in the topics that follow.

The syntax of a union

Figure 4-16 shows how to code a union. As the syntax shows, you create a union by connecting two or more SELECT statements with the UNION keyword. For this to work, the result of each SELECT statement must have the same number of columns, and the data types of the corresponding columns in each table must be compatible.

In this syntax, we have indented all of the SELECT statements that are connected by the UNION operator to make it easier to see how this statement works. However, in a production environment, it's common to see the SELECT statements and the UNION operator coded at the same level of indentation.

If you want to sort the result of a union operation, you can code an ORDER BY clause after the last SELECT statement. Note that the column names you use in this clause must be the same as those used in the first SELECT statement. That's because the column names you use in the first SELECT statement are the ones that are used in the result set.

By default, a union operation removes duplicate rows from the result set. If that's not what you want, you can include the ALL keyword. In most cases, though, you'll omit this keyword.

Unions that combine data from different tables

The example in this figure shows how to use a union to combine data from two different tables. In this case, the Active_Invoices table contains invoices with outstanding balances, and the Paid_Invoices table contains invoices that have been paid in full. Both of these tables have the same structure as the Invoices table you've seen in previous figures.

This union operation combines the rows in both tables that have an invoice date on or after June 1, 2008. Notice that the first SELECT statement includes a column named Source that contains the literal value "Active." The second SELECT statement includes a column by the same name, but it contains the literal value "Paid." This column is used to indicate which table each row in the result set came from.

Although this column is assigned the same name in both SELECT statements, you should realize that doesn't have to be the case. In fact, none of the columns have to have the same names. Corresponding columns do have to have compatible data types. But the corresponding relationships are determined by the order in which the columns are coded in the SELECT clauses, not by their names. When you use column aliases, though, you'll typically assign the same name to corresponding columns so that the statement is easier to understand.

The syntax for a union operation

```
    SELECT_statement_1
UNION [ALL]
    SELECT_statement_2
[UNION [ALL]
    SELECT_statement_3]...
[ORDER BY order_by_list]
```

A union that combines invoice data from two different tables

```
    SELECT 'Active' AS source, invoice_number, invoice_date, invoice_total
    FROM active_invoices
    WHERE invoice_date >= '01-JUN-2008'
UNION
    SELECT 'Paid' AS source, invoice_number, invoice_date, invoice_total
    FROM paid_invoices
    WHERE invoice_date >= '01-JUN-2008'
ORDER BY invoice_total DESC
```

The result set

	SOURCE	INVOICE_NUMBER	INVOICE_DATE	INVOICE_TOTAL
1	Active	40318	18-JUL-08	21842
2	Paid	P02-3772	03-JUN-08	7125.34
3	Paid	10843	04-JUN-08	4901.26
4	Paid	77290	04-JUN-08	1750
5	Paid	RTR-72-3662-X	04-JUN-08	1600
6	Paid	75C-90227	06-JUN-08	1367.5
7	Paid	P02-88D77S7	06-JUN-08	856.92
8	Active	I77271-OO1	05-JUN-08	662
9	Active	9982771	03-JUN-08	503.2

```
(22 rows selected)
```

Description

- A *union* combines the result sets of two or more SELECT statements into one result set.

- Each result set must return the same number of columns, and the corresponding columns in each result set must have compatible data types.

- By default, a union eliminates duplicate rows. If you want to include duplicate rows, code the ALL keyword.

- The column names in the final result set are taken from the first SELECT clause. Column aliases assigned by the other SELECT clauses have no effect on the final result set.

- To sort the rows in the final result set, code an ORDER BY clause after the last SELECT statement. This clause must refer to the column names assigned in the first SELECT clause.

Figure 4-16   How to combine data from different tables

Unions that combine data from the same table

Figure 4-17 shows how to use unions to combine data from a single table. In the first example, rows from the Invoices table that have a balance due are combined with rows from the same table that are paid in full. As in the example in the previous figure, a column named Source is added at the beginning of each interim table. That way, the final result set indicates whether each invoice is active or paid.

The second example in this figure shows how you can use a union with data that's joined from two tables. Here, each SELECT statement joins data from the Invoices and Vendors tables. The first SELECT statement retrieves invoices with totals greater than $10,000. Then, it calculates a payment of 33% of the invoice total. The two other SELECT statements are similar. The second one retrieves invoices with totals between $500 and $10,000 and calculates a 50% payment. And the third one retrieves invoices with totals less than $500 and sets the payment amount at 100% of the total. Although this is unrealistic, it helps illustrate the flexibility of union operations.

Notice in this example that the same column aliases are assigned in each SELECT statement. Although the aliases in the second and third SELECT statements have no effect on the query, they make the query easier to read. In particular, it makes it easy to see that the three SELECT statements have the same number and types of columns.

A union that combines information from the Invoices table

```
SELECT 'Active' AS source, invoice_number, invoice_date, invoice_total
FROM invoices
WHERE (invoice_total - payment_total - credit_total) > 0
UNION
SELECT 'Paid' AS source, invoice_number, invoice_date, invoice_total
FROM invoices
WHERE (invoice_total - payment_total - credit_total) <= 0
ORDER BY invoice_total DESC
```

The result set

	SOURCE	INVOICE_NUMBER	INVOICE_DATE	INVOICE_TOTAL
1	Paid	0-2058	08-MAY-08	37966.19
2	Paid	P-0259	16-APR-08	26881.4
3	Paid	0-2060	08-MAY-08	23517.58
4	Active	40318	18-JUL-08	21842
5	Active	P-0608	11-APR-08	20551.18
6	Active	0-2436	07-MAY-08	10976.06

`(114 rows selected)`

A union that combines payment data from the same joined tables

```
SELECT invoice_number, vendor_name, '33% Payment' AS payment_type,
    invoice_total AS total, (invoice_total * 0.333) AS payment
FROM invoices JOIN vendors
    ON invoices.vendor_id = vendors.vendor_id
WHERE invoice_total > 10000
UNION
SELECT invoice_number, vendor_name, '50% Payment' AS payment_type,
    invoice_total AS total, (invoice_total * 0.5) AS payment
FROM invoices JOIN vendors
    ON invoices.vendor_id = vendors.vendor_id
WHERE invoice_total BETWEEN 500 AND 10000
UNION
SELECT invoice_number, vendor_name, 'Full amount' AS payment_type,
    invoice_total AS Total, invoice_total AS Payment
FROM invoices JOIN vendors
    ON invoices.vendor_id = vendors.vendor_id
WHERE invoice_total < 500
ORDER BY payment_type, vendor_name, invoice_number
```

The result set

	INVOICE_NUMBER	VENDOR_NAME	PAYMENT_TYPE	TOTAL	PAYMENT
1	40318	Data Reproductions Corp	33% Payment	21842	7273.386
2	0-2058	Malloy Lithographing Inc	33% Payment	37966.19	12642.74127
3	0-2060	Malloy Lithographing Inc	33% Payment	23517.58	7831.35414
4	0-2436	Malloy Lithographing Inc	33% Payment	10976.06	3655.02798
5	P-0259	Malloy Lithographing Inc	33% Payment	26881.4	8951.5062
6	P-0608	Malloy Lithographing Inc	33% Payment	20551.18	6843.54294
7	509786	Bertelsmann Industry Svcs. Inc	50% Payment	6940.25	3470.125

`(114 rows selected)`

Figure 4-17   Unions that combine data from the same table

How to use the MINUS and INTERSECT operators

Like the UNION operator, the MINUS and INTERSECT operators work with two or more result sets, as shown in figure 4-18. Because of that, all three of these operators can be referred to as *set operators*. In addition, the MINUS and INTERSECT operators follow many of the same rules as the UNION operator.

The first query shown in this figure uses the MINUS operator to return the first and last names of all customers in the Customers table except any customers whose first and last names also exist in the Employees table. Since Thomas Hardy is the only name that's the same in both tables, this is the only record that's excluded from the result set for the query that comes before the MINUS operator.

The second query shown in this figure uses the INTERSECT operator to return the first and last names of all customers in the Customers table whose first and last names also exist in the Employees table. Since Thomas Hardy is the only name that exists in both tables, this is the only record that's returned for the result set for this query.

When you use the MINUS and INTERSECT operators, you must follow many of the same rules for working with the UNION operator. To start, both of the statements that are connected by these operators must return the same number of columns. In addition, the data types for these columns must be compatible. Finally, when two queries are joined by a MINUS or INTERSECT operator, the column names in the final result set are taken from the first query. When you code the ORDER BY clause, you can specify the column names in the first query (customer_last_name in our example), or you can specify the column position (2). If you understand how the UNION operator works, you shouldn't have any trouble understanding these rules.

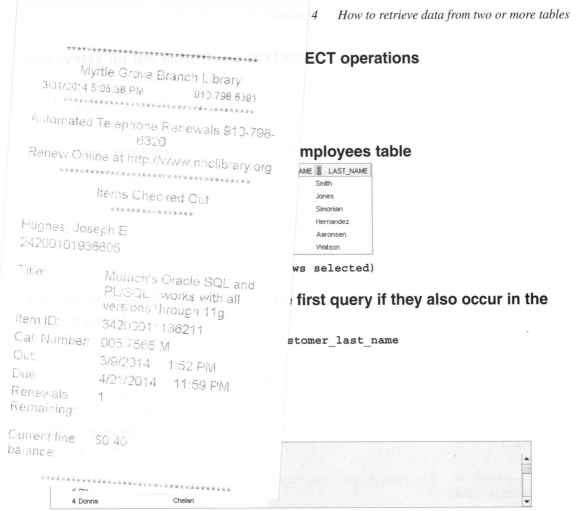

ECT operations

mployees table

...AME | LAST_NAME
Smith
Jones
Simonian
Hernandez
Aaronsen
Watson

...ws selected)

first query if they also occur in the

...stomer_last_name

(23 rows selected)

A query that only includes rows that occur in both queries

```
SELECT customer_first_name, customer_last_name
FROM customers
INTERSECT
SELECT first_name, last_name
FROM employees
```

The result set

CUSTOMER_FIRST_NAME	CUSTOMER_LAST_NAME
1 Thomas	Hardy

(1 rows selected)

Description

- The number of columns must be the same in both SELECT statements.
- The data types for each column must be compatible.
- The column names in the final result set are taken from the first SELECT statement.

Figure 4-18   How to use the MINUS and INTERSECT operators

Perspective

In this chapter, you learned a variety of techniques for combining data from two or more tables into a single result set. In particular, you learned how to use the SQL-92 syntax for combining data using inner joins. Of all the techniques presented in this chapter, this is the one you'll use most often. So you'll want to be sure you understand it thoroughly before you go on.

Terms

join	theta syntax
join condition	outer join
inner join	left outer join
ad hoc relationship	right outer join
qualified column name	full outer join
explicit syntax	equijoin
table alias	natural join
schema	cross join
user	Cartesian product
schema owner	union
self-join	set operator
implicit syntax	

Exercises

1. Write a SELECT statement that returns all columns from the Vendors table inner-joined with all columns from the Invoices table.

2. Write a SELECT statement that returns four columns:

vendor_name	vendor_name from the Vendors table
invoice_number	invoice_number from the Invoices table
invoice_date	invoice_date from the Invoices table
balance_due	invoice_total minus payment_total minus credit_total from the Invoices table

    The result set should have one row for each invoice with a non-zero balance. Sort the result set by vendor_name in ascending order.

3. Write a SELECT statement that returns three columns:

vendor_name	vendor_name from the Vendors table
default_account	default_account_number from the Vendors table
description	account_description from the General_Ledger_Accounts table

    The result set should have one row for each vendor, and it should be sorted by account_description and then by vendor_name.

4. Write a SELECT statement that returns five columns from three tables:

vendor_name	vendor_name from the Vendors table
invoice_date	invoice_date from the Invoices table
invoice_number	invoice_number from the Invoices table
li_sequence	invoice_sequence from the Invoice_Line_Items table
li_amount	line_item_amt from the Invoice_Line_Items table

   Use these aliases for the tables: Ven for the Vendors table, Inv for the Invoices table, and LI for the Invoice_Line_Items table. Also, sort the final result set by vendor_name, invoice_date, invoice_number, and invoice_sequence.

5. Write a SELECT statement that returns three columns:

vendor_id	vendor_id from the Vendors table
vendor_name	vendor_name from the Vendors table
contact_name	A concatenation of vendor_contact_first_name and vendor_contact_last_name with a space in between

   The result set should have one row for each vendor whose contact has the same last name as another vendor's contact, and it should be sorted by vendor_contact_last_name. *Hint: Use a self-join.*

6. Write a SELECT statement that returns two columns from the General_Ledger_Accounts table: account_number and account_description. The result set should have one row for each account number that has never been used. Sort the final result set by account_number. *Hint: Use an outer join to the Invoice_Line_Items table.*

7. Use the UNION operator to generate a result set consisting of two columns from the Vendors table: vendor_name and vendor_state. If the vendor is in California, the vendor_state value should be "CA"; otherwise, the VendorState value should be "Outside CA." Sort the final result set by vendor_name.

5

How to code summary queries

In this chapter, you'll learn how to code queries that summarize data. For example, you can use summary queries to report sales totals by vendor or state, or to get a count of the number of invoices that were processed each day of the month. You'll also learn how to use a special type of function called an aggregate function. Aggregate functions allow you to do jobs like calculate averages, summarize totals, or find the highest value for a given column.

How to work with aggregate functions

In chapter 3, you were introduced to *scalar functions*, which operate on a single value and return a single value. In this chapter, you'll learn how to use *aggregate functions*, which operate on a series of values and return a single summary value. Because aggregate functions typically operate on the values in columns, they are sometimes referred to as *column functions*. A query that contains one or more aggregate functions is typically referred to as a *summary query*.

How to code aggregate functions

Figure 5-1 presents the syntax of the most common aggregate functions. Since the purpose of these functions is self-explanatory, we'll focus mainly on how you use them.

All of these functions but one operate on an expression. In the query in this figure, for example, the expression that's coded for the SUM function calculates the balance due of an invoice using the invoice_total, payment_total, and credit_total columns. The result is a single value that represents the total amount due for all the selected invoices. If you look at the WHERE clause in this example, you'll see that it includes only those invoices with a balance due.

In addition to an expression, you can also code the ALL or DISTINCT keyword in these functions. ALL is the default, which means that all values are included in the calculation. The exceptions are null values, which are always excluded from these functions.

If you don't want duplicate values included, you can code the DISTINCT keyword. In most cases, you'll use DISTINCT only with the COUNT function. You'll see an example of that in the next figure. You won't use it with MIN or MAX because it has no effect on those functions. And it doesn't usually make sense to use it with the AVG and SUM functions.

Unlike the other aggregate functions, you can't use the ALL or DISTINCT keywords or an expression with COUNT(*). Instead, you code this function exactly as shown in the syntax. The value returned by this function is the number of rows in the base table that satisfy the search condition of the query, including rows with null values. The COUNT(*) function in the query in this figure, for example, indicates that the Invoices table contains 40 invoices with a balance due.

The syntax of the aggregate functions

Function syntax	Result
AVG([ALL|DISTINCT] expression)	The average of the non-null values in the expression.
SUM([ALL|DISTINCT] expression)	The total of the non-null values in the expression.
MIN([ALL|DISTINCT] expression)	The lowest non-null value in the expression.
MAX([ALL|DISTINCT] expression)	The highest non-null value in the expression.
COUNT([ALL|DISTINCT] expression)	The number of non-null values in the expression.
COUNT(*)	The number of rows selected by the query.

A summary query that counts unpaid invoices and calculates the total due

```
SELECT COUNT(*) AS number_of_invoices,
    SUM(invoice_total - payment_total - credit_total) AS total_due
FROM invoices
WHERE invoice_total - payment_total - credit_total > 0
```

	NUMBER_OF_INVOICES	TOTAL_DUE
1	40	66796.24

Description

- *Aggregate functions*, also called *column functions*, perform a calculation on the values in a set of selected rows. You specify the values to be used in the calculation by coding an expression for the function's argument. In many cases, the expression is just the name of a column.

- A SELECT statement that includes an aggregate function can be called a *summary query*.

- The expression you specify for the AVG and SUM functions must result in a numeric value. The expression for the MIN, MAX, and COUNT functions can result in a numeric, date, or string value.

- By default, all values are included in the calculation regardless of whether they're duplicated. If you want to omit duplicate values, code the DISTINCT keyword. This keyword is typically used only with the COUNT function.

- All of the aggregate functions except for COUNT(*) ignore null values.

- Aggregate functions are often used with the GROUP BY clause of the SELECT statement, which is used to group the rows in a result set. See figure 5-3 for more information.

- If you code an aggregate function in the SELECT clause, that clause can't include non-aggregate columns from the base table.

Figure 5-1   How to code aggregate functions

Queries that use aggregate functions

Figure 5-2 presents four more queries that use aggregate functions. Before we describe these queries, you should know that with two exceptions, a SELECT clause that contains an aggregate function can contain only aggregate functions. The first exception is if the column specification results in a literal value. This is illustrated by the first column in the first two queries in this figure. The second exception is if the query includes a GROUP BY clause. Then, the SELECT clause can include any columns specified in the GROUP BY clause. You'll see how you use the GROUP BY clause later in this chapter.

The first two queries in this figure use the COUNT(*) function to count the number of rows in the Invoices table that satisfy the search condition. In both cases, only those invoices with invoice dates after 1/1/2008 are included in the count. In addition, the first query uses the AVG function to calculate the average amount of those invoices and the SUM function to calculate the total amount of those invoices. In contrast, the second query uses the MIN and MAX functions to calculate the minimum and maximum invoice amounts.

Although the MIN, MAX, and COUNT functions are typically used on columns that contain numeric data, they can also be used on columns that contain character or date data. In the third query, for example, they're used on the vendor_name column in the Vendors table. Here, the MIN function returns the name of the vendor that's lowest in the sort sequence, the MAX function returns the name of the vendor that's highest in the sort sequence, and the COUNT function returns the total number of vendors. Note that since the vendor_name column can't contain null values, the COUNT(*) function would have returned the same result.

The fourth query illustrates how using the DISTINCT keyword can affect the result of a COUNT function. Here, the first COUNT function uses the DISTINCT keyword to count the number of vendors that have invoices dated 1/1/2008 or later in the Invoices table. To do that, it looks for distinct values in the vendor_id column. In contrast, because the second COUNT function doesn't include the DISTINCT keyword, it counts every invoice that's dated 1/1/2008 or later. Of course, you could accomplish the same thing using the COUNT(*) function. COUNT(vendor_id) is used here only to illustrate the difference between coding and not coding the DISTINCT keyword.

A summary query that uses the COUNT(*), AVG, and SUM functions

```
SELECT 'After 1/1/2008' AS selection_date,
    COUNT(*) AS number_of_invoices,
    ROUND(AVG(invoice_total), 2) AS avg_invoice_amt,
    SUM(invoice_total) AS total_invoice_amt
FROM invoices
WHERE invoice_date > '01-JAN-2008'
```

	SELECTION_DATE	NUMBER_OF_INVOICES	AVG_INVOICE_AMT	TOTAL_INVOICE_AMT
1	After 1/1/2008	114	1879.74	214290.51

A summary query that uses the MIN and MAX functions

```
SELECT 'After 1/1/2008' AS selection_date, COUNT(*) AS number_of_invoices,
    MAX(invoice_total) AS highest_invoice_total,
    MIN(invoice_total) AS lowest_invoice_total
FROM invoices
WHERE invoice_date > '01-JAN-2008'
```

	SELECTION_DATE	NUMBER_OF_INVOICES	HIGHEST_INVOICE_TOTAL	LOWEST_INVOICE_TOTAL
1	After 1/1/2008	114	37966.19	6

A summary query that works on non-numeric columns

```
SELECT MIN(vendor_name) AS first_vendor,
    MAX(vendor_name) AS last_vendor,
    COUNT(vendor_name) AS number_of_vendors
FROM vendors
```

	FIRST_VENDOR	LAST_VENDOR	NUMBER_OF_VENDORS
1	ASC Signs	Zylka Design	122

A summary query that uses the DISTINCT keyword

```
SELECT COUNT(DISTINCT vendor_id) AS number_of_vendors,
    COUNT(vendor_id) AS number_of_invoices,
    ROUND(AVG(invoice_total),2) AS avg_invoice_amt,
    SUM(invoice_total) AS total_invoice_amt
FROM invoices
WHERE invoice_date > '01-JAN-2008'
```

	NUMBER_OF_VENDORS	NUMBER_OF_INVOICES	AVG_INVOICE_AMT	TOTAL_INVOICE_AMT
1	34	114	1879.74	214290.51

Notes

- If you want to count all of the selected rows, you'll typically use the COUNT(*) function as illustrated by the first two examples above. An alternative is to code the name of any column in the base table that can't contain null values, as illustrated by the third example.
- If you want to count only the rows with unique values in a specified column, you can code the COUNT function with the DISTINCT keyword followed by the name of the column, as illustrated in the fourth example.

Figure 5-2   Queries that use aggregate functions

How to group and summarize data

Now that you understand how aggregate functions work, you're ready to learn how to group data and use aggregate functions to summarize the data in each group. To do that, you need to learn about two new clauses of the SELECT statement: GROUP BY and HAVING.

How to code the GROUP BY and HAVING clauses

Figure 5-3 presents the syntax of the SELECT statement with the GROUP BY and HAVING clauses. The GROUP BY clause determines how the selected rows are grouped, and the HAVING clause determines which groups are included in the final results. As you can see, these clauses are coded after the WHERE clause but before the ORDER BY clause. That makes sense because the search condition in the WHERE clause is applied before the rows are grouped, and the sort sequence in the ORDER BY clause is applied after the rows are grouped.

In the GROUP BY clause, you list one or more columns or expressions separated by commas. Then, the rows that satisfy the search condition in the WHERE clause are grouped by those columns or expressions in ascending sequence. That means that a single row is returned for each unique set of values in the GROUP BY columns. This will make more sense when you see the examples in the next figure that group by two columns. For now, take a look at the example in this figure that groups by a single column.

This example calculates the average invoice amount for each vendor who has invoices in the Invoices table that average over $2,000. To do that, it groups the invoices by vendor_id. Then, the AVG function calculates the average of the invoice_total column. Because this query includes a GROUP BY clause, this function calculates the average invoice total for each group rather than for the entire result set. In that case, the aggregate function is called a *vector aggregate*. In contrast, aggregate functions like the ones you saw earlier in this chapter that return a single value for all the rows in a result set are called *scalar aggregates*.

The example in this figure also includes a HAVING clause. The search condition in this clause specifies that only those vendors with invoices that average over $2,000 should be included. Note that this condition must be applied after the rows are grouped and the average for each group has been calculated.

In addition to the AVG function, the SELECT clause includes the vendor_id column. That makes sense since the rows are grouped by this column. However, the columns used in the GROUP BY clause don't have to be included in the SELECT clause.

The syntax of the SELECT statement with the GROUP BY and HAVING clauses

```
SELECT select_list
FROM table_source
[WHERE search_condition]
[GROUP BY group_by_list]
[HAVING search_condition]
[ORDER BY order_by_list]
```

A summary query that calculates the average invoice amount by vendor

```
SELECT vendor_id, ROUND(AVG(invoice_total), 2) AS average_invoice_amount
FROM invoices
GROUP BY vendor_id
HAVING AVG(invoice_total) > 2000
ORDER BY average_invoice_amount DESC
```

	VENDOR_ID	AVERAGE_INVOICE_AMOUNT
1	110	23978.48
2	72	10963.66
3	104	7125.34
4	99	6940.25
5	119	4901.26
6	122	2575.33
7	86	2433
8	100	2184.5

```
(8 rows selected)
```

Description

- The GROUP BY clause groups the rows of a result set based on one or more columns or expressions. It's typically used in SELECT statements that include aggregate functions.

- If you include aggregate functions in the SELECT clause, the aggregate is calculated for each set of values that result from the columns named in the GROUP BY clause.

- If you include two or more columns or expressions in the GROUP BY clause, they form a hierarchy where each column or expression is subordinate to the previous one.

- When a SELECT statement includes a GROUP BY clause, the SELECT clause can include aggregate functions, the columns used for grouping, and expressions that result in a constant value.

- A group-by list typically consists of the names of one or more columns separated by commas. However, it can contain any expression except for those that contain aggregate functions.

- The HAVING clause specifies a search condition for a group or an aggregate. This condition is applied after the rows that satisfy the search condition in the WHERE clause are grouped.

Figure 5-3   How to code the GROUP BY and HAVING clauses

Queries that use the GROUP BY and HAVING clauses

Figure 5-4 presents three more queries that group data. If you understood the query in the last figure, you shouldn't have any trouble understanding how the first query in this figure works. It groups the rows in the Invoices table by vendor_id and returns a count of the number of invoices for each vendor.

The second query in this figure illustrates how you can group by more than one column. Here, a join is used to combine the vendor_state and vendor_city columns from the Vendors table with a count and average of the invoices in the Invoices table. Because the rows are grouped by both state and city, a row is returned for each state and city combination. Then, the ORDER BY clause sorts the rows by city within state. Without this clause, the rows would be returned in no particular sequence.

The third query is identical to the second query except that it includes a HAVING clause. This clause uses the COUNT function to limit the state and city groups that are included in the result set to those that have two or more invoices. In other words, it excludes groups that have only one invoice.

A summary query that counts the number of invoices by vendor

```
SELECT vendor_id, COUNT(*) AS invoice_qty
FROM invoices
GROUP BY vendor_id
ORDER BY vendor_id
```

	VENDOR_ID	INVOICE_QTY
1	34	2
2	37	3
3	48	1
4	72	2

(34 rows selected)

A summary query that calculates the number of invoices and the average invoice amount for the vendors in each state and city

```
SELECT vendor_state, vendor_city, COUNT(*) AS invoice_qty,
    ROUND(AVG(invoice_total),2) AS invoice_avg
FROM invoices JOIN vendors
    ON invoices.vendor_id = vendors.vendor_id
GROUP BY vendor_state, vendor_city
ORDER BY vendor_state, vendor_city
```

	VENDOR_STATE	VENDOR_CITY	INVOICE_QTY	INVOICE_AVG
1	AZ	Phoenix	1	662
2	CA	Fresno	19	1208.75
3	CA	Los Angeles	1	503.2
4	CA	Oxnard	3	188

(20 rows selected)

A summary query that limits the groups to those with two or more invoices

```
SELECT vendor_state, vendor_city, COUNT(*) AS invoice_qty,
    ROUND(AVG(invoice_total),2) AS invoice_avg
FROM invoices JOIN vendors
    ON invoices.vendor_id = vendors.vendor_id
GROUP BY vendor_state, vendor_city
HAVING COUNT(*) >= 2
ORDER BY vendor_state, vendor_city
```

	VENDOR_STATE	VENDOR_CITY	INVOICE_QTY	INVOICE_AVG
1	CA	Fresno	19	1208.75
2	CA	Oxnard	3	188
3	CA	Pasadena	5	196.12
4	CA	Sacramento	7	253

(12 rows selected)

Note

- You can use a join with a summary query to group and summarize the data in two or more tables.

Figure 5-4   Queries that use the GROUP BY and HAVING clauses

How the HAVING clause compares to the WHERE clause

As you've seen, you can limit the groups included in a result set by coding a search condition in the HAVING clause. In addition, you can apply a search condition to each row before it's included in a group. To do that, you code the search condition in the WHERE clause just as you would for any SELECT statement. To make sure you understand the differences between search conditions coded in the HAVING and WHERE clauses, figure 5-5 presents two examples.

In the first example, the invoices in the Invoices table are grouped by vendor name, and a count and average invoice amount are calculated for each group. Then, the HAVING clause limits the groups in the result set to those that have an average invoice total greater than $500.

In contrast, the second example includes a search condition in the WHERE clause that limits the invoices included in the groups to those that have an invoice total greater than $500. In other words, the search condition in this example is applied to every row. In the previous example, it was applied to each group of rows.

Beyond this, there are also two differences in the expressions that you can include in the WHERE and HAVING clauses. First, the HAVING clause can include aggregate functions as you saw in the first example in this figure, but the WHERE clause can't. That's because the search condition in a WHERE clause is applied before the rows are grouped. Second, although the WHERE clause can refer to any column in the base tables, the HAVING clause can only refer to columns included in the SELECT clause. That's because it filters the summarized result set that's defined by the SELECT, FROM, WHERE, and GROUP BY clauses. In other words, it doesn't filter the base tables.

A summary query with a search condition in the HAVING clause

```
SELECT vendor_name, COUNT(*) AS invoice_qty,
    ROUND(AVG(invoice_total),2) AS invoice_avg
FROM vendors JOIN invoices
    ON vendors.vendor_id = invoices.vendor_id
GROUP BY vendor_name
HAVING AVG(invoice_total) > 500
ORDER BY invoice_qty DESC
```

	VENDOR_NAME	INVOICE_QTY	INVOICE_AVG
1	United Parcel Service	9	2575.33
2	Zylka Design	8	867.53
3	Malloy Lithographing Inc	5	23978.48
4	IBM	2	600.06

`(19 rows selected)`

A summary query with a search condition in the WHERE clause

```
SELECT vendor_name, COUNT(*) AS invoice_qty,
    ROUND(AVG(invoice_total),2) AS invoice_avg
FROM vendors JOIN invoices
    ON vendors.vendor_id = invoices.vendor_id
WHERE invoice_total > 500
GROUP BY vendor_name
ORDER BY invoice_qty DESC
```

	VENDOR_NAME	INVOICE_QTY	INVOICE_AVG
1	United Parcel Service	9	2575.33
2	Zylka Design	7	946.67
3	Malloy Lithographing Inc	5	23978.48
4	Ingram	2	1077.21

`(20 rows selected)`

Description

- When you include a WHERE clause in a SELECT statement that uses grouping and aggregates, the search condition is applied before the rows are grouped and the aggregates are calculated. That way, only the rows that satisfy the search condition are grouped and summarized.

- When you include a HAVING clause in a SELECT statement that uses grouping and aggregates, the search condition is applied after the rows are grouped and the aggregates are calculated. That way, only the groups that satisfy the search condition are included in the result set.

- A HAVING clause can only refer to a column included in the SELECT clause. A WHERE clause can refer to any column in the base tables.

- Aggregate functions can only be coded in the HAVING clause. A WHERE clause can't contain aggregate functions.

Figure 5-5   How the HAVING clause compares to the WHERE clause

How to code complex search conditions

You can code compound search conditions in a HAVING clause just as you can in a WHERE clause. This is illustrated by the first query in figure 5-6. This query groups invoices by invoice date and calculates a count of the invoices and the sum of the invoice totals for each date. In addition, the HAVING clause specifies three conditions. First, the invoice date must be between 5/1/2008 and 5/31/2008. Second, the invoice count must be greater than 1. And third, the sum of the invoice totals must be greater than $100.

Because the second and third conditions in the HAVING clause in this query include aggregate functions, they must be coded in the HAVING clause. The first condition, however, doesn't include an aggregate function, so it could be coded in either the HAVING or WHERE clause. The second statement in this figure, for example, shows this condition coded in the WHERE clause. Note that the query returns the same result set regardless of where you code this condition.

So how do you know where to code a search condition? In general, I think your code will be easier to read if you include all the search conditions in the HAVING clause. If, on the other hand, you prefer to code non-aggregate search conditions in the WHERE clause, that's OK, too.

Since a search condition in the WHERE clause is applied before the rows are grouped while a search condition in the HAVING clause isn't applied until after the grouping, you might expect a performance advantage by coding all search conditions in the HAVING clause. However, Oracle takes care of this performance issue for you when it optimizes the query. To do that, it automatically moves search conditions to whichever clause will result in the best performance, as long as that doesn't change the logic of your query. As a result, you can code search conditions wherever they result in the most readable code without worrying about system performance.

A summary query with a compound condition in the HAVING clause

```
SELECT
    invoice_date,
    COUNT(*) AS invoice_qty,
    SUM(invoice_total) AS invoice_sum
FROM invoices
GROUP BY invoice_date
HAVING invoice_date BETWEEN '01-MAY-2008' AND '31-MAY-2008'
    AND COUNT(*) > 1
    AND SUM(invoice_total) > 100
ORDER BY invoice_date DESC
```

The same query coded with a WHERE clause

```
SELECT
    invoice_date,
    COUNT(*) AS invoice_qty,
    SUM(invoice_total) AS invoice_sum
FROM invoices
WHERE invoice_date BETWEEN '01-MAY-2008' AND '31-MAY-2008'
GROUP BY invoice_date
HAVING COUNT(*) > 1
    AND SUM(invoice_total) > 100
ORDER BY invoice_date DESC
```

The result set returned by both queries

	INVOICE_DATE		INVOICE_QTY		INVOICE_SUM
1	31-MAY-08		3		11557.75
2	23-MAY-08		6		2761.17
3	22-MAY-08		2		442.5
4	20-MAY-08		3		308.64

```
(15 rows selected)
```

Description

- You can use the AND and OR operators to code compound search conditions in a HAVING clause just as you can in a WHERE clause.

- If a search condition includes an aggregate function, it must be coded in the HAVING clause. Otherwise, it can be coded in either the HAVING or the WHERE clause.

- In most cases, your code will be easier to read if you code all the search conditions in the HAVING clause, but you can code non-aggregate search conditions in the WHERE clause if you prefer.

Figure 5-6   How to code complex search conditions

How to summarize data using Oracle extensions

So far, this chapter has discussed standard SQL keywords and functions. However, you should also know about two extensions that Oracle provides for summarizing data: the ROLLUP and CUBE operators. You'll learn how to use these operators in the topics that follow.

How to use the ROLLUP operator

You can use the ROLLUP operator to add one or more summary rows to a result set that uses grouping and aggregates. The two examples in figure 5-7 illustrate how this works.

The first example shows how the ROLLUP operator works when you group by a single column. Here, the invoices in the Invoices table are grouped by vendor_id, and an invoice count and invoice total are calculated for each vendor. In addition, because the ROLLUP operator is included in the GROUP BY clause, a summary row is added at the end of the result set. This row summarizes all the aggregate columns in the result set. In this case, it summarizes the invoice_count and invoice_total columns. Because the vendor_id column can't be summarized, it's assigned a null value.

The second query in this figure shows how the ROLLUP operator works when you group by two columns. This query groups the vendors in the Vendors table by state and city and counts the number of vendors in each group. Then, in addition to a summary row at the end of the result set, summary rows are included for each state.

When you use an ORDER BY clause with the ROLLUP operator, the rows are sorted after the summary rows are added. Then, because null values come after other values in the Oracle sort sequence, the summary rows come after the rows that they summarize. Incidentally, if the ORDER BY clause in the second example were omitted, the only difference in the result set would be that the cities within each state wouldn't necessarily be in the right sequence.

You can also use another function, the GROUPING function, to work with null columns in a summary row. However, this function is typically used in conjunction with the CASE function, which you'll learn about in chapter 8. So we'll present the GROUPING function in that chapter.

A summary query that includes a final summary row

```
SELECT vendor_id, COUNT(*) AS invoice_count,
    SUM(invoice_total) AS invoice_total
FROM invoices
GROUP BY ROLLUP(vendor_id)
```

	VENDOR_ID	INVOICE_COUNT	INVOICE_TOTAL
1	34	2	1200.12
2	37	3	564
3	48	1	856.92
4	72	2	21927.31

```
(35 rows selected)
```

A summary query that includes a summary row for each grouping level

```
SELECT vendor_state, vendor_city, COUNT(*) AS qty_vendors
FROM vendors
WHERE vendor_state IN ('IA', 'NJ')
GROUP BY ROLLUP (vendor_state, vendor_city)
ORDER BY vendor_state, vendor_city
```

	VENDOR_STATE	VENDOR_CITY	QTY_VENDORS
1	IA	Fairfield	1
2	IA	Washington	1
3	IA	(null)	2
4	NJ	East Brunswick	2
5	NJ	Fairfield	1
6	NJ	Washington	1
7	NJ	(null)	4
8	(null)	(null)	6

Description

- You can use the ROLLUP operator in the GROUP BY clause to add summary rows to the final result set. A summary is provided for each aggregate column included in the select list. All other columns, except the ones that identify which group is being summarized, are assigned null values.

- The ROLLUP operator adds a summary row for each group specified in the GROUP BY clause except for the rightmost group, which is summarized by the aggregate functions. It also adds a summary row to the end of the result set that summarizes the entire result set. If the GROUP BY clause specifies a single group, only the final summary row is added.

- The sort sequence in the ORDER BY clause is applied after the summary rows are added.

- When you use the ROLLUP operator, you can't use the DISTINCT keyword in any of the aggregate functions.

- You can also use the GROUPING function with the ROLLUP operator to determine if a summary row has a null value assigned to a given column. See chapter 8 for details.

Figure 5-7   How to use the ROLLUP operator

How to use the CUBE operator

Figure 5-8 shows you how to use the CUBE operator. This operator is similar to the ROLLUP operator, except that it adds summary rows for every combination of groups. This is illustrated by the two examples in this figure. As you can see, these examples are the same as the ones in figure 5-7 except that they use the CUBE operator instead of the ROLLUP operator.

In the first example, the result set is grouped by a single column. In this case, a single row is added to the result set that summarizes all the groups. In other words, this works the same as it does with the ROLLUP operator. The only difference is that the summary row is at the start of the result set instead of the end of the result set.

In the second example, you can see how CUBE differs from ROLLUP when you group by two or more columns. In this case, the result set includes a summary row for each state just as it did when the ROLLUP operator was used. For instance, the third row in this example indicates that there are two vendors in the state of Iowa. In addition, though, the CUBE operator includes a summary row for each city. For instance, the ninth row in this example indicates that there are two vendors for the city of Fairfield. But if you look at the first and fifth rows in the result set, you'll see that one of those vendors is in Fairfield, Iowa and one is in Fairfield, New Jersey. Similarly, there are two vendors in two different states for the city named Washington. There are also two vendors in the city of East Brunswick, but both are in New Jersey.

Here again, the ORDER BY clause is applied after the summary rows are added. So in the second example, the ORDER BY clause has two effects. First, it insures that the cities are in sequence within the states. Second, it moves the four extra summary rows that are created by the CUBE operator from the start of the result set to the end of the result set.

Now that you've seen how the CUBE operator works, you may be wondering when you would use it. One obvious use is to add a summary row to a result set that's grouped by a single column, but you could just as easily use the ROLLUP operator for that. Beyond that, the CUBE operator can occasionally get useful information that you can't get any other way.

A summary query that includes a final summary row

```
SELECT vendor_id, COUNT(*) AS invoice_count,
    SUM(invoice_total) AS invoice_total
FROM invoices
GROUP BY CUBE(vendor_id)
```

	VENDOR_ID	INVOICE_COUNT	INVOICE_TOTAL
1	(null)	114	214290.51
2	34	2	1200.12
3	37	3	564
4	48	1	856.92

```
(35 rows selected)
```

A summary query that includes a summary row for each set of groups

```
SELECT vendor_state, vendor_city, COUNT(*) AS qty_vendors
FROM vendors
WHERE vendor_state IN ('IA', 'NJ')
GROUP BY CUBE(vendor_state, vendor_city)
ORDER BY vendor_state, vendor_city
```

	VENDOR_STATE	VENDOR_CITY	QTY_VENDORS
1	IA	Fairfield	1
2	IA	Washington	1
3	IA	(null)	2
4	NJ	East Brunswick	2
5	NJ	Fairfield	1
6	NJ	Washington	1
7	NJ	(null)	4
8	(null)	East Brunswick	2
9	(null)	Fairfield	2
10	(null)	Washington	2
11	(null)	(null)	6

Description

- You can use the CUBE operator in the GROUP BY clause to add summary rows to the final result set. A summary is provided for each aggregate column included in the select list. All other columns, except the ones that identify which group is being summarized, are assigned null values.

- The CUBE operator adds a summary row for every combination of groups specified in the GROUP BY clause. It also adds a summary row to the end of the result set that summarizes the entire result set.

- The sort sequence in the ORDER BY clause is applied after the summary rows are added.

- When you use the CUBE operator, you can't use the DISTINCT keyword in any of the aggregate functions.

- You can also use the GROUPING function with the CUBE operator to determine if a summary row has a null value assigned to a given column. See chapter 8 for details.

Figure 5-8   How to use the CUBE operator

Perspective

In this chapter, you learned how to code queries that group and summarize data. In most cases, you'll be able to use the techniques presented here to get the summary information you need.

Terms

scalar function
aggregate function
column function
summary query
scalar aggregate
vector aggregate

Exercises

1. Write a SELECT statement that returns one row for each vendor that contains these columns from the Invoices table:

    The vendor_id column

    The sum of the invoice_total column

    The result set should be sorted by vendor_id.

2. Write a SELECT statement that returns one row for each vendor that contains these columns:

    The vendor_name column from the Vendors table

    The sum of the payment_total column in the Invoices table.

    The result set should be sorted in descending sequence by the payment total sum for each vendor.

3. Write a SELECT statement that returns one row for each vendor that contains three columns:

    The vendor_name column from the Vendors table

    The count of the invoices for each vendor in the Invoices table

    The sum of the invoice_total column for each vendor in the Invoices table

    Sort the result set so the vendor with the most invoices appears first.

4. Write a SELECT statement that returns one row for each general ledger account number that contains three columns:

    The account_description column from the General_Ledger_Accounts table

    The count of the entries in the Invoice_Line_Items table that have the same account_number

The sum of the line item amounts in the Invoice_Line_Items table that have the same account-number

Filter the result set to include only those rows with a count greater than 1; group the result set by account description; and sort the result set in descending sequence by the sum of the line item amounts.

5. Modify the solution to exercise 4 to filter for invoices dated in the second quarter of 2008 (April 1, 2008 to June 30, 2008). *Hint: Join to the Invoices table to code a search condition based on invoice_date.*

6. Write a SELECT statement that answers this question: What is the total amount invoiced for each general ledger account number? Use the ROLLUP operator to include a row that gives the grand total. *Hint: Use the line_item_amt column of the Invoice_Line_Items table.*

7. Write a SELECT statement that answers this question: Which vendors are being paid from more than one account? Return two columns: the vendor name and the total number of accounts that apply to that vendor's invoices. *Hint: Use the DISTINCT keyword to count the account_number column in the Invoice_Line_Items table.*

6

How to code subqueries

A subquery is a SELECT statement that's coded within another SQL statement. As a result, you can use subqueries to build queries that would be difficult or impossible to do otherwise. In this chapter, you'll learn how to use subqueries within SELECT statements. Then, in the next chapter, you'll learn how to use them when you code INSERT, UPDATE, and DELETE statements.

An introduction to subqueries

Since you know how to code SELECT statements, you already know how to code a *subquery*. It's simply a SELECT statement that's coded within another SQL statement. The trick to using subqueries is knowing where and when to use them. You'll learn the specifics of using subqueries throughout this chapter. The two topics that follow, however, will give you an overview of where and when to use them.

How to use subqueries

In figure 6-1, you can see that a subquery can be coded, or *introduced*, in the WHERE, HAVING, FROM, or SELECT clause of a SELECT statement. The SELECT statement in this figure, for example, illustrates how you can use a subquery in the search condition of a WHERE clause. When it's used in a search condition, a subquery can be referred to as a *subquery search condition* or a *subquery predicate*.

The statement in this figure retrieves all the invoices from the Invoices table that have invoice totals greater than the average of all the invoices. To do that, the subquery calculates the average of all the invoices. Then, the search condition tests each invoice to see if its invoice total is greater than that average.

When a subquery returns a single value as it does in this example, you can use it anywhere you would normally use an expression. However, a subquery can also return a single-column result set with two or more rows. In that case, it can be used in place of a list of values, such as the list for an IN operator. In addition, if a subquery is coded within a FROM clause, it can return a result set with two or more columns. You'll learn about all of these different types of subqueries in this chapter.

You can also code a subquery within another subquery. In that case, the subqueries are said to be nested. Because *nested subqueries* can be difficult to read, you should use them only when necessary.

Four ways to introduce a subquery in a SELECT statement

1. In a WHERE clause as a search condition
2. In a HAVING clause as a search condition
3. In the FROM clause as a table specification
4. In the SELECT clause as a column specification

A SELECT statement that uses a subquery in the WHERE clause

```
SELECT invoice_number, invoice_date, invoice_total
FROM invoices
WHERE invoice_total >
    (SELECT AVG(invoice_total)
     FROM invoices)
ORDER BY invoice_total
```

The value returned by the subquery

```
1879.7413
```

The result set

	INVOICE_NUMBER	INVOICE_DATE	INVOICE_TOTAL
1	989319-487	18-APR-08	1927.54
2	97/522	30-APR-08	1962.13
3	989319-417	26-APR-08	2051.59
4	989319-427	25-APR-08	2115.81
5	989319-477	19-APR-08	2184.11

```
(21 rows)
```

Description

- A *subquery* is a SELECT statement that's coded within another SQL statement.

- A subquery can return a single value, a result set that contains a single column, or a result set that contains one or more columns.

- A subquery that returns a single value can be coded, or *introduced*, anywhere an expression is allowed. A subquery that returns a single column can be introduced in place of a list of values, such as the values for an IN phrase. And a subquery that returns one or more columns can be introduced in place of a table in the FROM clause.

- The syntax for a subquery is the same as for a standard SELECT statement. However, a subquery doesn't typically include the GROUP BY or HAVING clause, and it can't include an ORDER BY clause.

- A subquery that's used in a WHERE or HAVING clause is called a *subquery search condition* or a *subquery predicate*. This is the most common use for a subquery.

- Although you can introduce a subquery in a GROUP BY or ORDER BY clause, you usually won't need to.

- Subqueries can be *nested* within other subqueries. However, subqueries that are nested more than two or three levels deep can be difficult to read.

Figure 6-1   How to use subqueries

How subqueries compare to joins

In the last figure, you saw an example of a subquery that returns an aggregate value that's used in the search condition of a WHERE clause. This type of subquery provides for processing that can't be done any other way. However, most subqueries can be restated as joins, and most joins can be restated as subqueries. This is illustrated by the SELECT statements in figure 6-2.

Both SELECT statements in this figure return a result set that consists of selected rows and columns from the Invoices table. In this case, only the invoices for vendors in California are returned. The first statement uses a join to combine the Vendors and Invoices tables so the vendor_state column can be tested for each invoice. In contrast, the second statement uses a subquery to return a result set that consists of the vendor_id column for each vendor in California. Then, that result set is used with the IN operator in the search condition so that only invoices with a vendor_id in that result set are included in the final result set.

So if you have a choice, which technique should you use? In general, we recommend that you use the technique that results in the most readable code. For example, a join tends to be more intuitive than a subquery when it uses an existing relationship between two tables. That's the case with the Vendors and Invoices tables used in the examples in this figure. On the other hand, a subquery tends to be more intuitive when it uses an ad hoc relationship.

As your queries get more complex, you may find that they're easier to code by using subqueries, regardless of the relationships that are involved. Later in this chapter, for example, you'll see a couple examples of this.

You should also realize that when you use a subquery in a search condition, its results can't be included in the final result set. For instance, the second example in this figure can't be changed to include the vendor_name column from the Vendors table. That's because the Vendors table isn't named in the FROM clause of the outer query. So if you need to include information from both tables in the result set, you need to use a join.

A query that uses an inner join

```
SELECT invoice_number, invoice_date, invoice_total
FROM invoices JOIN vendors
    ON invoices.vendor_id = vendors.vendor_id
WHERE vendor_state = 'CA'
ORDER BY invoice_date
```

The same query restated with a subquery

```
SELECT invoice_number, invoice_date, invoice_total
FROM invoices
WHERE vendor_id IN
    (SELECT vendor_id
    FROM vendors
    WHERE vendor_state = 'CA')
ORDER BY invoice_date
```

The result set returned by both queries

	INVOICE_NUMBER		INVOICE_DATE		INVOICE_TOTAL	
1	QP58872		25-FEB-08		116.54	
2	Q545443		14-MAR-08		1083.58	
3	MABO1489		16-APR-08		936.93	
4	97/553B		26-APR-08		313.55	

`(40 rows)`

Advantages of joins

- The result of a join operation can include columns from both tables.
- A join tends to be more intuitive when it uses an existing relationship between the two tables, such as a primary key to foreign key relationship.

Advantages of subqueries

- You can use a subquery to pass an aggregate value to the outer query.
- A subquery tends to be more intuitive when it uses an ad hoc relationship between the two tables.
- Long, complex queries can sometimes be easier to code using subqueries.

Description

- Like a join, a subquery can be used to code queries that work with two or more tables.
- Most subqueries can be restated as joins and most joins can be restated as subqueries.

Figure 6-2   How subqueries compare to joins

How to code subqueries in search conditions

You can use a variety of techniques to work with a subquery in a search condition. You'll learn about those techniques in the topics that follow. As you read these topics, keep in mind that although all of the examples illustrate the use of subqueries in a WHERE clause, all of this information applies to the HAVING clause as well.

How to use subqueries with the IN operator

In chapter 3, you learned how to use the IN operator to test whether an expression is contained in a list of values. One way to provide that list of values is to use a subquery. This is illustrated in figure 6-3.

The example in this figure retrieves the vendors from the Vendors table that don't have invoices in the Invoices table. To do that, it uses a subquery to retrieve the vendor_id of each vendor in the Invoices table. The result is a result set like the one shown that contains just the vendor_id column. Then, this result set is used to filter the vendors that are included in the final result set.

Note that this subquery returns a single column. That's a requirement when a subquery is used with the IN operator. Note also that the subquery includes the DISTINCT keyword. That way, if more than one invoice exists for a vendor, the vendor_id for that vendor will be included only once. The keyword DISTINCT is optional, however. The final result set will be the same if you include it or omit it.

In the previous figure, you saw that a query that uses a subquery with the IN operator can be restated using an inner join. Similarly, a query that uses a subquery with the NOT IN operator can typically be restated using an outer join. The first query shown in this figure, for example, can be restated as shown in the second query. In this case, though, the query with the subquery is more readable.

The syntax of a WHERE clause that uses an IN phrase with a subquery

```
WHERE test_expression [NOT] IN (subquery)
```

A query that returns vendors without invoices

```
SELECT vendor_id, vendor_name, vendor_state
FROM vendors
WHERE vendor_id NOT IN
    (SELECT DISTINCT vendor_id
    FROM invoices)
ORDER BY vendor_id
```

The result of the subquery

	VENDOR_ID
1	34
2	123
3	100
4	83
5	121
6	113

`(34 rows)`

The result set

	VENDOR_ID		VENDOR_NAME	VENDOR_STATE
32		33	Nielson	OH
33		35	Cal State Termite	CA
34		36	Graylift	CA
35		38	Venture Communications Int'l	NY
36		39	Custom Printing Company	MO
37		40	Nat Assoc of College Stores	OH

`(88 rows)`

The query restated without a subquery

```
SELECT v.vendor_id, vendor_name, vendor_state
FROM vendors v LEFT JOIN invoices i
    ON v.vendor_id = i.vendor_id
WHERE i.vendor_id IS NULL
ORDER BY v.vendor_id
```

Description

- You can introduce a subquery with the IN operator to provide the list of values that are tested against the test expression.

- When you use the IN operator, the subquery must return a single column of values.

- A query that uses the NOT IN operator with a subquery can typically be restated using an outer join.

Figure 6-3　How to use subqueries with the IN operator

How to compare the result of a subquery with an expression

Figure 6-4 illustrates how you can use the comparison operators to compare an expression with the result of a subquery. In the example, the subquery returns the average balance due of the invoices in the Invoices table with a balance due greater than zero. Then, it uses that value to retrieve all invoices that have a balance due that's less than the average.

When you use a comparison operator as shown in this figure, the subquery must return a single value. In most cases, that means that it uses an aggregate function. However, you can also use the comparison operators with subqueries that return two or more values. To do that, you use the SOME, ANY, or ALL keyword to modify the comparison operator. You'll learn more about these keywords in the next two topics.

The syntax of a WHERE clause that compares an expression with the value returned by a subquery

```
WHERE expression comparison_operator [SOME|ANY|ALL] (subquery)
```

A query that returns invoices with a balance due less than the average

```
SELECT invoice_number, invoice_date,
    invoice_total - payment_total - credit_total AS balance_due
FROM invoices
WHERE invoice_total - payment_total - credit_total  > 0
    AND invoice_total - payment_total - credit_total <
    (
    SELECT AVG(invoice_total - payment_total - credit_total)
    FROM invoices
    WHERE invoice_total - payment_total - credit_total > 0
    )
ORDER BY invoice_total DESC
```

The value returned by the subquery

```
1669.906
```

The result set

	INVOICE_NUMBER	INVOICE_DATE	BALANCE_DUE
1	31359783	23-MAY-08	1575
2	97/553	27-APR-08	904.14
3	I77271-O01	05-JUN-08	662
4	31361833	23-MAY-08	579.42
5	9982771	03-JUN-08	503.2
6	97/553B	26-APR-08	313.55

```
(33 rows)
```

Description

- You can use a comparison operator in a search condition to compare an expression with the results of a subquery.

- If you code a search condition without the ANY, SOME, or ALL keyword, the subquery must return a single value.

- If you include the ANY, SOME, or ALL keyword, the subquery can return a list of values. See figures 6-5 and 6-6 for more information on using these keywords.

Figure 6-4   How to compare the result of a subquery with an expression

How to use the ALL keyword

Figure 6-5 shows you how to use the ALL keyword. This keyword modifies the comparison operator so the condition must be true for all the values returned by a subquery. This is equivalent to coding a series of conditions connected by AND operators. The table at the top of this figure describes how this works for some of the comparison operators.

If you use the greater than operator (>), the expression must be greater than the maximum value returned by the subquery. Conversely, if you use the less than operator (<), the expression must be less than the minimum value returned by the subquery. If you use the equal operator (=), the expression must be equal to all of the values returned by the subquery. And if you use the not equal operator (<>), the expression must not equal any of the values returned by the subquery. Note that a not equal condition could be restated using a NOT IN condition.

The query in this figure illustrates the use of the greater than operator with the ALL keyword. Here, the subquery selects the invoice_total column for all the invoices with a vendor_id value of 34. This results in a table with two rows, as shown in this figure. Then, the outer query retrieves the rows from the Invoices table that have invoice totals greater than all of the values returned by the subquery. In other words, this query returns all the invoices that have totals greater than the largest invoice for vendor number 34.

When you use the ALL operator, you should realize that if the subquery doesn't return any rows, the comparison operation will always be true. In contrast, if the subquery returns only null values, the comparison operation will always be false.

In many cases, a condition with the ALL keyword can be rewritten so it's easier to read and maintain. For example, the condition in the query in this figure could be rewritten to use the MAX function like this:

```
WHERE invoice_total >
    (SELECT MAX(invoice_total)
    FROM invoices
    WHERE vendor_id = 34)
```

Whenever you can, then, we recommend that you replace the ALL keyword with an equivalent condition.

How the ALL keyword works

Condition	Equivalent expression	Description
`x > ALL (1, 2)`	`x > 2`	*x* must be greater than all the values returned by the subquery, which means it must be greater than the maximum value.
`x < ALL (1, 2)`	`x < 1`	*x* must be less than all the values returned by the subquery, which means it must be less than the minimum value.
`x = ALL (1, 2)`	`(x = 1) AND (x = 2)`	This condition can evaluate to True only if the subquery returns a single value or if all the values returned by the subquery are the same. Otherwise, it evaluates to False.
`x <> ALL (1, 2)`	`(x <> 1) AND (x <> 2)`	This condition is equivalent to: `x NOT IN (1, 2)`

A query that returns invoices larger than the largest invoice for vendor 34

```
SELECT vendor_name, invoice_number, invoice_total
FROM invoices i JOIN vendors v ON i.vendor_id = v.vendor_id
WHERE invoice_total > ALL
    (SELECT invoice_total
    FROM invoices
    WHERE vendor_id = 34)
ORDER BY vendor_name
```

The result of the subquery

	INVOICE_TOTAL
1	116.54
2	1083.58

The result set

	VENDOR_NAME	INVOICE_NUMBER	INVOICE_TOTAL
1	Bertelsmann Industry Svcs. Inc	509786	6940.25
2	Cahners Publishing Company	587056	2184.5
3	Computerworld	367447	2433
4	Data Reproductions Corp	40318	21842

`(25 rows)`

Description

- You can use the ALL keyword to test that a comparison condition is true for all of the values returned by a subquery. This keyword is typically used with the comparison operators <, >, <=, and >=.

- If no rows are returned by the subquery, a comparison that uses the ALL keyword is always true.

- If all of the rows returned by the subquery contain a null value, a comparison that uses the ALL keyword is always false.

Figure 6-5   How to use the ALL keyword

How to use the ANY and SOME keywords

Figure 6-6 shows how to use the ANY and SOME keywords. You use these keywords to test if a comparison is true for any, or some, of the values returned by a subquery. This is equivalent to coding a series of conditions connected with OR operators. Because these keywords are equivalent, you can use whichever one you prefer. The table at the top of this figure describes how these keywords work with some of the comparison operators.

The example in this figure shows how you can use the ANY keyword with the less than operator. This statement is similar to the one you saw in the previous figure, except that it retrieves invoices with invoice totals that are less than at least one of the invoice totals for a given vendor. Like the statement in the previous figure, this condition could be rewritten using the MAX function, as follows:

```
WHERE invoice_total <
    (SELECT MAX(invoice_total)
    FROM invoices
    WHERE vendor_id = 115)
```

Because you can usually replace an ANY condition with an equivalent condition that's more readable, you probably won't use ANY often.

How the ANY and SOME keywords work

Condition	Equivalent expression	Description
`x > ANY (1, 2)`	`x > 1`	*x* must be greater than at least one of the values returned by the subquery list, which means that it must be greater than the minimum value returned by the subquery.
`x < ANY (1, 2)`	`x < 2`	*x* must be less than at least one of the values returned by the subquery list, which means that it must be less than the maximum value returned by the subquery.
`x = ANY (1, 2)`	`(x = 1) OR (x = 2)`	This condition is equivalent to: `x IN (1, 2)`
`x <> ANY (1, 2)`	`(x <> 1) OR (x <> 2)`	This condition will evaluate to True for any non-empty result set containing at least one non-null value that isn't equal to *x*.

A query that returns invoice amounts smaller than the largest invoice amount for vendor 115

```
SELECT vendor_name, invoice_number, invoice_total
FROM vendors JOIN invoices ON vendors.vendor_id = invoices.invoice_id
WHERE invoice_total < ANY
    (SELECT invoice_total
    FROM invoices
    WHERE vendor_id = 115)
```

The result of the subquery

	INVOICE_TOTAL
1	25.67
2	6
3	6
4	6

The result set

	VENDOR_NAME	INVOICE_NUMBER	INVOICE_TOTAL
1	Boucher Communications Inc	24863706	6
2	Reiter's Scientific & Pro Books	25022117	6
3	Champion Printing Company	24780512	6
4	Opamp Technical Books	21-4748363	9.95
5	Capital Resource Credit	21-4923721	9.95

`(17 rows)`

Description

- You can use the ANY or SOME keyword to test that a condition is true for one or more of the values returned by a subquery. ANY and SOME are equivalent keywords. SOME is the ANSI-standard keyword, but ANY is more commonly used.

- If no rows are returned by the subquery or all of the rows returned by the subquery contain a null value, a comparison that uses the ANY or SOME keyword is always false.

Figure 6-6 How to use the ANY and SOME keywords

How to code correlated subqueries

The subqueries you've seen so far in this chapter have been subqueries that are executed only once for the entire query. However, you can also code subqueries that are executed once for each row that's processed by the outer query. This type of query is called a *correlated subquery*, and it's similar to using a loop to do repetitive processing in a procedural programming language.

Figure 6-7 illustrates how correlated subqueries work. The example in this figure retrieves rows from the Invoices table for those invoices that have an invoice total that's greater than the average of all the invoices for the same vendor. To do that, the search condition in the WHERE clause of the subquery refers to the vendor_id value of the current invoice. That way, only the invoices for the current vendor will be included in the average.

Each time a row in the outer query is processed, the value in the vendor_id column for that row is substituted for the column reference in the subquery. Then, the subquery is executed based on the current value. If the vendor_id value is 95, for example, this subquery will be executed:

```
SELECT AVG(invoice_total)
FROM invoices inv_sub
WHERE inv_sub.vendor_id = 95
```

After this subquery is executed, the value it returns is used to determine whether the current invoice is included in the result set. For example, the value returned by the subquery for vendor 95 is 28.5016. Then, that value is compared with the invoice total of the current invoice. If the invoice total is greater than that value, the invoice is included in the result set. Otherwise, it's not. This process is repeated until each of the invoices in the Invoices table has been processed.

As you study this example, notice how the column names in the WHERE clause of the inner query are qualified to indicate whether they refer to a column in the inner query or the outer query. In this case, the same table is used in both the inner and outer queries, so aliases have been assigned to the tables. Then, those alias names are used to qualify the column names. Although you have to qualify a reference to a column in the outer query, you don't have to qualify a reference to a column in the inner query. However, it's common practice to qualify both names, particularly if they refer to the same table.

Because correlated subqueries can be difficult to code, you may want to test a subquery separately before using it within another SELECT statement. To do that, however, you'll need to substitute a constant value for the variable that refers to a column in the outer query. That's what we did to get the average invoice total for vendor 95. Once you're sure that the subquery works on its own, you can replace the constant value with a reference to the outer query so you can use it within a SELECT statement.

A query that uses a correlated subquery to return each invoice amount that's higher than the vendor's average invoice amount

```
SELECT vendor_id, invoice_number, invoice_total
FROM invoices inv_main
WHERE invoice_total >
    (SELECT AVG(invoice_total)
    FROM invoices inv_sub
    WHERE inv_sub.vendor_id = inv_main.vendor_id)
ORDER BY vendor_id, invoice_total
```

The value returned by the subquery for vendor 95

```
28.50166...
```

The result set

	VENDOR_ID	INVOICE_NUMBER	INVOICE_TOTAL
6	83	31359783	1575
7	95	111-92R-10095	32.7
8	95	111-92R-10093	39.77
9	95	111-92R-10092	46.21
10	110	P-0259	26881.4

(36 rows)

Description

- A *correlated subquery* is a subquery that is executed once for each row processed by the outer query. In contrast, a *noncorrelated subquery* is executed only once. All of the subqueries you've seen so far have been noncorrelated subqueries.

- A correlated subquery refers to a value that's provided by a column in the outer query. Because that value varies depending on the row that's being processed, each execution of the subquery returns a different result.

- To refer to a value in the outer query, a correlated subquery uses a qualified column name that includes the table name from the outer query. If the subquery uses the same table as the outer query, you must assign a table alias to one of the tables to remove ambiguity.

Note

- Because a correlated subquery is executed once for each row processed by the outer query, a query with a correlated subquery typically takes longer to run than a query with a noncorrelated subquery.

Figure 6-7   How to code correlated subqueries

How to use the EXISTS operator

Figure 6-8 shows you how to use the EXISTS operator with a subquery. This operator tests whether or not the subquery returns a result set. In other words, it tests whether the result set exists. When you use this operator, the subquery doesn't actually return a result set to the outer query. Instead, it returns an indication of whether any rows satisfy the search condition of the subquery. Because of that, queries that use this operator execute quickly.

You typically use the EXISTS operator with a correlated subquery, as illustrated in this figure. This query retrieves all the vendors in the Vendors table that don't have invoices in the Invoices table. Notice that this query returns the same vendors as the two queries you saw in figure 6-3 that use the IN operator with a subquery and an outer join. However, the query in this figure executes more quickly than either of the queries in figure 6-3.

In this example, the correlated subquery selects all invoices that have the same vendor_id value as the current vendor in the outer query. Because the subquery doesn't actually return a result set, it doesn't matter what columns are included in the SELECT clause. So it's customary to just code an asterisk.

After the subquery is executed, the search condition in the WHERE clause of the outer query uses NOT EXISTS to test whether any invoices were found for the current vendor. If not, the vendor row is included in the result set.

The syntax of a subquery that uses the EXISTS operator

```
WHERE [NOT] EXISTS (subquery)
```

A query that returns vendors without invoices

```
SELECT vendor_id, vendor_name, vendor_state
FROM vendors
WHERE NOT EXISTS
    (SELECT *
    FROM invoices
    WHERE invoices.vendor_id = vendors.vendor_id)
```

The result set

	VENDOR_ID		VENDOR_NAME	VENDOR_STATE
32		33	Nielson	OH
33		35	Cal State Termite	CA
34		36	Graylift	CA
35		38	Venture Communications Int'l	NY
36		39	Custom Printing Company	MO
37		40	Nat Assoc of College Stores	OH

```
(88 rows)
```

Description

- You can use the EXISTS operator to test that one or more rows are returned by the subquery. You can also use the NOT operator along with the EXISTS operator to test that no rows are returned by the subquery.

- When you use the EXISTS operator with a subquery, the subquery doesn't actually return any rows. Instead, it returns an indication of whether any rows meet the specified condition.

- Because no rows are returned by the subquery, it doesn't matter what columns you specify in the SELECT clause. So you typically just code an asterisk (*).

- Although you can use the EXISTS operator with either a correlated or a noncorrelated subquery, it's used most often with correlated subqueries. That's because it's usually better to use a join than a noncorrelated subquery with EXISTS.

Figure 6-8   How to use the EXISTS operator

Other ways to use subqueries

Although you'll typically use subqueries in the WHERE or HAVING clause of a SELECT statement, you can also use them in the FROM and SELECT clauses. You'll learn how to do that in the topics that follow.

How to code subqueries in the FROM clause

Figure 6-9 shows you how to code a subquery in a FROM clause. As you can see, you can code a subquery in place of a table specification. In this example, the results of the subquery are joined with another table. When you use a subquery in this way, it can return any number of rows and columns. In the Oracle documentation, this type of subquery is sometimes referred to as an *inline view* since it works like a view that's temporarily created and stored in memory.

Subqueries are typically used in the FROM clause to create inline views that provide summarized data to a summary query. The subquery in this figure, for example, creates an inline view that contains the vendor_id values and the average invoice totals for all vendors with invoice averages over 4900. To do that, it selects all vendors with invoice averages over 4900, and it groups the invoices by vendor_id. The inline view is then joined with the Invoices table, and the resulting rows are grouped by vendor_id. Finally, the maximum invoice date and average invoice total are calculated for the grouped rows, and the results are sorted by the maximum invoice date in descending sequence.

You should notice three things about this query. First, the inline view is assigned a table alias so it can be referred to from the outer query. Second, the result of the AVG function in the subquery is assigned a column alias. This is because an inline view can't have unnamed columns. Third, although you might think that you could use the average invoice totals calculated by the subquery in the select list of the outer query, you can't. That's because the outer query includes a GROUP BY clause, so only aggregate functions, columns named in the GROUP BY clause, and constant values can be included in this list. Because of that, the AVG function is repeated in the select list.

When used in the FROM clause, a subquery is similar to a view. As you learned in chapter 1, a view is a predefined SELECT statement that's saved with the database. Because it's saved with the database, a view typically performs more efficiently than an inline view. However, it isn't always practical to use a view. In those cases, inline views can be quite useful. In addition, inline views can be useful for testing possible solutions before creating a view. Then, once the inline view works the way you want it to, you can define the view based on the subquery you used to create the inline view.

A query that uses an inline view to retrieve all vendors with an average invoice total over 4900

```
SELECT i.vendor_id, MAX(invoice_date) AS last_invoice_date,
    AVG(invoice_total) AS average_invoice_total
FROM invoices i JOIN
    (
    SELECT vendor_id, AVG(invoice_total) AS average_invoice_total
    FROM invoices
    HAVING AVG(invoice_total) > 4900
    GROUP BY vendor_id
    ) v
    ON i.vendor_id = v.vendor_id
GROUP BY i.vendor_id
ORDER BY MAX(invoice_date) DESC
```

The result of the subquery (an inline view)

	VENDOR_ID	AVERAGE_INVOICE_TOTAL
1	72	10963.655
2	119	4901.26
3	110	23978.482
4	99	6940.25
5	104	7125.34

The result set

	VENDOR_ID	LAST_INVOICE_DATE	AVERAGE_INVOICE_TOTAL
1	72	18-JUL-08	10963.655
2	119	04-JUN-08	4901.26
3	104	03-JUN-08	7125.34
4	99	31-MAY-08	6940.25
5	110	08-MAY-08	23978.482

Description

- A subquery that's coded in the FROM clause returns a result set that can be referred to as an *inline view*. When you create an inline view, you must assign an alias to it. Then, you can use the inline view within the outer query just as you would any other table.

- When you code a subquery in the FROM clause, you must assign names to any calculated values in the result set.

- Inline views are most useful when you need to further summarize the results of a summary query.

- An inline view is like a view in that it retrieves selected rows and columns from one or more base tables. Because views are stored as part of the database, they're typically more efficient to use than inline views. However, it may not always be practical to construct and save a view in advance.

Figure 6-9   How to code subqueries in the FROM clause

How to code subqueries in the SELECT clause

Figure 6-10 shows you how to use subqueries in the SELECT clause. As you can see, you can use a subquery in place of a column specification. Because of that, the subquery must return a single value.

In most cases, the subqueries you use in the SELECT clause will be correlated subqueries. The subquery in this figure, for example, calculates the maximum invoice date for each vendor in the Vendors table. To do that, it refers to the vendor_id column from the Invoices table in the outer query.

Because subqueries coded in the SELECT clause are difficult to read, you shouldn't use them unless you can't find another solution. In most cases, though, you can replace the subquery with a join. The first query shown in this figure, for example, could be restated as shown in the second query. This query joins the Vendors and Invoices tables, groups the rows by vendor_name, and then uses the MAX function to calculate the maximum invoice date for each vendor. As you can see, this query is much easier to read than the one with the subquery.

A query that uses a correlated subquery in its SELECT clause to retrieve the most recent invoice for each vendor

```
SELECT vendor_name,
    (SELECT MAX(invoice_date) FROM invoices
    WHERE invoices.vendor_id = vendors.vendor_id) AS latest_inv
FROM vendors
ORDER BY latest_inv
```

The result set

	VENDOR_NAME	LATEST_INV
1	IBM	14-MAR-08
2	Wang Laboratories, Inc.	16-APR-08
3	Reiter's Scientific & Pro Books	17-APR-08
4	United Parcel Service	26-APR-08
5	Wakefield Co	26-APR-08
6	Zylka Design	01-MAY-08
7	Abbey Office Furnishings	02-MAY-08

```
(122 rows)
```

The same query restated using a join

```
SELECT vendor_name, MAX(invoice_date) AS latest_inv
FROM vendors v
    LEFT JOIN invoices i ON v.vendor_id = i.vendor_id
GROUP BY vendor_name
ORDER BY latest_inv
```

Description

- When you code a subquery for a column specification in the SELECT clause, the subquery must return a single value.

- A subquery that's coded within a SELECT clause is typically a correlated subquery.

- A query that includes a subquery in its SELECT clause can typically be restated using a join instead of the subquery. Because a join is usually faster and more readable, subqueries are seldom coded in the SELECT clause.

Figure 6-10   How to code subqueries in the SELECT clause

Guidelines for working with complex queries

So far, the examples you've seen of queries that use subqueries have been relatively simple. However, these types of queries can get complicated in a hurry, particularly if the subqueries are nested. Because of that, you'll want to be sure that you plan and test these queries carefully. You'll learn a procedure for doing that in a moment. But first, you'll see a complex query that illustrates the type of query we're talking about.

A complex query that uses subqueries

Figure 6-11 presents a query that uses three subqueries. The first subquery is used in the FROM clause of the outer query to create a result set that contains the state, name, and total invoice amount for each vendor in the Vendors table. The second subquery is also used in the FROM clause of the outer query to create a result set that's joined with the first result set. This result set contains the state and total invoice amount for the vendor in each state that has the largest invoice total. To create this result set, a third subquery is nested within the FROM clause of the subquery. This subquery is identical to the first subquery.

After the two result sets are created, they're joined based on the columns in each table that contain the state and the total invoice amount. The final result set includes the state, name, and total invoice amount for the vendor in each state with the largest invoice total. This result set is sorted by state.

As you can see, this query is quite complicated and difficult to understand. In fact, you might be wondering if there isn't an easier solution to this problem. For example, you might think that you could solve the problem simply by joining the Vendors and Invoices tables and creating a grouped aggregate. If you grouped by vendor state, however, you wouldn't be able to include the name of the vendor in the result set. And if you grouped by vendor state and vendor name, the result set would include all the vendors, not just the vendor from each state with the largest invoice total.

If you think about how else you might solve this query, we think you'll agree that the solution presented here is fairly straightforward. However, in figure 6-13, you'll learn one way to simplify this query. In particular, you'll learn how to code a single Summary subquery instead of coding the Summary1 and Summary2 subqueries shown here.

A query that uses three subqueries

```
SELECT summary1.vendor_state, summary1.vendor_name,
    top_in_state.sum_of_invoices
FROM
    (
    SELECT v_sub.vendor_state, v_sub.vendor_name,
        SUM(i_sub.invoice_total) AS sum_of_invoices
    FROM invoices i_sub JOIN vendors v_sub
        ON i_sub.vendor_id = v_sub.vendor_id
    GROUP BY v_sub.vendor_state, v_sub.vendor_name
    ) summary1
    JOIN
        (
        SELECT summary2.vendor_state,
            MAX(summary2.sum_of_invoices) AS sum_of_invoices
        FROM
            (
            SELECT v_sub.vendor_state, v_sub.vendor_name,
                SUM(i_sub.invoice_total) AS sum_of_invoices
            FROM invoices i_sub JOIN vendors v_sub
                ON i_sub.vendor_id = v_sub.vendor_id
            GROUP BY v_sub.vendor_state, v_sub.vendor_name
            ) summary2
        GROUP BY summary2.vendor_state
        ) top_in_state
    ON summary1.vendor_state = top_in_state.vendor_state AND
        summary1.sum_of_invoices = top_in_state.sum_of_invoices
ORDER BY summary1.vendor_state
```

The result set

	VENDOR_STATE	VENDOR_NAME	SUM_OF_INVOICES
1	AZ	Wells Fargo Bank	662
2	CA	Digital Dreamworks	7125.34
3	DC	Reiter's Scientific & Pro Books	600
4	MA	Dean Witter Reynolds	1367.5
5	MI	Malloy Lithographing Inc	119892.41
6	NV	United Parcel Service	23177.96
7	OH	Edward Data Services	207.78

```
(10 rows)
```

How the query works

- This query retrieves the vendor from each state that has the largest invoice total. To do that, it uses three subqueries: Summary1, Summary2, and Top_In_State. The Summary1 and Top_In_State subqueries are joined in the FROM clause of the outer query, and the Summary2 subquery is nested within the FROM clause of the Top_In_State subquery.

- The Summary1 and Summary2 subqueries are identical. They join data from the Vendors and Invoices tables and produce a result set that includes the sum of invoices for each vendor grouped by vendor name within state.

- The Top_In_State subquery produces a result set that includes the vendor state and the largest sum of invoices for any vendor in that state. This information is retrieved from the results of the Summary2 subquery.

Figure 6-11   A complex query that uses subqueries

A procedure for building complex queries

To build a complex query like the one in the previous figure, you can use a procedure like the one in figure 6-12. To start, you should state the problem to be solved so that you're clear about what you want the query to accomplish. In this case, the question is, "Which vendor in each state has the largest invoice total?"

Once you're clear about the problem, you should outline the query using *pseudocode*. Pseudocode is simply code that represents the intent of the query, but doesn't necessarily use SQL code. The pseudocode shown in this figure, for example, uses part SQL code and part English. Notice that this pseudocode identifies the two main subqueries. Because these subqueries define inline views, the pseudocode also indicates the alias that will be used for each: summary1 and top_in_state. That way, you can use these aliases in the pseudocode for the outer query to make it clear where the data it uses comes from.

If it isn't clear from the pseudocode how each subquery will be coded, or, as in this case, if a subquery is nested within another subquery, you can also write pseudocode for the subqueries. For example, the pseudocode for the top_in_state query is presented in this figure. Because this subquery has a subquery nested in its FROM clause, that subquery is identified in this pseudocode as Summary2.

The next step in the procedure is to code and test the actual subqueries to be sure they work the way you want them to. For example, the code for the Summary1 and Summary2 queries is shown in this figure, along with the results of these queries and the results of the top_in_state query. Once you're sure that the subqueries work the way you want them to, you can code and test the final query.

If you follow the procedure presented in this figure, you'll find it easier to build complex queries that use subqueries. Before you can use this procedure, of course, you need to have a thorough understanding of how subqueries work and what they can do. So you'll want to be sure to experiment with the techniques you learned in this chapter before you try to build a complex query like the one shown here.

A procedure for building complex queries

1. State the problem to be solved by the query in English.
2. Use pseudocode to outline the query. The pseudocode should identify the subqueries used by the query and the data they return. It should also include aliases used for any inline views.
3. If necessary, use pseudocode to outline each subquery.
4. Code the subqueries and test them to be sure that they return the correct data.
5. Code and test the final query.

The problem to be solved by the query in figure 6-11

Which vendor in each state has the largest invoice total?

Pseudocode for the query

```
SELECT summary1.vendor_state, summary1.vendor_name,
top_in_state.sum_of_invoices
FROM (inline view returning vendor_state, vendor_name, sum_of_invoices)
    AS summary1
    JOIN (inline view returning vendor_state, max(sum_of_invoices))
        AS top_in_state
    ON summary1.vendor_state = top_in_state.vendor_state AND
        summary1.sum_of_invoices = top_in_state.sum_of_invoices
ORDER BY summary1.vendor_state
```

Pseudocode for the Top_In_State subquery

```
SELECT summary2.vendor_state, MAX(summary2.sum_of_invoices)
FROM (inline view returning vendor_state, vendor_name, sum_of_invoices)
    AS summary2
GROUP BY summary2.vendor_state
```

The code for the Summary1 and Summary2 subqueries

```
SELECT v_sub.vendor_state, v_sub.vendor_name,
    SUM(i_sub.invoice_total) AS sum_of_invoices
FROM invoices i_sub JOIN vendors v_sub
    ON i_sub.vendor_id = v_sub.vendor_id
GROUP BY v_sub.vendor_state, v_sub.vendor_name
ORDER BY v_sub.vendor_state, v_sub.vendor_name
```

The result of the Summary1 and Summary2 subqueries

VENDOR_STATE	VENDOR_NAME	SUM_OF_INVOICES
1 AZ	Wells Fargo Bank	662
2 CA	Abbey Office Furnishings	17.5
3 CA	Bertelsmann Industry Svcs. Inc	6940.25

`(34 rows)`

The result of the Top_In_State subquery

VENDOR_STATE	SUM_OF_INVOICES
1 CA	7125.34
2 MA	1367.5
3 OH	207.78

`(10 rows)`

Figure 6-12   A procedure for building complex queries

Two more skills for working with subqueries

Now that you've learned how to code complex queries, you're ready to learn two more skills that are closely related to coding subqueries. These skills make it possible to simplify queries that could also be coded with subqueries.

How to code a subquery factoring clause

Subquery factoring allows you to name a block of code that contains a SELECT statement. Fox example, figure 6-13 shows how to use subquery factoring to simplify the complex query presented in figure 6-11. To start, the statement for the query begins with the WITH keyword to identify a subquery factoring clause. Then, it specifies Summary as the name for the first subquery, followed by the AS keyword, followed by an opening parenthesis, followed by a SELECT statement that defines the subquery, followed by a closing parenthesis. In this figure, for example, this statement returns the same result set as the subqueries named Summary1 and Summary2 that were presented in figure 6-11.

After the first subquery is defined, this example continues by defining a second subquery named top_in_state. To start, a comma is coded to separate the two subqueries. Then, this code specifies top_in_state as the name for the second subquery, followed by the AS keyword, followed by an opening parenthesis, followed by a SELECT statement that defines the subquery, followed by a closing parenthesis. Here, this SELECT statement refers to the first subquery, named Summary. When coding multiple subqueries within a subquery factoring clause, a subquery can refer to any subquery coded before it, but it can't refer to subqueries coded after it. For example, this statement wouldn't work if the two subqueries were coded in the reverse order.

Finally, the SELECT statement that's coded immediately after the two named subqueries uses both of these subqueries, just as if they were tables. To do that, this SELECT statement joins the two subqueries, specifies the columns to retrieve, and specifies the sort order. To avoid ambiguous references, each column is qualified by the name for the subquery.

If you compare figure 6-13 with figure 6-11, we think you'll agree that the code in figure 6-13 is easier to read. That's partly because the tables defined by the subqueries aren't nested within the SELECT statement. In addition, the code in figure 6-13 is easier to maintain because the Summary query is coded in one place, not in two.

When using the syntax shown here to define a subquery factoring clause, you must supply distinct names for all columns defined by the SELECT statement, including calculated values. That way, it's possible for other statements to refer to the columns in the result set. Most of the time, that's all you need to know to be able to work with a subquery factoring clause.

The syntax of a subquery factoring clause

```
WITH query_name1 AS (query_definition1)
[, query_name2 AS (query_definition2)]
[...]
sql_statement
```

Two query names and a query that uses them

```
WITH summary AS
(
    SELECT vendor_state, vendor_name, SUM(invoice_total) AS sum_of_invoices
    FROM invoices
        JOIN vendors ON invoices.vendor_id = vendors.vendor_id
    GROUP BY vendor_state, vendor_name
),
top_in_state AS
(
    SELECT vendor_state, MAX(sum_of_invoices) AS sum_of_invoices
    FROM summary
    GROUP BY vendor_state
)
SELECT summary.vendor_state, summary.vendor_name,
    top_in_state.sum_of_invoices
FROM summary JOIN top_in_state
    ON summary.vendor_state = top_in_state.vendor_state AND
        summary.sum_of_invoices = top_in_state.sum_of_invoices
ORDER BY summary.vendor_state
```

The result set

	VENDOR_STATE	VENDOR_NAME	SUM_OF_INVOICES
1	AZ	Wells Fargo Bank	662
2	CA	Digital Dreamworks	7125.34
3	DC	Reiter's Scientific & Pro Books	600
4	MA	Dean Witter Reynolds	1367.5
5	MI	Malloy Lithographing Inc	119892.41
6	NV	United Parcel Service	23177.96
7	OH	Edward Data Services	207.78

```
(10 rows)
```

Description

- A *subquery factoring clause* can be thought of as a named subquery block. This name can then be used multiple times in the query.

- To define a subquery factoring block, you code the WITH keyword followed by the definition of the subquery.

- To code multiple subquery factoring clauses, separate them with commas. Then, each clause can refer to itself and any previously defined subquery factoring clauses in the same WITH clause.

- You can use subquery factoring clauses with SELECT, INSERT, UPDATE, and DE-LETE statements. However, you're most likely to use them with SELECT statements, as shown in this figure.

Figure 6-13   How to code a subquery factoring clause

How to code a hierarchical query

A *hierarchical query* loops through a result set and returns rows in a hierarchical sequence. Hierarchical queries are often used to work with organizational charts and other hierarchies, in which a parent element may have one or more child elements, and each child element may have one or more child elements. In figure 6-14, for example, the query shows the hierarchical levels for the employees within a company.

The Employees table uses the manager_id column to identify the manager for each employee. Here, Cindy Smith is the top-level manager since she doesn't have a manager, Elmer Jones and Paulo Locario report to Cindy Smith, and so on.

In this figure, the hierarchical query uses the LEVEL pseudo column to return a column that identifies the level of the employee within the hierarchy. To start, this query uses the LEVEL pseudo column in the SELECT clause to identify the third column. In addition, this query uses the LEVEL pseudo column in the ORDER BY clause to sort by this column.

After the FROM clause, this query uses the START WITH clause to identify the row to be used as the root of the hierarchy. In this figure, for example, the query uses the employee_id column to identify Cindy Smith as the root of the hierarchy. However, if you wanted, you could use a difference expression after the START WITH keywords to identify this row or a different row.

Finally, the CONNECT BY clause specifies the condition that identifies the relationship between parent rows and child rows. In this figure, for example, the CONNECT BY clause is followed by the PRIOR keyword to specify that a row is a child row if the row's employee_id column equals the manager_id column of the other row.

A query that returns hierarchical data

```
SELECT select_list
FROM table_source
[WHERE search_condition]
START WITH row_specification
CONNECT BY PRIOR connect_expression
[ORDER BY order_by_list]
```

The Employees table

EMPLOYEE_ID	FIRST_NAME	LAST_NAME	DEPARTMENT_NUMBER	MANAGER_ID
1 Cindy	Smith		2	(null)
2 Elmer	Jones		4	1
3 Ralph	Simonian		2	2
4 Olivia	Hernandez		1	9
5 Robert	Aaronsen		2	4
6 Denise	Watson		6	8
7 Thomas	Hardy		5	2
8 Rhea	O'Leary		4	9
9 Paulo	Locario		6	1

A query that returns hierarchical data

```
SELECT employee_id,
    first_name || ' ' || last_name AS employee_name,
    LEVEL
FROM employees
START WITH employee_id = 1
CONNECT BY PRIOR employee_id = manager_id
ORDER BY LEVEL, employee_id
```

The result set

	EMPLOYEE_ID	EMPLOYEE_NAME	LEVEL
1	1 Cindy Smith		1
2	2 Elmer Jones		2
3	9 Paulo Locario		2
4	3 Ralph Simonian		3
5	4 Olivia Hernandez		3
6	7 Thomas Hardy		3
7	8 Rhea O'Leary		3
8	5 Robert Aaronsen		4
9	6 Denise Watson		4

Description

- A *hierarchical query* is a query that returns rows in a hierarchical order.
- You can use the LEVEL pseudocolumn to identify the level for each row.
- You can use the START WITH clause to identify the row to be used as the root of the hierarchical query.
- You can use the CONNECT BY clause followed by the PRIOR keyword to specify a condition that identifies the relationship between parent rows and child rows.

Figure 6-14   How to code a hierarchical query

Perspective

As you've seen in this chapter, subqueries provide a powerful tool for solving difficult problems. Before you use a subquery, however, remember that a subquery can often be restated more clearly by using a join. If so, you'll typically want to use a join instead of a subquery.

If you find yourself coding the same subqueries over and over, you should consider creating a view for that subquery, as described in chapter 11. This will help you develop queries more quickly since you can use the view instead of coding the subquery again. In addition, since views typically execute more quickly than subqueries, this may improve the performance of your queries.

Terms

subquery
introduce a subquery
subquery search condition
subquery predicate
nested subquery
correlated subquery
inline view
pseudocode
subquery factoring
hierarchical query

Exercises

1. Write a SELECT statement that returns the same result set as this SELECT statement but don't use a join. Instead, use a subquery in a WHERE clause that uses the IN keyword.

    ```
    SELECT DISTINCT vendor_name
    FROM vendors JOIN invoices
        ON vendors.vendor_id = invoices.vendor_id
    ORDER BY vendor_name
    ```

2. Write a SELECT statement that answers this question: Which invoices have a payment_total that's greater than the average payment_total for all paid invoices? Return the invoice_number and invoice_total for each invoice.

3. Write a SELECT statement that returns two columns from the General_Ledger_Accounts table: account_number and account_description. The result set should have one row for each account number that has never been used. Use a subquery introduced with the NOT EXISTS operator, and sort the final result set by account_number.

4. Write a SELECT statement that returns four columns: vendor_name, invoice_id, invoice_sequence, and line_item_amt for each invoice that has more than one line item in the Invoice_Line_Items table. *Hint: Use a subquery that tests for invoice_sequence > 1.*

5. Write a SELECT statement that returns a single value that represents the sum of the largest unpaid invoices for each vendor (just one for each vendor). Use an inline view that returns MAX(invoice_total) grouped by vendor_id, filtering for invoices with a balance due.

6. Rewrite exercise 6 so it uses subquery factoring.

7. Write a SELECT statement that returns the name, city, and state of each vendor that's located in a unique city and state. In other words, don't include vendors that have a city and state in common with another vendor.

8. Use a correlated subquery to return one row per vendor, representing the vendor's oldest invoice (the one with the earliest date). Each row should include these four columns: vendor_name, invoice_number, invoice_date, and invoice_total.

9. Rewrite exercise 8 so it gets the same result but doesn't use a correlated subquery.

7

How to insert, update, and delete data

In the last four chapters, you learned how to code the SELECT statement to retrieve and summarize data. Now, you'll learn how to code the INSERT, UPDATE, and DELETE statements to modify the data in a table. When you're done with this chapter, you'll know how to code the four statements that are used every day by professional application developers.

How to create test tables

As you practice coding INSERT, UPDATE, and DELETE statements, you need to make sure that your experimentation won't affect "live" data that's used by other people at your business or school. Two ways to get around that are presented next.

How to create the tables for this book

The first procedure in figure A-5 of appendix A shows how to create the tables that are used for the examples in this book. After you create these tables, you can modify them without worrying about how much you change them. If you ever want to restore the tables to their original data, you can use the second procedure in figure A-5.

How to create a copy of a table

If you want to test INSERT, UPDATE, and DELETE statements on tables that are running on a server that's available from your business or school, you can create a copy of some or all of a table before you do any testing. To do that, you can use the CREATE TABLE statement with an embedded SELECT statement as shown in figure 7-1. Then, you can experiment all you want with the test tables and delete them when you're done. When you use this technique, the result set that's defined by the SELECT statement is simply copied into a new table.

The three examples in this figure show some of the ways you can use this statement. Here, the first example copies all of the columns from all of the rows in the Invoices table into a new table named Invoices_Copy. The second example copies all of the columns in the Invoices table into a new table named Old_Invoices, but only for rows where the balance due is zero. And the third example creates a table that contains summary data from the Invoices table.

When you're done experimenting with test tables, you can use the DROP TABLE statement that's shown in this figure to delete any tables you don't need anymore. In this figure, for instance, the fourth example shows how to drop the Invoices_Copy table.

When you use this technique to create tables, though, only the column definitions and data are copied, which means that definitions like those of primary keys, foreign keys, and default values aren't retained. As a result, the results that you get when you test against copied tables may be slightly different than the results you would get with the original tables. You'll understand that better after you read chapters 9 and 10.

The syntax of the CREATE TABLE AS statement

```
CREATE TABLE table_name AS
SELECT select_list
FROM table_source
[WHERE search_condition]
[GROUP BY group_by_list]
[HAVING search_condition]
[ORDER BY order_by_list]
```

A statement that creates a complete copy of the Invoices table

```
CREATE TABLE invoices_copy AS
SELECT *
FROM invoices
```

A statement that creates a partial copy of the Invoices table

```
CREATE TABLE old_invoices AS
SELECT *
FROM invoices
WHERE invoice_total - payment_total - credit_total = 0
```

A statement that creates a table with summary rows from the Invoices table

```
CREATE TABLE vendor_balances AS
SELECT vendor_id, SUM(invoice_total) AS sum_of_invoices
FROM invoices
WHERE (invoice_total - payment_total - credit_total) <> 0
GROUP BY vendor_id
```

A statement that deletes a table

```
DROP TABLE invoices_copy
```

Description

- You can create a new table based on the result set defined by the SELECT statement. Since the definitions of the columns in the new table are based on the columns in the result set, the column names assigned in the SELECT clause must be unique.

- You can code the other clauses of the SELECT statement just as you would for any other SELECT statement, including grouping, aggregates, joins, and subqueries.

- If you use calculated values in the select list, you must name the column since that name is used in the definition of the new table.

- The table you name must not exist. If it does, you must delete the table by using the DROP TABLE statement before you execute the SELECT statement.

Warning

- When you use the SELECT statement to create a table, only the column definitions and data are copied. Definitions of primary keys, foreign keys, indexes, default values, and so on are not included in the new table.

Figure 7-1   How to create a table from another table

How to commit and rollback changes

When you use SQL Developer to execute INSERT, UPDATE, and DELETE statements, Oracle Database automatically adds those statements to a *transaction*. A transaction is a group of SQL statements that must all be executed successfully before they are saved to the database. To make the changes to the database permanent, you must explicitly *commit* the changes to the database. Otherwise, you can undo, or *rollback*, the changes.

For example, the INSERT statement in figure 7-2 adds a single row to the Invoices table. If you use SQL Developer to execute this statement, the row will be added to the Invoices table. Then, you will be able to see this row if you execute a SELECT statement that selects this row from the Invoices table. However, any other users who may be using this database won't be able to see this row until you commit this change to the database.

When you exit SQL Developer, the Oracle Database will automatically rollback all INSERT, UPDATE, and DELETE statements that haven't explicitly been committed. In other words, if you don't explicitly commit changes, they will be lost when you exit SQL Developer.

When you're practicing with INSERT, UPDATE, and DELETE statements, you may want them rolled back. If you want to make permanent changes to a production system, though, you'll need to make sure to commit the changes. For more information about working with transactions, see chapter 14.

How to commit changes

You can make the changes to the database permanent by executing the COMMIT statement shown in this figure. Or, if you're using SQL Developer, you can commit the changes by clicking on the Commit button or pressing F11. When you do, SQL Developer will display a message that indicates whether the commit succeeded.

Most of the time, you'll want to use one of these techniques to manually commit your changes. However, if you want SQL Developer to automatically commit changes immediately after they are made, you can enable the "Autocommit in SQL Worksheet" feature as described in this figure.

How to rollback changes

You can rollback any INSERT, UPDATE, and DELETE statements that haven't been committed yet by executing the ROLLBACK statement shown in this figure. Or, if you're using SQL Developer, you can undo the changes by clicking on the Rollback button or pressing F12. When you do, SQL Developer will display a message that indicates whether the rollback succeeded.

An INSERT statement that adds a new row to the Invoices table

```
INSERT INTO invoices
VALUES (115, 97, '456789', '01-AUG-08', 8344.50, 0, 0, 1, '31-AUG-08', NULL)
```

The response from the system

```
1 rows inserted
```

A COMMIT statement that commits the changes

```
COMMIT
```

The response from the system

```
COMMIT succeeded
```

A ROLLBACK statement that rolls back the changes

```
ROLLBACK
```

The response from the system

```
ROLLBACK succeeded
```

Description

- A *transaction* is a group of SQL statements that must all be executed together. By default, Oracle adds INSERT, UPDATE, and DELETE statements to a transaction.
- To *commit* the changes made by a transaction, you can issue the COMMIT statement. Or, if you're using SQL Developer, you can click on the Commit button or press F11.
- To *rollback* the changes made by a transaction, you can issue the ROLLBACK statement. Or, if you're using SQL Developer, you can click on the Rollback button or press F12.
- By default, if you don't explicitly commit the changes made to the database by a transaction, the Oracle Database will rollback the changes when you exit SQL Developer.
- If you want SQL Developer to automatically commit changes to the database immediately after each INSERT, UPDATE, or DELETE statement is executed, use the Tools→Preferences command. Then, expand the Database node, click on the Worksheet Parameters node, and check the "Autocommit in SQL Worksheet" check box.

Figure 7-2   How to rollback or commit changes

How to insert new rows

To add new rows to a table, you use the INSERT statement. This statement lets you insert a single row with the values you specify or selected rows from another table. You'll see how to use both forms of the INSERT statement in the topics that follow. In addition, you'll learn how to work with default values and null values when you insert new rows.

How to insert a single row

Figure 7-3 shows how to code an INSERT statement to insert a single row. The two examples in this figure insert a row into the Invoices table. The data this new row contains is defined near the top of this figure.

In the first example, you can see that you name the table in which the row will be inserted in the INSERT clause. Then, the VALUES clause lists the values to be used for each column. You should notice three things about this list. First, it includes a value for every column in the table. Second, the values are listed in the same sequence that the columns appear in the table. That way, Oracle knows which value to assign to which column. And third, a null value is assigned to the last column, payment_date, using the NULL keyword. You'll learn more about using this keyword in the next topic.

The second INSERT statement in this figure includes a column list in the INSERT clause. Notice that this list doesn't include the payment_date column since it allows a null value. In addition, the columns aren't listed in the same sequence as the columns in the Invoices table. When you include a list of columns, you can code the columns in any sequence you like. Then, you just need to be sure that the values in the VALUES clause are coded in the same sequence.

When you specify the values for the columns to be inserted, you must be sure that those values are compatible with the data types of the columns. For example, you must enclose literal values for dates and strings within single quotes. However, you don't need to enclose literal values for numbers in single quotes. You'll learn more about data types and how to work with them in the next chapter. For now, just realize that if any of the values aren't compatible with the data types of the corresponding columns, an error will occur and the row won't be inserted.

The syntax of the INSERT statement for inserting a single row

```
INSERT INTO table_name [(column_list)]
    VALUES (expression_1 [, expression_2]...)
```

The values for a new row to be added to the Invoices table

Column	Value	Column	Value
invoice_id	115	payment_total	0
vendor_id	97	credit_total	0
invoice_number	456789	terms_id	1
invoice_date	8/01/2008	invoice_due_date	8/31/2008
invoice_total	8,344.50	payment_date	null

An INSERT statement that adds the new row without using a column list

```
INSERT INTO invoices
VALUES (115, 97, '456789', '01-AUG-08', 8344.50, 0, 0, 1, '31-AUG-08', NULL)

(1 rows inserted)
```

An INSERT statement that adds the new row using a column list

```
INSERT INTO invoices
    (invoice_id, vendor_id, invoice_number, invoice_total, payment_total,
     credit_total, terms_id, invoice_date, invoice_due_date)
VALUES
    (115, 97, '456789', 8344.50, 0, 0, 1, '01-AUG-08', '31-AUG-08')

(1 rows inserted)
```

Description

- You use the INSERT statement to add a new row to a table.

- In the INSERT clause, you specify the name of the table that you want to add a row to, along with an optional column list. The INTO keyword is required.

- You specify the values to be inserted in the VALUES clause. The values you specify depend on whether you include a column list.

- If you don't include a column list, you must specify the column values in the same order as they appear in the table, and you must code a value for each column in the table.

- If you include a column list, you must specify the column values in the same order as they appear in the column list. You can omit columns with default values and columns that accept null values.

- To insert a null value into a column, you can use the NULL keyword. To insert a default value, you can use the DEFAULT keyword. See figure 7-4 for more information on using these keywords.

Figure 7-3   How to insert a single row

How to insert default values and null values

If a column allows null values, you'll want to know how to insert a null value into that column. Similarly, if a column is defined with a default value, you'll want to know how to insert that value. The technique you use depends on whether the INSERT statement includes a column list, as shown by the examples in figure 7-4.

All of these INSERT statements use a table named Color_Sample. This table contains the three columns shown at the top of this figure. The first column, color_id, represents the internal ID for the column. The second column, color_number, is defined with a default value of 0. And the third column, color_name, is defined so that it allows null values.

The first two statements illustrate how you assign a default value or a null value using a column list. To do that, you simply omit the column from the list. In the first statement, for example, the column list names only the color_number column, so the color_name column is assigned a null value. Similarly, the column list in the second statement names only the color_name column, so the color_number is assigned its default value.

The next three statements show how you assign a default or null value to a column without including a column list. As you can see, you do that by using the DEFAULT and NULL keywords. For example, the third statement specifies a value for the color_name column, but uses the DEFAULT keyword for the color_number column. Because of that, Oracle will assign a value of zero to this column. The fourth statement assigns a value of 808 to the color_number column, and it uses the NULL keyword to assign a null value to the color_name column. Finally, the fifth statement uses both the DEFAULT and NULL keywords to assign a value of zero to the color_number column and a null value to the color_name column.

The definition of the Color_Sample table

Column name	Data Type	Not Null	Default Value
color_id	NUMBER	Yes	
color_number	NUMBER	Yes	0
color_name	VARCHAR2		

Five INSERT statements for the Color_Sample table

```
INSERT INTO color_sample (color_id, color_number)
VALUES (1, 606)

INSERT INTO color_sample (color_id, color_name)
VALUES (2, 'Yellow')

INSERT INTO color_sample
VALUES (3, DEFAULT, 'Orange')

INSERT INTO color_sample
VALUES (4, 808, NULL)

INSERT INTO color_sample
VALUES (5, DEFAULT, NULL)
```

The Color_Sample table after the rows are inserted

COLOR_ID	COLOR_NUMBER	COLOR_NAME
1	606	(null)
2	0	Yellow
3	0	Orange
4	808	(null)
5	0	(null)

Description

- If a column is defined so it allows null values, you can use the NULL keyword in the list of values to insert a null value into that column.

- If a column is defined with a default value, you can use the DEFAULT keyword in the list of values to insert the default value for that column.

- If you include a column list, you can omit columns with default values and null values. Then, the default value or null value is assigned automatically.

Figure 7-4   How to insert default values and null values

How to use a subquery to insert multiple rows

Instead of using the VALUES clause of the INSERT statement to specify the values for a single row, you can use a subquery to select the rows you want to insert from another table. Figure 7-5 shows you how to do that.

Both examples in this figure retrieve rows from the Invoices table and insert them into a table named Invoice_Archive. This table is defined with the same columns as the Invoices table. However, the payment_total and credit_total columns aren't defined with default values. Because of that, you must include values for these columns.

The first example in this figure shows how you can use a subquery in an INSERT statement without coding a column list. In this example, the SELECT clause of the subquery is coded with an asterisk so that all the columns in the Invoices table will be retrieved. Then, after the search condition in the WHERE clause is applied, all the rows in the result set are inserted into the Invoice_Archive table.

The second example shows how you can use a column list in the INSERT clause when you use a subquery to retrieve rows. Just as when you use the VALUES clause, you can list the columns in any sequence. However, the columns must be listed in the same sequence in the SELECT clause of the subquery. In addition, you can omit columns that are defined with default values or that allow null values.

Notice that the subqueries in these statements aren't coded within parentheses as a subquery in a SELECT statement is. That's because they're not coded within a clause of the INSERT statement. Instead, they're coded in place of the VALUES clause.

Before you execute INSERT statements like the ones shown in this figure, you'll want to be sure that the rows and columns retrieved by the subquery are the ones you want to insert. To do that, you can execute the SELECT statement by itself. Then, when you're sure it retrieves the correct data, you can add the INSERT clause to insert the rows into another table.

The syntax of the INSERT statement for inserting rows selected from another table

```
INSERT [INTO] table_name [(column_list)]
SELECT column_list
FROM table_source
[WHERE search_condition]
```

An INSERT statement that inserts paid invoices in the Invoices table into the Invoice_Archive table

```
INSERT INTO invoice_archive
SELECT *
FROM invoices
WHERE invoice_total - payment_total - credit_total = 0

(74 rows inserted)
```

The same INSERT statement with a column list

```
INSERT INTO invoice_archive
    (invoice_id, vendor_id, invoice_number, invoice_total, credit_total,
    payment_total, terms_id, invoice_date, invoice_due_date)
SELECT
    invoice_id, vendor_id, invoice_number, invoice_total, credit_total,
    payment_total, terms_id, invoice_date, invoice_due_date
FROM invoices
WHERE invoice_total - payment_total - credit_total = 0

(74 rows inserted)
```

Description

- To insert rows selected from one or more tables into another table, you can code a subquery in place of the VALUES clause. Then, the rows in the derived table that result from the subquery are inserted into the table.

- If you don't code a column list in the INSERT clause, the subquery must return values for all the columns in the table where the rows will be inserted, and the columns must be returned in the same order as they appear in that table.

- If you include a column list in the INSERT clause, the subquery must return values for those columns in the same order as they appear in the column list. You can omit columns with default values and columns that accept null values. However, it is good programming practice to always include a column list.

Figure 7-5   How to use a subquery to insert multiple rows

How to update existing rows

To modify the data in one or more rows of a table, you use the UPDATE statement. Although most of the UPDATE statements you code will perform simple updates, you can also code more complex UPDATE statements that include subqueries.

How to update rows

Figure 7-6 presents the syntax of the UPDATE statement. As you can see in the examples, most UPDATE statements include just the UPDATE, SET, and WHERE clauses. The UPDATE clause names the table to be updated, the SET clause names the columns to be updated and the values to be assigned to those columns, and the WHERE clause specifies the condition a row must meet to be updated. Although the WHERE clause is optional, you'll almost always include it. If you don't, all of the rows in the table will be updated, which usually isn't what you want.

The first UPDATE statement in this figure modifies the values of two columns in the Invoices table: payment_date and payment_total. Because the WHERE clause in this statement identifies a specific invoice number, only the columns in that invoice will be updated. Notice in this example that the value to be assigned to payment_date is coded as a literal. You should realize, however, that you can assign any valid expression to a column as long as it evaluates to a value that's compatible with the data type of the column. You can also use the NULL keyword to assign a null value to a column that allows nulls, and you can use the DEFAULT keyword to assign the default value to a column that's defined with one.

The second UPDATE statement modifies a single column in the Invoices table: terms_id. This time, however, the WHERE clause specifies that all the rows for vendor 95 should be updated. Because this vendor has six rows in the Invoices table, all six rows will be updated.

The third UPDATE statement illustrates how you can use an expression to assign a value to a column. In this case, the expression increases the value of the credit_total column by 100. Like the first UPDATE statement, this statement updates a single row.

Before you execute an UPDATE statement, you'll want to be sure that you've selected the correct rows. To do that, you can execute a SELECT statement with the same search condition. Then, if the SELECT statement returns the correct rows, you can change it to an UPDATE statement.

The syntax of the UPDATE statement

```
UPDATE table_name
SET column_name_1 = expression_1 [, column_name_2 = expression_2]...
[WHERE search_condition]
```

An UPDATE statement that assigns new values to two columns of a single row in the Invoices table

```
UPDATE invoices
SET payment_date = '21-SEP-08',
    payment_total = 19351.18
WHERE invoice_number = '97/522'

(1 rows updated)
```

An UPDATE statement that assigns a new value to one column of all invoices for a vendor

```
UPDATE invoices
SET terms_id = 1
WHERE vendor_id = 95

(6 rows updated)
```

An UPDATE statement that uses an arithmetic expression to assign a value to a column

```
UPDATE invoices
SET credit_total = credit_total + 100
WHERE invoice_number = '97/522'

(1 rows updated)
```

Description

- You use the UPDATE statement to modify one or more rows in the table named in the UPDATE clause.

- You name the columns to be modified and the value to be assigned to each column in the SET clause. You can specify the value for a column as a literal or an expression.

- You can specify the conditions that must be met for a row to be updated in the WHERE clause.

- You can use the DEFAULT keyword to assign the default value to a column that has one, and you can use the NULL keyword to assign a null value to a column that allows nulls. For more information, see figure 7-4.

Warning

- If you omit the WHERE clause, all rows in the table will be updated.

Figure 7-6   How to update rows

How to use a subquery in an UPDATE statement

Figure 7-7 presents three UPDATE statements that illustrate how you can use subqueries in an update operation. In the first statement, a subquery is used in the SET clause to retrieve the maximum invoice due date from the Invoices table. Then, that value is assigned to the invoice_due_date column for invoice number 97/522.

In the second statement, a subquery is used in the WHERE clause to identify the invoices to be updated. This subquery returns the vendor_id value for the vendor in the Vendors table with the name "Pacific Bell." Then, all the invoices with that vendor_id value are updated.

The third UPDATE statement also uses a subquery in the WHERE clause. This subquery returns a list of the vendor_id values for all vendors in California, Arizona, and Nevada. Then, the IN operator is used to update all the invoices with vendor_id values in that list. Note that although the subquery returns 80 vendors, many of these vendors don't have invoices. As a result, the UPDATE statement only affects 51 invoices.

An UPDATE statement that assigns the maximum due date in the Invoices table to a specific invoice

```
UPDATE invoices
SET credit_total = credit_total + 100,
    invoice_due_date = (SELECT MAX(invoice_due_date) FROM invoices)
WHERE invoice_number = '97/522'

(1 rows updated)
```

An UPDATE statement that updates all invoices for a vendor based on the vendor's name

```
UPDATE invoices
SET terms_id = 1
WHERE vendor_id =
   (SELECT vendor_id
    FROM vendors
    WHERE vendor_name = 'Pacific Bell')

(6 rows updated)
```

An UPDATE statement that changes the terms of all invoices for vendors in three states

```
UPDATE invoices
SET terms_id = 1
WHERE vendor_id IN
   (SELECT vendor_id
    FROM vendors
    WHERE vendor_state IN ('CA', 'AZ', 'NV'))

(51 rows updated)
```

Description

- You can code a subquery in the SET or WHERE clause of an UPDATE statement.
- You can use a subquery in the SET clause to return the value that's assigned to a column.
- You can code a subquery in the WHERE clause to provide one or more values used in the search condition.

Figure 7-7   How to use subqueries in an UPDATE statement

How to delete existing rows

To delete one or more rows from a table, you use the DELETE statement. Just as you can with the UPDATE statement, you can use subqueries in a DELETE statement to help identify the rows to be deleted.

How to delete rows

Figure 7-8 presents the syntax of the DELETE statement along with three examples that illustrate some basic delete operations. As you can see, you specify the name of the table that contains the rows to be deleted in the DELETE clause. You can also code the FROM keyword in this clause, but this keyword is optional so it can be omitted.

To identify the rows to be deleted, you code a search condition in the WHERE clause. Although this clause is optional, you'll almost always include it. If you don't, all of the rows in the table are deleted. This is a common coding mistake, and it can be disastrous if you're working with live data.

If you want to make sure that you've selected the correct rows before you issue the DELETE statement, you can issue a SELECT statement with the same search condition. Then, if the correct rows are retrieved, you can use the same search for the DELETE statement.

The first DELETE statement in this figure deletes a single row from the Invoice_Line_Items table. To do that, it specifies the invoice_id value of the row to be deleted and the invoice_sequence value in the WHERE clause.

The second DELETE statement deletes four rows from the Invoice_Line_Items table. To do that, it specifies 100 as the invoice_id value of the row to be deleted in the WHERE clause. Since the invoice for this ID has four line items, this deletes all four line items for the invoice.

If you try to delete a row that has one or more child rows that are defined with a foreign-key constraint, Oracle will return an error message and won't delete the row. For example, if you attempt to delete a row from the Vendors table that has child rows in the Invoices and Invoice_Line_Items tables, Oracle will return an error message that indicates that an integrity constraint was violated, and it won't delete the vendor. Usually, that's what you want.

How to use a subquery in a DELETE statement

If you really want to delete a row that has one or more child rows from the Vendors table, you can start by deleting all of the invoices and line items for that vendor. To do that, you can use a statement like the third one in this figure to delete the line items for the vendor from the Invoice_Line_Items table. Note how this statement uses a subquery to delete all line items for the vendor with the ID of 115. Then, you can use a similar statement to delete all of the invoices for that vendor from the Invoices table. Finally, you can use a simple DELETE statement to delete the row for the vendor from the Vendors table.

The syntax of the DELETE statement

```
DELETE [FROM] table_name
[WHERE search_condition]
```

A DELETE statement that deletes one row

```
DELETE FROM invoice_line_items
WHERE invoice_id = 100 AND invoice_sequence = 1
```
```
(1 rows deleted)
```

A DELETE statement that deletes four rows

```
DELETE FROM invoice_line_items
WHERE invoice_id = 100
```
```
(4 rows deleted)
```

A DELETE statement that uses a subquery to delete all invoice line items for a vendor

```
DELETE FROM invoice_line_items
WHERE invoice_id IN
    (SELECT invoice_id
    FROM invoices
    WHERE vendor_id = 115)
```
```
(4 rows deleted)
```

Description

- You can use the DELETE statement to delete one or more rows from the table you name in the DELETE clause.
- You specify the conditions that must be met for a row to be deleted in the WHERE clause.
- You can use a subquery within the WHERE clause.
- A foreign-key constraint may prevent you from deleting a row. In that case, you can only delete the row if you delete all child rows for that row first.

Warning

- If you omit the WHERE clause from a DELETE statement, all the rows in the table will be deleted.

Figure 7-8   How to delete rows

Perspective

In this chapter, you learned how to use the INSERT, UPDATE, and DELETE statements to modify the data in a database. In chapters 9 and 10, you'll learn more about the table definitions that can affect the way these statements work. And in chapter 14, you'll learn more about executing groups of INSERT, UPDATE, and DELETE statements as a single transaction.

Terms

transaction
rollback
commit

Exercises

To test whether a table has been modified correctly as you do these exercises, you can write and run an appropriate SELECT statement. Or, when you're using Oracle SQL Developer, you can click on a table name in the Connections window and then on the Data tab to display the data for all of the columns in the table. To refresh the data on this tab, click the Refresh button.

1. Write an INSERT statement that adds this row to the Invoices table:

invoice_id	The next id in sequence (find out what this should be)
vendor_id:	32
invoice_number:	AX-014-027
invoice_date:	8/1/2008
invoice_total:	$434.58
payment_total:	$0.00
credit_total:	$0.00
terms_id:	2
invoice_due_date:	8/31/2008
payment_date:	null

2. Write an UPDATE statement that modifies the Vendors table. Change the default account number to 403 for each vendor that has a default account number of 400.

3. Write an UPDATE statement that modifies the Invoices table. Change the terms_id to 2 for each invoice that's for a vendor with a default_terms_id of 2.

4. Write a DELETE statement that deletes the row that you added to the Invoices table in exercise 1.

5. After you have verified that all of the modifications for the first four exercises have been successful, rollback the changes. Then, verify that they have been rolled back.

8

How to work with data types and functions

In chapter 3, you were introduced to some of the built-in scalar functions such as the SUBSTR, TO_CHAR, and SYSDATE functions. Now, this chapter expands on that coverage by presenting more of the built-in scalar functions. Because most of these functions work with specific data types, this chapter begins by describing the data types for an Oracle database.

The built-in data types

A column's *data type* specifies the type of information that the column is intended to store. A column's data type also determines the types of operations that can be performed on the data.

Data type overview

The Oracle data types can be divided into the five categories shown in the first table in figure 8-1. In this chapter, you'll learn how to work with the most important data types in the first three categories. Then, you can learn more about working with the data types in the temporal category in chapter 17, and you can learn how to work with the data types in the large object category in chapter 18.

The *character data types* are used to store a string of one or more characters that can include letters, numbers, or special characters like the pound sign (#) or the at sign (@). The terms *character*, *string*, and *text* are used interchangeably to describe this type of data.

The *numeric data types* are used to store numbers that can be used for mathematical calculations. These numbers can be *integers*, which are numbers that don't contain decimal places, or they can be numbers that contain decimal places. They can also be *floating-point numbers* that are used to store approximate values for very large and very small numbers.

The *temporal data types* are used primarily to store dates and times. In Oracle terminology, these data types are referred to as the *datetime*, *date/time*, or just *date* types. Remember, though that these types always include a time component as well as a date component. Besides dates and times, the temporal data types include time intervals and timestamps, which you can learn more about in chapter 17.

The *large object (LOB) data types* are used to store large amounts of text, images, sound, video, and so on. In the old days (you know, way back in the 80s and 90s), databases were primarily used to store character, numeric, and date/time data. Today, however, you can use the large object types to store other types of data. That's why we show how to use these data types in chapter 18.

The *rowid data types* are used to store an address for each row in a database. If you want, you can view the address for a row by using the ROWID pseudocolumn. However, since most developers don't need to view these addresses, these data types aren't presented in this book. For more information about the rowid data types, look up "Rowid Datatypes" in the Oracle Database SQL Reference manual.

Most of the Oracle data types correspond to the ANSI-standard data types. These data types are listed in the second table in this figure. Here, the second column lists the Oracle data type names, and the first column lists the synonyms Oracle provides for the ANSI-standard data types. Although you can use these synonyms instead of the Oracle data types, there's no reason to do that. If you do, Oracle simply maps the synonyms to the corresponding Oracle data types.

Built-in data type categories

Category	Description	Chapter
Character	Strings of characters	8
Numeric	Integer, decimal, and floating-point numbers	8
Temporal	Dates, times, time intervals, and timestamps	8 and 17
Large object (LOB)	Text, images, sound, and video	18
Rowid	Addresses for each row in the database	(not covered)

ANSI data types and Oracle equivalents

ANSI synonyms	Oracle data type
CHARACTER (n)	CHAR (n)
CHAR (n)	
CHARACTER VARYING (n)	VARCHAR2 (n)
CHAR VARYING (n)	
NATIONAL CHARACTER (n)	NCHAR (n)
NATIONAL CHAR (n)	
NCHAR (n)	
NATIONAL CHARACTER VARYING (n)	NVARCHAR2 (n)
NATIONAL CHAR VARYING (n)	
NCHAR VARYING (n)	
NUMERIC (p,s)	NUMBER (p,s)
DECIMAL (p,s)	
INTEGER	NUMBER (38)
INT	
SMALLINT	
FLOAT	FLOAT (126)
DOUBLE PRECISION	FLOAT (126)
REAL	FLOAT (63)

Description

- Oracle provides built-in *data types* that can be divided into the five categories shown above.

- Oracle provides a synonym for each of the ANSI-standard data types. These are the SQL data types that are specified by the American National Standards Institute.

- When you use the synonym for an ANSI data type, it's mapped to the appropriate Oracle data type indicated in the table above.

Figure 8-1   Data type overview

The character data types

Figure 8-2 presents the four character data types. The CHAR and VARCHAR2 types store strings of characters defined by the *ASCII character set*. This character set uses one byte per character but only defines 256 characters, which is usually adequate for working with the English language.

The NCHAR and NVARCHAR2 data types store strings of characters defined by the *Unicode character set*. These types of characters require two or three bytes per character, depending on the type of encoding that's used. However, this character set defines over 65,000 characters including most characters from most of the world's languages. Since the Unicode characters are commonly referred to as *national characters*, these data types begin with the prefix *n*.

You use the CHAR and NCHAR data types to store *fixed-length strings*. Data stored using these data types always occupies the same number of bytes, regardless of the actual length of the string. These data types are typically used to define columns that have a fixed number of characters. For example, the vendor_state column in the Vendors table is defined as CHAR(2) because it always contains two characters.

You use the VARCHAR2 and NVARCHAR2 data types to store *variable-length strings*. Data stored using these data types occupies only the number of bytes needed to store the string. These types are typically used to define columns whose lengths vary from one row to the next. In general, variable-length strings are more efficient than fixed-length strings because the database only uses the amount of disk space required by the value. For example, if you define a column as VARCHAR2(50) and it stores a value that's three characters long, the database only stores the three characters. In contrast, if you define the column as CHAR(50) and it stores a value that's three characters long, the database stores 50 characters, padding the value with 47 space characters.

Although you typically store numeric values using numeric data types, the character data types may be a better choice for some numeric values. For example, you typically store zip codes, telephone numbers, and social security numbers in character columns even though they contain only numbers. That's because their values aren't used in arithmetic operations. In addition, if you store these numbers in numeric columns, leading zeroes are stripped, which usually isn't what you want.

The character data types used to store standard characters

Type	Description
CHAR[(size [BYTE|CHAR])]	Fixed-length strings of character data where size is the number of characters or bytes between 1 and 2000. The default is 1 character.
VARCHAR2(size [BYTE|CHAR])	Variable-length strings of character data where size is the maximum number of characters or bytes between 1 and 4000. The size argument is required.

The character data types used to store Unicode characters

Type	Description
NCHAR[(size)]	Fixed-length Unicode characters where size is the number of characters. The default and minimum size is 1. Maximum size is determined by the national character set definition, with an upper limit of 2000 bytes.
NVARCHAR2(size)	Variable-length Unicode characters where size is the maximum number of characters. The size argument is required. Maximum size is determined by the national character set definition, with an upper limit of 4000 bytes.

Description

- The *ASCII character set* provides for 256 characters with 1 byte per character.
- The CHAR and VARCHAR2 types use the ASCII character set.
- The *Unicode character set* provides for over 65,000 characters, usually with 2 bytes per character. In the Unicode character set, the first 256 characters correspond with the 256 ASCII characters.
- The NCHAR and NVARCHAR types use the Unicode character set, which is commonly referred to as the *national character set*.
- The CHAR and NCHAR data types are typically used for *fixed-length strings*. These data types use the same amount of storage regardless of the actual length of the string. If you insert a value that's shorter than the specified type, the end of the value will be padded with spaces.
- The VARCHAR and NVARCHAR data types are typically used for *variable-length strings*. These data types use only the amount of storage needed for a given string.

Figure 8-2   The character data types

The numeric data types

Figure 8-3 presents the numeric data types supported by Oracle. The NUMBER data type is used to store positive and negative numbers with a fixed number of digits. When you specify this data type, you give the precision and scale in parentheses. The *precision* is the total number of digits that can be stored in the column, and the *scale* is the number of digits that can be stored to the right of the decimal point. For business applications, this will probably be the only numeric data type that you will need.

For columns that contain integers, you code the NUMBER data type with just the precision. For example, a column defined as NUMBER(5) allows for an integer value of up to 99999. In contrast, you code both the precision and scale for numbers that contain decimal positions. For example, a column defined as NUMBER(7, 2) allows for a number seven digits long with two digits to the right of the decimal point. As a result, the maximum value for the column is 99999.99.

In contrast to the fixed numbers stored by the NUMBER data type, the FLOAT data type is used to store *floating-point numbers*. These numbers are useful for storing the values for very large or small numbers, but with a limited number of significant digits. As a result, the FLOAT data type doesn't always provide for exact values.

To express the value of a floating-point number, you can use *scientific notation*. To use this notation, you type the letter E followed by a power of 10. For instance, 3.65E+9 is equal to 3.65 x 109, or 3,650,000,000. If you have a scientific or mathematical background, of course, you're already familiar with this notation. And if you aren't already familiar with this notation, you probably aren't going to need to use floating-point numbers.

The BINARY_FLOAT and BINARY_DOUBLE data types were introduced with Oracle Database 10g to conform to the IEEE (Institute of Electrical and Electronic Engineers) standard for floating-point arithmetic. BINARY_FLOAT is used to represent *single-precision*, 32-bit, floating-point numbers, while BINARY_DOUBLE is used to represent *double-precision*, 64-bit, floating-point numbers.

The numeric data types

Type	Bytes	Description
NUMBER [(p[, s])]	1 to 22	Stores zero as well as positive and negative fixed numbers with absolute values from 1.0×10^{-130} to, but not including, 1.0×10^{126}. The precision (p) can range from 1 to 38. The scale (s) can range from -84 to 127.
FLOAT [(p)]	1 to 22	Stores floating-point numbers. The precision (p) can range from 1 to 126 bits. A FLOAT value is represented internally as a NUMBER value.
BINARY_FLOAT	5	Stores single-precision, 32-bit, floating-point values.
BINARY_DOUBLE	9	Stores double-precision, 64-bit, floating-point.

Description

- The numeric data types are used to store numbers.

- The *precision* of a NUMBER type indicates the total number of digits that can be stored in the data type. The *scale* indicates the number of decimal digits that can be stored to the right of the decimal point.

- For integers, you use the NUMBER type with just the precision in parentheses. For decimal numbers, you use the NUMBER type with both the precision and scale in parentheses.

- A *floating-point number* provides for very large and very small numbers that require decimal positions, but with a limited number of significant digits.

- A *single-precision* floating-point number provides for up to 7 significant digits. A *double-precision* floating-point number provides for up to 16 significant digits.

- The BINARY_FLOAT and BINARY_DOUBLE types were introduced with Oracle 10g.

Figure 8-3   The numeric data types

The temporal data types

Figure 8-4 presents the temporal data types that are used to store dates and times. Of these data types, the DATE type is the oldest and the most commonly used. This data type stores the century, year, month, day, hour, minute and second.

When you use a SELECT statement to select a column that's defined with the DATE type, the date is displayed with the default format that's used by the database. On most Oracle systems, that means that August 19, 2008 is displayed as "19-AUG-08". Later in this chapter, though, you'll learn how to use functions to display date values in other formats such as "2008-08-19" or "8/19/08".

When you store a DATE value, the value includes a time component, but this component isn't displayed by default. Later in this chapter, you'll learn how to use functions to work with the time component of a DATE value. For example, you'll learn how to display the time component in a format like 04:20:36 PM or 16:20:36.

When Oracle Database 9i was released, it provided several new data types for working with temporal data. To start, it introduced the three TIMESTAMP types shown in this figure. These data types provide two advantages over the DATE type. First, you can use them to store fractional seconds. Second, you can use them to store a time zone.

Oracle Database 9i also introduced the INTERVAL types shown in this figure. These data types make it easier to work with time intervals like 2 days, 2 hours, and 12 minutes. Before these data types were introduced, you usually used the NUMBER type to store intervals of time.

Since the DATE type is the most widely used temporal type, you'll learn how to work with it in this chapter. For some applications, this is the only temporal type that you will need. However, if you want to learn how to use the TIMESTAMP and INTERVAL types, you can refer to chapter 17.

The date/time data types

Type	Bytes	Description
DATE	7	Stores date and time information using fixed-length fields to store the century, year, month, day, minute, hour, and second. Valid dates range from January 1, 4712 BC, to December 31, 9999 AD. This type does not have fractional seconds or a time zone.
TIMESTAMP [(fsp)]	7 to 11	An extension of DATE. Stores year, month, day, hour, minute, second, and (optionally) the fractional part of a second where the fractional second precision (fsp) is the number of decimal places used to store the fractional part of a second. The fsp can range from 0 to 9, and the default is 6. This type does not have a time zone.
TIMESTAMP [(fsp)] WITH TIME ZONE	13	Works like TIMESTAMP except that it includes either a time zone region name or a time zone offset.
TIMESTAMP [(fsp)] WITH LOCAL TIME ZONE	7 to 11	Works like TIMESTAMP WITH TIME ZONE except that the time zone is set to the database time zone when it is stored in the database, and the user sees the session time zone when data is retrieved.
INTERVAL YEAR [(yp)] TO MONTH	5	Stores a time interval in years and months. Year precision (yp) is the number of digits in the year, and the default is 2.
INTERVAL DAY [(dp)] TO SECOND [(fsp)]	11	Stores a time interval in days, hours, minutes and seconds. Day precision (dp) is the maximum number of digits in the day, and the default is 2. The fsp (fractional second precision) can range from 0 to 9, and the default is 6.

Description

- The *temporal data types* are typically referred to as the *date/time*, *datetime*, or simply *date* types.
- The default date format is determined by the NLS_DATE_FORMAT and NLS_TERRITORY parameters. For more information about these parameters, you can refer to the Oracle Database Globalization Support Guide.
- In this chapter, you'll learn how to work with the most common temporal data type, the DATE type. To learn how to work with the other temporal data types, see chapter 17.

Figure 8-4   The temporal data types

The large object data types

Figure 8-5 presents the new large object (LOB) data types that were introduced with Oracle Database 8. These data types make it easier to store large amounts of character or binary data. For example, they can be used to store text, XML, Word, PDF, image, sound, and video files.

The CLOB (Character Large Object) and NCLOB (National Character Large Object) types can store character data. These data types are commonly used to store large text and XML files. The primary difference between these types is that the CLOB type uses 1 byte per character to store characters in the ASCII character set while the NCLOB type uses 2 or 3 bytes per character to store characters in the Unicode character set.

The BLOB (Binary Large Object) type can store any kind of data in binary format. It can be used to store binary files such as PDF files, and it can be used to store image, sound, and video files.

The BFILE (Binary File) type stores a pointer to a binary file that's stored outside of the database. These binary files can be stored anywhere that's accessible through the host computer's file system.

This figure finishes by presenting the old data types for storing large objects that were used prior to Oracle Database 8. These data types are provided primarily for backward compatibility. As a result, you should use one of the new LOB data types for any new development.

The large object data types

Type	Description
CLOB	Character large object. Stores up to 8 terabytes of character data inside the database.
NCLOB	National character large object. Stores up to 8 terabytes of national character data inside the database.
BLOB	Binary large object. Stores up to 8 terabytes of unstructured binary data inside the database.
BFILE	Binary file. Stores a pointer to a large binary file stored outside the database in the file system of the host computer.

The old data types for large objects

Type	Description
RAW(size)	Stores up to 2000 bytes of binary data that is not intended to be converted by Oracle when moving data between different systems.
LONG	Stores up to 2 gigabytes of character data.
LONG RAW	Stores up to 2 gigabytes of row binary data that is not intended to be converted.

Description

- The *large object* (*LOB*) data types can store large and unstructured data such as text, images, sound, and video.
- For more information about large object data types, see chapter 18.

Figure 8-5   The large object data types

How to convert data from one type to another

As you work with the various data types, you'll find that you frequently need to convert a value from one data type to another. To do that, you can use the functions that are described next.

How to convert characters, numbers, and dates

Figure 8-6 shows how to use three of the Oracle functions to convert data from one type to another. The TO_CHAR function converts an expression to the VARCHAR2 data type. The TO_NUMBER function converts an expression to the NUMBER type. And the TO_DATE function converts an expression to the DATE type.

As the syntax summaries and examples for these functions show, you can code these functions with or without format specifications. When you code a format specification, it determines how the data is converted. Otherwise, the default format for the system is used. In the next two figures, you'll learn how to code the format specifications for converting numbers and dates.

To show how these functions work, these examples use literal values to specify numbers and dates. As a result, date literals are enclosed in single quotation marks, and numeric literals aren't enclosed. In practice, though, you're more likely to use these functions on columns or expressions.

In the first two examples, you can see how the TO_CHAR function can be used to convert a numeric value to character data. In the next two examples, you can see how the system date is converted to character data with and without a format specification. In the third example, only the date is shown. In the fourth example, both the date and time are shown with a 24-hour clock. In both cases, the system date includes the date and time, but the default date format doesn't show the time.

In the last four examples, you can see how the TO_NUMBER and TO_DATE functions work. In the seventh example, the TO_DATE function converts the characters "15-APR-08" to a DATE data type with a time value of 00:00:00. In the eighth example, this DATE data type is converted back to characters with a format that shows both the date and time with a 24-hour clock.

Besides the three TO functions in this figure, Oracle provides TO functions for all of its built-in types. For example, you can use the TO_NCHAR function to convert a number or date/time value to an NVARCHAR2 type, and you can use the TO_TIMESTAMP function to convert a character type to a TIMESTAMP type. For more information about TO functions, navigate to the "Functions" section of the Oracle Database SQL Reference manual and scroll down to the functions that begin with TO.

One other way to convert data is to use the CAST function that's shown in this figure. This is an ANSI-standard function that lets you convert, or *cast*, an expression to the data type you specify. In the example, the SELECT statement

Oracle functions for converting data

Function	Description
`TO_CHAR(expr[, format])`	Converts the result of an expression to a value of the VARCHAR2 type.
`TO_NUMBER(expr[, format])`	Converts the result of an expression to a value of NUMBER type.
`TO_DATE(expr[, format])`	Converts the result of an expression to a value of DATE type.

Examples that use the Oracle TO functions

Example	Resulting Value
`TO_CHAR(1975.5)`	`1975.5`
`TO_CHAR(1975.5, '$99,999.99')`	`$1,975.50`
`TO_CHAR(SYSDATE)`	`15-APR-08`
`TO_CHAR(SYSDATE, 'DD-MON-YYYY HH24:MI:SS')`	`15-APR-2008 10:53:56`
`TO_NUMBER('1975.5')`	`1975.5`
`TO_NUMBER('$1,975.5', '$99,999.99')`	`1975.5`
`TO_DATE('15-APR-08')`	`15-APR-2008 00:00:00`
`TO_CHAR(TO_DATE('15-APR-08'), 'DD-MON-YYYY HH24:MI:SS')`	`15-APR-2008 00:00:00`

A statement that uses ANSI-standard CAST functions

```
SELECT invoice_id, invoice_date, invoice_total,
    CAST(invoice_date AS VARCHAR2(9)) AS varchar_date,
    CAST(invoice_total AS NUMBER(9)) AS integer_total
FROM invoices
```

Description

- If a format element is specified, the TO functions use that format element to format the value that's returned. Otherwise, these functions use the default formats for the system.
- Although this figure only lists three of the TO functions, Oracle provides TO functions for most of the built-in data types.
- CAST is an ANSI-standard function that you can use for simple conversions, but the TO functions give you more control over the conversions that are done.
- For more information on the format elements for TO functions, please see the next two figures.
- For more information about TO functions, navigate to the "Functions" section of the Oracle Database SQL Reference manual and scroll down to the functions that begin with TO.

Figure 8-6   How to convert characters, numbers, and dates

casts the invoice_date column to the VARCHAR2(9) data type, and it casts the invoice_total column to the NUMBER(9) type. Although this can be useful, you're usually better off using the TO functions because they give you more control over the conversions.

Common number format elements

Figures 8-7 summarizes the most common number format elements and provides some examples. These examples show how to specify the currency symbols, group separators, and signs that are used to format numbers. Here, if you specify a format that's too short to accommodate the number, the database will return one or more # characters.

Since these format elements often provide several ways to get the same result, you can use the format element that makes the most sense for your situation. For example, if you always want the currency symbol to be a dollar sign ($), you can use this sign to specify the currency symbol. However, if you want to use the default currency symbol for the database, you can use one of the other elements to specify the currency symbol. Then, the symbol that's used will vary depending on the NLS parameters that are stored within the database.

When coding some format elements, you can code the element before or after the format for the number. For example, you can code the MI element before or after the format for the number. In other cases, you must code the format element before the format for the number. For example, you must code the FM element before the format for the number.

Number format elements

Element	Description
9	Digits
.	Decimal point
D	Decimal point
,	Comma
G	Group separator
0	Leading or trailing zeros
$	Dollar sign
L	Local currency symbol
U	Dual currency symbol
C	Currency symbol
S	Minus sign for negative numbers, plus sign for positive numbers
MI	Minus sign for negative numbers
PR	Negative numbers in brackets, one space before and after positive numbers
FM	Removes leading or trailing spaces or zeros
EEEE	Scientific notation

Number format examples

Value	Format	Output
1975.5	(none specified)	1975.5
1975.5	999	###
1975.5	9999	1976
1975.5	9,999.9	1,975.5
1975.5	9G999D9	1,975.5
1975.5	99,999.99	1,975.50
1975.5	09,999.990	01,975.500
1975.5	$99,999.99	$1,975.50
1975.5	L9,999.99	$1,975.50
1975.5	U9,999.99	$1,975.50
1975.5	C9,999.99	USD1,975.50
1975.5	S9,999.99	+1,975.50
-1975.5	9,999.99S	1,975.50-
-1975.5	9,999.99MI	1,975.50-
1975.5	9,999.99MI	1,975.50
-1975.5	9,999.99PR	<1,975.50>
1975.5	9,999.99PR	1,975.50
01975.50	FM9,999.99	1,975.5
1975.5	9.99EEEE	1.98E+03

Description

- For more information, look up "Number Format Elements" in the Oracle Database SQL Reference manual.

Figure 8-7   Common number format elements

Common date/time format elements

Figures 8-8 shows how to use the most common date/time format elements. After you read through the list of format elements, you shouldn't have much trouble understanding how the examples work.

However, the RR format element requires some explanation. This element allows you to use a two-digit year to specify years in two different centuries. For this century, for example, years from 00 to 49 are interpreted as 2000 to 2049, and years 50 through 99 are interpreted as 1950 through 1999. As a result, 98 is interpreted as 1998, not 2098. In most cases, that's what you want. If that isn't what you want, you can use the YY format to specify the year.

In addition, note that the FF format element works with the fractional seconds component, which isn't available from the DATE type. As a result, you will only use this element when you're working with the TIMESTAMP and INTERVAL types that are described in chapter 17.

If you study the summary and examples in this figure, you will see that you can include periods when using the BC, AD, AM, and PM elements. If, for example, you specify "B.C." as a format element, the formatted date will include a value of "B.C" or "A.D.", depending on whether the date is before or after the birth of Christ.

You will also see that the MONTH and DAY elements pad the end of the value that's returned with spaces to accommodate the longest value that can be returned. Since this makes it easy to align the month and day elements of a date in columns, this is often what you want. If it isn't what you want, you can use the TRIM function described later in this chapter to trim the spaces from the ends of these elements.

Last, if a format element returns letters, the capitalization that you use when you specify the format element corresponds with the capitalization for the returned value. If, for example, you specify "MONTH", the month will be returned in all caps (AUGUST). If you specify "Month", the month will be returned with an initial cap (August). And if you specify "month", the month will be returned in lowercase (august). Note that this also applies to the date format elements for both the full and abbreviated names of months and days.

Common date/time format elements

Element	Description	Element	Description
AD	Anno Domini	DAY	Name of day padded with spaces
BC	Before Christ	DY	Abbreviated name of day
CC	Century	DDD	Day of year (1-366)
YEAR	Year spelled out	DD	Day of month (01-31)
YYYY	Four-digit year	D	Day of week (1-7)
YY	Two-digit year	HH	Hour of day (01-12)
RR	Two-digit round year	HH24	Hour of day (01-24)
Q	Quarter of year (1-4)	MI	Minute (00-59)
MONTH	Name of month padded with spaces	SS	Second (00-59)
MON	Abbreviated name of month	SSSSS	Seconds past midnight (0-86399)
MM	Month (01-12)	FF[1-9]	Fractional seconds
WW	Week of year (1-52)	PM	Post Meridian
W	Week of month (1-5)	AM	Ante Meridian

Common date and time formats

Format	Example
(none specified)	19-AUG-08
DD-MON-YY	19-AUG-08
DD-MON-RR	19-AUG-08
DD-Mon-YY	19-Aug-08
MM/DD/YY	08/19/08
YYYY-MM-DD	2008-08-19
Dy Mon DD, YY	Tue Aug 19, 08
MONTH DD, YYYY BC	AUGUST 19, 2008 AD
Month DD, YYYY B.C.	August 19, 2008 A.D.
HH:MI	04:20
HH24:MI:SS	16:20:36
HH:MI AM	04:20 PM
HH:MI A.M.	04:20 P.M.
HH:MI:SS	04:20:36
HH:MI:SS.FF5	04:20:36.12345
HH:MI:SS.FF4	04:20:36.1234
YYYY-MM-DD HH:MI:SS AM	2008-08-19 04:20:36 PM

Description

- If you use the RR format, years from 00 to 49 are interpreted as 2000 to 2049, and years 50 through 99 are interpreted as 1950 through 1999.

- For more information about date/time format elements, look up "Datetime Format Elements" in the Oracle Database SQL Reference manual.

Figure 8-8   Common date/time format elements

How to convert characters to and from their numeric codes

Figure 8-9 shows three functions that are used to convert characters to and from their equivalent numeric code. The CHR and ASCII functions work with standard ASCII characters.

For instance, the CHR function in this figure converts the number 97 to its equivalent ASCII code, the letter *a*. Conversely, the ASCII function converts the letter *a* to its numeric equivalent of 97. Although the string in the ASCII function can include more than one character, please note that only the first character is converted.

The NCHR function works like the CHR function. However, since it usually works with the Unicode character set, it's able to convert thousands of characters.

The CHR function is frequently used to output ASCII control characters that can't be typed on your keyboard. The three most common control characters are presented in this figure. These characters can be used to format output so it's easier to read. The SELECT statement in this figure, for example, uses the CHR(13) control character to start a new line after the vendor name and vendor address in the output.

Three functions for converting characters to and from their numeric codes

Function	Description
ASCII(string)	Returns a NUMBER value that corresponds to the first character in the specified string of the CHAR, VARCHAR2, NCHAR, or NVARCHAR2 type.
CHR(number)	Returns a VARCHAR2 value that corresponds to the specified NUMBER value in the ASCII character set.
NCHR(number)	Returns a VARCHAR2 value that corresponds to the specified NUMBER value in the national character set.

Examples that use the ASCII, CHR, and NCHR functions

Example	Result
ASCII('a')	97
ASCII('abc')	97
CHR(97)	a
NCHR(97)	a
NCHR(332)	ō

ASCII codes for common control characters

Control character	Value
Tab	CHR(9)
Line feed	CHR(10)
Carriage return	CHR(13)

A SELECT statement that uses the CHR function to format output

```
SELECT vendor_name || CHR(13)
    || vendor_address1 || CHR(13)
    || vendor_city || ', ' || vendor_state || ' ' || vendor_zip_code
    AS vendor_address
FROM vendors
WHERE vendor_id = 1
```

The value that's returned

```
VENDOR_ADDRESS
-----------------------------------------------------------------
US Postal Service
Attn:  Supt. Window Services
Madison, WI 53707
```

Figure 8-9   How to convert characters to and from their numeric codes

How to work with character data

Now that you know how to convert the number and date/time data types to and from the character data types, you're read to learn some additional functions for working with character data.

How to use the common character functions

Figure 8-10 shows how to use some of the common character functions available from Oracle. To start, you can use the LTRIM and RTRIM functions to remove leading or trailing characters from the left or right side of a string. Or, you can use the TRIM function to remove leading and trailing characters from both sides of a string. Most of the time, you'll use these functions to remove leading and trailing spaces. However, you can also use these functions to remove other characters such as zeros (0), periods (.), and so on.

Conversely, you can use the LPAD and RPAD functions to add leading or trailing characters to the left or right side of a string. Again, most of the time, you'll use these functions to add leading and trailing spaces. However, you can also use these functions to add other characters.

You can use the LOWER and UPPER functions to convert the characters in a string to lower or uppercase. In addition, you can use the INITCAP function to convert the characters in a string so the initial letter in each word is capitalized and the rest of the word is lowercase.

You can use the NVL and NVL2 functions to provide a substitute string if the string value is a NULL value. For example, you can use these functions to display a value of "Unknown" instead of displaying the default value of null.

You can use the last four functions presented in this figure to modify a string. To start, you can use the SUBSTR function to return the specified number of characters from anywhere in a string. When you use this function, you can use the second argument to specify the starting point where 1 is the first character in the string. In addition, you can use the third argument to specify the number of characters that you want to return. If you don't specify this argument, this function will return all characters from the starting point to the end of the string.

To specify the starting point and length arguments for the SUBSTR function, it's common to use the INSTR and LENGTH functions to return integer values. For example, if you want to find the position of the first space in a string, you can use an INSTR function to return an integer value for its position. Then, if necessary, you can perform arithmetic operations on this integer, and you can nest the resulting expression within a SUBSTR function. Similarly, you can use the LENGTH function to return the number of characters in a string, you can include this function in an arithmetic expression, and you can nest the expression within a SUBSTR function.

Finally, you can use the REPLACE function to replace a substring within a string with another substring. For example, you might want to use this function to replace hypens (-) with periods (.).

Some common character functions

Function	Description
LTRIM(string[, trim_string])	By default, this function removes any spaces from the left side of the specified string. If you specify a trim string, this function removes all characters specified in the trim string.
RTRIM(string[, trim_string])	Same as LTRIM but removes characters from the right side of the string instead of the left.
TRIM([trim_char FROM]string)	Removes any spaces from the left and right sides of the specified string. If you specify a trim character, this function removes the trim character from both sides of the string.
LPAD(string, length[, pad_string])	Pads the left side of the string to the specified length with spaces or with the characters specified by the pad string.
RPAD(string, length[, pad_string])	Pads the right side of the string to the specified length with spaces or with the characters specified by the pad string.
LOWER(string)	Converts the string to lowercase letters.
UPPER(string)	Converts the string to uppercase letters.
INITCAP(string)	Converts the initial letter in each word to uppercase.
NVL(string, value)	Returns the value argument if the specified string is a null value. Otherwise, this function returns the specified string.
NVL2(string, value1, value2)	Returns the value1 argument if the specified string is a null value. Otherwise, this function returns the value2 argument.
SUBSTR(string, start[, length])	Returns the specified number of characters (length) from the string (string) at the specified starting position (start).
LENGTH(string)	Returns an integer for the number of characters in the specified string.
INSTR(string, find [,start])	Returns an integer for the position of the first occurrence of the specified find string in the specified string starting at the specified position. If the starting position isn't specified, the search starts at the beginning of the string. If the string isn't found, the function returns zero.
REPLACE(string, find, replace)	Returns the string with all occurrences of the specified find string replaced with the specified replace string.

Figure 8-10   How to use the common character functions (part 1 of 2)

Part 2 of figure 8-10 shows examples of the string functions described in part 1. To start, the LTRIM and RTRIM examples remove spaces from the left and right sides of a string. Then, the TRIM example removes spaces from both sides of a string. Here, the result column uses single quotes to identify strings. This distinguishes string values from number values, and it shows the leading and trailing spaces for the result.

The second LTRIM example shows how to remove other characters besides spaces from a string. Here, the second argument specifies that all dollar signs and zeros should be removed from the left side of the string. This shows that the second argument of the LTRIM and RTRIM functions allows you to trim multiple characters.

Conversely, the second TRIM example uses a different syntax that only allows you to specify a single character. Here, you must specify that character, followed by the FROM keyword, followed by the string.

The LPAD and RPAD examples show how to add spaces or other characters to the left or right side of a string. If you want, you can use these functions to align the columns of a result set. In particular, note how the LPAD function can be used to align numbers with the right side of a column.

The LOWER, UPPER, and INITCAP examples show how to change the case of a string. Note how the INITCAP example works the same regardless of whether the input string is uppercase or lowercase.

The NVL and NVL2 examples show how to substitute a string for a NULL value. In these examples, string literals are used to specify a string value, and the NULL keyword is used to specify a NULL value.

The SUBSTR examples show how to return part of a string. To start, the first example returns the first five characters of a string. To do that, the second argument specifies 1 as the position for first character in the string, and the second argument specifies 5 as the length of the string. The second SUBSTR example works similarly, but it returns a string that begins at the seventh character and is three characters long. Unlike the first two examples, the third SUBSTR example doesn't include a third argument. As a result, it returns all characters in the string from the seventh character to the end of the string.

The INSTR examples show how to search for a string within a string and to return an integer value for its starting position. To start, the first example shows how to return an integer for the position of the first space in a string. In this case, the space is the sixth character of the string. Then, the second example shows how to return an integer for the first hyphen in the string. Next, the third example shows how to return an integer for the second hyphen in the string. To do that, this example uses the third argument of the INSTR function to start the search at the fifth character in the string. Finally, the fourth example shows how to return the position for a string literal of "1212". This shows that you can use this function to search for a single character or a string of multiple characters.

The LENGTH examples show how to return an integer for the length of a string. Note that this includes any leading or trailing spaces.

The REPLACE examples show how to replace part of a string with another string. Here, the first example replaces all of the hyphens within the string with periods. Then, the second example replaces all of the hypens within the string

Character function examples

Example	Result
`LTRIM('   John Smith   ')`	`'John Smith   '`
`RTRIM('   John Smith   ')`	`'   John Smith'`
`TRIM('   John Smith   ')`	`'John Smith'`
`LTRIM('$0019.99', '$0')`	`'19.99'`
`TRIM('$' FROM '$0019.99')`	`'0019.99'`
`LPAD('$19.99', 15)`	`'         $19.99'`
`LPAD('$2150.78', 15)`	`'       $2150.78'`
`LPAD('$2150.78', 15, '.')`	`'.......$2150.78'`
`RPAD('John', 15)`	`'John           '`
`RPAD('John', 15, '.')`	`'John...........'`
`LOWER('CA')  'ca'`	
`UPPER('ca')  'CA'`	
`INITCAP('john smith')`	`'John Smith'`
`INITCAP('JOHN SMITH')`	`'John Smith'`
`NVL('Fresh Corn Records', 'Unknown Company Name')`	`'Fresh Corn Records'`
`NVL(NULL, 'Unknown Company Name')`	`'Unknown Company Name'`
`NVL2('Fresh Corn Records', 'Known', 'Unknown')`	`'Known'`
`NVL2(NULL, 'Known', 'Unknown')`	`'Unknown'`
`SUBSTR('(559) 555-1212', 1, 5)`	`'(559)'`
`SUBSTR('(559) 555-1212', 7, 3)`	`'555'`
`SUBSTR('(559) 555-1212', 7)`	`'555-1212'`
`INSTR('(559) 555-1212', ' ')`	6
`INSTR('559-555-1212', '-')`	4
`INSTR('559-555-1212', '-', 5)`	8
`INSTR('559-555-1212', '1212')`	9
`LENGTH('(559) 555-1212')`	14
`LENGTH('   (559) 555-1212   ')`	18
`REPLACE('559-555-1212', '-', '.')`	`'559.555.1212'`
`REPLACE('559-555-1212', '-', '')`	`'5595551212'`

Description

- For more information about these and other functions, you can look them up in the Oracle Database SQL Reference manual. To do that, you can start by navigating to the "Functions" topic. Then, you can navigate to the function you want to learn more about.

Figure 8-10   How to use the common character functions (part 2 of 2)

with nothing. To do that, the third example uses two single quotes with nothing between them to specify a value of nothing. Although these examples use a string that contains a single character for the second and third arguments, you can specify a string that contains multiple characters for these arguments.

How to parse a string

Figure 8-11 shows how to parse a string. To start, the first SELECT statement shows how you can use the SUBSTR function to format columns in a result set. Here, the second column begins by getting the first name of the vendor contact and appending a space to the end of this name. Then, it uses the SUBSTR function to return the first initial of the last name for the vendor contract and appends this initial to the string. Finally, this column adds a period after the initial for the last name.

The third column displays the vendor's phone number without an area code. To accomplish that, this column specification uses the SUBSTR function to return all characters of the vendor_phone column starting at the seventh character. Of course, this only works correctly because all of the phone numbers are stored in the same format with the area code in parentheses.

This SELECT statement also shows how you can use a function in the search condition of a WHERE clause. This condition uses the SUBSTRING function to select only those rows with an area code of 559. To do that, it retrieves three characters from the vendor_phone column starting with the second character. Again, this assumes that the phone numbers are all in the same format and that the area code is enclosed in parentheses.

The second SELECT statement shows how to extract multiple values from a single column. In this example, both a first and a last name are stored in the Name column of the String_Sample table. As a result, if you want to work with the first and last names independently, you have to parse the string using the string functions. In this example, the first name is considered to be every non-blank character up to the first blank, and the last name is considered to be every character after the first blank.

To extract the first name, this statement uses the SUBSTR and INSTR functions. First, it uses the INSTR function to locate the first space in the Name column. Then, it uses the SUBSTR function to extract all of the characters up to that space. Note that a value of one is subtracted from the value that's returned by the INSTR function, so the space itself isn't included in the first name.

To extract the last name, this statement uses the same functions. First, it uses the INSTR function to locate the first space in the Name column. Then, it uses the SUBSTR function to extract all of the characters from that space to the end of the string. Note that a value of one is added to the value that's returned by the INSTR function, so the space itself isn't included in the last name.

As you review this example, you should keep in mind that I kept it simple so that you can focus on how the string functions are used. You should realize, however, that this code won't work for all names. If, for example, a first name contains a space, such as in the name Jean Paul, this code won't work properly.

A SELECT statement that uses the SUBSTR function

```
SELECT vendor_name,
       vendor_contact_first_name || ' ' ||
           SUBSTR(vendor_contact_last_name, 1, 1) || '.'
           AS contact_name,
       SUBSTR(vendor_phone, 7) AS phone
FROM vendors
WHERE SUBSTR(vendor_phone, 2, 3) = '559'
ORDER BY vendor_name
```

The result set

	VENDOR_NAME	CONTACT_NAME	PHONE
1	Abbey Office Furnishings	Kyra F.	555-8300
2	BFI Industries	Erick K.	555-1551
3	Bill Marvin Electric Inc	Kaitlin H.	555-5106
4	Cal State Termite	Demetrius H.	555-1534
5	California Business Machines	Anders R.	555-5570

```
(34 rows selected)
```

The String_Sample table

	ID	NAME
1	1	Lizbeth Darien
2	2	Darnell O'Sullivan
3	17	Lance Pinos-Potter
4	20	Jean Paul Renard
5	3	Alisha von Strump

A SELECT statement that parses a string

```
SELECT SUBSTR(name, 1, (INSTR(name, ' ') - 1)) AS first_name,
       SUBSTR(name, (INSTR(name, ' ') + 1)) AS last_name
FROM string_sample
```

The result set

	FIRST_NAME	LAST_NAME
1	Lizbeth	Darien
2	Darnell	O'Sullivan
3	Lance	Pinos-Potter
4	Jean	Paul Renard
5	Alisha	von Strump

Description

- When parsing strings, it's common to nest one function within another.

Figure 8-11   How to parse a string

That illustrates the importance of designing a database so that this type of problem doesn't occur. You'll learn more about that in section 3. For now, just realize that if a database is designed correctly, you won't have to worry about this type of problem.

How to sort a string in numerical sequence

Figure 8-12 addresses a common problem that occurs when you store numeric data in a character column and then want to sort the column in numeric sequence. In this figure, the columns in the String_Sample table are defined with character data types. As a result, the first example sorts the values in the ID column in alphabetical sequence instead of numeric sequence, which isn't what you want.

One way to solve this problem is to convert the values in the ID column to integers for sorting purposes as shown in the SELECT statement in the second example. To do that, this example uses the TO_NUMBER function to convert the ID column to a NUMBER value. As a result, this example sorts the rows in numeric sequence.

Another way to solve this problem is to pad the numbers with leading zeros or spaces as shown in the third example. To do that, this example uses the LPAD function to pad the left side of the ID column with zeros. When it does, it specifies an alias for this column of lpad_id. Then, it sorts the result set by this alias, which causes the rows to be returned in numeric sequence.

How to sort mixed-case columns in alphabetical sequence

You may remember from chapter 3 that uppercase letters come before lowercase letters when you sort a string in ascending sequence. As a result, a vendor name like "ASC Signs" comes before "Abbey Office Furnishings."

Now that you know how to use the LOWER and UPPER functions, though, this problem is easy to fix. Just convert the strings to all uppercase or all lower-case before you sort them as in

```
ORDER BY LOWER(vendor_name)
```
or
```
ORDER BY UPPER(vendor_name)
```
Either way, the rows will be sorted in the correct alphabetical sequence.

A table sorted by a character column

```
SELECT * FROM string_sample
ORDER BY id
```

The result set

	ID		NAME
1	1		Lizbeth Darien
2	17		Lance Pinos-Potter
3	2		Darnell O'Sullivan
4	20		Jean Paul Renard
5	3		Alisha von Strump

A table sorted by a character column treated as a numeric column

```
SELECT * FROM string_sample
ORDER BY TO_NUMBER(id)
```

The result set

	ID		NAME
1	1		Lizbeth Darien
2	2		Darnell O'Sullivan
3	3		Alisha von Strump
4	17		Lance Pinos-Potter
5	20		Jean Paul Renard

A table sorted by a character column that's padded with leading zeros

```
SELECT LPAD(id, 2, '0') AS lpad_id, name
FROM string_sample
ORDER BY lpad_id
```

The result set

	LPAD_ID		NAME
1	01		Lizbeth Darien
2	02		Darnell O'Sullivan
3	03		Alisha von Strump
4	17		Lance Pinos-Potter
5	20		Jean Paul Renard

Description

- If you sort by a character column that contains numbers, you may receive unexpected results. To avoid that, you can convert the string column to a numeric value or you can pad the left side of the character column with leading zeros or spaces.

Figure 8-12   How to sort a string in numerical sequence

How to work with numeric data

In addition to the character functions, Oracle provides several functions for working with numeric data. Although you'll probably use only a couple of these functions regularly, you should be aware of them in case you ever need them.

How to use the common numeric functions

Figure 8-13 summarizes some of the common numeric functions that Oracle provides. The function you'll probably use most often is the ROUND function. This function rounds a number to the precision specified by the length argument. Note that you can round the digits to the left of the decimal point by coding a negative value for this argument. However, you're more likely to code a positive number to round the digits to the right of the decimal point.

Another function that you might use regularly is the TRUNC function. This function works like the ROUND function, but it truncates the number instead of rounding to the nearest number. In other words, this function chops off the end of the number without doing any rounding. For example, if you round 19.99 to the nearest integer, you get a value of 20. However, if you truncate 19.99, you get a value of 19.

If you study the examples in this figure, you shouldn't have much trouble understanding how they work. For instance, you can easily see how a negative length argument causes the ROUND and TRUNC functions to round and truncate to the left of the decimal point.

In addition to the functions shown in this figure, Oracle provides many other functions for performing mathematical calculations. In particular, it provides many functions for performing trigonometric calculations. Since you're not likely to use these functions for business applications, they aren't presented in this book. However, if you need a function that isn't shown here, you can search for the function in the Oracle Database SQL Reference manual.

Some common numeric functions

Function	Description
ROUND(number[, length])	Returns the number rounded to the precision specified by the length argument. If the length argument is positive, the digits to the right of the decimal point are rounded. If it's negative, the digits to the left of the decimal point are rounded.
TRUNC(number[, length])	Returns the number truncated as specified by the length argument. If the length argument is omitted, this function truncates all numbers to the right of the decimal point. If it's negative, this function truncates the specified number of digits to the left of the decimal point.
CEIL(number)	Returns the smallest integer that is greater than or equal to number.
FLOOR(number)	Returns the largest integer that is less than or equal to number.
ABS(number)	Returns the absolute value of number.
SIGN(number)	Returns -1 if the number is less than 0, 0 if the number is equal to 0, and 1 if the number is greater than 0.
MOD(number, number_divisor)	Returns the remainder after the number argument is divided by the divisor.
POWER(number, number_exponent)	Returns the number after it has been raised to the power of the specified exponent.
SQRT(number)	Returns the square root of the number.

Examples that use the numeric functions

Example	Result	Example	Result
ROUND(12.5)	13	ABS(1.25)	1.25
ROUND(12.4999, 0)	12	ABS(-1.25)	1.25
ROUND(12.4999, 1)	12.5		
ROUND(12.4944, 2)	12.49	SIGN(1.25)	1
ROUND(1264.99, -2)	1300	SIGN(0)	0
		SIGN(-1.25)	-1
TRUNC(12.5)	12		
TRUNC(12.4999, 1)	12.4	MOD(10, 10)	0
TRUNC(12.4944, 2)	12.49	MOD(10, 9)	1
TRUNC(1264.99, -2)	1200		
		POWER(2, 2)	4
CEIL(1.25)	2	POWER(2, 2.5)	5.65685…
CEIL(-1.25)	-1		
FLOOR(1.25)	1	SQRT(4)	2
FLOOR(-1.25)	-2	SQRT(5)	2.23606…

Note

- You can use these functions to work with any numeric data type or any nonnumeric type that can be implicitly converted to a numeric type.

Figure 8-13   How to use the common numeric functions

How to search for floating-point numbers

Earlier in this chapter, you learned that floating-point numbers don't always contain exact values. From a practical point of view, though, that means that you don't want to search for an exact value when you're working with floating-point numbers. If you do, you'll miss values that are essentially equal to the value you want.

To illustrate, consider the Float_Sample table shown in figure 8-14. This table includes a column named float_value that's defined with the BINARY_DOUBLE data type. Here, the first example shows what happens when a SELECT statement retrieves all rows where the value stored in the float_value column is equal to 1. As you can see, the result set includes only the second row, even though the first and third rows also contain a value that's approximately equal to 1.

To solve this problem, you can search for an approximate value when you perform a search on a column with a floating-point data type. To do that, you can search for a range of values as shown by the second example in this figure. This SELECT statement searches for values between .99 and 1.01.

Another alternative is to round the value that you're searching for. This is illustrated by the third example. In both the second and third examples, the statement returns the three rows in the Float_Sample table that have a float value that's approximately equal to 1.

The Float_Sample table

	FLOAT_ID	FLOAT_VALUE
1	1	0.999999999999999
2	2	1.0
3	3	1.000000000000001
4	4	1234.56789012345
5	5	999.04440209348
6	6	24.04849

A SELECT statement that searches for an exact value

```
SELECT * FROM float_sample
WHERE float_value = 1
```

The result set

	FLOAT_ID	FLOAT_VALUE
1	2	1.0

A SELECT statement that searches for a range of values

```
SELECT * FROM float_sample
WHERE float_value BETWEEN 0.99 AND 1.01
```

The result set

	FLOAT_ID	FLOAT_VALUE
1	1	0.999999999999999
2	2	1.0
3	3	1.000000000000001

A SELECT statement that searches for rounded values

```
SELECT * FROM float_sample
WHERE ROUND(float_value, 2) = 1
```

The result set

	FLOAT_ID	FLOAT_VALUE
1	1	0.999999999999999
2	2	1.0
3	3	1.000000000000001

Description

- Because the values of floating-point numbers aren't always exact, you'll want to search for approximate values when you retrieve floating-point numbers. To do that, you can specify a range of values, or you can use the ROUND function to search for rounded values.

Figure 8-14   How to search for floating-point numbers

How to work with date/time data

In the topics that follow, you'll learn how to use some of the functions that Oracle provides for working with dates and times. As you'll see, these include functions for extracting different parts of a date/time value and for performing operations on dates and times.

How to use the common date/time functions

Figure 8-15 shows how the date/time functions work and how the plus and minus signs can be used to work with dates. If you study the summaries and examples, you shouldn't have much trouble using these functions.

To get the current date and time, you can use the SYSDATE or CURRENT_DATE function, although the SYSDATE function is more commonly used. In most cases, both of these functions return the same value. However, if a session time zone has been set, the value returned by the CURRENT_DATE function will be adjusted to accommodate that time zone.

When you use the ROUND and TRUNC functions without a date format, the default is to round or truncate to a date at 00:00:00 on a 24-hour clock. But when you specify a date format like MI for minutes, the date/time value is rounded or truncated to that time component.

When you use the MONTHS_BETWEEN function, it returns a whole number of months when the day component is the same for both date arguments. However, if the day component isn't the same for both date arguments, this function returns a decimal number.

When you use the ADD_MONTHS function, you can specify a positive value to add months to the specified date or a negative number to subtract months from the specified date. If necessary, the function will increase or decrease the year component.

When you use the NEXT_DAY function, you specify a day of the week as the second argument. Then, the function returns the next day of the week that comes after the specified date. For instance, the first example of this function returns the first Friday after August 15, 2008, which is August 22, and the second example returns the first Thursday after August 15, 2008, which is August 21. Note that you can use full or abbreviated names for the second argument.

When you use the addition (+) and subtraction (-) operators, you can add a specific number of days to a date or subtract a specific number of days from a date. You can also use the subtraction operator to subtract one date from another. If the first date comes after the second date, a positive integer is returned. Otherwise, a negative integer is returned.

Some common date/time functions

Function	Description
SYSDATE	Returns the current local date and time based on the operating system's clock.
CURRENT_DATE	Returns the local date and time adjusted for the current session time zone.
ROUND(date[, date_format])	Returns the date rounded to the unit specified by the date format. If the format is omitted, rounds to the nearest day.
TRUNC(date[, date_format])	Works like the ROUND function but truncates the date.
MONTHS_BETWEEN(date1, date2)	Returns the number of months between date1 and date2.
ADD_MONTHS(date, integer_months)	Adds the specified number of months to the specified date and returns the resulting date.
LAST_DAY(date)	Returns the date for last day of the month for the specified date.
NEXT_DAY(date, day_of_week)	Returns the date for the next day of the week that comes after the specified date.

Two operators for working with dates

Operator	Description
+	Adds the specified number of days to a date.
-	Subtracts a specified number of days from a date. Or, subtracts one date from another and returns the number of days between the two dates.

Examples that use the date/time functions

Example	Result
SYSDATE	19-AUG-08 04:20:36 PM
ROUND(SYSDATE)	20-AUG-08 12:00:00 AM
TRUNC(SYSDATE, 'MI')	19-AUG-08 04:20:00 PM
MONTHS_BETWEEN('01-SEP-08','01-AUG-08')	1
MONTHS_BETWEEN('15-SEP-08','01-AUG-08')	1.4516129032258064...
ADD_MONTHS('19-AUG-08', -1)	19-JUL-08
ADD_MONTHS('19-AUG-08', 11)	19-JUL-09
LAST_DAY('15-FEB-08')	29-FEB-08
NEXT_DAY('15-AUG-08', 'FRIDAY')	22-AUG-08
NEXT_DAY('15-AUG-08', 'THURS')	21-AUG-08
SYSDATE - 1	18-AUG-08
SYSDATE + 7	26-AUG-08
SYSDATE - TO_DATE('01-JAN-08')	231
TO_DATE('01-JAN-08') - SYSDATE	-231

Figure 8-15   How to use the common date/time functions

How to parse dates and times

Figure 8-16 shows you how to use the TO_CHAR function to return the various parts of a DATE value as a string. To do that, you specify the appropriate date format element for the part of the DATE value that you want to return. For example, the "MONTH" element returns a string that spells out the month in uppercase, the "Month" element spells out the month with an initial cap, and the "MM" element returns a string that contains the number for the month.

If you need to get an integer value for part of the date, you can use the TO_CHAR function with the appropriate date format element to return a string that contains numeric characters. Then, you can use the TO_NUMBER function to convert that string to an integer value. For example, you can use the TO_CHAR function with the "MM" element to return a string that contains the the number for the month. Then, you can use the TO_NUMBER function to convert the string that's returned to an integer value.

Examples that parse a date/time value

Example	Result
TO_CHAR(SYSDATE, 'DD-MON-RR HH:MI:SS')	19-AUG-08 04:20:36 PM
TO_CHAR(SYSDATE, 'YEAR')	TWO THOUSAND EIGHT
TO_CHAR(SYSDATE, 'YEAR')	Two Thousand Eight
TO_CHAR(SYSDATE, 'YYYY')	2008
TO_CHAR(SYSDATE, 'YY')	08
TO_CHAR(SYSDATE, 'MONTH')	AUGUST
TO_CHAR(SYSDATE, 'MON')	AUG
TO_CHAR(SYSDATE, 'MM')	08
TO_CHAR(SYSDATE, 'DD')	19
TO_CHAR(SYSDATE, 'DAY')	TUESDAY
TO_CHAR(SYSDATE, 'DY')	TUES
TO_CHAR(SYSDATE, 'HH24')	16
TO_CHAR(SYSDATE, 'HH')	04
TO_CHAR(SYSDATE, 'MI')	20
TO_CHAR(SYSDATE, 'SS')	36
TO_CHAR(SYSDATE, 'CC')	21
TO_CHAR(SYSDATE, 'Q')	3
TO_CHAR(SYSDATE, 'WW')	34
TO_CHAR(SYSDATE, 'W')	3
TO_CHAR(SYSDATE, 'DDD')	232
TO_CHAR(SYSDATE, 'D')	3

How to convert a date component to a numeric value

Example	Result
TO_NUMBER(TO_CHAR(SYSDATE, 'HH24'))	16
TO_NUMBER(TO_CHAR(SYSDATE, 'HH'))	4
TO_NUMBER(TO_CHAR(SYSDATE, 'SS'))	36

Description

- You can use the TO_CHAR method to retrieve any part of a date as a string.
- If you need to perform mathematical operations on a part of a date, you can use the TO_NUMBER function to convert any numeric part of a date to a NUMBER value.

Figure 8-16   How to parse dates and times

How to perform a date search

Because date/time values always contain both a date and a time component, you may need to ignore the time component when you search for a date value. In figure 8-17, for example the Date_Sample table has a date_id column defined with the NUMBER type and a start_date column defined with the DATE type. In this table, the time components in the first three rows have a zero value. In contrast, the time components in the next three rows have non-zero time components.

The first SELECT statement shows a typical problem that you can encounter when searching for dates. Here, the statement searches for rows in the Date_Sample table that have a date value of "28-FEB-06". Since a time component isn't specified by the date literal in the WHERE clause, a default time component of 00:00:00 is added to the date when it is converted to a DATE value. However, because the one row with this date has a time that isn't 00:00:00, no rows are returned by this statement.

To solve this problem, you can search for a range of dates that includes only the dates you're looking for as shown by the second SELECT statement in this figure. In this statement, the search is for any date greater than or equal to February 28, 2006, and less than March 1, 2006. As a result, this search will find any date on February 28, no matter what the time component is.

Another alternative is to use the TRUNC function to truncate the time component from the date/time values as shown in the third SELECT statement in this figure. In this statement, the time components of the start dates are set to 00:00:00, which is the same as the time component for the date literal.

A third approach to this problem is to extract the month, day, and year components of each date in the WHERE clause using the techniques in the previous figure. Then, the condition in the WHERE clause can search for the right month and day and year values. Usually, though, you won't need this technique because the techniques in this figure are easier to use.

The Date_Sample table

	DATE_ID	START_DATE
1	1	01-MAR-1979 00:00:00
2	2	28-FEB-1999 00:00:00
3	3	31-OCT-2003 00:00:00
4	4	28-FEB-2005 10:00:00
5	5	28-FEB-2006 13:58:32
6	6	01-MAR-2006 09:02:25

A SELECT statement that fails to return a row

```
SELECT * FROM date_sample
WHERE start_date = '28-FEB-06'
```

A SELECT statement that searches for a range of dates

```
SELECT * FROM date_sample
WHERE start_date >= '28-FEB-06' AND start_date < '01-MAR-06'
```

The result set

	DATE_ID	START_DATE
1	5	28-FEB-06

A SELECT statement that uses the TRUNC function to remove time values

```
SELECT * FROM date_sample
WHERE TRUNC(start_date) = '28-FEB-06'
```

The result set

	DATE_ID	START_DATE
1	5	28-FEB-06

Description

- If you perform a search using a date string that doesn't include the time, the date string is converted implicitly to a date/time value of 12:00:00 AM (midnight) or 00:00:00 on a 24-hour clock. Then, if the date columns you're searching have time values other than 12:00:00 AM, you have to accommodate the times in the search condition.
- You can accommodate non-zero time components by searching for a range of dates rather than specific dates or by using the TRUNC function to remove the time component.

Figure 8-17   How to perform a date search

How to perform a time search

When you search for a time value without specifying a date component, Oracle automatically uses a default date of January 1 for the current year. That's why the first SELECT statement in figure 8-18 doesn't return any rows. In other words, even though one row has the correct time value in its search condition, that row doesn't have the correct date value.

The second SELECT statement in this figure shows how you can solve this problem. Here, the search condition in this statement uses the TO_CHAR function to convert the date/time values in the start_date column to string values that don't contain a date component. To do that, it uses a date format element of "HH24:MI:SS". That way, the string that's returned will match the string literal for the time that's specified in the search condition.

Like the first SELECT statement, the third SELECT statement doesn't return any rows. The problem, of course, is the same as in the first statement. To solve this problem, you can use the TO_CHAR function to remove the date component as shown in the fourth SELECT statement. Once you do that, this SELECT statement will return all rows that have a time within the range that's specified in the search condition.

The Date_Sample table

	DATE_ID	START_DATE
1	1	01-MAR-1979 00:00:00
2	2	28-FEB-1999 00:00:00
3	3	31-OCT-2003 00:00:00
4	4	28-FEB-2005 10:00:00
5	5	28-FEB-2006 13:58:32
6	6	01-MAR-2006 09:02:25

A SELECT statement that fails to return a row

```
SELECT * FROM date_sample
WHERE start_date = TO_DATE('10:00:00', 'HH24:MI:SS')
```

A SELECT statement that ignores the date component

```
SELECT * FROM date_sample
WHERE TO_CHAR(start_date, 'HH24:MI:SS') = '10:00:00'
```

The result set

	DATE_ID	START_DATE
1	4	28-FEB-05

Another SELECT statement that fails to return a row

```
SELECT * FROM date_sample
WHERE start_date >= TO_DATE('09:00:00', 'HH24:MI:SS')
  AND start_date  < TO_DATE('12:59:59', 'HH24:MI:SS')
```

Another SELECT statement that ignores the date component

```
SELECT * FROM date_sample
WHERE TO_CHAR(start_date, 'HH24:MI:SS') >= '09:00:00'
  AND TO_CHAR(start_date, 'HH24:MI:SS')  < '12:59:59'
```

The result set

	DATE_ID	START_DATE
1	4	28-FEB-05
2	6	01-MAR-06

Description

- If you use the TO_DATE function to return a date that only contains a time component, the date is converted implicitly to the first day of the current year. For 2006, for example, the date is converted to January 1, 2006. Then, if the date columns you're searching have dates other than that date, you have to accommodate those dates in the search condition.

- To ignore the date component of a date/time value, you can convert the DATE type to a CHAR type and only return the part of the time value that you want to use.

Figure 8-18   How to perform a time search

Other functions you should know about

In addition to the functions presented so far in this chapter, Oracle provides some other general purpose functions that you should know about.

How to use the CASE function

Figure 8-19 presents the two formats of the CASE function. This function returns a value that's determined by the conditions you specify. The two examples in this figure show how this function works.

The first example uses a simple CASE function. When you use this function, Oracle compares the input expression you code in the CASE clause with the expressions you code in the WHEN clauses. In this example, the input expression is the value in the terms_id column of the Invoices table, and the WHEN expressions are the valid values for this column. When Oracle finds a WHEN expression that's equal to the input expression, it returns the expression specified in the matching THEN clause. If the value of the terms_id column is 3, for example, this function returns the value "Net due 30 days." Although it's not shown in this example, you can also code an ELSE clause at the end of the CASE function. Then, if none of the when expressions are equal to the input expression, the function returns the value specified in the ELSE clause.

The simple CASE function is typically used with columns that can contain a limited number of values, such as the terms_id column used in this example. In contrast, the searched CASE function can be used for a wide variety of purposes. For example, you can test for conditions other than equal with this function. In addition, each condition can be based on a different column or expression. The second example in this figure shows how this function works.

This example determines the status of the invoices in the Invoices table. To do that, the searched CASE function determines the number of days between the current date and the invoice due date. If the difference is greater than 30, the CASE function returns the value "Over 30 days past due." Similarly, if the difference is greater than 0, the function returns the value "1 to 30 days past due." Note that if an invoice is 45 days old, both of these conditions are true. In that case, the function returns the expression associated with the first condition since this condition is evaluated first. In other words, the sequence of the conditions is critical to getting logical results. If neither of the conditions is true, the function uses the ELSE clause to return a value "Current."

The syntax of the simple CASE expression

```
CASE input_expression
    WHEN when_expression_1 THEN result_expression_1
    [WHEN when_expression_2 THEN result_expression_2]...
    [ELSE else_result_expression]
END
```

The syntax of the searched CASE expression

```
CASE
    WHEN conditional_expression_1 THEN result_expression_1
    [WHEN conditional_expression_2 THEN result_expression_2]...
    [ELSE else_result_expression]
END
```

A SELECT statement that uses a simple CASE expression

```
SELECT invoice_number, terms_id,
    CASE terms_id
        WHEN 1 THEN 'Net due 10 days'
        WHEN 2 THEN 'Net due 20 days'
        WHEN 3 THEN 'Net due 30 days'
        WHEN 4 THEN 'Net due 60 days'
        WHEN 5 THEN 'Net due 90 days'
    END AS terms
FROM invoices
```

The result set

	INVOICE_NUMBER	TERMS_ID	TERMS
1	QP58872	4	Net due 60 days
2	Q545443	4	Net due 60 days
3	P-0608	5	Net due 90 days

A SELECT statement that uses a searched CASE expression

```
SELECT invoice_number, invoice_total, invoice_date, invoice_due_date,
    CASE
        WHEN (SYSDATE - invoice_due_date) > 30 THEN 'Over 30 days past due'
        WHEN (SYSDATE - invoice_due_date) > 0  THEN '1 to 30 days past due'
        ELSE 'Current'
    END AS status
FROM invoices
WHERE invoice_total - payment_total - credit_total > 0
```

The result set

	INVOICE_NUMBER	INVOICE_TOTAL	INVOICE_DATE	INVOICE_DUE_DATE	STATUS
37	547480102	224	19-MAY-08	24-JUN-08	1 to 30 days past due
38	547481328	224	20-MAY-08	25-JUN-08	1 to 30 days past due
39	40318	21842	18-JUL-08	20-JUL-08	Current
40	31361833	579.42	23-MAY-08	09-JUN-08	Over 30 days past due

Note

- The last example assumes the SYSDATE function returns July 18, 2008.

Figure 8-19   How to use the CASE expression

How to use the COALESCE, NVL, and NVL2 functions

Figure 8-20 presents three functions that you can use to substitute non-null values for null values: COALESCE, NVL, and NVL2. Although these functions are similar, COALESCE is the most flexible because it lets you specify a list of values. Then, it returns the first non-null value in the list. In contrast, the NVL and NVL2 functions aren't as flexible since they only let you substitute a single non-null value for a null value. Still, these functions are useful in some situations.

The first example uses the COALESCE function to return the value of the payment_date column if that column doesn't contain a null value. Otherwise, it returns the value of the invoice_due_date column if that column doesn't contain a null value. Otherwise, it returns a date of January 1, 1900. Note that all of the arguments for this function must be of the same date type. In this case, all three arguments are of the DATE type.

The second example performs a similar task using the NVL function. In this example, the NVL function substitutes a string value of "Unpaid" for a null payment date. Since both arguments must be of the same data type, this example uses the TO_CHAR function to convert the payment_date column to a string.

The third example performs a similar task using the NVL2 function. In this example, the NVL2 function substitutes a string value of "Unpaid" for a null payment date, and it substitutes a string value of "Paid" for a non-null payment date. With the NVL2 function, only the second and third arguments need to be of the same data type. As a result, in this example, it isn't necessary to convert the first argument to a string.

The syntax of the COALESCE, NVL, and NVL2 functions

```
COALESCE(expression1 [, expression2][, expression3]...)
NVL(expression, null_replacement)
NVL2(expression, not_null_replacement, null_replacement)
```

A SELECT statement that uses the COALESCE function

```
SELECT payment_date, invoice_due_date,
       COALESCE(payment_date, invoice_due_date, TO_DATE('01-JAN-1900'))
       AS payment_date_2
FROM invoices
```

The result set

PAYMENT_DATE	INVOICE_DUE_DATE	PAYMENT_DATE_2
1 11-APR-08	22-APR-08	11-APR-08
2 14-MAY-08	23-MAY-08	14-MAY-08
3 (null)	30-JUN-08	30-JUN-08
4 12-MAY-08	16-MAY-08	12-MAY-08
5 13-MAY-08	16-MAY-08	13-MAY-08
6 (null)	26-JUN-08	26-JUN-08

A SELECT statement that uses the NVL function

```
SELECT payment_date,
       NVL(TO_CHAR(payment_date), 'Unpaid') AS payment_date_2
FROM invoices
```

The result set

PAYMENT_DATE	PAYMENT_DATE_2
1 11-APR-08	11-APR-08
2 14-MAY-08	14-MAY-08
3 (null)	Unpaid
4 12-MAY-08	12-MAY-08

A SELECT statement that uses the NVL2 function

```
SELECT payment_date,
       NVL2(payment_date, 'Paid', 'Unpaid') AS payment_date_2
FROM invoices
```

The result set

PAYMENT_DATE	PAYMENT_DATE_2
1 11-APR-08	Paid
2 14-MAY-08	Paid
3 (null)	Unpaid
4 12-MAY-08	Paid

Description

- The COALESCE, NVL, and NVL2 functions let you substitute non-null values for null values.

- The COALESCE function returns the first expression in a list of expressions that isn't null. All of the expressions in the list must have the same data type. If all of the expressions are null, this function returns a null value.

Figure 8-20   How to use the COALESCE, NVL, and NVL2 functions

How to use the GROUPING function

In chapter 5, you learned how to use the ROLLUP and CUBE operators to add summary rows to a summary query. When you do that, a null value is assigned to any column in a summary row that isn't being summarized.

If you want to assign a value other than null to these columns, you can do that by using the GROUPING function, as illustrated in figure 8-21. This function accepts the name of a column as its argument. The column you specify must be one of the columns named in a GROUP BY clause that includes the ROLLUP or CUBE operator.

The example in this figure shows how you can use the GROUPING function in a summary query that summarizes vendors by state and city. This is the same summary query that was described in chapter 5. However, instead of simply retrieving the values of the vendor_state and vendor_city columns from the base table, this query uses the GROUPING function within a CASE function to determine the values that are assigned to those columns. If a row is added to summarize the vendor_state column, for example, the value of the GROUPING function for that column is 1. Then, the CASE function assigns a literal string value of "========" to that column. Otherwise, it retrieves the value of the column from the Vendors table. Similarly, if a row is added to summarize the vendor_city column, a literal string value of "========" is assigned to that column. As you can see in the result set shown here, this makes it more obvious which columns are being summarized.

This technique is particularly useful if the columns you're summarizing can contain null values. In that case, it would be difficult to determine which rows are summary rows and which rows simply contain null values. Then, you may not only want to use the GROUPING function to replace the null values in summary rows, but you may want to use the COALESCE or NVL function to replace null values retrieved from the base table.

The syntax of the GROUPING function

```
GROUPING(column_name)
```

A summary query that uses the GROUPING function

```
SELECT
    CASE
        WHEN GROUPING(vendor_state) = 1 THEN '=========='
        ELSE vendor_state
    END AS vendor_state,
    CASE
        WHEN GROUPING(vendor_city) = 1 THEN '=========='
        ELSE vendor_city
    END AS vendor_city,
    COUNT(*) AS qty_vendors
FROM vendors
WHERE vendor_state IN ('IA', 'NJ')
GROUP BY ROLLUP(vendor_state, vendor_city)
ORDER BY vendor_state DESC, vendor_city DESC
```

The result set

	VENDOR_ST...	VENDOR_CITY	QTY_VENDORS
1	NJ	Washington	1
2	NJ	Fairfield	1
3	NJ	East Brunswick	2
4	NJ	==========	4
5	IA	Washington	1
6	IA	Fairfield	1
7	IA	==========	2
8	==========	==========	6

Description

- You can use the GROUPING function to determine when a null value is assigned to a column as the result of the ROLLUP or CUBE operator. The column you name in this function must be one of the columns named in the GROUP BY clause.

- If a null value is assigned to the specified column as the result of the ROLLUP or CUBE operator, the GROUPING function returns a value of 1. Otherwise, the GROUPING function returns a value of 0.

- You typically use the GROUPING function with the CASE expression. Then, if the GROUPING function returns a value of 1, you can assign a value other than null to the column.

Figure 8-21   How to use the GROUPING function

How to use the ranking functions

Figure 8-22 shows how to use the Oracle *ranking functions*. These functions provide a variety of ways that you can rank the rows that are returned by a result set. All four of these functions have a similar syntax and work similarly.

The first example shows how to use the ROW_NUMBER function. Here, the SELECT statement retrieves two columns from the Vendors table. The first column uses the ROW_NUMBER function to sort the result set by vendor_name and to number each row in the result set. To show that the first column has been sorted and numbered correctly, the second column displays the vendor_name.

To accomplish the sorting and numbering, you code the name of the ROW_NUMBER function, followed by a set of parentheses, followed by the OVER keyword and a second set of parentheses. Within the second set of parentheses, you code the required ORDER BY clause that specifies the sort order. In this example, for instance, the ORDER BY clause sorts by vendor_name in ascending order. However, you can code more complex ORDER BY clauses if necessary. In addition, you can code an ORDER BY clause that applies to the entire result set. In that case, the ORDER BY clause within the ranking function is used to number the rows and the ORDER BY clause outside the ranking function is used to sort the rows after the numbering has been applied.

The second example shows how to use the optional PARTITION BY clause of a ranking function. This clause allows you to specify a column that's used to divide the result set into groups. In this example, for instance, the PARTITION BY clause uses a column within the Vendors table to group vendors by state and to sort these vendors by name within each state.

However, you can also use the PARTITION BY clause when a SELECT statement joins one or more tables, like this:

```
SELECT vendor_name, invoice_number,
       ROW_NUMBER() OVER(PARTITION BY vendor_name
                         ORDER BY invoice_number) AS row_number
FROM vendors JOIN invoices
   ON vendors.vendor_id = invoices.vendor_id
```

Here, the invoices will be grouped by vendor and sorted within each vendor by invoice number. As a result, if a vendor has three invoices, these invoices will be sorted by invoice number and numbered from 1 to 3.

The syntax for the four ranking functions

```
ROW_NUMBER()              OVER ([partition_by_clause] order_by_clause)
RANK()                    OVER ([partition_by_clause] order_by_clause)
DENSE_RANK()              OVER ([partition_by_clause] order_by_clause)
NTILE(integer_expression) OVER ([partition_by_clause] order_by_clause)
```

A query that uses the ROW_NUMBER function

```
SELECT ROW_NUMBER() OVER(ORDER BY vendor_name) AS row_number, vendor_name
FROM vendors
```

The result set

ROW_NUMBER	VENDOR_NAME
1	1 ASC Signs
2	2 AT&T
3	3 Abbey Office Furnishings
4	4 American Booksellers Assoc
5	5 American Express

A query that uses the PARTITION BY clause

```
SELECT ROW_NUMBER()
       OVER(PARTITION BY vendor_state ORDER BY vendor_name)
       AS row_number, vendor_name, vendor_state
FROM vendors
```

The result set

ROW_NUMBER	VENDOR_NAME	VENDOR_STATE
1	1 AT&T	AZ
2	2 Computer Library	AZ
3	3 Wells Fargo Bank	AZ
4	1 ASC Signs	CA
5	2 Abbey Office Furnishings	CA
6	3 American Express	CA

Description

- The ROW_NUMBER, RANK, DENSE_RANK, and NTILE functions are known as *ranking functions*.
- The ROW_NUMBER function returns the sequential number of a row within a partition of a result set, starting at 1 for the first row in each partition.
- The ORDER BY clause of a ranking function specifies the sort order in which the ranking function is applied.
- The optional PARTITION BY clause of a ranking function specifies the column that's used to divide the result set into groups.

Figure 8-22   How to use the ranking functions (part 1 of 2)

The third example shows how the RANK and DENSE_RANK functions work. You can use these functions to rank the rows in a result set. In this example, both the RANK and the DENSE_RANK functions sort all invoices in the Invoices table by the invoice total. Since the first three rows have the same invoice total, both of these functions give these three rows the same rank, 1. However, the fourth row has a different value. To calculate the value for this row, the RANK function adds 1 to the total number of previous rows. In other words, since the first three rows are tied for first place, the fourth row gets fourth place and is assigned a rank of 4.

The DENSE_RANK function, on the other hand, calculates the value for the fourth row by adding 1 to the rank for the previous row. As a result, this function assigns a rank of 2 to the fourth row. In other words, since the first three rows are tied for first place, the fourth row gets second place.

The fourth example shows how the NTILE function works. You can use this function to divide the rows in a partition into the specified number of groups. When the rows can be evenly divided into groups, this function is easy to understand. For example, if a result set returns 100 rows, you can use the NTILE function to divide this result set into 10 groups of 10. However, when the rows can't be evenly divided into groups, this function is a little more difficult to understand. In this figure, for example, the NTILE function is used to divide a result set that contains 5 rows. Here, the first NTILE function divides this result into 2 groups with the first having 3 rows and the second having 2 rows. The second NTILE function divides this result set into 3 groups with the first having 2 rows, the second having 2 rows, and the third having 1 row. And so on. Although this doesn't result in groups with even numbers of rows, the NTILE function creates the number of groups specified by its argument.

In this figure, the examples for the RANK, DENSE_RANK, and NTILE functions don't include PARTITION BY clauses. As a result, these functions are applied to the entire result set. However, whenever necessary, you can use the PARTITION BY clause to divide the result set into groups just as shown in the second example for the ROW_NUMBER function.

A query that uses the RANK and DENSE_RANK functions

```
SELECT RANK() OVER (ORDER BY invoice_total) AS rank,
       DENSE_RANK() OVER (ORDER BY invoice_total) AS dense_rank,
       invoice_total, invoice_number
FROM invoices
```

The result set

	RANK	DENSE_RANK	INVOICE_TOTAL	INVOICE_NUMBER
1	1	1	6	25022117
2	1	1	6	24863706
3	1	1	6	24780512
4	4	2	9.95	21-4748363
5	4	2	9.95	21-4923721
6	6	3	10	4-342-8069

Description

- The RANK and DENSE_RANK functions both return the rank of each row within the partition of a result set.

- If there is a tie, both of these functions give the same rank to all rows that are tied.

- To determine the rank for the next distinct row, the RANK function adds 1 to the total number of rows, while the DENSE_RANK function adds 1 to the rank for the previous row.

A query that uses the NTILE function

```
SELECT terms_description,
    NTILE(2) OVER (ORDER BY terms_id) AS tile2,
    NTILE(3) OVER (ORDER BY terms_id) AS tile3,
    NTILE(4) OVER (ORDER BY terms_id) AS tile4
FROM terms
```

The result set

	TERMS_DESCRIPTION	TILE2	TILE3	TILE4
1	Net due 10 days	1	1	1
2	Net due 20 days	1	1	1
3	Net due 30 days	1	2	2
4	Net due 60 days	2	2	3
5	Net due 90 days	2	3	4

Description

- The NTILE function divides the rows in a partition into the specified number of groups.

- If the rows can't be evenly divided into groups, the later groups may have one less row than the earlier groups.

Figure 8-22   How to use the ranking functions (part 2 of 2)

Perspective

In this chapter, you learned about the most common Oracle data types. You also learned how to use the common functions for working with strings, numbers, and dates. At this point, you have the essential skills you need to write SQL statements at a professional level.

However, there's more to learn about Oracle data types and functions. In particular, chapter 17 shows how to work with other temporal types, and chapter 18 shows how to work with the large object (LOB) types. From that point on, you should be able to use the Oracle Database SQL Reference manual to learn about the data types and functions that aren't presented in this book.

Terms

data type	ASCII character
character data type	Unicode character
string data type	national character
text data type	fixed-length string
numeric data type	variable-length string
integer	precision
floating-point number	scale
temporal data type	scientific notation
date/time data type	single-precision number
datetime data type	double-precision number
date data type	casting
large object (LOB) data type	ranking functions
rowid data type	

Exercises

1. Write a SELECT statement that returns these columns from the Invoices table:

    The invoice_total column

    Use the TO_CHAR function to return the invoice_total column with 2 digits to the right of the decimal point.

    Use the TO_CHAR function to return the invoice_total column with no digits to the right of the decimal point and no decimal point

    Use the CAST function to return the invoice_total column as an integer with seven digits

2. Write a SELECT statement that returns these columns from the Invoices table:

    The invoice_date column

    Use the TO_CHAR function to return the invoice_date column with its full date and time including a four-digit year on a 24-hour clock

Use the TO_CHAR function to return the invoice_date column with its full date and time including a four-digit year on a 12-hour clock with an am/pm indicator

Use the CAST function to return the invoice_date column as VARCHAR2(10)

3. Write a SELECT statement that returns these columns from the Vendors table:

    The vendor_name column

    The vendor_name column in all capital letters

    The vendor_phone column

    The last four digits of each phone number

When you get that working right, add the columns that follow to the result set. This is more difficult because these columns require the use of functions within functions.

    The second word in each vendor name if there is one; otherwise, blanks

    The vendor_phone column with the parts of the number separated by dots as in 555.555.5555

4. Write a SELECT statement that returns these columns from the Invoices table:

    The invoice_number column

    The invoice_date column

    The invoice_date column plus 30 days

    The payment_date column

    A column named days_to_pay that shows the number of days between the invoice date and the payment date

    The number of the invoice_date's month

    The four-digit year of the invoice_date

    The last day of the invoice date's month

When you've got this working, add a WHERE clause that retrieves just the invoices for the month of May based on the invoice date, not the number of the invoice month.

5. Write a SELECT statement that returns these columns from the Invoices table:

    The invoice_number column

    The balance due (invoice total minus payment total minus credit total) with commas, a decimal point, and two decimal positions

    A column named "Balance Rank" that uses the RANK function to return a column that ranks the balance due in descending order.

Section 3

Database design and implementation

In large programming shops, database administrators are usually responsible for designing the databases that are used by production applications, and they may also be responsible for the databases that are used for testing those applications. Often, though, programmers are asked to design, create, or maintain small databases that are used for testing. And in a small shop, programmers may also be responsible for the production databases.

So whether you're a database administrator or a SQL programmer, you need the skills and knowledge presented in this section. That's true even if you aren't ever called upon to design or maintain a database. By understanding what's going on behind the scenes, you'll be able to use SQL more effectively.

So in chapter 9, you'll learn how to design a database. In chapter 10, you'll learn how to use the Data Definition Language (DDL) statements to create and maintain the tables, indexes, and sequences of a database. In chapter 11, you'll learn how to create and maintain views, which are database objects that provide another way to look at tables. Finally, in chapter 12, you'll learn how to design the security for your database by creating users that have restricted access to your database.

9

How to design a database

In this chapter, you'll learn how to design a new database. This is useful information whether or not you ever design a database on your own. To illustrate this process, I'll use the accounts payable (AP) database that you've seen throughout this book.

How to design a data structure

Databases are often designed by database administrators (DBAs) or design specialists. This is especially true for large, multiuser databases. How well this is done can directly affect your job as a SQL programmer. In general, a well designed database is easy to understand and query, while a poorly designed database is difficult to work with. In fact, when you work with a poorly designed database, you will often need to figure out how it is designed before you can code your queries appropriately.

The topics that follow will teach you a basic approach for designing a *data structure*. We use that term to refer to a model of the database rather than the database itself. Once you design the data structure, you can use the techniques presented in the next two chapters to create a database with that design. By understanding the right way to design a database, you'll work more effectively as a SQL programmer.

The basic steps for designing a data structure

In many cases, you can design a data structure based on an existing real-world system. The illustration at the top of figure 9-1 presents a conceptual view of how this works. Here, you can see that all of the information about the people, documents, and facilities within a real-world system is mapped to the tables, columns, and rows of a database system.

As you design a data structure, each table represents one object, or *entity*, in the real-world system. Then, within each table, each column stores one item of information, or *attribute*, for the entity, and each row stores one occurrence, or *instance*, of the entity.

This figure also presents the six steps you can follow to design a data structure. You'll learn more about each of these steps in the topics that follow. In general, though, step 1 is to identify all the data elements that need to be stored in the database. Step 2 is to break complex elements down into smaller components whenever that makes sense. Step 3 is to identify the tables that will make up the system and to determine which data elements are assigned as columns in each table. Step 4 is to define the relationships between the tables by identifying the primary and foreign keys. Step 5 is to normalize the database to reduce data redundancy. And step 6 is to identify the indexes that are needed for each table.

To model a database system after a real-world system, you can use a technique called *entity-relationship (ER) modeling*. Because this is a complex subject of its own, I won't present it in this book. However, I have applied some of the basic elements of this technique to the design diagrams presented in this chapter. In effect, then, you'll be learning some of the basics of this modeling technique.

A database system is modeled after a real-world system

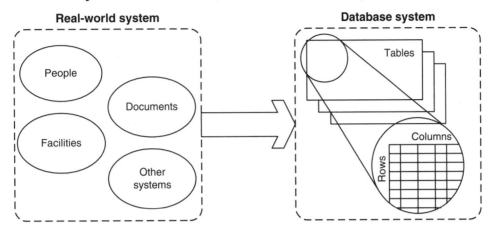

The six basic steps for designing a data structure

Step 1: Identify the data elements

Step 2: Subdivide each element into its smallest useful components

Step 3: Identify the tables and assign columns

Step 4: Identify the primary and foreign keys

Step 5: Review whether the data structure is normalized

Step 6: Identify the indexes

Description

- A relational database system should model the real-world environment where it's used. The job of the designer is to analyze the real-world system and then map it onto a relational database system.

- A table in a relational database typically represents an object, or *entity*, in the real world. Each column of a table is used to store an *attribute* associated with the entity, and each row represents one *instance* of the entity.

- To model a database and the relationships between its tables after a real-world system, you can use a technique called *entity-relationship (ER) modeling*. Some of the diagrams you'll see in this chapter apply the basic elements of ER modeling.

Figure 9-1 The basic steps for designing a data structure

How to identify the data elements

The first step for designing a data structure is to identify the data elements required by the system. You can use several techniques to do that, including analyzing the existing system if there is one, evaluating comparable systems, and interviewing anyone who will be using the system. One particularly good source of information are the documents used by an existing system.

In figure 9-2, for example, you can see an invoice that's used by an accounts payable system. We'll use this document as the main source of information for the database design presented in this chapter. Keep in mind, though, that you'll want to use all available resources when you design your own database.

If you study this document, you'll notice that it contains information about three different entities: vendors, invoices, and line items. First, the form itself has preprinted information about the vendor who issued the invoice, such as the vendor's name and address. If this vendor were to issue another invoice, this information wouldn't change.

This document also contains specific information about the invoice. Some of this information, such as the invoice number, invoice date, and invoice total, is general in nature. Although the actual information will vary from one invoice to the next, each invoice will include this information. In addition to this general information, each invoice includes information about the items that were purchased. Although each line item contains similar information, each invoice can contain a different number of line items.

One of the things you need to consider as you review a document like this is how much information your system needs to track. For an accounts payable system, for example, you may not need to store detailed data such as the information about each line item. Instead, you may just need to store summary data like the invoice total. As you think about what data elements to include in the database, then, you should have an idea of what information you'll need to get back out of the system.

An invoice that can be used to identify data elements

Acme Fabrication, Inc.

Custom Contraptions, Contrivances and Confabulations	Invoice Number:	I01-1088
1234 West Industrial Way East Los Angeles California 90022	Invoice Date:	10/05/08
800.555.1212 fax 562.555.1213 www.acmefabrication.com	Terms:	Net 30

Part No.	Qty.	Description	Unit Price	Extension
CUST345	12	Design service, hr	100.00	1200.00
457332	7	Baling wire, 25x3ft roll	79.90	559.30
50173	4375	Duct tape, black, yd	1.09	4768.75
328771	2	Rubber tubing, 100ft roll	4.79	9.58
CUST281	7	Assembly, hr	75.00	525.00
CUST917	2	Testing, hr	125.00	250.00
		Sales Tax		245.20

Your salesperson:	Ruben Goldberg, ext 4512
Accounts receivable:	Inigo Jones, ext 4901

$7,557.83
PLEASE PAY THIS AMOUNT

Thanks for your business!

The data elements identified on the invoice document

Vendor name	Invoice date	Item extension
Vendor address	Invoice terms	Vendor sales contact name
Vendor phone number	Item part number	Vendor sales contact extension
Vendor fax number	Item quantity	Vendor AR contact name
Vendor web address	Item description	Vendor AR contact extension
Invoice number	Item unit price	Invoice total

Description

- Depending on the nature of the system, you can identify data elements in a variety of ways, including interviewing users, analyzing existing systems, and evaluating comparable systems.

- The documents used by a real-world system, such as the invoice shown above, can often help you identify the data elements of the system.

- As you identify the data elements of a system, you should begin thinking about the entities that those elements are associated with. That will help you identify the tables of the database later on.

Figure 9-2   How to identify the data elements

How to subdivide the data elements

Some of the data elements you identify in step 1 of the design procedure will consist of multiple components. The next step, then, is to divide these elements into their smallest useful values. Figure 9-3 shows how you can do that.

The first example in this figure shows how you can divide the name of the sales contact for a vendor. Here, the name is divided into two elements: a first name and a last name. When you divide a name like this, you can easily perform operations like sorting by last name and using the first name in a salutation, such as "Dear Ruben." In contrast, if the full name is stored in a single column, you have to use the string functions to extract the component you need. But as you learned in the last chapter, that can lead to inefficient and complicated code. In general, then, you should separate a name like this whenever you'll need to use the name components separately. Later, when you need to use the full name, you can combine the first and last names using concatenation.

The second example shows how you typically divide an address. Notice in this example that the street number and street name are stored in a single column. Although you could store these components in separate columns, that usually doesn't make sense since these values are typically used together. That's what I mean when I say the data elements should be divided into their smallest *useful* values.

With that guideline in mind, you might even need to divide a single string into two or more components. A bulk mail system, for example, might require a separate column for the first three digits of the zip code. And a telephone number could require as many as four columns: one for the area code, one for the three-digit prefix, one for the four-digit number, and one for the extension.

As in the previous step, knowledge of the real-world system and of the information that will be extracted from the database is critical. In some circumstances, it may be okay to store data elements with multiple components in a single column. That can simplify your design and reduce the overall number of columns. In general, though, most designers divide data elements as much as possible. That way, it's easy to accommodate almost any query, and you don't have to change the database design later on when you realize that you need to use just part of a column value.

A name that's divided into first and last names

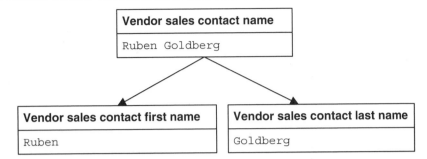

An address that's divided into street address, city, state, and zip code

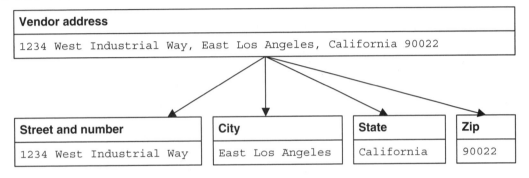

Description

- If a data element contains two or more components, you should consider subdividing the element into those components. That way, you won't need to parse the element each time you use it.

- The extent to which you subdivide a data element depends on how it will be used. Because it's difficult to predict all future uses for the data, most designers subdivide data elements as much as possible.

- When you subdivide a data element, you can easily rebuild it when necessary by concatenating the individual components.

Figure 9-3   How to subdivide the data elements

How to identify the tables and assign columns

Figure 9-4 presents the three main entities for the accounts payable system and lists the possible data elements that can be associated with each one. In most cases, you'll recognize the main entities that need to be included in a data structure as you identify the data elements. As I reviewed the data elements represented on the invoice document in figure 9-2, for example, I identified the three entities shown in this figure: vendors, invoices, and invoice line items. Although you may identify additional entities later on in the design process, it's sufficient to identity the main entities at this point. These entities will become the tables of the database.

After you identify the main entities, you need to determine which data elements are associated with each entity. These elements will become the columns of the tables. In many cases, the associations are obvious. For example, it's easy to determine that the vendor name and address are associated with the vendors entity and the invoice date and invoice total are associated with the invoices entity. Some associations, however, aren't so obvious. In that case, you may need to list a data element under two or more entities. In this figure, for example, you can see that the invoice number is included in both the invoices and invoice line items entities and the account number is included in all three entities. Later, when you normalize the data structure, you may be able to remove these repeated elements. For now, though, it's okay to include them.

Before I go on, I want to point out the notation I used in this figure. To start, any data elements I included that weren't identified in previous steps are shown in italics. Although you should be able to identify most of the data elements in the first two steps of the design process, you'll occasionally think of additional elements during the third step. In this case, since the initial list of data elements was based on a single document, I added several data elements to this list.

Similarly, you may decide during this step that you don't need some of the data elements you've identified. For example, I decided that I didn't need the fax number or web address of each vendor. So I used the strikethrough feature of my word processor to indicate that these data elements should not be included.

Finally, I identified the data elements that are included in two or more tables by coding an asterisk after them. Although you can use any notation you like for this step of the design process, you'll want to be sure that you document your design decisions. For a complicated design, you will probably want to use a *CASE (computer-aided software engineering)* tool.

By the way, a couple of the new data elements I added may not be clear to you if you haven't worked with a corporate accounts payable system before. "Terms" refers to the payment terms that the vendor offers. For example, the terms might be net 30 (the invoice must be paid in 30 days) or might include a discount for early payment. "Account number" refers to the general ledger accounts that a company uses to track its expenses. For example, one account number might be assigned for advertising expenses, while another might be for office supplies. Each invoice that's paid is assigned to an account, and in some cases, different line items on an invoice are assigned to different accounts.

Possible tables and columns for an accounts payable system

Vendors	Invoices	Invoice line items
Vendor name	Invoice number*	Invoice number*
Vendor address	Invoice date	~~Item part number~~
Vendor city	Terms*	Item quantity
Vendor state	Invoice total	Item description
Vendor zip code	*Payment date*	Item unit price
Vendor phone number	*Payment total*	Item extension
~~Vendor fax number~~	*Invoice due date*	*Account number**
~~Vendor web address~~	*Credit total*	*Sequence number*
Vendor contact first name	Account number*	
Vendor contact last name		
~~Vendor contact phone~~		
~~Vendor AR first name~~		
~~Vendor AR last name~~		
~~Vendor AR phone~~		
*Terms**		
*Account number**		

Description

- After you identify and subdivide all of the data elements for a database, you should group them by the entities with which they're associated. These entities will later become the tables of the database, and the elements will become the columns.

- If a data element relates to more than one entity, you can include it under all of the entities it relates to. Then, when you normalize the database, you may be able to remove the duplicate elements.

- As you assign the elements to entities, you should omit elements that aren't needed, and you should add any additional elements that are needed.

The notation used in this figure

- Data elements that were previously identified but aren't needed are crossed out.
- Data elements that were added are displayed in italics.
- Data elements that are related to two or more entities are followed by an asterisk.
- You can use a similar notation or develop one of your own. You can also use a *CASE (computer-aided software engineering)* tool if one is available to you.

Figure 9-4   How to identify the tables and assign columns

How to identify the primary and foreign keys

Once you identify the entities and data elements of a system, the next step is to identify the relationships between the tables. To do that, you need to identify the primary and foreign keys as shown in figure 9-5.

As you know, a primary key is used to uniquely identify each row in a table. In some cases, you can use an existing column as the primary key. For example, you might consider using the vendor_name column as the primary key of the Vendors table. Because the values for this column can be long, however, and because it would be easy to enter a value like that incorrectly, that's not a good candidate for a primary key. Instead, you should use an ID column like vendor_id that's incremented by one for each new record.

Similarly, you might consider using the invoice_number column as the primary key of the Invoices table. However, it's possible for different vendors to use the same invoice number, so this value isn't necessarily unique. Because of that, another ID column like invoice_id can be used as the primary key.

To uniquely identify the rows in the Invoice_Line_Items table, this design uses a composite key. This composite key uses two columns to identify each row. The first column is the invoice_id column from the Invoices table, and the second column is the invoice_sequence column. This is necessary because this table may contain more than one row (line item) for each invoice. And that means that the invoice_id value by itself may not be unique.

After you identify the primary key of each table, you need to identify the relationships between the tables and add foreign key columns as necessary. In most cases, two tables will have a one-to-many relationship with each other. For example, each vendor can have many invoices, and each invoice can have many line items. To identify the vendor that each invoice is associated with, a vendor_id column is included in the Invoices table. Because the Invoice_Line_Items table already contains an invoice_id column, it's not necessary to add another column to this table.

The diagram at the top of this figure illustrates the relationships I identified between the tables in the accounts payable system. As you can see, the primary keys are displayed in bold. Then, the lines between the tables indicate how the primary key in one table is related to the foreign key in another table. Here, a small, round connector indicates the one side of the relationship, and the connector with three lines indicates the many side of the relationship.

In addition to the one-to-many relationships shown in this diagram, you can also use many-to-many relationships and one-to-one relationships. The second diagram in this figure, for example, shows a many-to-many relationship between an Employees table and a Committees table. As you can see, this type of relationship can be implemented by creating a *linking table*, also called a *connecting table* or an *associate table*. This table contains the primary key columns from the two tables. Then, each table has a one-to-many relationship with the linking table. Notice that the linking table doesn't have its own primary key. Because this table doesn't correspond to an entity and because it's used only in conjunction with the Employees and Committees tables, a primary key isn't needed.

The relationships between the tables in the accounts payable system

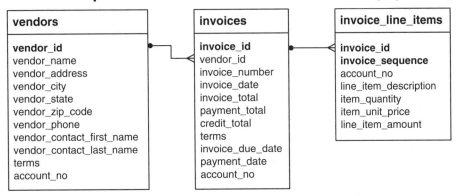

Two tables with a many-to-many relationship

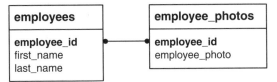

Linking table

Two tables with a one-to-one relationship

Description

- Each table should have a primary key that uniquely identifies each row. If possible, you should use an existing column for the primary key.

- The values of the primary keys should seldom, if ever, change. The values should also be short and easy to enter correctly.

- If a suitable column doesn't exist for a primary key, you can create an ID column that is incremented by one for each new row as the primary key.

- If two tables have a one-to-many relationship, you may need to add a foreign key column to the table on the "many" side. The foreign key column must have the same data type as the primary key column it's related to.

- If two tables have a many-to-many relationship, you'll need to define a *linking table* to relate them. Then, each of the tables in the many-to-many relationship will have a one-to-many relationship with the linking table. The linking table doesn't usually have a primary key.

- If two tables have a one-to-one relationship, they should be related by their primary keys. This type of relationship is typically used to improve performance. Then, columns with large amounts of data can be stored in a separate table.

Figure 9-5   How to identify the primary and foreign keys

The third example illustrates two tables that have a one-to-one relationship. With this type of relationship, both tables have the same primary key, which means that the information could be stored in a single table. This type of relationship is often used when a table contains one or more columns with large amounts of data. In this case, the Employee_Photos table contains a large binary column with a photo of each employee. Because this column is used infrequently, storing it in a separate table will make operations on the Employees table more efficient. Then, when this column is needed, it can be combined with the columns in the Employees table using a join.

How to enforce the relationships between tables

Although the primary keys and foreign keys indicate how the tables in a database are related, the database management system doesn't always enforce those relationships automatically. In that case, any of the operations shown in the table at the top of figure 9-6 would violate the *referential integrity* of the tables. If you deleted a row from a primary key table, for example, and the foreign key table included rows related to that primary key, the referential integrity of the two tables would be destroyed. In that case, the rows in the foreign key table that no longer have a related row in the primary key table would be *orphaned*. Similar problems can occur when you insert a row into the foreign key table or update a primary key or foreign value.

To enforce those relationships and maintain the referential integrity of the tables, Oracle provides for *declarative referential integrity*. To use it, you define *foreign key constraints* that indicate how the referential integrity between the tables is enforced. You'll learn more about defining foreign key constraints in the next chapter. For now, just realize that these constraints can prevent all of the operations listed in this figure that violate referential integrity.

Operations that can violate referential integrity

This operation...	Violates referential integrity if...
Delete a row from the primary key table	The foreign key table contains one or more rows related to the deleted row
Insert a row in the foreign key table	The foreign key value doesn't have a matching primary key value in the related table
Update the value of a foreign key	The new foreign key value doesn't have a matching primary key value in the related table
Update the value of a primary key	The foreign key table contains one or more rows related to the row that's changed

Description

- *Referential integrity* means that the relationships between tables are maintained correctly. That means that a table with a foreign key doesn't have rows with foreign key values that don't have matching primary key values in the related table.

- In Oracle, you can enforce referential integrity by using declarative referential integrity or by defining triggers.

- To use *declarative referential integrity (DRI)*, you define *foreign key constraints*. You'll learn how to do that in the next chapter.

- When you define foreign key constraints, you can specify how referential integrity is enforced when a row is deleted from the primary key table. The options are to return an error, to delete the related rows in the foreign key table, or to set the foreign key values in the related rows to null.

- If referential integrity isn't enforced and a row is deleted from the primary key table that has related rows in the foreign key table, the rows in the foreign key table are said to be *orphaned*.

Figure 9-6   How to enforce the relationships between tables

How normalization works

The next step in the design process is to review whether the data structure is *normalized*. To do that, you look at how the data is separated into related tables. If you follow the first four steps for designing a database that are presented in this chapter, your database will already be partially normalized when you get to this step. However, almost every design can be normalized further.

Figure 9-7 illustrates how *normalization* works. The first two tables in this figure show some of the problems caused by an *unnormalized* data structure. In the first table, you can see that each row represents an invoice. Because an invoice can have one or more line items, however, the item_description column must be repeated to provide for the maximum number of line items. But since most invoices have fewer line items than the maximum, this can waste storage space.

In the second table, each line item is stored in a separate row. That eliminates the problem caused by repeating the item_description column, but it introduces a new problem: the invoice number must be repeated in each row. This, too, can cause storage problems, particularly if the repeated column is large. In addition, it can cause maintenance problems if the column contains a value that's likely to change. Then, when the value changes, each row that contains the value must be updated. And if a repeated value must be reentered for each new row, it would be easy for the value to vary from one row to another.

To eliminate the problems caused by *data redundancy*, you can normalize the data structure. To do that, you apply the *normal forms* you'll learn about later in this chapter. As you'll see, there are a total of seven normal forms. However, it's common to apply only the first three. The diagram in this figure, for example, shows the accounts payable system in third normal form. Although it may not be obvious at this point how this reduces data redundancy, that will become clearer as you learn about the different normal forms.

A table that contains repeating columns

INVOICE_NUMBER	ITEM_DESCRIPTION_1	ITEM_DESCRIPTION_2	ITEM_DESCRIPTION_3
1 112897	VB ad	SQL ad	Library directory
2 97/552	Catalogs	SQL flyer	(null)
3 97/553B	Card revision	(null)	(null)

A table that contains redundant data

INVOICE_NUMBER	ITEM_DESCRIPTION
1 112897	VB ad
2 112897	SQL ad
3 97/533B	Card revisions
4 112897	Library directory
5 97/522	Catalogs
6 97/522	SQL flyer

The accounts payable system in third normal form

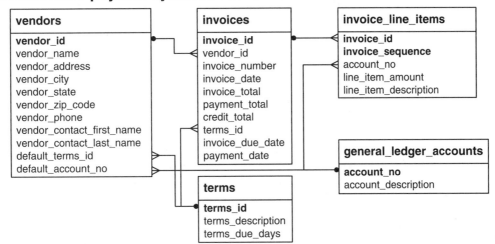

Description

- *Normalization* is a formal process you can use to separate the data in a data structure into related tables. Normalization reduces *data redundancy*, which can cause storage and maintenance problems.

- In an *unnormalized data structure*, a table can contain information about two or more entities. It can also contain repeating columns, columns that contain repeating values, and data that's repeated in two or more rows.

- In a *normalized data structure*, each table contains information about a single entity, and each piece of information is stored in exactly one place.

- To normalize a data structure, you apply the *normal forms* in sequence. Although there are a total of seven normal forms, a data structure is typically considered normalized if the first three normal forms are applied.

Figure 9-7   How normalization works

How to identify the columns to be indexed

The last step in the design process is to identify the columns that should be indexed. An *index* is a structure that provides for locating one or more rows directly. Without an index, a database management system has to perform a *table scan*, which involves searching through the entire table.

Just as the index of a book has page numbers that direct you to a specific subject, a database index has pointers that direct the system to a specific row. This can speed performance not only when you're searching for rows based on a search condition, but also when you're joining data from tables. If a join is done based on a primary key to foreign key relationship, for example, and an index is defined for the foreign key column, the database management system can use that index to locate the rows for each primary key value.

When you use Oracle, an index is automatically created for the primary key in each table that you create. But you should consider creating indexes for other columns in some of the tables based on the guidelines at the top of figure 9-8.

To start, you should index a column if it will be used frequently in search conditions or joins. Since you use foreign keys in most joins, you should typically index each foreign key column. The column should also contain mostly distinct values, and the values in the column should be updated infrequently. If these conditions aren't met, the overhead of maintaining the index will probably outweigh the advantages of using it.

When you create indexes, you should be aware that Oracle must update the indexes whenever you add, update, or delete rows. Because that can affect performance, you don't want to define more indexes than you need.

As you identify the indexes for a table, keep in mind that, like a key, an index can consist of two or more columns. This type of index is called a *composite index*.

When to create an index

- When the column is a foreign key
- When the column is used frequently in search conditions or joins
- When the column contains a large number of distinct values
- When the column is updated infrequently

Description

- Oracle automatically creates an index for a primary key.
- An *index* provides a way for a database management system to locate information more quickly. When it uses an index, the database management system can go directly to a specific row rather than having to search through all the rows until it finds it.
- Indexes speed performance when searching and joining tables.
- You can create *composite indexes* that include two or more columns. You should use this type of index when the columns in the index are updated infrequently or when the index will cover almost every search condition on the table.
- Because indexes must be updated each time you add, update, or delete a row, you shouldn't create more indexes than you need.

Figure 9-8   How to identify the columns to be indexed

How to normalize a data structure

The topics that follow describe the seven normal forms and teach you how to apply the first three. As I said earlier, you apply these three forms to some extent in the first four database design steps, but these topics will give you more insight into the process. Then, the last topic explains when and how to denormalize a data structure. When you finish these topics, you'll have the basic skills for designing databases that are efficient and easy to use.

The seven normal forms

Figure 9-9 summarizes the seven normal forms. Each normal form assumes that the previous forms have already been applied. Before you can apply the third normal form, for example, the design must already be in the second normal form.

Strictly speaking, a data structure isn't normalized until it's in the fifth or sixth normal form. However, the normal forms past the third normal form are applied infrequently. Because of that, I won't present those forms in detail here. Instead, I'll just describe them briefly so you'll have an idea of how to apply them if you need to.

The *Boyce-Codd normal form* can be used to eliminate *transitive dependencies*. With this type of dependency, one column depends on another column, which depends on a third column. To illustrate, consider the city, state, and zip code columns in the Vendors table. Here, a zip code identifies a city and state, which means that the city and state are dependent on the zip code. The zip code, in turn, is dependent on the vendor_id column. To eliminate this dependency, you could store the city and state values in a separate table that uses zip code as its primary key.

The fourth normal form can be used to eliminate multiple *multivalued dependencies* from a table. A multivalued dependency is one where a primary key column has a one-to-many relationship with a non-key column. To illustrate, consider the vendor contact phone number in the Vendors table. If you wanted to accommodate alternate phone numbers, such as a cellular or home phone, you could add extra columns for each type of number. However, this creates a multivalued dependency between the phone numbers and the vendor_id. To be in fourth normal form, therefore, you'd need to store phone numbers in a separate table that uses vendor_id as a foreign key.

To apply the fifth normal form, you continue to divide the tables of the data structure into smaller tables until all redundancy has been removed. When further splitting would result in tables that couldn't be used to reconstruct the original table, the data structure is in fifth normal form. In this form, most tables consist of little more than key columns with one or two data elements.

The *domain-key normal form*, sometimes called the sixth normal form, is only of academic interest since no database system has implemented a way to apply it. For this reason, even normalization purists might consider a database to be normalized in fifth normal form.

The seven normal forms

Normal form	Description
First (1NF)	The value stored at the intersection of each row and column must be a scalar value, and a table must not contain any repeating columns.
Second (2NF)	Every non-key column must depend on the entire primary key.
Third (3NF)	Every non-key column must depend only on the primary key.
Boyce-Codd (BCNF)	A non-key column can't be dependent on another non-key column. This prevents *transitive dependencies*, where column A depends on column C and column B depends on column C. Since both A and B depend on C, A and B should be moved into another table with C as the key.
Fourth (4NF)	A table must not have more than one *multivalued dependency*, where the primary key has a one-to-many relationship to non-key columns. This form gets rid of misleading many-to-many relationships.
Fifth (5NF)	The data structure is split into smaller and smaller tables until all redundancy has been eliminated. If further splitting would result in tables that couldn't be joined to recreate the original table, the structure is in fifth normal form.
Domain-key (DKNF) or Sixth (6NF)	Every constraint on the relationship is dependent only on key constraints and domain constraints, where a *domain* is the set of allowable values for a column. This form prevents the insertion of any unacceptable data by enforcing constraints at the level of a relationship, rather than at the table or column level. DKNF is less a design model than an abstract "ultimate" normal form.

The benefits of normalization

- Since a normalized database has more tables than an unnormalized database, and since each table has an index on its primary key, the database has more indexes. That makes data retrieval more efficient.

- Since each table contains information about a single entity, each index has fewer columns (usually one) and fewer rows. That makes data retrieval and insert, update, and delete operations more efficient.

- Each table has fewer indexes, which makes insert, update, and delete operations more efficient.

- Data redundancy is minimized, which simplifies maintenance and reduces storage.

Description

- Each normal form assumes that the design is already in the previous normal form.

- A database is typically considered to be normalized if it is in third normal form. The other four forms are not commonly used and are not covered in detail in this book.

Figure 9-9   The seven normal forms

Figure 9-9 also lists the benefits of normalizing a data structure. To summarize, normalization produces smaller, more efficient tables. In addition, it reduces data redundancy, which makes the data easier to maintain and reduces the amount of storage needed for the database. Because of these benefits, you should always consider normalizing your data structures.

You should also be aware that the subject of normalization is a contentious one in the database community. In the academic study of computer science, normalization is considered a form of design perfection that should always be strived for. In practice, though, database designers and DBAs tend to use normalization as a flexible design guideline.

How to apply the first normal form

Figure 9-10 illustrates how you apply the first normal form to an unnormalized invoice data structure consisting of the data elements that are shown in figure 9-2. The first two tables in this figure illustrate structures that aren't in first normal form. Both of these tables contain a single row for each invoice. Because each invoice can contain one or more line items, however, the first table allows for repeating values in the item_description column. The second table is similar, except it includes a separate column for each line item description. Neither of these structures is acceptable in first normal form.

The third table in this figure has eliminated the repeating values and columns. To do that, it includes one row for each line item. Notice, however, that this has increased the data redundancy. Specifically, the vendor name and invoice number are now repeated for each line item. This problem can be solved by applying the second normal form.

Before I describe the second normal form, I want you to realize that I intentionally omitted many of the columns in the invoice data structure from the examples in this figure and the next figure. In addition to the columns shown here, for example, each of these tables would also contain the vendor address, invoice date, invoice total, etc. By eliminating these columns, it will be easier for you to focus on the columns that are affected by applying the normal forms.

The invoice data with a column that contains repeating values

	VENDOR_NAME	INVOICE_NUMBER	ITEM_DESCRIPTION
1	Cahners Publishing	112897	VB ad, SQL ad, Library directory
2	Zylka Design	97/522	Catalogs, SQL Flyer
3	Zylka Design	97/533B	Card revision

The invoice data with repeating columns

	VENDOR_NAME	INVOICE_NUMBER	ITEM_DESCRIPTION_1	ITEM_DESCRIPTION_2	ITEM_DESCRIPTION_3
1	Cahners Publishing	112897	VB ad	SQL ad	Library directory
2	Zylka Design	97/552	Catalogs	SQL flyer	(null)
3	Zylka Design	97/553B	Card revision	(null)	(null)

The invoice data in first normal form

	VENDOR_NAME	INVOICE_NUMBER	ITEM_DESCRIPTION
1	Cahners Publishing	112897	VB ad
2	Cahners Publishing	112897	SQL ad
3	Cahners Publishing	97/533B	Card revisions
4	Zylka Design	112897	Library directory
5	Zylka Design	97/522	Catalogs
6	Zylka Design	97/522	SQL flyer

Description

- For a table to be in first normal form, its columns must not contain repeating values. Instead, each column must contain a single, scalar value. In addition, the table must not contain repeating columns that represent a set of values.

- A table in first normal form often has repeating values in its rows. This can be resolved by applying the second normal form.

Figure 9-10   How to apply the first normal form

How to apply the second normal form

Figure 9-11 shows how to apply the second normal form. To be in second normal form, every column in a table that isn't a key column must be dependent on the entire primary key. This form only applies to tables that have composite primary keys, which is often the case when you start with data that is completely unnormalized. The table at the top of this figure, for example, shows the invoice data in first normal form after key columns have been added. In this case, the primary key consists of the invoice_id and invoice_sequence columns. The invoice_sequence column is needed to uniquely identify each line item for an invoice.

Now, consider the three non-key columns shown in this table. Of these three, only one, item_description, depends on the entire primary key. The other two, vendor_name and invoice_number, depend only on the invoice_id column. Because of that, these columns should be moved to another table. The result is a data structure like the second one shown in this figure. Here, all of the information related to an invoice is stored in the Invoices table, and all of the information related to an individual line item is stored in the Invoice_Line_Items table.

Notice that the relationship between these tables is based on the invoice_id column. This column is the primary key of the Invoices table, and it's the foreign key in the Invoice_Line_Items table that relates the rows in that table to the rows in the Invoices table. This column is also part of the primary key of the Invoice_Line_Items table.

When you apply second normal form to a data structure, it eliminates some of the redundant row data in the tables. In this figure, for example, you can see that the invoice number and vendor name are now included only once for each invoice. In first normal form, this information was included for each line item.

The invoice data in first normal form with keys added

INVOICE_ID	VENDOR_NAME	INVOICE_NUMBER	INVOICE_SEQUENCE	ITEM_DESCRIPTION
1	1 Cahners Publishing	112897	1	VB ad
2	2 Cahners Publishing	112897	2	SQL ad
3	3 Cahners Publishing	112897	3	Library directory
4	4 Zylka Design	97/522	1	Catalogs
5	5 Zylka Design	97/522	2	SQL flyer
6	6 Zylka Design	97/533B	1	Card revision

The invoice data in second normal form

INVOICE_NUMBER	VENDOR_NAME	INVOICE_ID
1 11287	Cahners Publishing	1
2 97/522	Zylka Design	2
3 97/533B	Zylka Design	3

INVOICE_ID	INVOICE_SEQUENCE	ITEM_DESCRIPTION
1	1	1 VB ad
2	1	2 SQL ad
3	1	3 Library directory
4	2	1 Catalogs
5	2	2 SQL flyer
6	3	1 Card revision

Description

- For a table to be in second normal form, every non-key column must depend on the entire primary key. If a column doesn't depend on the entire key, it indicates that the table contains information for more than one entity. This is reflected by the table's composite key.

- To apply second normal form, you move columns that don't depend on the entire primary key to another table and then establish a relationship between the two tables.

- Second normal form helps remove redundant row data, which can save storage space, make maintenance easier, and reduce the chance of storing inconsistent data.

Figure 9-11   How to apply the second normal form

How to apply the third normal form

To apply the third normal form, you make sure that every non-key column depends *only* on the primary key. Figure 9-12 illustrates how you can apply this form to the data structure for the accounts payable system. At the top of this figure, you can see all of the columns in the Invoices and Invoice_Line_Items tables in second normal form. Then, you can see a list of questions that you might ask about some of the columns in these tables when you apply third normal form.

First, does the vendor information depend only on the invoice_id column? Another way to phrase this question is, "Will the information for the same vendor change from one invoice to another?" If the answer is no, the vendor information should be stored in a separate table. That way, can you be sure that the vendor information for each invoice for a vendor will be the same. In addition, you will reduce the redundancy of the data in the Invoices table. This is illustrated by the diagram in this figure that shows the accounts payable system in third normal form. Here, a Vendors table has been added to store the information for each vendor. This table is related to the Invoices table by the vendor_id column, which has been added as a foreign key to the Invoices table.

Second, does the terms column depend only on the invoice_id column? The answer to that question depends on how this column is used. In this case, I'll assume that this column is used not only to specify the terms for each invoice, but also to specify the default terms for a vendor. Because of that, the terms information could be stored in both the Vendors and the Invoices tables. To avoid redundancy, however, the information related to different terms can be stored in a separate table, as illustrated by the Terms table in this figure. As you can see, the primary key of this table is an identity column named terms_id. Then, a foreign key column named default_terms_id has been added to the Vendors table, and a foreign key column named terms_id has been added to the Invoices table.

Third, does the account_no column depend only on the invoice_id column? Again, that depends on how this column is used. In this case, it's used to specify the general ledger account number for each line item, so it depends on the invoice_id and the invoice_sequence columns. In other words, this column should be stored in the Invoice_Line_Items table. In addition, each vendor has a default account number, which should be stored in the Vendors table. Because of that, another table named General_Ledger_Accounts has been added to store the account numbers and account descriptions. Then, foreign key columns have been added to the Vendors and Invoice_Line_Items tables to relate them to this table.

Fourth, can the invoice_due_date column in the Invoices table and the line_item_amount column in the Invoice_Line_Items table be derived from other data in the database? If so, they depend on the columns that contain that data rather than on the primary key columns. In this case, the value of the line_item_amount column can always be calculated from the item_quantity and item_unit_price columns. Because of that, this column could be omitted.

The accounts payable system in second normal form

invoices

---

invoice_id
vendor_name	invoice_date
vendor_address	invoice_total
vendor_city	payment_total
vendor_state	credit_total
vendor_zip_code	terms
vendor_phone	invoice_due_date
vendor_contact_first_name	payment_date
vendor_contact_last_name	account_no
invoice_number	

invoice_line_items

---

invoice_id
invoice_sequence
account_no
invoice_line_item_description
item_quantity
item_unit_price
line_item_amount

Questions about the structure

1. Does the vendor information (vendor_name, vendor_address, etc.) depend only on the invoice_id column?
2. Does the terms column depend only on the invoice_id column?
3. Does the account_no column depend only on the invoice_id column?
4. Can the invoice_due_date and line_item_amount columns be derived from other data?

The accounts payable system in third normal form

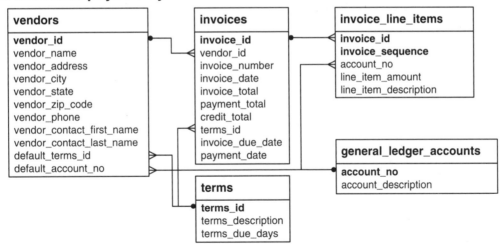

Description

- For a table to be in third normal form, every non-key column must depend *only* on the primary key.
- If a column doesn't depend only on the primary key, it implies that the column is assigned to the wrong table or that it can be computed from other columns in the table. A column that can be computed from other columns contains *derived data*.

Figure 9-12   How to apply the third normal form

Alternatively, you could omit the item_quantity and item_unit_price columns and keep just the line_item_amount column. That's what I did in the data structure shown in this figure. The solution you choose, however, depends on how the data will be used.

In contrast, although the invoice_due_date column could be calculated from the invoice_date column in the Invoices table and the terms_due_days column in the related row of the Terms table, the system also allows this date to be overridden. Because of that, the invoice_due_date column should not be omitted. If the system didn't allow this value to be overridden, however, this column could be safely omitted.

When and how to denormalize a data structure

Denormalization is the deliberate deviation from the normal forms. Most denormalization occurs beyond the third normal form. In contrast, the first three normal forms are almost universally applied.

To illustrate when and how to denormalize a data structure, figure 9-13 presents the design of the accounts payable system in fifth normal form. Here, the vendor zip codes are stored in a separate table that contains the city and state for each zip code. In addition, the area codes are stored in a separate table. Because of that, a query that retrieves vendor addresses and phone numbers would require two joins. In contrast, if you left the city, state, and area code information in the Vendors table, no joins would be required, but the Vendors table would be larger. In general, you should denormalize based on the way the data will be used. In this case, we'll seldom need to query phone numbers without the area code. Likewise, we'll seldom need to query city and state without the zip code. For these reasons, I've denormalized my design by eliminating the Zip_Codes and Area_Codes tables.

You might also consider denormalizing a table if the data it contains is updated infrequently. In that case, redundant data isn't as likely to cause problems.

Finally, you should consider including derived data in a table if that data is used frequently in search conditions. For example, if you frequently query the Invoices table based on invoice balances, you might consider including a column that contains the balance due. That way, you won't have to calculate this value each time it's queried. Keep in mind, though, that if you store derived data, it's possible for it to deviate from the derived value. For this reason, you may need to protect the derived column so it can't be updated directly. Alternatively, you could update the table periodically to reset the value of the derived column.

Because normalization eliminates the possibility of data redundancy errors and optimizes the use of storage, you should carefully consider when and how to denormalize a data structure. In general, you should denormalize only when the increased efficiency outweighs the potential for redundancy errors and storage problems. Of course, your decision to denormalize should also be based on your knowledge of the real-world environment in which the system will be used. If you've carefully analyzed the real-world environment as outlined in this chapter, you'll have a good basis for making that decision.

The accounts payable system in fifth normal form

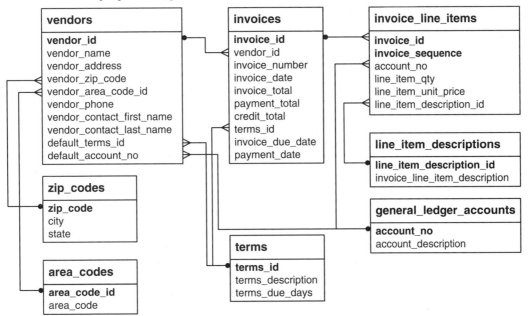

When to denormalize

- When a column from a joined table is used repeatedly in search criteria, you should consider moving that column to the primary key table if it will eliminate the need for a join.
- If a table is updated infrequently, you should consider denormalizing it to improve efficiency. Because the data remains relatively constant, you don't have to worry about data redundancy errors once the initial data is entered and verified.
- Include columns with derived values when those values are used frequently in search conditions. If you do that, you need to be sure that the column value is always synchronized with the value of the columns it's derived from.

Description

- Data structures that are normalized to the fourth normal form and beyond typically require more joins than tables normalized to the third normal form and can therefore be less efficient.
- SQL statements that work with tables that are normalized to the fourth normal form and beyond are typically more difficult to code and debug.
- Most designers *denormalize* data structures to some extent, usually to the third normal form.
- *Denormalization* can result in larger tables, redundant data, and reduced performance.
- Only denormalize when necessary. It is better to adhere to the normal forms unless it is clear that performance will be improved by denormalizing.

Figure 9-13   When and how to denormalize a data structure

Perspective

Database design is a complicated subject. Because of that, it's impossible to teach you everything you need to know in a single chapter. With the skills you've learned in this chapter, however, you should now be able to design simple databases of your own. More important, you should be able to evaluate the design of any database that you work with. That way, you can be sure that the queries you code will be as efficient and as effective as possible.

One aspect of database design that isn't covered in this chapter is designing the security of the database. Among other things, that involves creating database users and assigning permissions for each user. In chapter 12, you'll learn how to implement database security.

Terms

data structure	foreign key constraint
entity	orphaned row
attribute	normalization
instance	data redundancy
entity-relationship (ER) modeling	unnormalized data structure
CASE (computer-aided software engineering)	normalized data structure
linking table	normal forms
connecting table	index
associate table	composite index
referential integrity	derived data
declarative referential integrity (DRI)	denormalization

Exercises

Design a database for tracking memberships

1. Draw a database diagram for a database that tracks the memberships for an association and for the groups within the association. Assume that each member can belong to any number of groups and that each group can have any number of members.

2. Modify your design for exercise 2 to keep track of the *role* served by each individual in each group. Assume that each individual can only serve one role within a group and that each group has its own set of roles that members can fulfill.

10

How to create tables, indexes, and sequences

Now that you've learned how to design a database, you're ready to learn how to implement your design. To do that, you use the set of SQL statements that are known as the data definition language (DDL). In this chapter, you'll learn how to use the DDL statements that work with tables, indexes, and sequences.

This chapter begins by teaching you how to code these DDL statements yourself. This is useful because it's common to store the DDL statements that create a database in a script. This chapter finishes by showing how to use SQL Developer to work with these database objects.

How to work with tables

This topic shows how to code the DDL statements that work with the tables of a database. If you're working on a large database project, you probably won't need to code DDL statements like these because that will be handled by a database administrator (DBA). For small projects, though, the SQL programmer may often have to serve as the DBA too. And even when working with large projects, the SQL programmer often needs to use DDL to create tables that are needed for testing.

Because the syntax for the statements presented in this chapter is complex, this chapter doesn't present complete syntax diagrams for the statements. Instead, the diagrams present only the commonly used clauses. If you're interested in the complete syntax of any statement, though, you can refer to the Oracle Database SQL Reference manual.

How to create a table

Figure 10-1 presents a simplified syntax for the CREATE TABLE statement. By default, this statement creates a new table in the current schema. If that's not what you want, you can qualify the table name with the schema name. For example, you can qualify the Vendors table with the EX schema like this:

```
CREATE TABLE ex.vendors
```

In its simplest form, the CREATE TABLE statement consists of the name of the new table followed by the names and data types of its columns. This is illustrated by the first example in this figure. However, in most cases, you'll code one or more *attributes* for each column as illustrated by the second example. For instance, to indicate that a column doesn't accept null values, you can code the NOT NULL attribute. If you omit this attribute, the column will allow null values.

To indicate that each row in a column must contain a unique value, you can code the UNIQUE attribute. Since two null values aren't considered to be the same, a unique column can contain null values. However, it's common to use the NOT NULL and UNIQUE attributes to define a column that can't contain null values and where each value in the column must be unique.

Finally, to specify a default value for a column, you can use the DEFAULT attribute. This value is used if another value isn't specified when a row is added to the database. The default value you specify must correspond to the data type for the column. For example, the default value for the invoice_date column is set to the value that's returned by the SYSDATE function. Similarly, the default value for the payment_total column is set to a value of zero.

Before I continue, you should realize that if you run the statements shown in this figure against the AP schema, the statements will fail. That's because the AP schema already contains tables named Vendors and Invoices. As a result, if you want to test these statements, you can run them against the EX schema. Then, the Vendors and Invoices tables will be created in that schema.

The syntax of the CREATE TABLE statement

```
CREATE TABLE [schema_name.]table_name
(
  column_name_1 data_type [column_attributes]
  [, column_name_2 data_type [column_attributes]]...
  [, table_level_constraints]
)
```

Common column attributes

Attribute	Description
NOT NULL	Indicates that the column doesn't accept null values. If omitted, the column can accept null values.
UNIQUE	Specifies that each value stored in the column must be unique.
DEFAULT default_value	Specifies a default value for the column.

A statement that creates a table without column attributes

```
CREATE TABLE vendors
(
  vendor_id     NUMBER,
  vendor_name   VARCHAR2(50)
)
```

A statement that creates a table with column attributes

```
CREATE TABLE vendors
(
  vendor_id     NUMBER        NOT NULL    UNIQUE,
  vendor_name   VARCHAR2(50)  NOT NULL    UNIQUE
)
```

Another statement that creates a table with column attributes

```
CREATE TABLE invoices
(
  invoice_id       NUMBER        NOT NULL    UNIQUE,
  vendor_id        NUMBER        NOT NULL,
  invoice_number   VARCHAR2(50)  NOT NULL,
  invoice_date     DATE                      DEFAULT SYSDATE,
  invoice_total    NUMBER(9,2)   NOT NULL,
  payment_total    NUMBER(9,2)               DEFAULT 0
)
```

Description

- The CREATE TABLE statement creates a table based on the column definitions, column *attributes*, and table attributes you specify.

- You can also assign one or more constraints to a column or to the entire table as described later in this chapter.

- To review the complete syntax of the CREATE TABLE statement, you can use the Oracle Database SQL Reference manual.

- To test the code in this figure and in the figures that follow, you can connect to the EX schema.

Figure 10-1   How to create a table

If you review the CREATE TABLE syntax in figure 10-1, you'll see that you can code table-level constraints after the columns of the table. You'll see some examples of these constraints in figure 10-2.

How to code a primary key constraint

Whether you realize it or not, the NOT NULL and UNIQUE keywords are examples of *constraints*. A constraint restricts the type of data that can be stored in a column. For example, the NOT NULL keyword prevents null values from being stored in a column, and the UNIQUE keyword only allows unique values.

Now, figure 10-2 shows how to code another type of constraint that's known as a *primary key constraint*. The easiest way to define a primary key is to code the PRIMARY KEY keywords after the data type for the column as shown in the first example. When you identify a column as the primary key, two of the column's attributes are changed automatically. First, the column is forced to be NOT NULL. Second, the column is forced to contain a unique value for each row. In addition, an index is automatically created based on the column.

Although the first example is the easiest way to code a primary key constraint, it's generally considered a good programming practice to provide a name for the primary key constraint. This makes it easier to work with the constraint if that becomes necessary later on. To provide a name, you can use the CONSTRAINT keyword at the column level or at the table level.

To show how to provide a name for a constraint, the second example uses the CONSTRAINT keyword to provide names for the three constraints that are defined in the first example. Here, the first constraint provides a name of vendors_pk for the primary key of the Vendors table. Note how the names provided here begin with a table name or a column name and use a two-letter suffix to identify the type of constraint. Since these constraints are coded after the column name, they are known as *column-level constraints*.

The third example shows how to code *table-level constraints*. In this figure, the vendors_pk and vendor_name_uq constraints work the same regardless of whether they are coded at the column level or the table level. As a result, where you decide to code these constraints is largely a matter of personal preference. I prefer to name primary key and unique key constraints, and I prefer to code these constraints at the table level as shown in the third example.

However, a table-level constraint does provide one capability that isn't available from column-level constraints: it can refer to multiple columns in the table. As a result, if you need to refer to multiple columns, you must use a table-level constraint. For example, to create a primary key based on two or more columns, you must code PRIMARY KEY at the table level as shown in the fourth example.

When you code a constraint at the table level, you must code a comma at the end of the preceding column definition. If you don't, you will get an error when you try to run the statement.

The syntax of a column-level primary key constraint

```
[CONSTRAINT constraint_name] PRIMARY KEY
```

The syntax of a table-level primary key constraint

```
[CONSTRAINT constraint_name]
PRIMARY KEY (column_name_1 [, column_name_2]...)
```

A table with column-level constraints

```
CREATE TABLE vendors
(
  vendor_id      NUMBER          PRIMARY KEY,
  vendor_name    VARCHAR2(50)    NOT NULL    UNIQUE
)
```

A table with named column-level constraints

```
CREATE TABLE vendors
(
  vendor_id      NUMBER          CONSTRAINT vendors_pk PRIMARY KEY,
  vendor_name    VARCHAR2(50)    CONSTRAINT vendor_name_nn NOT NULL
                                 CONSTRAINT vendor_name_un UNIQUE
)
```

A table with table-level constraints

```
CREATE TABLE vendors
(
  vendor_id      NUMBER,
  vendor_name    VARCHAR2(50)    NOT NULL,
  CONSTRAINT vendors_pk PRIMARY KEY (vendor_id),
  CONSTRAINT vendor_name_uq UNIQUE (vendor_name)
)
```

A table with a two-column primary key constraint

```
CREATE TABLE invoice_line_items
(
  invoice_id             NUMBER        NOT NULL,
  invoice_sequence       NUMBER        NOT NULL,
  line_item_description  VARCHAR2(100) NOT NULL,
  CONSTRAINT line_items_pk PRIMARY KEY (invoice_id, invoice_sequence)
)
```

Description

- *Constraints* are used to enforce the integrity of the data in a table by defining rules about the values that can be stored in the columns of the table.

- You code a *column-level constraint* as part of the definition of the column it constrains. You code a *table-level constraint* as if it is a separate column definition, and you name the columns it constrains within that definition.

- A *not null constraint* prevents null values from being stored in the column. A *unique constraint* requires that each row has a unique value in the column but allows null values to be stored in the column.

- A *primary key constraint* requires that each row has a unique value for the column or columns for the primary key, and it does not allow null values.

Figure 10-2   How to code a primary key constraint

How to code a foreign key constraint

Figure 10-3 shows how to code a *foreign key constraint*, which is also known as a *reference constraint*. This type of constraint is used to define the relationships between tables and to enforce referential integrity.

To create a foreign key constraint at the column level, you code the REFER-ENCES keyword followed by the name of the related table and the name of the related column in parentheses. In this figure, for instance, the first example creates a table with a vendor_id column that includes a REFERENCES clause that identifies the vendor_id column in the Vendors table as the related column.

The second example shows how to code the same primary and foreign key constraints shown in the first example at the table level. When you use this syntax, you must include the CONSTRAINT keyword followed by a name, followed by the FOREIGN KEY keywords. Although this requires a little more code, it forces you to provide a name for the foreign key, which is a good programming practice. It also lets you reference a foreign key that consists of multiple columns.

The third example in this figure shows what happens when you try to insert a row into the Invoices table with a vendor_id value that isn't matched by the vendor_id column in the Vendors table. Because of the foreign key constraint, the system enforces referential integrity by refusing to do the operation. It also displays an error message that indicates the constraint that was violated.

Similarly, if you try to delete a row from the Vendors table that has related rows in the Invoices table, the delete operation will fail and the system will display an error message. Since this prevents rows in the Invoices table from being orphaned, this is usually what you want.

In some cases, though, you may want to automatically delete the related rows in the Invoices table when the related row in the Vendors table is deleted. To do that, you can code the ON DELETE clause with the foreign key con-straint as illustrated by the fourth example. Here, this clause is coded with the CASCADE option. Then, when you delete a row from the primary key table, the delete is *cascaded* to the related rows in the foreign key table. If, for example, you delete a row from the Vendors table, all related rows in the Invoices table will also be deleted. Because a *cascading delete* makes it easier to delete data that you didn't intend to delete, you should use it with caution.

The other option for the ON DELETE clause is SET NULL. Then, when you delete a row from the primary key table, the values in the foreign key column of the foreign key table are set to null. Since this creates rows in the foreign key table that aren't related to the primary key table, you'll rarely want to use this option.

The syntax of a column-level foreign key constraint

```
[CONSTRAINT constraint_name]
  REFERENCES table_name (column_name)
  [ON DELETE {CASCADE|SET NULL}]
```

The syntax of a table-level foreign key constraint

```
[CONSTRAINT constraint_name]
  FOREIGN KEY (column_name_1 [, column_name_2]...)
  REFERENCES table_name (column_name_1 [, column_name_2]...)
  [ON DELETE {CASCADE|SET NULL}]
```

A table with a column-level foreign key constraint

```
CREATE TABLE invoices
(
  invoice_id      NUMBER        PRIMARY KEY,
  vendor_id       NUMBER        REFERENCES vendors (vendor_id),
  invoice_number  VARCHAR2(50)  NOT NULL    UNIQUE
)
```

A table with a table-level foreign key constraint

```
CREATE TABLE invoices
(
  invoice_id      NUMBER        NOT NULL,
  vendor_id       NUMBER        NOT NULL,
  invoice_number  VARCHAR2(50)  NOT NULL    UNIQUE,
  CONSTRAINT invoices_pk
    PRIMARY KEY (invoice_id),
  CONSTRAINT invoices_fk_vendors
    FOREIGN KEY (vendor_id) REFERENCES vendors (vendor_id)
)
```

An INSERT statement that fails because a related row doesn't exist

```
INSERT INTO invoices
VALUES (1, 1, '1')
```

The response from the system

```
SQL Error: ORA-02291: integrity constraint (EX.INVOICES_FK_VENDORS) violated
- parent key not found
*Cause:    A foreign key value has no matching primary key value.
*Action:   Delete the foreign key or add a matching primary key.
```

A constraint that uses the ON DELETE clause

```
CONSTRAINT invoices_fk_vendors
  FOREIGN KEY (vendor_id) REFERENCES vendors (vendor_id)
  ON DELETE CASCADE
```

Description

- A *foreign key constraint* requires values in one table to match values in another table. This defines the relationship between two tables and enforces referential integrity.

- To define a relationship that consists of two or more columns, you must define the constraint at the table level.

Figure 10-3   How to code a foreign key constraint

How to code a check constraint

Figure 10-4 shows how to code a *check constraint*. A check constraint allows you to code a Boolean expression that checks values before they are stored in the column and only stores them if they satisfy the Boolean expression.

The first example in this figure uses a column-level check constraint to limit the values in the invoice_total column to numbers greater than zero. This works similarly to the constraints you saw in the previous figures. Note that if you try to store a negative value in this column as illustrated by the INSERT statement in the third example, the system responds with an error and the insert operation is terminated.

The second example shows how to code the same constraint at the table level. Note how the AND keyword is used to combine both Boolean expressions into a single Boolean expression. Note also that this example provides a name of invoices_ck for the constraint and that this name is used by the error message that's returned by the system. This shows why it's helpful to name your constraints.

In general, you should use check constraints to restrict the values in a column whenever possible. In some situations, however, check constraints can be too restrictive. As an example, consider a telephone number that's constrained to the "(000) 000-0000" format used for US phone numbers. The problem with this constraint is that it doesn't let you store phone numbers with extensions (although you could store extensions in a separate column) or phone numbers with an international format.

For this reason, check constraints aren't used by all database designers. That way, the database can store values with formats that weren't predicted when the database was designed. However, this flexibility comes at the cost of allowing some invalid data. For some systems, this tradeoff is acceptable.

Keep in mind, too, that application programs that add and update data can also include data validation. In that case, check constraints may not be necessary. Because you can't always assume that an application program will check for valid data, though, you should include check constraints whenever that makes sense.

The syntax of a check constraint

```
[CONSTRAINT constraint_name] CHECK (condition)
```

A statement that creates a table with two column-level check constraints

```
CREATE TABLE invoices
(
  invoice_id      NUMBER        PRIMARY KEY,
  invoice_total   NUMBER(9,2)   NOT NULL    CHECK (invoice_total >= 0),
  payment_total   NUMBER(9,2)   DEFAULT 0   CHECK (payment_total >= 0)
)
```

The same statement with the check constraints coded at the table level

```
CREATE TABLE invoices
(
  invoice_id      NUMBER        PRIMARY KEY,
  invoice_total   NUMBER(9,2)   NOT NULL,
  payment_total   NUMBER(9,2)   DEFAULT 0,
  CONSTRAINT invoices_ck CHECK (invoice_total >= 0 AND payment_total >= 0)
)
```

An INSERT statement that fails due to the check constraint

```
INSERT INTO invoices
VALUES (1, 99.99, -10)
```

The response from the system

```
SQL Error: ORA-02290: check constraint (EX.INVOICES_CK) violated
02290. 00000 -  "check constraint (%s.%s) violated"
*Cause:    The values being inserted do not satisfy the named check
*Action:   do not insert values that violate the constraint.
```

Description

- *Check constraints* limit the values that can be stored in the columns of a table.

- The condition you specify for a check constraint is evaluated as a Boolean expression. If the expression is true, the insert or update operation proceeds. Otherwise, it fails.

- A check constraint that's coded at the column level can refer only to that column. A check constraint that's coded at the table level can refer to any column in the table.

Figure 10-4   How to code a check constraint

How to alter the columns of a table

After you create tables, you may need to change the columns of a table. For example, you may need to add, modify, or drop a column. To do that, you can use the ALTER TABLE statement shown in figure 10-5.

The first example in this figure shows how to add a new column to a table. As you can see, you code the column definition the same way you do when you create a new table. To start, you specify the column name. Then, you code the data type and its attributes.

The second example shows how to drop an existing column. Note that Oracle prevents you from dropping some columns. For example, you can't drop a column if it's the primary key column.

The third example shows how to modify the length of the data type for an existing column. In this case, a column that was defined as VARCHAR2(50) is changed to VARCHAR2(100). Since the new data type is bigger than the old data type, you can be sure that the existing data will still fit.

The fourth example shows how to change the data type to a different data type. In this case, a column that was defined as VARCHAR2(100) is changed to CHAR(100). Since these data types both store the same type of characters, you know that no data will be lost.

The fifth example shows how to change the default value for a column. In this case, a default value of 'New Vendor' is assigned to the vendor_name column.

In the first five statements, Oracle can alter the table without losing any data. As a result, these statements execute successfully and alter the table. However, if the change will result in a loss of data, it's not allowed. For example, the sixth statement attempts to change the length of the vendor_name column to a length that's too small for existing data that's stored in this column. As a result, Oracle doesn't modify the column, and the system returns an error message like the one shown in this figure.

The syntax for modifying the columns of a table

```
ALTER TABLE [schema_name.]table_name
{
ADD          column_name data_type [column_attributes] |
DROP COLUMN column_name |
MODIFY       column_name data_type [column_attributes]
}
```

A statement that adds a new column

```
ALTER TABLE vendors
ADD last_transaction_date DATE;
```

A statement that drops a column

```
ALTER TABLE vendors
DROP COLUMN last_transaction_date;
```

A statement that changes the length of a column

```
ALTER TABLE vendors
MODIFY vendor_name VARCHAR2(100);
```

A statement that changes the data type of a column

```
ALTER TABLE vendors
MODIFY vendor_name CHAR(100);
```

A statement that changes the default value of a column

```
ALTER TABLE vendors
MODIFY vendor_name DEFAULT 'New Vendor';
```

A statement that fails because it would cause data to be lost

```
ALTER TABLE vendors
MODIFY vendor_name VARCHAR2(10);
```

The response from the system

```
SQL Error: ORA-01441: cannot decrease column length because some value is
too big
```

Description

- You can use the ALTER TABLE statement to modify the columns of an existing table.
- Oracle won't allow you to change a column if that change would cause data to be lost.

Warning

- You should never alter a table or other database object in a production database without first consulting the DBA.

Figure 10-5   How to alter the columns of a table

How to alter the constraints of a table

After you create tables, you may need to change the constraints of a table. For example, you may need to add or drop a constraint. Or, you may want to disable or enable a constraint. To do that, you can use the ALTER TABLE command as shown in figure 10-6.

The first example shows how to add a check constraint to a table. In this case, if the invoice_total column contains existing values that don't satisfy the check constraint, Oracle won't add the check constraint and will return an error message.

The second example shows how to drop the check constraint that was added in the first example. To do that, you have to know the name of the constraint. Since I supplied a name for the constraint in the first example, it's easy to drop this constraint later. If you don't name your constraints, Oracle will automatically generate a name for the constraint such as SYS_C0012769. In that case, before you can drop a constraint, you'll need to use the SQL Developer tool to look up its name as shown later in this chapter.

The third example shows how to use the DISABLE keyword to add a new check constraint that's disabled. Since this check constraint is disabled, Oracle won't check to make sure existing values satisfy this constraint. As a result, the constraint will be added even if there are existing values in the column that don't satisfy the constraint.

The fourth example shows how to use the ENABLE and NOVALIDATE keywords to enable a constraint for new values only. In this case, the code enables the check constraint that was added in the third example without validating existing values against the check constraint. If you want to validate values when you enable the constraint, you can omit the NOVALIDATE keyword.

The fifth example shows how to use the DISABLE keyword to disable an existing constraint. In some cases, this is useful if you need to temporarily disable a constraint while you update the data in the column. Then, you can enable the constraint when you're done.

The last three examples show how to add other types of constraints. In particular, the sixth example shows how to add a foreign key constraint; the seventh example shows how to add a unique constraint; and the eighth example shows how to add a not null constraint. Note that a not null constraint uses a different syntax than the previous types of constraints. Note also that this syntax is a cross between the syntax for modifying a column and the syntax for modifying other types of constraints.

The syntax for modifying the constraints of a table

```
ALTER TABLE table_name
{
ADD         CONSTRAINT   constraint_name constraint_definition [DISABLE] |
DROP        CONSTRAINT   constraint_name |
ENABLE    [NOVALIDATE]   constraint_name |
DISABLE                  constraint_name
}
```

A statement that adds a new check constraint

```
ALTER TABLE invoices
ADD CONSTRAINT invoice_total_ck CHECK (invoice_total >= 0);
```

A statement that drops a check constraint

```
ALTER TABLE invoices
DROP CONSTRAINT invoice_total_ck;
```

A statement that adds a disabled constraint

```
ALTER TABLE invoices
ADD CONSTRAINT invoice_total_ck CHECK (invoice_total >= 1) DISABLE;
```

A statement that enables a constraint for new values only

```
ALTER TABLE invoices
ENABLE NOVALIDATE CONSTRAINT invoice_total_ck;
```

A statement that disables a constraint

```
ALTER TABLE invoices
DISABLE CONSTRAINT invoice_total_ck;
```

A statement that adds a foreign key constraint

```
ALTER TABLE invoices
ADD CONSTRAINT invoices_fk_vendors
FOREIGN KEY (vendor_id) REFERENCES vendors (vendor_id);
```

A statement that adds a unique constraint

```
ALTER TABLE vendors
ADD CONSTRAINT vendors_vendor_name_uq
UNIQUE (vendor_name);
```

A statement that adds a not null constraint

```
ALTER TABLE vendors
MODIFY vendor_name
CONSTRAINT vendors_vendor_name_nn NOT NULL;
```

Description

- You use the ALTER TABLE statement to add or drop the constraints of an existing table.
- To drop a constraint, you must know its name. If you don't know its name, you can use SQL Developer to look up the name as shown later in this chapter.
- By default, Oracle verifies that existing data satisfies a new constraint. If that's not what you want, you can add a disabled constraint. Then, you can enable the constraint without validating existing data.

Figure 10-6   How to alter the constraints of a table

How to rename, truncate, and drop a table

Figure 10-7 shows how to use the RENAME, TRUNCATE TABLE, and DROP TABLE statements. When you use these statements, use them cautiously, especially when you're working on a production database.

To start, you can use the RENAME statement to rename an existing table. This is useful if you want to change the name of a table without modifying its column definitions or the data that's stored in the table. In this figure, for instance, the first example changes the name of the Vendors table to Vendor. However, if you rename a table, you should probably update the names of any constraints that use the name of the table.

On the other hand, you can use the TRUNCATE TABLE statement to delete all of the data from a table without deleting the column definitions for the table. In this figure, for instance, the second example deletes all rows from the newly renamed Vendor table.

Finally, you can use the DROP TABLE statement to delete all of the data from a table and also delete the definition of the table, including the constraints for the table. In this figure, for instance, the third and fourth examples drop the Vendor table. However, the fourth example explicitly specifies that it is dropping the Vendor table that's stored in the EX schema, not the Vendor table in another schema such as the AP schema.

When you issue a DROP TABLE statement, Oracle checks to see if other tables depend on the table you're trying to delete. If they do, Oracle won't allow the deletion. For example, you can't delete the Vendors table if a foreign key constraint in the Invoices table refers to the Vendors table. In that case, you must drop the Invoices table before you can drop the Vendors table.

When you drop a table, any indexes or triggers that have been defined for the table are also dropped. In a moment, you'll learn how to create indexes for a table, and you'll learn how to create triggers for a table in chapter 16.

A statement that renames a table

```
RENAME vendors TO vendor
```

A statement that deletes all data from a table

```
TRUNCATE TABLE vendor
```

A statement that deletes a table from the current schema

```
DROP TABLE vendor
```

A statement that qualifies the table to be deleted

```
DROP TABLE ex.vendor
```

Description

- You can use the RENAME statement to change the name of an existing table.

- You can use the TRUNCATE TABLE statement to delete all data from a table without deleting the definition for the table.

- You can use the DROP TABLE statement to delete a table from the current database/ schema. To delete a table from another schema, you must qualify the table name with the schema name.

- You can't truncate or drop a table if a foreign key constraint in another table refers to that table.

- When you drop a table, all of its data, constraints, and indexes are deleted.

Warnings

- You should not use these statements on a production database without first consulting the DBA.

Figure 10-7   How to rename, truncate, and drop a table

How to work with indexes

An *index* speeds up joins and searches by providing a way for a database management system to go directly to a row rather than having to search through all the rows until it finds the one you want. By default, Oracle creates indexes for the primary keys and unique constraints of a table, which is usually what you want. In addition, you may want to create indexes for foreign keys and other columns that are used frequently in search conditions or joins. However, you'll want to avoid creating indexes on columns that are updated frequently since this slows down insert, update, and delete operations.

How to create an index

Figure 10-8 presents the basic syntax of the CREATE INDEX statement, which creates an index based on one or more columns of a table. This syntax omits some of the optional clauses that you can use for tuning the indexes for better performance. This tuning is often done by DBAs working with large databases, but usually isn't necessary for small databases.

To create an index, you name the table and columns that the index will be based on in the ON clause. For each column, you can specify the ASC or DESC keyword to indicate whether you want the index sorted in ascending or descending sequence. If you don't specify a sort order, ASC is the default. In addition, you can use the UNIQUE keyword to specify that an index contains only unique values.

In these examples, the names follow a standard naming convention that's used by many developers. To start, the index name specifies the name of the table, followed by the name of the column or columns, followed by a suffix of IX. The only exception in this figure is the second example, which had to be shortened so it wouldn't exceed the maximum number of characters allowed for a name. This naming convention makes it easy to see which columns of which tables have been indexed.

The fifth and sixth examples show how to create a *function-based index*, which is an index that's based on an expression. This expression may include one or more functions. To enable function-based indexes, you may need to set the QUERY_REWRITE_ENABLED parameter for the system to true as shown in the seventh example.

How to drop an index

The eighth example shows how to use the DROP INDEX statement to drop an index. You may want to drop an index if you suspect that it isn't speeding up your joins and searches and that it may be slowing down your insert, update, and delete operations.

The syntax of the CREATE INDEX statement

```
CREATE [UNIQUE] INDEX index_name
   ON table_name (column_name_1 [ASC|DESC] [, column_name_2 [ASC|DESC]]...)
```

A statement that creates an index based on a single column

```
CREATE INDEX invoices_vendor_id_ix
   ON invoices (vendor_id);
```

A statement that creates an index based on two columns

```
CREATE INDEX invoices_vendor_id_inv_no_ix
   ON invoices (vendor_id, invoice_number);
```

A statement that creates a unique index

```
CREATE UNIQUE INDEX vendors_vendor_phone_ix
   ON vendors (vendor_phone);
```

A statement that creates an index that's sorted in descending order

```
CREATE INDEX invoices_invoice_total_ix
   ON invoices (invoice_total DESC);
```

A statement that creates a function-based index

```
CREATE INDEX vendors_vendor_name_upper_ix
   ON vendors (UPPER(vendor_name));
```

Another statement that creates a function-based index

```
CREATE INDEX invoices_balance_due_ix
   ON invoices (invoice_total - payment_total - credit_total DESC);
```

How to enable function-based indexes

```
CONNECT system/system;
ALTER SYSTEM SET QUERY_REWRITE_ENABLED=TRUE;
```

A statement that drops an index

```
DROP INDEX vendors_vendor_state_ix
```

Description

- Oracle automatically creates an index for primary key constraints and for unique constraints.

- You can use the CREATE INDEX statement to create other *indexes* for a table. An index can improve performance when the Oracle searches for rows in the table.

- You can use the CREATE INDEX statement to create *function-based indexes* for a table. A function-based index is an index that's based on an expression that may include one or more functions.

- You can use the DROP INDEX statement to drop an index.

Figure 10-8   How to create and drop an index

How to work with sequences

In Oracle, a *sequence* is a database object that automatically generates a sequence of integer values. Typically, a sequence is used to generate a value for the primary key of a table.

How to create a sequence

Figure 10-9 shows how to create a sequence. Most of the time, you can create a sequence by coding the CREATE SEQUENCE statement followed by the name of the sequence. In the first example, for instance, the CREATE SEQUENCE statement creates a sequence named vendor_id_seq that can be used to get a value for the primary key of the Vendors table.

This creates a sequence that starts with 1, is incremented by a value of 1, has no maximum or minimum value, and caches the next 20 generated numbers. In addition, this sequence doesn't cycle back to the first number when it reaches the last number in the sequence, and it doesn't guarantee that sequence numbers are generated in order of request. In most cases, these settings are adequate.

If you need to create a sequence that works differently, you can use any of the optional clauses of the CREATE SEQUENCE statement to modify the sequence. For example, the script that creates the AP database inserts 123 rows into the Vendors table. As a result, it makes sense to use the STARTS WITH clause to start the sequence that's used to generate values for the vendor_id column at 124 or higher.

Although you'll rarely ever need to use the other clauses, the third example illustrates how these clauses work. This example generates a sequence that begins with 100, is incremented by a value of 10, has a minimum value of 0, has a maximum value of 1,000,000, cycles back to the beginning of the sequence when it reaches the end, and guarantees that sequence numbers are generated in order of request.

How to use a sequence

Once you've created a sequence, you typically use it within an INSERT statement as shown in the fourth example. Here, the NEXTVAL pseudo column gets the next value from the sequence so it can be inserted into the vendor_id column of the Vendors table. Then, the fifth example shows how to use the CURRVAL pseudo column to check the current value of the sequence.

When you use these pseudo columns, you should be aware that Oracle doesn't initialize the sequence until you call the NEXTVAL pseudo column for the first time. As a result, you can't call the CURRVAL pseudo column until you've called the NEXTVAL pseudo column at least once.

The syntax of the CREATE SEQUENCE statement

```
CREATE SEQUENCE sequence_name
   [START WITH starting_integer]
   [INCREMENT BY increment_integer]
   [{MAXVALUE maximum_integer | NOMAXVALUE}]
   [{MINVALUE minimum_integer | NOMINVALUE}]
   [{CYCLE|NOCYCLE}]
   [{CACHE cache_size|NOCACHE}]
   [{ORDER|NOORDER}]
```

A statement that creates a sequence of integers that starts with 1 and is incremented by 1

```
CREATE SEQUENCE vendor_id_seq
```

A statement that specifies a starting integer for a sequence

```
CREATE SEQUENCE vendor_id_seq
   START WITH 124
```

A statement that specifies all optional parameters for a sequence

```
CREATE SEQUENCE test_seq
   START WITH 100 INCREMENT BY 10
   MINVALUE 0 MAXVALUE 1000000
   CYCLE CACHE 10 ORDER;
```

A statement that uses the NEXTVAL pseudo column to get the next value for a sequence

```
INSERT INTO vendors
VALUES (vendor_id_seq.NEXTVAL, 'Acme Co.', '123 Main St.', NULL,
   'Fresno', 'CA', '93711', '(800) 221-5528',
   'Wiley' , 'Coyote');
```

A statement that uses the CURRVAL pseudo column to get the current value of the sequence

```
SELECT vendor_id_seq.CURRVAL from dual;
```

Description

- You use the CREATE SEQUENCE statement to generate integer values for a primary key.
- By default, the CREATE SEQUENCE statement creates a sequence that starts with 1, is incremented by a value of 1, has no maximum or minimum value, caches the next 20 generated numbers, doesn't restart the sequence when the end is reached, and doesn't guarantee that sequence numbers are generated in order of request.
- You can use the NEXTVAL pseudo column to get the next value in the sequence.
- You can use the CURRVAL pseudo column to get the current value in the sequence.

Figure 10-9   How to create and use a sequence (part 1 of 2)

How to alter a sequence

Once you've created a sequence, you can use the ALTER SEQUENCE statement to alter the attributes of a sequence. This works similarly to the CREATE SEQUENCE statement. However, you can't change the starting value, and you can't set the minimum and maximum attributes to values that don't make sense. For example, if the current value of the sequence is 99, you can't set the maximum value to 98.

How to drop a sequence

When you drop a table, all indexes related to the table are also dropped. However, the sequences that are used by the table aren't dropped. As a result, if you want to drop a sequence, you must use the DROP SEQUENCE statement. In this figure, for instance, the last example drops the sequence named test_seq that was created in part 1 of this figure.

The syntax of the ALTER SEQUENCE statement

```
ALTER SEQUENCE sequence_name
   [sequence_attributes]
```

A statement that alters a sequence

```
ALTER SEQUENCE test_seq
   INCREMENT BY 9
   MINVALUE 99 MAXVALUE 999999
   NOCYCLE CACHE 9 NOORDER;
```

A statement that drops a sequence

```
DROP SEQUENCE test_seq;
```

Description

- You can use the ALTER SEQUENCE statement to alter the attributes of a sequence. However, you can't change the starting value, and you can't set the minimum and maximum attributes to values that don't make sense.

- You can use the DROP SEQUENCE statement to drop a sequence.

Figure 10-9   How to create and use a sequence (part 2 of 2)

The script used to create the AP schema

Figure 10-10 presents the DDL statements that are used to create the AP schema that's used throughout this book. In this figure, these statements are coded as part of a script.

An introduction to scripts

As you learned in the earlier chapters, a *script* is a file that contains one or more SQL statements. In addition, a script can store PL/SQL code. Scripts are often used to create the objects for a database as shown in this figure.

When you code a script, you code a semicolon at the end of each SQL statement. In addition, you code a front slash at the end of each block of PL/SQL code that's stored in the script. At any point in the script, you can code a COMMIT statement to commit the changes to the database. However, DDL statements such as CREATE and DROP statements are automatically committed immediately after they're executed. As a result, you don't need to code a COMMIT statement after DDL statements like the ones shown in this figure.

How the DDL statements work

The CONNECT command that begins this script connects as the AP user with a password of AP. As a result, the rest of the statements in the script are executed against the AP schema.

After the CONNECT command, an anonymous block of PL/SQL code is used to drop any existing sequences and tables that might already exist in the AP schema. Note that the DROP SEQUENCE and DROP TABLE statements are coded after the EXECUTE IMMEDIATE keywords within single quotes. This is necessary to execute DDL statements from within a block of PL/SQL code. At any rate, if these objects exist, this code drops them. If not, this code suppresses any error messages that would be displayed when you try to drop an object that doesn't exist.

After the block of PL/SQL code, a COMMIT statement is used to commit any changes that have been made to the database. For example, if the PL/SQL code dropped the sequences and tables, this statement will make sure that the changes are committed to the database.

After the COMMIT statement, I have coded the CREATE TABLE statements for the five main tables of the AP schema. For each CREATE TABLE statement, I have coded the primary key column (or columns) first. Although this isn't required, it's a good programming practice. Since the order in which you declare the columns defines the default order for the columns, I have defined these columns in a logical order. That way, when you use a SELECT * statement to retrieve all of the columns, they're returned in this order.

The SQL script that creates the AP schema

Page 1

```
CONNECT ap/ap;

-- Use an anonymous PL/SQL script to
-- drop all tables and sequences in the current schema and
-- suppress any error messages that may be displayed
-- if these objects don't exist
BEGIN
  EXECUTE IMMEDIATE 'DROP SEQUENCE vendor_id_seq';
  EXECUTE IMMEDIATE 'DROP SEQUENCE invoice_id_seq';

  EXECUTE IMMEDIATE 'DROP TABLE invoice_archive';
  EXECUTE IMMEDIATE 'DROP TABLE invoice_line_items';
  EXECUTE IMMEDIATE 'DROP TABLE invoices';
  EXECUTE IMMEDIATE 'DROP TABLE vendor_contacts';
  EXECUTE IMMEDIATE 'DROP TABLE vendors';
  EXECUTE IMMEDIATE 'DROP TABLE terms';
  EXECUTE IMMEDIATE 'DROP TABLE general_ledger_accounts';
EXCEPTION
  WHEN OTHERS THEN
    DBMS_OUTPUT.PUT_LINE('');
END;
/

CREATE TABLE general_ledger_accounts
(
  account_number        NUMBER         NOT NULL,
  account_description    VARCHAR2(50)   NOT NULL,
  CONSTRAINT gl_accounts_pk
    PRIMARY KEY (account_number),
  CONSTRAINT gl_account_description_uq
    UNIQUE (account_description)
);

CREATE TABLE terms
(
  terms_id             NUMBER         NOT NULL,
  terms_description    VARCHAR2(50)   NOT NULL,
  terms_due_days       NUMBER         NOT NULL,
  CONSTRAINT terms_pk
    PRIMARY KEY (terms_id)
);
```

Figure 10-10   The script used to create the AP schema (part 1 of 3)

When you create tables, you must create the tables that don't have foreign keys first. That way, the other tables can define foreign keys that refer to them. In this figure, for example, you can see that I created the Terms and General_Ledger_Accounts tables first since they don't have foreign keys. Then, I coded the Vendors table, which has foreign keys that refer to these tables. And so on.

Conversely, when you drop tables, you must drop the last table that was created first. Then, you can work back to the first table that was created. Otherwise, the foreign keys might not allow you to delete the tables. In this figure, for example, the PL/SQL script deletes the Invoice_Line_Items table and works back from there.

For most of the columns in these tables, I have coded a NOT NULL constraint or a DEFAULT attribute. In general, I only allow a column to accept null values when I want to allow for unknown values. If, for example, a vendor doesn't supply an address, the address is unknown. In that case, you can store a null value in the vendor_address1 and vendor_address2 columns.

Another option is to store an empty string for these columns. To do that, I could have defined the vendor address columns like this:

```
vendor_address1    VARCHAR2(50)    DEFAULT '',
vendor_address2    VARCHAR2(50)    DEFAULT '',
```

In this case, empty strings will be stored for these columns unless other values are assigned to them.

In practice, a null value is a more intuitive representation of an unknown value than a default value is. Conversely, it makes sense to use a default value like an empty string to indicate that a value is known but the column is empty. For example, an empty string might indicate that a vendor hasn't provided its street address. Although how you use nulls and empty strings is largely a matter of personal preference, it does of course affect the way you query a table.

The SQL script that creates the AP schema   **Page 2**

```
CREATE TABLE vendors
(
  vendor_id                    NUMBER          NOT NULL,
  vendor_name                  VARCHAR2(50)    NOT NULL,
  vendor_address1              VARCHAR2(50),
  vendor_address2              VARCHAR2(50),
  vendor_city                  VARCHAR2(50)    NOT NULL,
  vendor_state                 CHAR(2)         NOT NULL,
  vendor_zip_code              VARCHAR2(20)    NOT NULL,
  vendor_phone                 VARCHAR2(50),
  vendor_contact_last_name     VARCHAR2(50),
  vendor_contact_first_name    VARCHAR2(50),
  default_terms_id             NUMBER          NOT NULL,
  default_account_number       NUMBER          NOT NULL,
  CONSTRAINT vendors_pk
    PRIMARY KEY (vendor_id),
  CONSTRAINT vendors_vendor_name_uq
    UNIQUE (vendor_name),
  CONSTRAINT vendors_fk_terms
    FOREIGN KEY (default_terms_id)
    REFERENCES terms (terms_id),
  CONSTRAINT vendors_fk_accounts
    FOREIGN KEY (default_account_number)
    REFERENCES general_ledger_accounts (account_number)
);

CREATE TABLE invoices
(
  invoice_id        NUMBER          NOT NULL,
  vendor_id         NUMBER          NOT NULL,
  invoice_number    VARCHAR2(50)    NOT NULL,
  invoice_date      DATE            NOT NULL,
  invoice_total     NUMBER(9,2)     NOT NULL,
  payment_total     NUMBER(9,2)                      DEFAULT 0,
  credit_total      NUMBER(9,2)                      DEFAULT 0,
  terms_id          NUMBER          NOT NULL,
  invoice_due_date  DATE            NOT NULL,
  payment_date      DATE,
  CONSTRAINT invoices_pk
    PRIMARY KEY (invoice_id),
  CONSTRAINT invoices_fk_vendors
    FOREIGN KEY (vendor_id)
    REFERENCES vendors (vendor_id),
  CONSTRAINT invoices_fk_terms
    FOREIGN KEY (terms_id)
    REFERENCES terms (terms_id)
);
```

Figure 10-10   The script used to create the AP schema (part 2 of 3)

Since Oracle automatically creates an index for each primary key and unique constraint, I provided names for all primary key and unique constraints. I also followed a strict convention for naming these constraints that begins with the name of the table or an abbreviated name for the table.

In addition to the indexes that are created automatically, I used CREATE INDEX statements to create six more indexes to improve the performance of the database. Here again, I followed the naming conventions that I used for the primary key and unique constraints. As a result, if you view the indexes for the schema as shown later in this chapter, it's easy to determine how the indexes relate to the tables.

As you review this script, note that the first five of these indexes are based on the foreign keys that each referring table uses to relate to another table. For example, since the vendor_id column in the Invoices table refers to the vendor_id column in the Vendors table, I created an index on vendor_id in the Invoices table. Finally, I created an index for the invoice_date column in the Invoices table because this column is frequently used to search for rows in this table.

After the indexes, I coded the CREATE SEQUENCE statements for the sequences that are used for the Vendors and Invoices tables. These statements use the STARTS WITH clause to specify a starting number that's larger than the existing primary key values for these tables. To get the starting values, I checked the INSERT statements that are used to initially populate the database. Although these statements aren't shown in this figure, they are coded in the script that creates the AP schema after the DDL statements that are shown in this figure.

The SQL script that creates the AP schema   **Page 3**

```
CREATE TABLE invoice_line_items
(
  invoice_id              NUMBER        NOT NULL,
  invoice_sequence        NUMBER        NOT NULL,
  account_number          NUMBER        NOT NULL,
  line_item_amt           NUMBER(9,2)   NOT NULL,
  line_item_description   VARCHAR2(100) NOT NULL,
  CONSTRAINT line_items_pk
    PRIMARY KEY (invoice_id, invoice_sequence),
  CONSTRAINT line_items_fk_invoices
    FOREIGN KEY (invoice_id) REFERENCES invoices (invoice_id),
  CONSTRAINT line_items_fk_acounts
    FOREIGN KEY (account_number)
      REFERENCES general_ledger_accounts (account_number)
);

-- Create the indexes
CREATE INDEX vendors_terms_id_ix
  ON vendors (default_terms_id);
CREATE INDEX vendors_account_number_ix
  ON vendors (default_account_number);

CREATE INDEX invoices_vendor_id_ix
  ON invoices (vendor_id);
CREATE INDEX invoices_terms_id_ix
  ON invoices (terms_id);
CREATE INDEX line_items_account_number_ix
  ON invoice_line_items (account_number);
CREATE INDEX invoices_invoice_date_ix
  ON invoices (invoice_date DESC);

-- Create the sequences
CREATE SEQUENCE vendor_id_seq
  START WITH 124;
CREATE SEQUENCE invoice_id_seq
  START WITH 115;
```

Description

- Instead of creating database objects one at a time, you can write a *script* that contains all of the statements needed to create the tables, indexes, sequences, and other database objects for a schema.

- Each SQL statement in the script ends with a semicolon.

- Each block of PL/SQL code ends with a front slash (/).

- When you create tables, you must create the tables that don't have foreign keys first. That way, the other tables can define foreign keys that refer to them.

- When you drop tables, you start by dropping the last table that was created and then work back to the first table that was created. Otherwise, the foreign keys might not allow you to delete the tables.

Figure 10-10   The script used to create the AP schema (part 3 of 3)

How to use SQL Developer

Since you often use a script to create tables and other database objects, it's important to understand the DDL skills presented in this chapter. Once you understand these skills, it's easy to learn how to use a graphical user interface such as SQL Developer to work with *database objects* such as tables, indexes, and sequences. For example, it's often useful to view these database objects before writing SELECT, INSERT, UPDATE, or DELETE statements that use them.

How to work with the columns of a table

Figure 10-11 shows how to work with the column definitions of a table. To start, you can view the column definitions for a table by clicking on the table to display it in the main window. In this figure, for example, the Invoices table is shown in the main window. Here, you can see the name, data type, and other attributes of each column in the Invoices table. For example, you can see that the payment_total and credit_total columns specify a default value of 0. In addition, the payment_date column allows null values. As a result, you don't need to specify these columns in an INSERT statement for this table.

If you want to modify the definition for a column, you can right-click on the table and select the Edit command. Then, you can use the resulting dialog box to edit the column or columns that you want to edit. Although this dialog box isn't shown in this figure, you shouldn't have any trouble using it if you understand the DDL statements presented earlier in this chapter.

If you need to add a new table, you can right-click on the Tables folder and select the New Table command. Then, you can use the resulting dialog box to create a new table. Again, you shouldn't have any trouble using this dialog box if you understand how to use DDL to create a table.

How to work with the data of a table

When you view the column definitions of a table, you use the Columns tab of the main window. Then, if you want to view the data for a table, you can click on the Data tab. You can also use the buttons at the top of this tab to insert new rows, update the data in existing rows, and delete existing rows.

The column definitions for the Invoices table

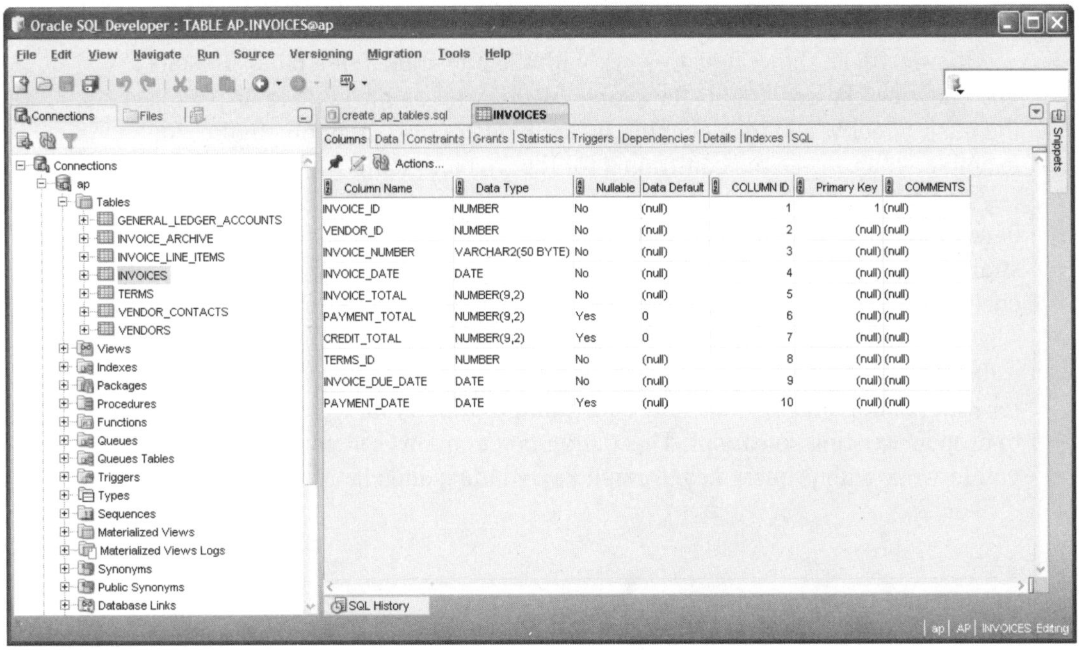

Description

- To view the column definitions for a table, click on the table to display it in the main window.

- To modify the definition for a column, right-click on the table and select the Edit command. Then, use the resulting dialog box to edit the column or columns that you want to edit.

- To add a new table, right-click on the Tables folder and select the New Table command. Then, use the resulting dialog box to create a new table.

- To work with the data for a table, click on the table to display it in the main window, and click on the Data tab. Then, you can view the data for the table, and you can insert, update, and delete rows.

Figure 10-11   How to work with the columns of a table

How to work with the constraints of a table

Figure 10-12 shows how to work with the constraints of a table. To start, you can view the constraints for a table by clicking on the table to display it in the main window and then clicking on the Constraints tab. In this figure, for example, you can see the constraints for the Invoices table. Here, the primary key and foreign key constraints have been named, but the not null constraints haven't been named. As a result, Oracle has generated names for these constraints that begin with SYS_C. Note that these not null constraints are actually check constraints that don't allow null values to be stored in these columns.

Although there are several ways to work constraints, one of the easiest is to right-click on the table and select the Edit command. Then, you can use the resulting dialog box to add a new constraint, to modify an existing constraint, or to drop an existing constraint. This dialog box contains categories that allow you to work with primary key, foreign key, unique, and check constraints.

The constraints for the Invoices table

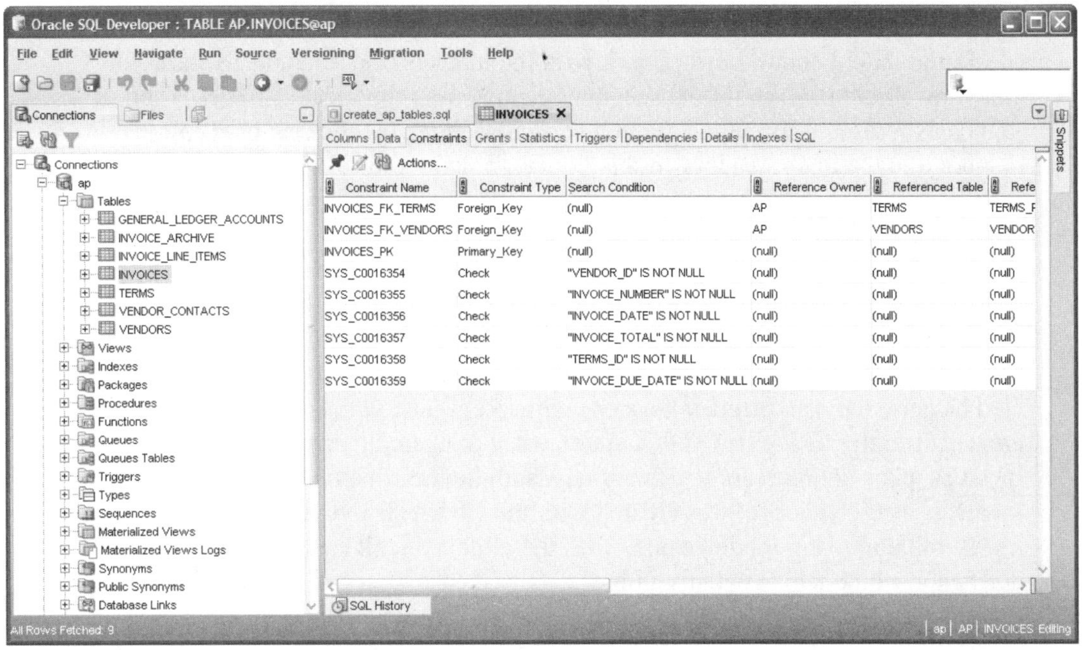

Description

- To view the constraints for a table, click on the table to display it in the main window, and click on the Constraints tab. Then, you can view the constraints for the table, add a new constraint, and alter or drop an existing constraint.

- To work with the constraints for a table, right-click on the table and select the Edit command. Then, you can use the resulting dialog box to work with the primary key, foreign key, unique, and check constraints of the table.

Figure 10-12   How to work with the constraints of a table

How to work with indexes

Figure 10-13 shows how to work with the indexes of a schema. To start, you can view all the indexes for the schema by expanding the Indexes folder. Then, you can get more information about a particular index by clicking on it to display it in the main window. In this figure, for example, all indexes for the AP schema are shown and the index named invoices_pk is displayed in the main window.

Since the script that created the AP schema starts the name for each index with the name of its table, it's easy to find the index that you're looking for. In addition, the suffixes that are used for primary keys (PK), unique keys (UQ), and indexes (IX) make it easy to see which indexes were automatically generated because they are primary keys or unique keys, and which indexes were created with the CREATE INDEX statement. For example, the index named invoices_pk is an index for a primary key, and the index named invoices_invoice_date_ix was created with the CREATE INDEX statement.

If you don't begin index names with the table name, it can be difficult to determine which table contains an index. In that case, you can view the indexes for a particular table by expanding the Tables folder and clicking on the table to display it in the main window. Then, you can click on the Indexes tab to display the indexes for the table.

If you want to work with an existing index, you can right-click on the index, select the appropriate command, and respond to the resulting dialog box. For example, to edit an index, right-click on the index, select the Edit command, and use the resulting dialog box to edit the index.

Finally, if you want to add a new index, you can right-click on the Indexes folder and select the New Index command. Then, you can use the resulting dialog box to add the index.

The indexes for the AP schema

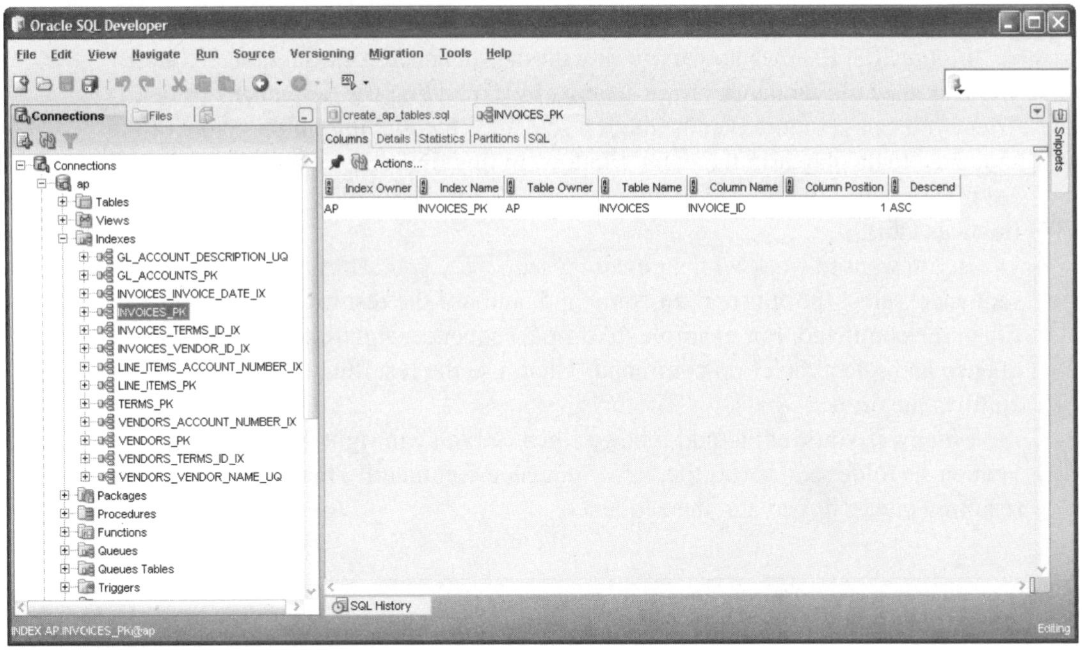

Description

- To view all indexes for a schema, expand the Indexes folder. Then, to get more information about a particular index, click on it to display it in the main window.

- To view the indexes for a particular table, expand the Tables folder and click on the table to display it in the main window. Then, click on the Indexes tab to display the indexes for the table.

- To edit an index, right-click on the index and select the Edit command. Then, use the resulting dialog box to edit the index.

- To drop an index, right-click on the index and select the Drop command. Then, use the resulting dialog box to confirm the drop.

- To add a new index, right-click on the Indexes folder and select the New Index command. Then, use the resulting dialog box to add the index.

Figure 10-13   How to work with indexes

How to work with sequences

Figure 10-14 shows how to work with the sequences of a schema. To start, you can view the sequences for a schema by expanding the Sequences folder. Then, you can get more details about a sequence by clicking on the name of the sequence to display it in the main window. In this figure, for example, you can see the sequence that's used to generate values for the invoice_id column of the Invoices table.

If you want to work with an existing sequence, you can right-click on the sequence, select the appropriate command, and use the resulting dialog box to finish the command. For example, to drop a sequence, right-click on the sequence and select the Drop command. Then, use the resulting dialog box to confirm the drop.

Finally, if you want to add a new sequence, you can right-click on the Sequences folder and select the New Sequence command. Then, you can use the resulting dialog box to add the sequence.

The sequences for the AP schema

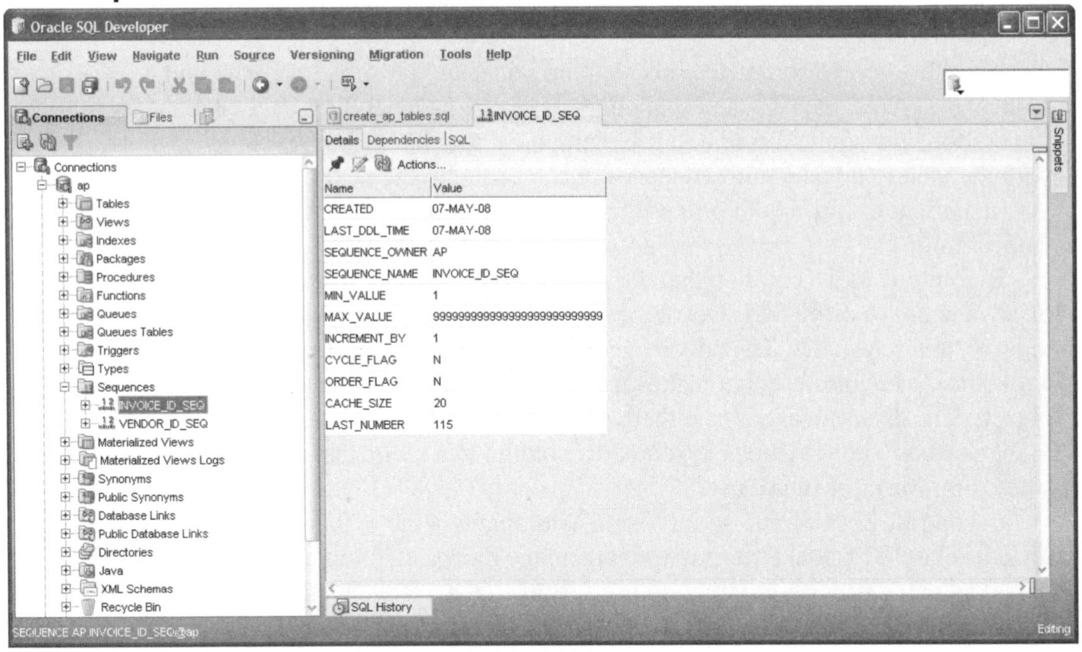

Description

- To view the sequences for a schema, expand the Sequences folder. Then, to get more information about a sequence, click on the name of the sequence to display it in the main window.

- To edit a sequence, right-click on the sequence and select the Edit command. Then, use the resulting dialog box to edit the sequence.

- To drop a sequence, right-click on the sequence and select the Drop command. Then, use the resulting dialog box to confirm the drop.

- To add a new sequence, right-click on the Sequences folder and select the New Sequence command. Then, use the resulting dialog box to add the sequence.

Figure 10-14   How to work with sequences

Perspective

Now that you've completed this chapter, you should be able to create and modify the tables, indexes, and sequences of a schema by coding DDL statements. In addition, you should be able to use a graphical tool like SQL Developer to work with the tables, indexes, and sequences of a schema. In the next two chapters, you'll learn how to use both of these techniques to work with other types of database objects.

Before you move on, though, take a moment to consider the advantages and disadvantages of using SQL Developer to work with database objects like tables, indexes, and sequences. The advantage, of course, is that SQL Developer provides a graphical user interface that makes it easy to view and work with database objects. The disadvantage is that there is no record of any changes that you make to the database. For example, if you add a column to a table, that change isn't stored anywhere for future use.

In contrast, if you use a script to add a column to a table, that change is stored for future use. This makes it easy to recreate the database if you ever need to do that. And that's why it's common to use scripts to make any changes to the structure of a database. On the other hand, the SQL Developer is an excellent tool for quickly viewing the objects of a database or for quickly creating temporary tables or other objects that won't need to be recreated later.

Terms

attribute	reference constraint
constraint	cascading delete
column-level constraint	check constraint
table-level constraint	index
not null constraint	function-based index
unique constraint	sequence
primary key constraint	script
foreign key constraint	database object

Exercises

Add constraints and an index to the AP schema

1. Write an ALTER TABLE statement that adds two new check constraints to the Invoices table of the AP schema. The first should allow (1) payment_date to be null only if payment_total is zero and (2) payment_date to be not null only if payment_total is greater than zero. The second constraint should prevent the sum of payment_total and credit_total from being greater than invoice_total.

2. Add an index to the AP schema for the zip code field in the Vendors table.

Implement a database design

3. Write the CREATE TABLE statements needed to implement the following design in the EX schema:

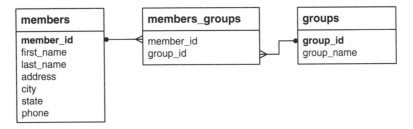

These tables provide for members of an association, and each member can be registered in one or more groups within the association. There should be one row for each member in the Members table and one row for each group in the Groups table. The member ID and group ID columns are the primary keys for the Members and Groups tables. And the Members_Groups table relates each member to one or more groups.

When you create the tables, be sure to include the key constraints. Also, include any null or default constraints that you think are necessary.

4. Write INSERT statements that add two rows to the Members table for member IDs 1 and 2, two rows to the Groups table for group IDs 1 and 2, and three rows to the Group_Membership table: one row for member 1 and group 2; one for member 2 and group 1; and one for member 2 and group 2. Then, write a SELECT statement that joins the three tables and retrieves the group name, member last name, and member first name.

5. Create sequences that can be used to number the member ID and group ID values starting with 3 (since you already added members and groups for IDs 1 and 2).

6. Write an INSERT statement that adds another row to the Groups table. This statement should use the NEXTVAL pseudo column to get the value for the next group ID from the sequence that you created in exercise 5. Then, write a SELECT statement that gets all of the data for all of the rows in the Groups table to make sure your sequence worked correctly.

7. Write an ALTER TABLE statement that adds two new columns to the Members table: one column for annual dues that provides for three digits to the left of the decimal point and two to the right; and one column for the payment date. The annual dues column should have a default value of 52.50.

8. Write an ALTER TABLE statement that modifies the Groups table so the group name in each row has to be unique. Then, re-run the INSERT statement that you used in exercise 6 to make sure this works.

11

How to create views

As you've seen throughout this book, SELECT queries can be complicated, particularly if they use multiple joins, subqueries, or complex functions. Because of that, you may want to save the queries you use regularly. One way to do that is to store the statement in a script file. Another way is to create a view.

Unlike scripts, which are stored in files, views are stored as part of the database. As a result, they can be used by SQL programmers and by custom applications that have access to the database. This provides some advantages over using tables directly.

An introduction to views

Before you learn the details for working with a view, it's helpful to get a general idea of how a view works. In addition, it's helpful to consider some of the benefits of views so you can determine whether you want to use them.

How views work

A *view* is a SELECT statement that's stored in the database as a database object. To create a view, you use a CREATE VIEW statement like the one shown in figure 11-1. This statement creates a view named vendors_min that retrieves the vendor_name, vendor_state, and vendor_phone columns from the Vendors table.

You can think of a view as a virtual table that consists only of the rows and columns specified in its CREATE VIEW statement. The table or tables that are listed in the FROM clause are called the *base tables* for the view. Since the view refers back to the base tables, it doesn't store any data itself, and it always reflects the most current data in the base tables.

To use a view, you refer to it from another SQL statement. In this figure, for example, the SELECT statement uses the vendors_min view in the FROM clause instead of a table. As a result, this SELECT statement extracts its result set from the virtual table that the view represents. In this case, all the rows for vendors in California are retrieved from the view.

When you create a view like the one in this figure, the view is updateable. As a result, it's possible to use the view in an INSERT, UPDATE, or DELETE statement. In this figure, for example, the UPDATE statement uses the vendors_min view to update the vendor_phone column in the Vendors table for the specified vendor.

To drop a view, you can use the DROP VIEW statement as shown in this figure. This works similarly to the DROP statements for tables, indexes, and sequences that you learned about in the previous chapter.

Because a view is stored as an object in a database, it can be used by anyone who has access to the database. That includes users who have access to the database through applications that provide for ad hoc queries and report generation. In addition, that includes custom applications that are written specifically to work with the data in the database. In fact, views are often designed to be used with these types of applications.

A CREATE VIEW statement for a view named Vendors_Min

```
CREATE VIEW vendors_min AS
  SELECT vendor_name, vendor_state, vendor_phone
  FROM vendors;
```

The virtual table that's represented by the view

	VENDOR_NAME	VENDOR_STATE	VENDOR_PHONE
1	US Postal Service	WI	(800) 555-1205
2	National Information Data Ctr	DC	(301) 555-8950
3	Register of Copyrights	DC	NULL
4	Jobtrak	CA	(800) 555-8725
5	Newbrige Book Clubs	NJ	(800) 555-9980

```
(122 rows)
```

A SELECT statement that uses the Vendors_Min view

```
SELECT * FROM vendors_min
WHERE vendor_state = 'CA'
ORDER BY vendor_name
```

The result set that's returned by the SELECT statement

	VENDOR_NAME	VENDOR_STATE	VENDOR_PHONE
1	ASC Signs	CA	NULL
2	Abbey Office Furnishings	CA	(559) 555-8300
3	American Express	CA	(800) 555-3344
4	Aztek Label	CA	(714) 555-9000
5	BFI Industries	CA	(559) 555-1551

```
(75 rows)
```

An UPDATE statement that uses a view to update the base table

```
UPDATE vendors_min
SET vendor_phone = '(800) 555-3941'
WHERE vendor_name = 'Register of Copyrights'
```

The response from the system

```
1 rows updated
```

A statement that drops a view

```
DROP VIEW vendors_min
```

Description

- A *view* consists of a SELECT statement that's stored as an object in the database. The tables referenced in the SELECT statement are called the *base tables* for the view.

- When you create a view, you can refer to the view anywhere you would normally use a table in any of the data manipulation statements: SELECT, INSERT, UPDATE, and DELETE.

- Although a view behaves like a virtual table, it doesn't store any data. Instead, a view always refers back to its base tables.

- A view can also be referred to as a *viewed table* because it provides a view to the underlying base tables.

Figure 11-1   How views work

Benefits of using views

Figure 11-2 describes some of the advantages of using views. To start, you can use views to limit the exposure of the tables in your database to external users and applications. To illustrate, suppose a view refers to a table that you've decided to divide into two tables. To accommodate this change, you simply modify the view. In other words, you don't have to modify any statements that refer to the view. That means that users who query the database using the view don't have to be aware of the change in the database structure, and application programs that use the view don't have to be modified.

You can also use views to restrict access to a database. To do that, you include just the columns and rows you want a user or an application to have access to in the view. Then, you let the user or application access the data only through the views. For example, let's assume you have an Employees table that has a salary column that contains information about each employee's salary. In this case, you can create a view that doesn't include the salary column for the users who need to view and maintain this table, but who should not be able to view salaries. Then, you can create another view that includes the salary column for the users who need to view and maintain salary information.

In addition, you can use views to hide the complexity of a SELECT statement. For example, if you have a long and unwieldy SELECT statement that joins multiple tables, you can create a view for that statement. This makes it easier for you and other database users to work with this data.

Finally, when you create a view, you can allow data in the base table to be updated through the view. To do that, you use INSERT, UPDATE, or DELETE statements to work with the view.

Some of the benefits provided by views

Benefit	Description
Design independence	Views can limit the exposure of tables to external users and applications. As a result, if the design of the tables changes, you can modify the view as necessary so the users and applications that use the view don't need to be modified.
Data security	Views can restrict access to the data in a table by using the SELECT clause to not include all columns of a table or by using the WHERE clause to not include all rows in a table.
Simplified queries	Views can be used to hide the complexity of retrieval operations. Then, the data can be retrieved using simple SELECT statements that specify a view in the FROM clause.
Updatability	With certain restrictions, views can be used to update, insert, and delete data from a base table.

Description

- You can create a view based on almost any SELECT statement. That means that you can code views that join tables, summarize data, and use subqueries and functions.

Figure 11-2   Benefits of using views

How to work with views

Now that you have a general understanding of how views work and of the benefits that they provide, you're ready to learn the details for working with them.

How to create a view

Figure 11-3 presents the CREATE VIEW statement that you use to create a view. In its simplest form, you code the CREATE VIEW keywords, followed by the name of the view, followed by the AS keyword and the SELECT statement that defines the view. In this figure, for instance, the first statement creates a view named vendors_phone_list. This view includes four columns from the Vendors table for all vendors with invoices.

If you execute the first CREATE VIEW statement and a view with that name doesn't already exist in the current database/schema, Oracle will add the view, and it will display a message to indicate that the statement was successful. However, if a statement with this name already exists, Oracle won't add the view, and it will display a message that indicates that the name is already in use. In that case, you will need to specify a new name for the view, or you will need to drop the view that's already using that name.

When you code a CREATE VIEW statement, you can specify that you want to automatically drop any views that have the same name as the view that you're creating. To do that, you can specify the OR REPLACE keywords after the CREATE keyword as shown in all of the examples in this figure except for the first.

The SELECT statement for a view can use most of the features of a normal SELECT statement. In this figure, for instance, the second example creates a view that joins data from two tables. Similarly, the third statement creates a view that uses a subquery and the ROWNUM pseudo column.

By default, the columns in a view are given the same names as the columns in the base tables. If a view contains a calculated column, however, you'll want to name that column just as you do in other SELECT statements. In addition, you'll need to rename columns from different tables that have the same name. To do that, you can code the column names in the CREATE VIEW clause as shown in the fourth example. Or, you can use the AS clause as shown in the fifth example.

Note that you have to name all of the columns in the fourth example. In contrast, in the fifth example, you only have to name the columns you need to rename. As a result, you'll typically want to use the technique presented in the fifth example.

The syntax of the CREATE VIEW statement

```
CREATE [OR REPLACE] [{FORCE|NOFORCE}] VIEW view_name
  [(column_alias_1[, column_alias_2]...)]
AS
  select_statement
  [WITH {READ ONLY|CHECK OPTION} [CONSTRAINT constraint_name]]
```

A CREATE VIEW statement that creates a view of vendors that have invoices

```
CREATE VIEW vendors_phone_list AS
  SELECT vendor_name, vendor_contact_last_name,
         vendor_contact_first_name, vendor_phone
  FROM vendors
  WHERE vendor_id IN (SELECT vendor_id FROM invoices)
```

A CREATE VIEW statement that uses a join

```
CREATE OR REPLACE VIEW vendor_invoices AS
  SELECT vendor_name, invoice_number, invoice_date, invoice_total
  FROM vendors
    JOIN invoices ON vendors.vendor_id = invoices.vendor_id
```

A CREATE VIEW statement that uses a subquery

```
CREATE OR REPLACE VIEW top5_invoice_totals AS
  SELECT vendor_id, invoice_total
  FROM (SELECT vendor_id, invoice_total FROM invoices
        ORDER BY invoice_total DESC)
  WHERE ROWNUM <= 5
```

A statement that names all the view columns in its CREATE VIEW clause

```
CREATE OR REPLACE VIEW invoices_outstanding
  (invoice_number, invoice_date, invoice_total, balance_due)
AS
  SELECT invoice_number, invoice_date, invoice_total,
         invoice_total - payment_total - credit_total
  FROM invoices
  WHERE invoice_total - payment_total - credit_total > 0
```

A statement that names just the calculated column in its SELECT clause

```
CREATE OR REPLACE VIEW invoices_outstanding AS
  SELECT invoice_number, invoice_date, invoice_total,
         invoice_total - payment_total - credit_total AS balance_due
  FROM invoices
  WHERE invoice_total - payment_total - credit_total > 0
```

Figure 11-3   How to create a view (part 1 of 2)

The first example in part 2 of this figure creates a view that summarizes the rows in the Invoices table by vendor. This shows that a view can use aggregate functions and the GROUP BY clause to summarize data. In this case, the rows are grouped by vendor name, and a count of the invoices and the invoice total are calculated for each vendor.

If you attempt to create a view for a base table that doesn't exist, Oracle will display an error message that indicates that the base table doesn't exist. Since this prevents you from creating views for tables that don't exist, this is usually what you want. However, if you want to create a view first and create a table later, you can use the FORCE option to create a view for a table that doesn't exist as shown in the second example in part 2 of this figure. Of course, this view won't display any data until a table named Products is created and the product_description and product_price columns are filled with some data.

When you code views, the SELECT statement you code within the definition of a view can refer to another view. In other words, views can be *nested*. In theory, *nested views* can make it easier to present data to your users. In practice, using nested view can make the dependencies between tables and views confusing, which can make your code difficult to maintain. As a result, if you use nested views, you should use them carefully.

Although this figure shows most of the skills that you'll need for creating views, it doesn't show how to use the WITH READ ONLY or WITH CHECK OPTION clauses. Instead, the next two figures show how to use those clauses.

A CREATE VIEW statement that summarizes invoices by vendor

```
CREATE OR REPLACE VIEW invoice_summary AS
  SELECT vendor_name,
    COUNT(*) AS invoice_count,
    SUM(invoice_total) AS invoice_total_sum
  FROM vendors
    JOIN invoices ON vendors.vendor_id = invoices.vendor_id
  GROUP BY vendor_name
```

A CREATE VIEW statement that uses the FORCE option

```
CREATE FORCE VIEW products_list AS
  SELECT product_description, product_price
  FROM products
```

Description

- You use the CREATE VIEW statement to create a view.

- If you include the OR REPLACE keyword, the CREATE VIEW statement will replace any existing view that has the same name. Otherwise, you must specify a new name for the view.

- If you include the FORCE keyword, the CREATE VIEW statement will create the view even if the underlying tables don't exist. Otherwise, you must specify underlying tables that exist.

- If you name the columns of a view in the CREATE VIEW clause, you have to name all of the columns. In contrast, if you name the columns in the SELECT clause, you can name just the columns you need to rename.

- You can create a view that's based on another view rather than on a table. This is known as a *nested view*.

Figure 11-3   How to create a view (part 2 of 2)

How to create an updatable view

Once you create a view, you can refer to it in a SELECT statement. In addition, you can refer to it in INSERT, UPDATE, and DELETE statements to modify the data that's stored in an underlying table. To do that, the view must be updatable. Figure 11-4 lists the requirements for creating *updatable views*.

The first two requirements have to do with what you can code in the select list of the SELECT statement that defines the view. In particular, the select list can't include the DISTINCT clause, and it can't include aggregate functions. In addition, the SELECT statement can't include a GROUP BY or HAVING clause, and two SELECT statements can't be joined by a union operation.

The first CREATE VIEW statement in this figure creates a view that's updatable. This view adheres to all of the requirements for updatable views. As a result, you can refer to it in an INSERT, UPDATE, or DELETE statement. For example, you can use the first UPDATE statement shown in this figure to update the credit_total column in the Invoices base table.

However, you can't update any calculated columns that are used by the view. For example, you can't use the second UPDATE statement shown in this figure to update the balance_due column that's calculated from the other columns in the view.

In addition, when you update data through a view, you can only update the data in a single base table, even if the view refers to two or more tables. In this figure, for instance, the view includes data from two base tables, the Vendors and Invoices tables. However, since the first UPDATE statement only refers to columns in the Invoices table, it is able to update data in that table.

How to create a read-only view

If you don't follow the requirements for creating an updateable view, Oracle will automatically add the WITH READ ONLY clause to the view to create a *read-only view*. Then, you won't be able to use a view to update any columns in the base table. If you attempt to do this, you'll get an error message.

If you want to make sure that a view is a read-only view, you can add the WITH READ ONLY clause to the CREATE VIEW statement. In this figure, for instance, the last example creates a read-only view. As a result, your users won't be able to use this view to update data in the Invoices table.

Requirements for creating updatable views

- The select list can't include a DISTINCT clause.
- The select list can't include an aggregate function.
- The SELECT statement can't include a GROUP BY or HAVING clause.
- The view can't include the UNION operator.

A CREATE VIEW statement that creates an updatable view

```
CREATE OR REPLACE VIEW balance_due_view AS
   SELECT vendor_name, invoice_number,
         invoice_total, payment_total, credit_total,
         invoice_total - payment_total - credit_total AS balance_due
   FROM vendors JOIN invoices ON vendors.vendor_id = invoices.vendor_id
   WHERE invoice_total - payment_total - credit_total > 0
```

An UPDATE statement that uses the view to update data

```
UPDATE balance_due_view
SET credit_total = 300
WHERE invoice_number = '989319-497'
```

The response from the system

```
1 rows updated
```

An UPDATE statement that attempts to use the view to update a calculated column

```
UPDATE balance_due_view
SET balance_due = 0
WHERE invoice_number = '989319-497';
```

The response from the system

```
SQL Error: ORA-01733: virtual column not allowed here
```

A CREATE VIEW statement that creates a read-only view

```
CREATE OR REPLACE VIEW balance_due_view AS
   SELECT vendor_name, invoice_number,
         invoice_total, payment_total, credit_total,
         invoice_total - payment_total - credit_total AS balance_due
   FROM vendors JOIN invoices ON vendors.vendor_id = invoices.vendor_id
   WHERE invoice_total - payment_total - credit_total > 0
WITH READ ONLY;
```

Description

- An *updatable view* is a view that can be used in an INSERT, UPDATE, or DELETE statement to update the data in the base table.
- A *read-only view* is a view that cannot be used to update the data in the base table. To create a read-only view, you can code the WITH READ ONLY clause.
- The requirements for coding updatable views are more restrictive than for coding read-only views. That's because Oracle must be able to unambiguously determine which base tables and columns are affected.

Figure 11-4   How to create updatable and read-only views

How to use the WITH CHECK OPTION clause

Figure 11-5 shows an example of an updateable view that uses the WITH CHECK OPTION clause to prevent an update if it causes the row to be excluded from the view. To start, the CREATE VIEW statement creates an updatable view named vendor_payment that joins data from the Vendors and Invoices tables and displays all invoices that have a balance due that's greater than zero.

Then, the first UPDATE statement uses this view to modify the payment_date and payment_total columns for a specific invoice. This works because this UPDATE statement doesn't exclude the row from the view.

However, the second UPDATE statement causes the balance due to become less than zero. As a result, this statement fails due to the WITH CHECK OPTION clause and an error is displayed. Since this can prevent users from storing invalid data in a database, this clause can be useful in some situations.

An updatable view that has a WITH CHECK OPTION clause

```
CREATE OR REPLACE VIEW vendor_payment AS
  SELECT vendor_name, invoice_number, invoice_date, payment_date,
         invoice_total, credit_total, payment_total
  FROM vendors JOIN invoices ON vendors.vendor_id = invoices.vendor_id
  WHERE invoice_total - payment_total - credit_total >= 0
WITH CHECK OPTION
```

A SELECT statement that displays a row from the view

```
SELECT * FROM vendor_payment
WHERE invoice_number = 'P-0608'
```

The result set

	VENDOR_NAME	INVOICE_NUM...	INVOICE_DATE	PAYMENT_DATE	INVOICE_TOTAL	CREDIT_TOTAL	PAYMENT_TOTAL
1	Malloy Lithographing...	P-0608	11-APR-08	(null)	20551.18	1200	0

An UPDATE statement that updates the view

```
UPDATE vendor_payment
SET payment_total = 400.00,
    payment_date = '01-AUG-08'
WHERE invoice_number = 'P-0608'
```

The response from the system

```
1 rows updated
```

The same row data after the update

	VENDOR_NAME	INVOICE_NUM...	INVOICE_DATE	PAYMENT_DATE	INVOICE_TOTAL	CREDIT_TOTAL	PAYMENT_TOTAL
1	Malloy Lithographing...	P-0608	11-APR-08	01-AUG-08	20551.18	1200	400

An UPDATE statement that attempts to update the view

```
UPDATE vendor_payment
SET payment_total = 30000.00,
    payment_date = '01-AUG-08'
WHERE invoice_number = 'P-0608';
```

The response from the system

```
SQL Error: ORA-01402: view WITH CHECK OPTION where-clause violation
```

Description

- If you don't include a WITH CHECK OPTION clause when you create a view, a change you make through the view can cause the modified rows to no longer be included in the view.

- If you specify a WITH CHECK OPTION clause when you create a view, an error will occur if you try to modify a row in such a way that it would no longer be included in the view.

Figure 11-5   How to use the WITH CHECK OPTION clause

How to insert or delete rows through a view

In the previous figures, you learned how to use a view to update data in the underlying tables. Now, figure 11-6 shows how to use a view to insert or delete data in an underlying view. In general, this works the same as it does for a table. However, due to table constraints, using a view to insert or delete rows often results in errors like the ones shown in this figure. As a result, it's generally more common to work directly with base tables when inserting or deleting rows.

To insert rows through a view, you can use the INSERT statement as shown in figure 11-6. At the top of this figure, you can see a CREATE VIEW statement for a view named ibm_invoices. This view retrieves columns and rows from the Invoices table for the vendor named IBM, which has a vendor_id of 34. Then, the INSERT statement attempts to insert a row into the Invoices table through this view.

This insert operation fails, though, because the view and the INSERT statement don't include all of the required columns for the Invoices table. In this case, a value is required for the other columns in the Invoices table including the invoice_id and invoice_due_date columns. As a result, to be able to use a view to insert rows, you must design a view that includes all required columns for the underlying table.

In addition, an INSERT statement that uses a view can insert rows into only one table. That's true even if the view is based on two or more tables and all of the required columns for those tables are included in the view. In that case, you could use a separate INSERT statement to insert rows into each table through the view.

Figure 11-6 also shows how to delete rows through a view. To do that, you use a DELETE statement like the one shown here. To start, the first DELETE statement attempts to delete an invoice from the Invoices table through the ibm_invoices view. However, this DELETE statement fails because the invoice contains line items. This causes an error message like the one in this figure to be displayed. As a result, to get this DELETE statement to work, you must delete the related line items for the specified invoice before you use the ibm_invoices view to delete the invoice as shown by the last two DELETE statements in this figure.

A statement that creates an updatable view

```
CREATE OR REPLACE VIEW ibm_invoices AS
  SELECT invoice_number, invoice_date, invoice_total
  FROM invoices
  WHERE vendor_id = 34;
```

The contents of the view

	INVOICE_NUMBER	INVOICE_DATE	INVOICE_TOTAL
1	QP58872	25-FEB-08	116.54
2	Q545443	14-MAR-08	1083.58

An INSERT statement that fails due to columns with null values

```
INSERT INTO ibm_invoices
  (invoice_number, invoice_date, invoice_total)
VALUES
  ('RA23988', '31-JUL-08', 417.34)
```

The response from the system

```
SQL Error: ORA-01400: cannot insert NULL into
("AP"."INVOICES"."INVOICE_ID")
```

A DELETE statement that fails due to a foreign key constraint

```
DELETE FROM ibm_invoices
WHERE invoice_number = 'Q545443'
```

The response from the system

```
SQL Error: ORA-02292: integrity constraint (AP.LINE_ITEMS_FK_INVOICES)
violated - child record found
```

Two DELETE statements that succeed

```
DELETE FROM invoice_line_items
WHERE invoice_id = (SELECT invoice_id FROM invoices
                    WHERE invoice_number = 'Q545443');

DELETE FROM ibm_invoices
WHERE invoice_number = 'Q545443';
```

The response from the system

```
1 rows deleted
```

Description

- You can use the INSERT statement to insert rows into a base table through a view. To do that, you name the view in the INSERT clause. Both the view and the INSERT statement must include all of the columns from the base table that require a value.

- If the view names more than one base table, an INSERT statement can insert data into only one of those tables.

- You can use the DELETE statement to delete rows from a base table through a view. To do that, you name the view in the DELETE clause. For this to work, the view must be based on a single table.

Figure 11-6   How to insert or delete rows through a view

How to alter or drop a view

Although Oracle supports an ALTER VIEW statement, it's usually easier to alter a view by using the CREATE OR REPLACE VIEW statement to replace the existing view with a new one. In figure 11-7, for instance, the first example uses a CREATE VIEW statement to create a view named vendors_sw that retrieves rows from the Vendors table for vendors located in four states. Then, the second example uses the CREATE OR REPLACE VIEW statement to modify this view so it includes vendors in two additional states and is read-only.

To drop a view, you use the DROP VIEW statement to name the view you want to drop. In this figure, for instance, the third example drops the view named vendors_sw. Like the other statements for dropping database objects, this statement permanently deletes the view. As a result, you should be careful when you use it.

A statement that creates a view

```
CREATE VIEW vendors_sw AS
SELECT *
FROM vendors
WHERE vendor_state IN ('CA','AZ','NV','NM')
```

A statement that replaces the view with a new read-only view

```
CREATE OR REPLACE VIEW vendors_sw AS
SELECT *
FROM vendors
WHERE vendor_state IN ('CA','AZ','NV','NM','UT','CO')
WITH READ ONLY;
```

A statement that drops the view

```
DROP VIEW vendors_sw
```

Description

- To alter a view, use the CREATE OR REPLACE VIEW statement to replace the existing view with a new one.
- To delete a view from the database, use the DROP VIEW statement.

Figure 11-7   How to alter or drop a view

How to use SQL Developer

Once you understand how to write SQL code that creates and drops views, it's easy to learn how to use a graphical user interface such as SQL Developer to work with views. If you experiment with SQL Developer, I think you'll find that it's particularly useful for getting information about existing views.

How to get information about a view

Figure 11-8 shows how to use SQL Developer to get information about an existing view. To start, you can expand the Views folder to see a list of all views that are stored in a schema. In this figure, for example, the Views folder shows all of the views in the AP schema that were created by the SQL statements presented earlier in this chapter. Here, the balance_due_view is selected and displayed in the main window, and the Columns tab presents information about the columns of this view.

If you want to view the data that's retrieved by a view, you can click on the Data tab. Then, if the view is updateable, you can use the buttons at the top of this tab to insert, update, and delete rows.

If you want to get other information about a view, you can click on the appropriate tab. In particular, you can click on the Grants tab to see the users that have been granted privileges for working with the view. You can click on the Dependencies tab to view the tables that the view depends on. You can view the Details tab to get miscellaneous information about the view. And you can click on the SQL tab to see the SQL code that was used to create the view.

How to drop a view

Using SQL Developer to drop a view works the same as using SQL Developer to drop any other type of database object. To start, right-click the view and select the Drop command. Then, use the resulting dialog box to confirm the drop.

How to alter or create a view

To alter the design of an existing view, you can right-click on the view and select the Edit command. Or, to create a new view, you can right-click on the Views folder and select the New View command. Then, with a little experimentation, you should be able to use the resulting dialog box to alter or create the view. This dialog box allows you to directly modify the SQL code, and it allows you to generate SQL code by selecting tables and columns from the graphical user interface.

SQL Developer with the views for the AP schema displayed

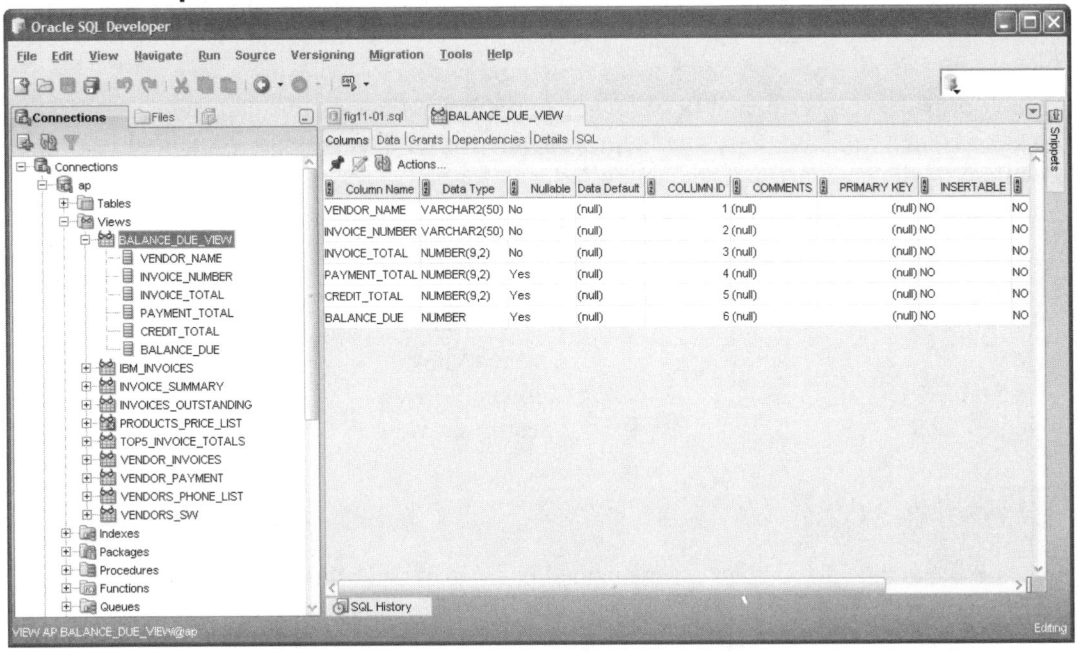

Description

- To examine the columns of a view, expand the Views folder and click on the view to display it in the main window. Then, if necessary, click on the Columns tab.

- To work with the data for a view, click on the view to display it in the main window, and click on the Data tab. Then, you can view the data for the table, and you can insert, update, and delete rows if the view is updateable.

- To get other information about a view, click on the view to display it in the main window. Then, click on the Grants, Dependencies, Details, or SQL tab.

- To drop a view, right-click on the view and select the Drop command. Then, use the resulting dialog box to confirm the drop.

- To modify the design of an existing view, right-click on the view and select the Edit command. Then, use the resulting dialog box to modify the view.

- To create a new view, right-click on the Views folder and select the New View command. Then, use the resulting dialog box to create a new view.

Figure 11-8   How to use SQL Developer to work with views

Perspective

In this chapter, you learned how to create and use views. As you've seen, views provide a powerful and flexible way to predefine the data that can be retrieved from a database. By using them, you can restrict the access to a database while providing a consistent and simplified way for end users and application programs to access that data.

Terms

view	nested view
base table	updatable view
viewed table	read-only view

Exercises

1. Create a view that defines a view named open_items that shows the invoices that haven't been paid. This view should return four columns from the Vendors and Invoices tables: vendor_name, invoice_number, invoice_total, and balance_due (invoice_total – payment_total – credit_total). However, a row should only be returned when the balance due is greater than zero, and the rows should be in sequence by vendor_name. Then, run the script to create the view, and use SQL Developer to review the data that it returns. (You may have to click on the Refresh button in the Connections window after you click on the Views node to show the view you just created.)

2. Write a SELECT statement that returns all of the columns in the open_items view that you created in exercise 1, with one row for each invoice that has a balance due of $1000 or more.

3. Create a view named open_items_summary that returns one summary row for each vendor that contains invoices with unpaid balance dues. Each row should include vendor_name, open_item_count (the number of invoices with a balance due), and open_item_total (the total of the balance due amounts), and the rows should be sorted by the open item totals in descending sequence. Then, run the script to create the view, and use SQL Developer to review the data that it returns.

4. Write a SELECT statement that returns just the first 5 rows in the open_items_summary view that you created in exercise 3.

5. Create an updatable view named vendor_address that returns the vendor_id, both address columns, and the city, state, and zip code columns for each vendor. Then, use SQL Developer to review the data in this view.

6. Write an UPDATE statement that changes the address for the row with vendor ID 4 so the suite number (Ste 260) is stored in vendor_address2 instead of vendor_address1. Then, use SQL Developer to verify the change (you may need to click the Refresh button at the top of the Data tab to see the change). If this works correctly, go back to the tab for the UPDATE statement and click the Commit button to commit the change.

12

How to manage
database security

If you have installed Oracle XE on your own computer, and you have only been working with sample databases, security hasn't been of concern. However, when you use Oracle in a production environment, you must configure security to prevent misuse of your data. In this chapter, you'll learn how to do that by writing SQL statements to create users that have restricted access to your database. In addition, you'll learn how to use SQL Developer to perform many of the security-related tasks that you can perform with SQL code.

An introduction to database security

Before you learn the details of coding security-related SQL statements, it's helpful to understand some of the general concepts for working with security.

How to create an admin user

Figure 12-1 begins by presenting a script that creates an administrative (or admin) user that has all privileges for working with the objects of a database. In this script, the first statement connects to the database as a user that has all privileges, including the capability to create users and grant privileges. In this case, that user is the system user that's created when Oracle is installed. If you don't have access to this user, you may need to consult your DBA to learn how to connect as a user with suitable privileges.

After this script connects to the database, it creates a user named AR with a password of AR. In addition, this statement sets the default tablespace for the AR user to the Users tablespace. A *tablespace* is a container that can store users and other database objects such as tables and views. Typically, each tablespace is stored in a separate file.

The Users tablespace is created when Oracle is installed, and it's a good place to store users. In this figure, for example, the code stores the AR user and all of its objects in the Users tablespace. Although it's possible to store users and their objects in the System tablespace, this is generally considered a bad practice since the System tablespace should be reserved for internal use by Oracle.

After the script creates the AR user, it grants all privileges to this user. As a result, this user will be able to execute DDL statements to create tables, sequences, views, and other database objects. In addition, this user will be able to execute DML statements such as the SELECT, INSERT, UPDATE, and DELETE statements.

After this script grants privileges to the AR user, it connects as the AR user. Then, it uses the CREATE TABLE statement to create a table named Customers. Since this statement doesn't specify a schema for the table, the table is stored in a schema with the same name as the user. As a result, the Customers table is stored in the AR schema, which is stored in the Users tablespace. A *schema* helps to group the tables in a database.

After this script creates the Customers table, it uses three INSERT statements to insert three rows into the table. Since the script is still connected as the AR user, there's no need to qualify the table name with the schema name in these statements. However, if you were connected as another user, you would need to qualify the table name with the schema name like this:

```
INSERT INTO ar.customers VALUES (1, 'Jack', 'Samson');
```

Finally, this figure shows how to drop a user. To do that, you can use the DROP USER statement. However, if the user contains tables or other database objects, Oracle will display an error message like the one shown in this figure,

A script that creates a user named AR and a table named Customers

```
-- connect as the SYSTEM user and create the AR user
CONNECT system/system;
CREATE USER ar IDENTIFIED BY ar DEFAULT TABLESPACE users;
GRANT ALL PRIVILEGES TO ar;

-- connect as the AR user and create the Customers table
CONNECT ar/ar;
CREATE TABLE customers
(
  customer_id              NUMBER           NOT NULL,
  customer_first_name      VARCHAR2(50)     NOT NULL,
  customer_last_name       VARCHAR2(50)     NOT NULL,
  CONSTRAINT customers_pk
    PRIMARY KEY (customer_id)
);
INSERT INTO customers VALUES (1, 'Jack', 'Samson');
INSERT INTO customers VALUES (2, 'Joan', 'Redding');
INSERT INTO customers VALUES (3, 'Jim', 'Abbot');
```

A statement that attempts to drop the AR user

```
DROP USER ar
```

The response from the system

```
SQL Error: ORA-01922: CASCADE must be specified to drop 'AR'
*Cause:    Cascade is required to remove this user from the system.  The
           user own's object which will need to be dropped.
*Action:   Specify cascade.
```

A statement that drops the AR user and the table

```
DROP USER ar CASCADE
```

Description

- In a script, you can use the CONNECT command to connect to a database with the specified username/password.

- You can use the CREATE USER statement to create a username and password for a user. When you do that, it's a good practice to specify a default tablespace for the user. A *tablespace* is a container for tables and other database objects.

- You can use the GRANT ALL PRIVILEGES statement to grant all privileges to an administrative (or admin) user.

- If a user connects to a database and adds a table or other database object without specifying a schema, the database object is stored in a schema with the same name as the user. A *schema* helps to group the tables in a database.

- You use the DROP USER statement to drop a user. If you use add the optional CASCADE keyword with this statement, it deletes all objects that have been created by the user.

Figure 12-1   How to create an admin user

and it won't drop the user. Since this prevents you from accidentally dropping database objects, this is usually what you want. However, if you want to drop the user and all database objects stored in the user's schema, you can specify the CASCADE keyword as shown in the last statement.

How to use SQL Developer to view database objects for a schema

In chapter 2, you learned how to use SQL Developer to create connections for the AP, OM, and EX users. Then, as you progressed through this book, you learned how to use SQL Developer to work with these user connections.

Now, figure 12-2 reviews this information by showing how to create a connection for the AR user that was created by the script presented in the previous figure. Once you create a connection for this user, you can use SQL Developer to view and work with the database objects that are stored in the user's schema. In this figure, for example, the AR schema is displayed in the Connections window, and the Tables folder is expanded to show the Customers table that was created by the script in figure 12-1. In addition, the main window shows the results for a SELECT statement that has been executed against this table.

SQL Developer with a connection for the AR user

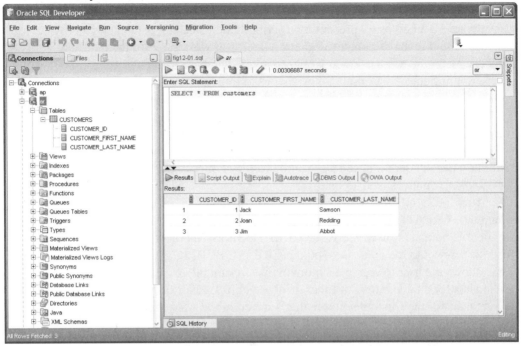

How to create a connection for an admin user

1. Right-click the Connections node in the Connections window and select the New Connection command to display the dialog box for creating database connections.

2. Enter a connection name, username, and password for the connection.

3. Click the Test button to test the connection. If the connection works, a success message is displayed.

4. Click the Save button to save the connection. When you do, the connection will be added to the dialog box and to the Connections window.

Description

*   Once you create an admin user, you can use SQL Developer to create a connection for that user. Then, you can use SQL Developer to view tables and other database objects that have been created by that user.

Figure 12-2   How to use SQL Developer to view database objects for a schema

How to create end users

Figure 12-3 begins by presenting a script that creates end users that can use the database, but may not have all the privileges for working with the database objects. Here, the first statement connects to the database as the AR user. Since the script in figure 12-1 grants all privileges to this user, this user can create other users and grant them privileges.

After the script connects as the AR user, it creates a role named ar_user. A *role* is a database object that allows you to group users. If, for example, you're working with a database that contains multiple users, you can use roles to group similar types of users. Those roles can be for developers, administrators, managers, application users, and so on.

After the script creates the role, it grants privileges to the role. To start, it grants the CREATE SESSION and CREATE PUBLIC SYNONYM privileges to the role named ar_user. Here, the CREATE SESSION privilege allows the user to connect to the database, and the CREATE PUBLIC SYNONYM privilege allows the user to create a synonym that's available to all users. A *synonym* is an alias for a table, view, or other database object. Later on, this script creates a synonym for the Customers table that's stored in the AR schema so users can access that table without qualifying it with the schema name.

After granting the CREATE SESSION and CREATE PUBLIC SYNONYM privileges, the script grants the SELECT and INSERT privileges on the Customers table to the ar_user role. As a result, any user that is granted the ar_user role can select data from this table and insert rows into this table. However, this role doesn't let the user update or delete data in this table.

After the script finishes granting privileges to the role, it creates three users in the Users tablespace, and it specifies a password of sesame for all three users. Then, it grants the ar_user role to all three users. As a result, all three users will have the privileges that have been granted to the ar_user role. In addition, the last GRANT statement grants the DELETE privilege on the Customers table to the user named John.

After the script, this figure shows how to revoke privileges. This shows that you can use the REVOKE statement to revoke privileges from a role or a user. For instance, the first REVOKE statement revokes the CREATE PUBLIC SYNONYM privilege from the ar_user role, and the second REVOKE statement revokes the ar_user role from the user named Jim. The last REVOKE statement shows that you can also revoke a privilege directly from a user. This statement revokes the DELETE privilege on the Customers table from the user named John.

A script that creates three end users and grants them privileges

```
-- connect as the AR user
CONNECT ar/ar;

-- create the role
CREATE ROLE ar_user;

GRANT CREATE SESSION TO ar_user;
GRANT CREATE PUBLIC SYNONYM TO ar_user;
GRANT SELECT ON customers TO ar_user;
GRANT INSERT ON customers TO ar_user;

-- create the users
CREATE USER john IDENTIFIED BY sesame DEFAULT TABLESPACE users;
CREATE USER jane IDENTIFIED BY sesame DEFAULT TABLESPACE users;
CREATE USER jim  IDENTIFIED BY sesame DEFAULT TABLESPACE users;

GRANT ar_user TO john, jane, jim;

GRANT DELETE ON customers TO john;

-- create the public synonym
CONNECT john/sesame;
CREATE PUBLIC SYNONYM customers FOR ar.customers;
```

A statement that revokes privileges from a role

```
REVOKE CREATE PUBLIC SYNONYM FROM ar_user
```

A statement that revokes a role from a user

```
REVOKE ar_user FROM jim
```

A statement that revokes a privilege from a user

```
REVOKE DELETE ON customers FROM john
```

Description

- You can use the CREATE USER statement to create a user.
- You can use the CREATE ROLE statement to create a role for a user. A *role* is a database object that allows you to group users.
- You can use the CREATE PUBLIC SYNONYM statement to create a synonym that can be used by all users. A *synonym* is an alias for a table, view, or other database object.
- You can use the GRANT statement to grant privileges to a user or a role. You can also use this statement to grant a role to a user.
- You can use the REVOKE statement to revoke privileges from a user or a role. You can also use this statement to revoke a role from a user.
- For a partial list of privileges that can be granted or revoked, see figure 12-5.

Figure 12-3   How to create end users

How to use SQL*Plus to test end users

In chapter 2, you learned how to use SQL*Plus to connect to a database and execute SQL statements. Now, figure 12-4 reviews this information by showing how to use SQL*Plus to connect as an end user. This provides a quick way for you to test the username and password for a user, and it allows you to verify that a user has appropriate privileges.

In this figure, for example, I began by logging in as the user named Jane. Then, I selected data from the Customers table to make sure that Jane can select data from this table. This shows that Jane has the SELECT privilege on the Customers table, and it shows that the script in figure 12-3 has successfully created a public synonym for the Customers table so that Jane doesn't need to qualify this table with the schema name. Finally, I used the CONNECT command to log out as Jane and to log in as John.

SQL*Plus after you have connected as Jane

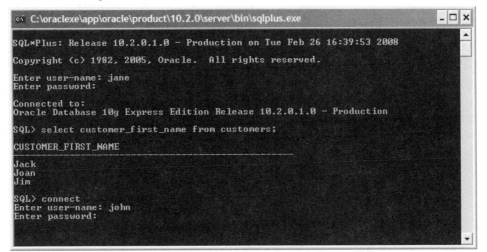

Description

- SQL*Plus is a command-line tool that's installed with the Oracle Database. You can use it to work with an Oracle database.

- To start SQL*Plus, select the Run command from the Start menu, enter "sqlplus", and select the OK button.

- To connect to a database, enter the username and password. If necessary, you can enter the CONNECT command to have SQL*Plus prompt you for a username and password.

- To run a SQL statement, you type it, type a semicolon, and press the Enter key. By default, you must specify the schema name for tables and other database objects.

Figure 12-4   How to use SQL*Plus to test end users

System privileges and object privileges

Figure 12-5 lists the privileges that you can code in either the GRANT or REVOKE statement. To start, *system privileges* allow the user to connect to a database and to create, alter, or drop database objects such as tables, sequences, views, and stored procedures. Although this figure doesn't show them all, Oracle provides system privileges for most types of DDL statements. For example, Oracle provides a CREATE INDEX privilege, a CREATE TRIGGER privilege, and so on. To see a complete list of privileges, you can look up the GRANT statement in the Oracle Database SQL Reference manual.

For most privileges, you can use the ANY keyword to apply the privilege to any schema. For example, if you grant the CREATE TABLE privilege to a user named John, he can only create a table in the schema named John. However, if you grant the CREATE ANY TABLE privilege to John, he can create a table in any schema on the current server. To do that, though, John must qualify the name of the table with the name of the schema.

For most CREATE privileges, there is a corresponding DROP and ALTER privilege. For example, Oracle provides a DROP TABLE privilege and an ALTER TABLE privilege. Like the CREATE TABLE privilege, you can use the ANY keyword to apply these privileges to any schema. Otherwise, they will only apply to the user's current schema.

When you work with system privileges, granting a CREATE privilege often implicitly grants the corresponding ALTER and DROP privilege. In most cases, this works the way you want. However, if it doesn't, you can explicitly grant or revoke the corresponding ALTER and DROP privilege. For example, if you grant the CREATE TABLE privilege to a user but you don't want the user to be able to drop tables, you can explicitly revoke the DROP TABLE privilege.

While system privileges allow a user to create database objects, *object privileges* allow a user to use database objects such as tables, views, sequences, and stored procedures after they have been created. In other words, object privileges allow a user to execute DML statements such as the SELECT, UP-DATE, INSERT, and DELETE statements. In addition, the EXECUTE privilege lets the user run a stored procedure or a function. For more information about stored procedures and functions, see chapter 15.

When you work with object privileges, you'll find that each privilege can be granted only for certain types of objects. For example, you can grant a SELECT privilege only to an object from which you can select data, such as a table or view. Likewise, you can grant an EXECUTE privilege only to an object that you can execute, such as a stored procedure or function.

Finally, note that the syntax for working with system privileges is a little different than the syntax for working with object privileges. In particular, for object privileges, you need to specify the ON keyword followed by the object that you're working with. For system privileges, though, you don't need to use the ON keyword to specify the object. In a moment, you'll learn more about how this syntax works.

System privileges

Privilege	Description
CREATE SESSION	Lets the user connect to the database.
CREATE TABLE	Lets the user create a table in the current schema.
CREATE ANY TABLE	Lets the user create a table in any schema.
DROP TABLE	Lets the user drop a table in the current schema.
DROP ANY TABLE	Lets the user drop a table in any schema.
UNLIMITED TABLESPACE	Lets the user create objects such as tables that need to allocate space in the current tablespace.
CREATE SEQUENCE	Lets the user create a sequence in the current schema.
CREATE VIEW	Lets the user create a view in the current schema.
CREATE PROCEDURE	Lets the user create a stored procedure, function, or package in the current schema.
CREATE PUBLIC SYNONYM	Lets the user create a synonym in the current schema that's available to all users.

Object privileges

Privilege	Description
SELECT	Lets the user select data from the specified object. This applies to tables, sequences, and views.
UPDATE	Lets the user update data. This applies to tables and views.
INSERT	Lets the user insert data. This applies to tables and views.
DELETE	Lets the user delete data. This applies to tables and views.
EXECUTE	Lets the user execute a stored procedure or a function.

A statement that grants a system privilege to a role

```
GRANT CREATE SESSION TO ar_user
```

A statement that grants an object privilege to a role

```
GRANT SELECT ON customers TO ar_user
```

Description

- *System privileges* allow the user to connect to a database and to create, alter, or drop database objects such as tables, views, sequences, and stored procedures.
- *Object privileges* allow the user to work with database objects such as tables, views, sequences, and stored procedures. The privileges that are available for an object depend on the type of object.
- For a complete list of privileges, look up the GRANT statement in the Oracle Database SQL Language Reference.

Figure 12-5   System privileges and object privileges

How to manage database security

Now that you have a general idea of how database security works, you're ready to learn the details for coding the SQL statements that create database users and assign privileges to them.

How to create, alter, and drop users

Figure 12-6 shows how to work with users. Here, the first statement shows how to create a user named AR with a password of AR in the tablespace named Users. As I mentioned earlier, unless a DBA has created a tablespace for you to use, it's a good practice to store users in the Users tablespace.

If you don't use the DEFAULT TABLESPACE clause to specify a tablespace, the user will be stored in the default tablespace for the system. Unfortunately, though, the default tablespace on many systems is the System tablespace. But as I mentioned earlier, it's a good practice to reserve this tablespace for database objects that are created by Oracle.

The second statement in this figure shows how to create a user named Joel with a password of sesame. This statement stores this user in the Users tablespace, and it specifies the Temp tablespace as the temporary tablespace for this user. The Temp tablespace is usually created when you install Oracle, and it's a good practice to use this tablespace as the temporary tablespace for a user. However, since this tablespace is the default temporary tablespace on many systems, you usually don't need to specify it when you create a user.

The QUOTA clause in the second statement lets the user allocate an unlimited amount of disk space in the Users tablespace. Then, if the user is granted appropriate privileges, the user will be able to create tables and other database objects that allocate disk space. By default, though, a user isn't allocated any disk space. As a result, the user can't create database objects even if that user is granted the privilege to create an object.

The third and fourth statements in this figure show how to change the amount of disk space that's allocated to a user. Here, the third statement changes the amount of disk space for Joel from unlimited to 10 megabytes. Then, the fourth statement changes the amount of disk space for Joel to 0 bytes. As a result, Joel won't be able to create any more database objects. However, any existing objects that were created by Joel will remain.

When you create an admin user such as the AR user as shown in figure 12-1, one of the privileges that's granted to the admin user is the UNLIMITED TABLESPACE privilege. As a result, you don't need to use the QUOTA clause for an admin user. However, if you wanted to prevent an admin user from creating any database objects, you could revoke this privilege from the admin user.

Although it isn't shown in this figure, you can use the UNLIMITED keyword to specify an unlimited amount of disk space within an ALTER USER statement. Conversely, you can provide a specific number of megabytes in the QUOTA clause of the CREATE USER statement.

Three tablespaces that are created when Oracle is installed

Tablespace	Description
SYSTEM	A tablespace for storing permanent objects such tables and views that are created and used internally by Oracle.
USERS	A tablespace for storing users and other permanent objects such tables and views.
TEMP	A tablespace for storing temporary objects that are created when users work with a database.

The syntax of the CREATE USER statement

```
CREATE USER username IDENTIFIED BY password
[DEFAULT    TABLESPACE tablespace_name]
[TEMPORARY TABLESPACE tablespace_name]
[QUOTA {quota_size|UNLIMITED} ON tablespace_name]
```

A statement that creates a user

```
CREATE USER ar IDENTIFIED BY ar DEFAULT TABLESPACE users
```

Another statement that creates a database user

```
CREATE USER joel IDENTIFIED BY sesame
DEFAULT TABLESPACE users
TEMPORARY TABLESPACE temp
QUOTA UNLIMITED ON users
```

A statement that changes a user's disk space allocation quota

```
ALTER USER joel QUOTA 10M ON users
```

A statement that doesn't allow the user to allocate disk space

```
ALTER USER joel QUOTA 0 ON users
```

A statement that changes a user's password

```
ALTER USER john IDENTIFIED BY secret
```

A statement that forces the user to change his or her password

```
ALTER USER john PASSWORD EXPIRE
```

A statement that locks a users account

```
ALTER USER john ACCOUNT LOCK
```

A statement that unlocks a users account

```
ALTER USER john ACCOUNT UNLOCK
```

A statement that drops a user

```
DROP USER john
```

A statement that drops a user and all of its objects

```
DROP USER ar CASCADE
```

Figure 12-6   How to work with users

The fifth and sixth statements in figure 12-6 show how to work with a user's password. Here, the fifth statement changes the password for John to secret. Then, the sixth statement causes the password for John to expire. As a result, the next time a user logs in as John, he or she will have to enter the old password and create a new password.

The seventh and eighth statements show how to lock or unlock a user's account. If, for example, you want to temporarily lock John out of the database, you can use the seventh statement. Or, if a user enters an invalid password more than three times in a row, the user's account may become locked so you need to unlock it.

The last two statements show how to drop a user. If the user hasn't created any objects, you can use the DROP statement without the CASCADE keyword. But if the user has created objects, you must add the CASCADE keyword to drop the user. Then, Oracle will delete the user and all of the objects that are stored in the schema for the user. In other words, the last statement will delete the entire AR schema! So please be careful when you use this statement.

How to create and drop roles

As you learned earlier in this chapter, you can use a role to make it easier to work with users. To do that, you use the CREATE ROLE statement that's shown in figure 12-7. Here, the second CREATE ROLE statement uses the IDENTI-FIED BY clause to supply a password for a role. Although you can use this clause to provide an additional level of security, passwords are rarely assigned to roles. Instead, they are typically assigned to users as shown in the previous figure.

Once you've created a role, you can grant privileges to it, and you can grant the role to a user. You'll learn how to do that next. Later, if you want to drop a role, you can use the DROP ROLE statement shown in this figure.

A statement that creates a role

```
CREATE ROLE ap_user
```

Another statement that creates a role

```
CREATE ROLE ap_admin IDENTIFIED BY secret
```

A statement that drops a role

```
DROP ROLE ap_user
```

Another statement that drops a role

```
DROP ROLE ap_admin
```

Description

- You use the CREATE ROLE statement to create roles. Although you can use the IDENTIFIED BY clause to specify a password for a role, this clause is rarely used.
- You use the DROP ROLE statement to drop roles.

Figure 12-7   How to work with roles

How to grant privileges

Figure 12-8 shows how to use the GRANT statement to grant system and object privileges to a role or a user. To start, the first two statements show how to grant system privileges. Here, the first statement grants the CREATE SESSION privilege to the role named ap_user. Then, the second statement grants the same privilege to the role named ap_developer. However, since this statement includes the WITH ADMIN OPTION clause, any user in the ap_developer role can grant the specified privilege to other users.

The third and fourth statements show how to grant object privileges. Here, the third statement grants the SELECT privilege on the Vendors table to the ap_user role, and the fourth statement grants the same privilege to the role named ap_manager. However, since this fourth statement includes the WITH GRANT OPTION clause, any user in the ap_manager role can grant the specified privilege to other users.

The fifth statement shows that you can grant multiple privileges by separating the privileges with commas. This statement grants the SELECT, INSERT, UPDATE, and DELETE privileges on the Vendors table to the ap_user role. Although it isn't shown, you can use a similar technique for granting multiple system privileges. You can also grant privileges to multiple roles and users by separating them with commas.

The sixth statement shows how to use the ALL keyword to grant most of the privileges for the specified database object. This statement grants all privileges on the Vendors table to the ap_user role, which grants all of the privileges that are granted by the fifth example: SELECT, INSERT, UPDATE, and DELETE. In addition, this statement grants several other privileges such as FLASHBACK and DEBUG. The advantage of using the ALL keyword is that you write less code to grant all privileges on an object. The disadvantage is that you may accidentally grant a user more privileges than the user needs, which could open a hole in the security of your database.

Before you can grant privileges, you must connect as an appropriate user. In this figure, for instance, the examples assume that you are connected as the AP user for two reasons. First, this user has the necessary privileges to grant all system and object privileges to other roles and users. Second, the database objects shown in this figure are stored in the schema for this user. As a result, you don't need to qualify the names of these objects with the schema name. In this figure, that means that you don't need to qualify the Vendors and Invoices tables with the AP schema. However, if you weren't connected as the AP user, you would need to qualify these object names with the schema name.

Finally, note that you can grant privileges to specific columns for an object that has columns, such as a table. However, it's usually easier to create a view that provides access to the columns that you want to grant to the user. Then, you can grant privileges on the view but not on the table.

The syntax of the GRANT statement for system privileges

```
GRANT system_privilege[, ...]
TO user_or_role [, ...]
[WITH ADMIN OPTION]
```

The syntax of the GRANT statement for object privileges

```
GRANT object_privilege[, ...]
ON [schema_name.]object_name [(column [, ...])]
TO user_or_role [, ...]
[WITH GRANT OPTION]
```

A statement that grants a system privilege to a role

```
GRANT CREATE SESSION TO ap_user
```

A statement that grants a system privilege with the admin option

```
GRANT CREATE SESSION TO ap_developer WITH ADMIN OPTION
```

A statement that grants an object privilege to a role

```
GRANT SELECT ON vendors TO ap_user
```

A statement that grants an object privilege to a role with the grant option

```
GRANT SELECT ON vendors TO ap_manager WITH GRANT OPTION
```

A statement that grants all object privileges for a table to a role

```
GRANT SELECT, INSERT, UPDATE, DELETE ON invoices TO ap_user;
```

Another way to grant all object privileges for a table to a role

```
GRANT ALL ON invoices TO ap_user;
```

A statement that grants a role to multiple users

```
GRANT ap_user TO john, jane;
```

A statement that grants a role to another role

```
GRANT ap_user TO ap_developer;
```

Description

- You use the GRANT statement to grant system or object privileges to users or roles.
- For a partial list of system and object privileges, refer back to figure 12-5.
- The WITH ADMIN OPTION clause allows the user or role to grant the specified system privileges to other users or roles.
- The WITH GRANT OPTION clause allows the user or role to grant the specified object privileges to other users or roles.

Figure 12-8   How to grant privileges

How to revoke privileges

Figure 12-9 shows how to use the REVOKE statement to revoke system or object privileges. As you can see, this statement is similar to the GRANT statement, but it reverses the action of a GRANT statement.

To start, the first REVOKE statement in this figure shows how to revoke a system privilege. This statement revokes the DROP ANY VIEW privilege from the user role named ap_developer.

In contrast, the second statement shows how to revoke an object privilege. This statement revokes the SELECT privilege on the Invoices table from the ap_user role.

The third statement shows that you can revoke multiple object privileges by separating each privilege with a comma. This statement revokes the INSERT, UPDATE, and DELETE privileges on the Invoices table from the ap_user role.

The fourth statement shows how to use the ALL keyword to revoke all privileges on a database object. This works similarly to the previous two statements. However, it also revokes any other privileges that may have been granted on the Invoices table from the ap_user role. If you need to make sure that you've revoked all privileges on an object, this is the way to do it.

The fifth statement shows how to revoke a role from multiple users. In particular, it revokes the ap_users role from the users named John and Jane.

The sixth statement shows how to revoke one role from another role. Specifically, it revokes the ap_users role from the ap_developer role. As a result, the ap_developer role will no longer have the privileges that have been granted to the ap_user role.

The syntax of the REVOKE statement for system privileges

```
REVOKE system_privilege [, ...]
FROM user_or_role [, ...]
```

The syntax of the REVOKE statement for object privileges

```
REVOKE object_privilege
ON [schema_name.]object_name [(column [, ...])]
FROM user_or_role [, ...]
```

A statement that revokes a system privilege from a role

```
REVOKE DROP ANY VIEW FROM ap_developer;
```

A statement that revokes an object privilege from a role

```
REVOKE SELECT ON invoices FROM ap_user;
```

A statement that revokes multiple object privileges from a role

```
REVOKE INSERT, UPDATE, DELETE ON invoices FROM ap_user
```

A statement that revokes all object privileges from a role

```
REVOKE ALL ON invoices FROM ap_user
```

A statement that revokes a role from multiple users

```
REVOKE ap_user FROM john, jane
```

A statement that revokes a role from another role

```
REVOKE ap_user FROM ap_developer
```

Description

- You can use the REVOKE statement to revoke privileges from a user or role.
- For a partial list of privileges that can be revoked, see figure 12-5.

Figure 12-9   How to revoke privileges

How to work with private synonyms

Earlier in this chapter, you learned that a *synonym* is an alias for a table, view, or other database object. Now, figure 12-10 shows how to work with a *private synonym*, which is a synonym that's only available to the current user.

The primary benefit of using a synonym is that it allows applications to work without modification regardless of which schema a table or view is stored in. To illustrate, the first example in this figure shows what happens when a user named John tries to use the Vendors table in the AP schema without qualifying the table name. In this case, an error message is displayed and the statement fails.

To solve this problem, you can create a synonym for a user as shown by the second and third examples. To start, you need to connect as an admin user and grant the CREATE SYNONYM privilege to the user. Then, you can connect as the user named John and use the CREATE SYNONYM statement to create a synonym for the ap.vendors table.

At this point, John can use the same code as the AP user to refer to the Vendors table as shown in the fourth example. In other words, any statements that work on the Vendors table for the AP user will now work for John without any modification. This assumes, however, that John has all necessary privileges for working with the Vendors table. For example, to select data from this table, John must have the SELECT privilege on the Vendors table.

The last statement in this figure shows how to drop a synonym. Since this works like most other DROP statements described in this book, you shouldn't have any trouble using it.

A SELECT statement that fails because it doesn't specify the schema name for the table

```
CONNECT john/sesame;
SELECT vendor_name FROM vendors WHERE vendor_id = 1;
```

The error message that's displayed

```
SQL Error: ORA-00942: table or view does not exist
```

How to grant the CREATE SYNONYM privilege

```
CONNECT ap/ap;
GRANT CREATE SYNONYM TO john;
```

How to create a synonym for a single user

```
CONNECT john/sesame;
CREATE SYNONYM vendors FOR ap.vendors;
```

A SELECT statement that succeeds due to the synonym

```
SELECT vendor_name FROM vendors WHERE vendor_id = 1
```

The result set

	VENDOR_NAME
1	US Postal Service

How to drop a synonym

```
DROP SYNONYM vendors
```

Description

- A *private synonym* is a synonym that's only available to the current user.
- Synonyms allow applications to work without modification regardless of which user owns the table or view.
- If a user has the CREATE SYNONYM privilege, the user can use the CREATE SYNONYM statement to create a private synonym.
- Before a user can use a synonym, the user must have appropriate privileges on the underlying object.

Figure 12-10 How to work with private synonyms

How to work with public synonyms

If you only need to create a synonym for a single user, you can use a private synonym as described in the previous figure. However, for multi-user databases, you often need to create a synonym for all users in the database. In that case, you can use a *public synonym* as described in figure 12-11.

Once you understand how to work with private synonyms, you shouldn't have any trouble working with public synonyms. The main difference is that you use the PUBLIC keyword before the SYNONYM keyword. In this figure, for instance, the third statement uses the CREATE PUBLIC SYNONYM statement to create a public synonym. Similarly, the last statement uses the DROP PUBLIC SYNONYM statement to drop a public synonym.

In this figure, please note that the third example creates a public synonym for the user named John. However, this allows the user named Jane to access the Vendors table without specifying the schema name as shown by the fourth example. This shows that a public synonym is available to all users, not just to John.

A SELECT statement that fails because it doesn't specify the schema name for the table

```
CONNECT john/sesame;
SELECT vendor_name FROM vendors WHERE vendor_id = 1;
```

The error message that's displayed

```
SQL Error: ORA-00942: table or view does not exist
```

How to grant the CREATE PUBLIC SYNONYM privilege

```
CONNECT ap/ap;
GRANT CREATE PUBLIC SYNONYM TO ap_user;
```

How to create a synonym for all users

```
CONNECT john/sesame;
CREATE PUBLIC SYNONYM vendors FOR ap.vendors;
```

A SELECT statement that succeeds due to the public synonym

```
CONNECT jane/sesame;
SELECT vendor_name FROM vendors WHERE vendor_id = 1
```

The result set

VENDOR_NAME
1 US Postal Service

How to drop a synonym

```
DROP PUBLIC SYNONYM vendors
```

Description

- A *public synonym* is a synonym that's available to all users.
- If a user has the CREATE PUBLIC SYNONYM privilege, the user can use the CREATE PUBLIC SYNONYM statement to create a public synonym that's available to all users.

Figure 12-11   How to work with public synonyms

A script that creates roles and users

Figure 12-12 shows a script that creates roles and users that can work with the tables and other database objects in the AP schema. To start, this script connects as the AP user, which has appropriate privileges for creating roles, creating users, and granting privileges. Then, it uses an anonymous PL/SQL script to drop any existing users, roles, or synonyms that are created by the script. Note that the DROP USER statement for Joel includes the CASCADE keyword so it drops any database objects that exist within the schema named Joel.

After the script drops any existing objects, it creates three roles: ap_user, ap_manager, and ap_developer. Then, the script grants privileges to these three roles.

The ap_user role has the fewest privileges. It can connect to the database and create a public synonym. It can select and modify data in the Vendors, Invoices, and Invoice_Line_Items tables. It can select data from the Terms and General_Ledger_Accounts tables. And it can use the sequences for the Vendors and Invoices tables. In short, this role has all of the privileges needed for a user to work with an Accounts Payable application.

The ap_manager role has all of the privileges of the ap_user role, and it has a few more privileges. In particular, it can grant the ap_user role to other users, and it can modify data in the Terms and General_Ledger_Accounts tables. In short, this role has all of the privileges needed for a manager to perform managerial functions with an Accounts Payable application.

A script that sets up the roles and users for a database   **Page 1**

```
CONNECT ap/ap;

-- Use an anonymous PL/SQL script to
-- drop all end users, roles, and synonyms in the current database
-- and suppress any error messages that may be displayed
-- if these objects don't exist
BEGIN
  EXECUTE IMMEDIATE 'DROP USER john';
  EXECUTE IMMEDIATE 'DROP USER jane';
  EXECUTE IMMEDIATE 'DROP USER jim';
  EXECUTE IMMEDIATE 'DROP USER joel CASCADE';

  EXECUTE IMMEDIATE 'DROP ROLE ap_user';
  EXECUTE IMMEDIATE 'DROP ROLE ap_manager';
  EXECUTE IMMEDIATE 'DROP ROLE ap_developer';

  EXECUTE IMMEDIATE 'DROP PUBLIC SYNONYM vendors';
  EXECUTE IMMEDIATE 'DROP PUBLIC SYNONYM invoices';
  EXECUTE IMMEDIATE 'DROP PUBLIC SYNONYM invoice_line_items';
  EXECUTE IMMEDIATE 'DROP PUBLIC SYNONYM general_ledger_accounts';
  EXECUTE IMMEDIATE 'DROP PUBLIC SYNONYM terms';
EXCEPTION
  WHEN OTHERS THEN
    DBMS_OUTPUT.PUT_LINE('');
END;
/

-- create the roles
CREATE ROLE ap_user;
CREATE ROLE ap_manager;
CREATE ROLE ap_developer;

-- grant privileges to the ap_user role
GRANT CREATE SESSION TO ap_user;
GRANT CREATE PUBLIC SYNONYM TO ap_user;
GRANT ALL ON vendors TO ap_user;
GRANT SELECT, INSERT, UPDATE, DELETE ON invoices TO ap_user;
GRANT SELECT, INSERT, UPDATE, DELETE ON invoice_line_items TO ap_user;
GRANT SELECT ON general_ledger_accounts TO ap_user;
GRANT SELECT ON terms TO ap_user;
GRANT SELECT ON invoice_id_seq TO ap_user;
GRANT SELECT ON vendor_id_seq TO ap_user;

-- grant privileges to the ap_manager role
GRANT ap_user TO ap_manager WITH ADMIN OPTION;
GRANT ALL ON general_ledger_accounts TO ap_manager;
GRANT ALL ON terms TO ap_manager;
```

Figure 12-12   A script that creates the roles and users for a database (part 1 of 2)

The ap_developer role has all of the privileges of the ap_manager role, and it has a few more privileges. In particular, it can create and drop tables, views, and sequences from any schema in the database. Although this role doesn't have all the privileges that are available to the AP user, it has all enough privileges for a developer to work with the tables, views, and sequences of the Accounts Payable application.

After this script grants privileges to the roles, it creates some users. In particular, it creates four users named John, Jane, Jim, and Joel. It creates a password of sesame for all of them. And it sets the Users tablespace as the default tablespace for these users. As a result, these users and any objects that they create will be stored in the Users tablespace.

After this script creates the users, it assigns them to their roles. Here, John and Jane are assigned to the ap_user role, Jim is assigned to the ap_manager role, and Joel is assigned to the ap_developer role. This shows that multiple users can be assigned to a role.

To keep this script easy to understand, it only creates four users. However, for a real-world application, you might need to create hundreds of users. To do that, you might want to use PL/SQL to write code that queries an existing database of users, creates the users, and assigns them to the appropriate role. To learn more about PL/SQL, see chapter 13.

After this script assigns roles for the users, it alters the user named Joel so he can allocate up to 10MB of disk space in the Users tablespace. Without this statement, Joel would not be able to create tables or views or other objects that allocate disk space even though the ap_developer role was granted the CREATE ANY TABLE and CREATE ANY VIEW privileges earlier in the script.

By contrast, the AP user has the UNLIMITED TABLESPACE privilege. As a result, there is no limit to the amount of disk space that the AP user can allocate.

After this script sets the disk space quota for Joel, it connects to the database as Joel and creates public synonyms for the tables in the AP schema. Since these synonyms are public, they are also available to John, Jane, Jim, and any other users that are created later.

Finally, this script connects as the AP user, and alters the password for each user so it is expired. This forces each user to change his or her password when he or she connects to the database for the first time. To start, the user needs to specify the sesame password that's created earlier in the script. Then, the user can create a new password. This secures the database by forcing users to generate their own unique passwords that are different than the one that's stored in the script.

A script that sets up the roles and users for a database   **Page 2**

```
-- grant privileges to the ap_developer role
GRANT
  ap_manager,
  CREATE ANY TABLE,
  DROP ANY TABLE,
  CREATE ANY VIEW,
  DROP ANY VIEW,
  CREATE ANY SEQUENCE,
  DROP ANY SEQUENCE
TO ap_developer;

-- create the users
CREATE USER john IDENTIFIED BY sesame DEFAULT TABLESPACE users;
CREATE USER jane IDENTIFIED BY sesame DEFAULT TABLESPACE users;
CREATE USER jim IDENTIFIED BY sesame DEFAULT TABLESPACE users;
CREATE USER joel IDENTIFIED BY sesame DEFAULT TABLESPACE users;

-- assign the users to their roles
GRANT ap_user TO john, jane;
GRANT ap_manager TO jim;
GRANT ap_developer TO joel;

-- allow joel to create tables
ALTER USER joel QUOTA 10M ON users;

-- create synonyms for all users
CONNECT joel/sesame;
CREATE PUBLIC SYNONYM vendors FOR ap.vendors;
CREATE PUBLIC SYNONYM invoices FOR ap.invoices;
CREATE PUBLIC SYNONYM invoice_line_items FOR ap.invoice_line_items;
CREATE PUBLIC SYNONYM general_ledger_accounts FOR
                     ap.general_ledger_accounts;
CREATE PUBLIC SYNONYM terms FOR ap.terms;

-- require the users to change their passwords when they log in
CONNECT ap/ap;
ALTER USER john PASSWORD EXPIRE;
ALTER USER jane PASSWORD EXPIRE;
ALTER USER jim PASSWORD EXPIRE;
ALTER USER joel PASSWORD EXPIRE;
```

Description

- When you create a database, you can use a script to create the users and roles and assign privileges to them.

Figure 12-12   A script that creates the roles and users for a database (part 2 of 2)

How to view the privileges for users and roles

Figure 12-13 shows how you can use SELECT statements to view the privileges that have been granted to a user. In the first example, the user connects as the AP user and grants one system privilege and one object privilege directly to the user named John. That way, the second and third examples return one row each when you view the privileges for John. Otherwise, these two examples wouldn't return any rows.

Since the rest of the statements in this figure work with the current user, you start by connecting to the database as the user whose privileges you want to view. So after the first example, I connected to the database as John. As a result, John is the user for all of the other examples in this figure.

The second example shows how to view the system privileges for the current user. As a result, this statement returns all of the privileges that have been granted to John. In this case, the only system privilege that has been granted directly to John is the CREATE PROCEDURE privilege that was granted by the first example.

The third example shows how to view the object privileges for the current user. Like the previous statement, this statement returns a single privilege that was granted directly to John by the first example.

The fourth example shows how to view the role privileges for the current user. This statement shows that John is a member of the ap_user role.

The fifth example shows how to view the system privileges that are granted to John through the roles. In this case, that shows all of the system privileges that are granted to John through his only role, the ap_user role. These system privileges include the two that were granted by the script in the previous figure: the CREATE SESSION and CREATE PUBLIC SYNONYM privileges.

If John had been assigned multiple roles, the result set would include all of the system privileges from each role. In that case, if you wanted to narrow the result set to a single role, you could include a WHERE clause like this:

```
SELECT * FROM role_sys_privs WHERE role = 'AP_USER'
```

For this to work, though, you must use all caps when coding the name of the role. Otherwise, Oracle won't return any data.

The sixth example works like the fourth one, but it displays all object privileges that are granted to John though his roles. Here, the result set shows the first four rows of the 16 object privileges that were granted by the script shown in the previous figure.

Some code that grants system and object privileges directly to a user

```
CONNECT ap/ap;
GRANT CREATE PROCEDURE TO john;
GRANT SELECT ON vendors TO john;
```

A SELECT statement that views system privileges for the current user

```
SELECT * FROM user_sys_privs
```

The result set

	USERNAME	PRIVILEGE	ADMIN_OPTION
1	JOHN	CREATE PROCEDURE	NO

A SELECT statement that views object privileges for the current user

```
SELECT * FROM user_tab_privs
```

The result set

	GRANTEE	OWNER	TABLE_NAME	GRANTOR	PRIVILEGE	GRANTABLE	HIERARCHY
1	JOHN	AP	VENDORS	AP	SELECT	NO	NO

A SELECT statement that views role privileges for the current user

```
SELECT * FROM user_role_privs
```

The result set

	USERNAME	GRANTED_ROLE	ADMIN_OPTION	DEFAULT_ROLE	OS_GRANTED
1	JOHN	AP_USER	NO	YES	NO

A SELECT statement that views all system privileges for the ap_user role

```
SELECT * FROM role_sys_privs
```

The result set

	ROLE	PRIVILEGE	ADMIN_OPTION
1	AP_USER	CREATE PUBLIC SYNONYM	NO
2	AP_USER	CREATE SESSION	NO

A SELECT statement that views all object privileges for the ap_user role

```
SELECT * FROM role_tab_privs
```

The result set

	ROLE	OWNER	TABLE_NAME	COLUMN_NAME	PRIVILEGE	GRANTABLE
1	AP_USER	AP	INVOICES	(null)	INSERT	NO
2	AP_USER	AP	INVOICES	(null)	UPDATE	NO
3	AP_USER	AP	INVOICES	(null)	SELECT	NO
4	AP_USER	AP	INVOICE_LINE_ITEMS	(null)	UPDATE	NO

Figure 12-13   How to view the privileges for users and roles

How to use SQL Developer

Since you often use a script to set up the security for a database or to view the privileges that have been granted to a user, it's important to understand the SQL statements presented in this chapter. Once you understand them, it's easy to learn how to use a graphical user interface such as SQL Developer to work with security. For example, it's easy to use SQL Developer to drop or alter an existing user or to grant or revoke the privileges for a user.

How to work with users

Figure 12-14 shows how to use SQL Developer to work with users. To start, you can view the users for a database by expanding the Other Users folder for any connection in the Connections window.

However, before you can use SQL Developer to work with users, you need to create a connection for the system user as described in figure 12-2. Otherwise, you won't have appropriate privileges, and the options in the dialog boxes will be grayed out. In this figure, for example, note that a connection named system is displayed at the top of the Connections window. This is the connection for the system user.

If you want to drop a user, you can right-click on the user and select the Drop User command. Then, you can use the resulting dialog box to confirm the drop.

If you want to edit a user, you can right-click on the user, select the Edit User command, and click on the User tab in the resulting dialog box. In this figure, for example, you can see the dialog box for the user named John. Note here that the default tablespace for John is the Users tablespace and that the temporary tablespace is the Temp tablespace. Most of the time, this is what you want. But if it isn't, you can use this dialog box to select new tablespaces for John.

At this point, you can create a new password for John by entering and confirming the password and clicking on the Apply button. You can force John to change his password the next time he logs in by checking the Password Expired check box. Or, you can lock or unlock John's account by checking or unchecking the Account Is Locked check box.

The dialog box for working with users

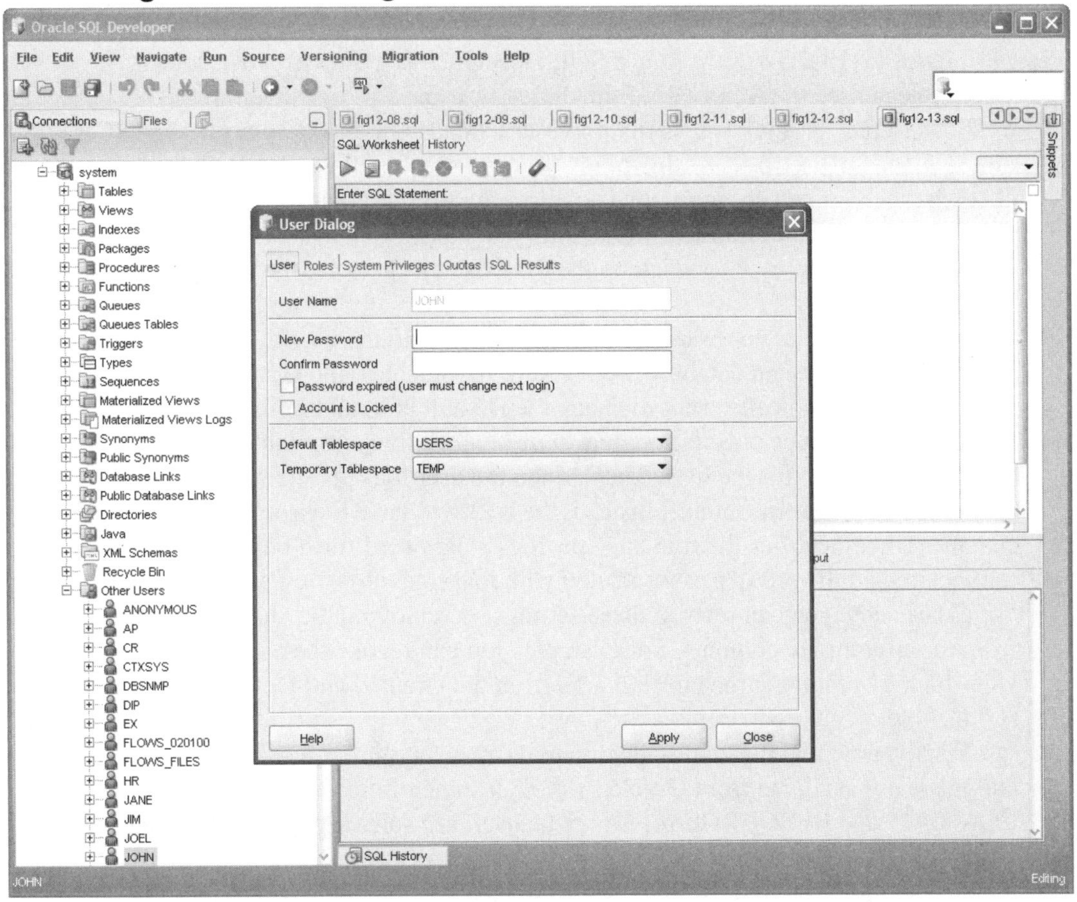

Description

- To display the users for a database, you can use SQL Developer to connect to the database. Then, you can expand the Other Users folder to see all users.

- To work with a user, you must connect as the system user. To do that, you can create a new connection as described in figure 12-2.

- To drop a user, right-click on the user and select the Drop User command. Then, use the resulting dialog box to confirm the drop.

- To edit a user, right-click on the user, select the Edit User command, and click on the User tab in the resulting dialog box. Then, you can (1) set the password, (2) force the user to change the password on the next login, (3) lock or unlock the users account, or (4) change the tablespace settings for the user.

Figure 12-14   How to use SQL Developer to work with users

How to grant and revoke roles

Figure 12-15 shows how to use SQL Developer to grant or revoke roles. Here, you can see the Roles tab of the dialog box that was displayed in the previous figure. This tab shows that the user named John has only been granted one role, the ap_user role. At this point, you can grant additional roles by checking the Granted column; you can allow the user to grant the role to other users by checking the Admin column; and you make a role available to a user by default when the user connects to the database by checking the Default column.

Most of the time, you want a role to be available to the user by default when the user connects to the database. As a result, if you check the Granted column for a role, you'll typically want to check the Default column too. However, if you want to introduce an additional level of security for roles, you can deselect the Default column for the user. Then, when the user logs on, the role won't be available to the user by default. Instead, the user will have to issue a SET ROLE statement that identifies the role and specifies a password for it before the user will be granted the privileges associated with that role.

Conversely, you can reverse these settings by removing the check mark from the appropriate columns. For example, you can revoke the ap_user role from John by removing the check marks from the Granted and Default columns for this role.

Finally, note that this dialog box displays many system roles that are automatically available from Oracle. Although some of these roles such as the CONNECT and RESOURCE roles may be useful in some situations, they may change if you upgrade to a new version of Oracle. As a result, I don't recommend using them, especially since it's fairly easy to create your own roles that provide the privileges that are necessary for your applications.

The dialog box for working with roles

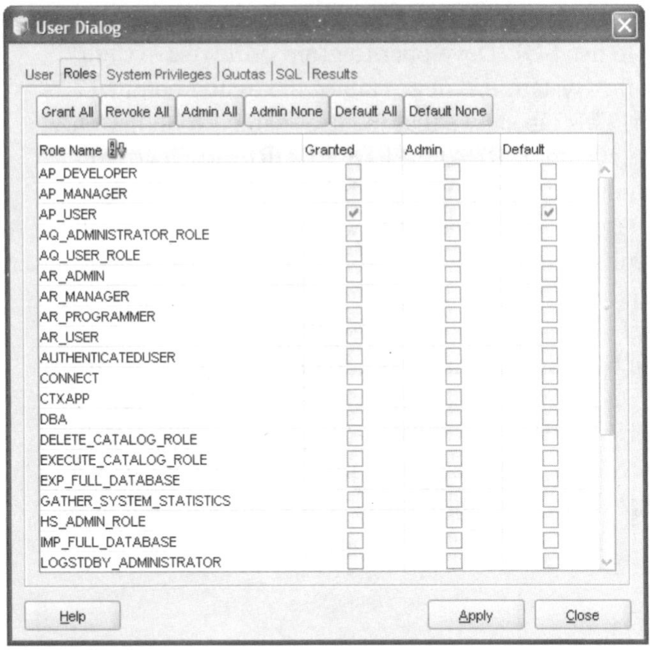

Description

- To work with the roles that are assigned to a user, right-click on the user, select the Edit User command, and click on the Roles tab in the resulting dialog box.

- You can use the Roles tab of the User Dialog box to (1) view the roles that are assigned to the user, (2) grant or revoke a role, (3) grant or revoke the admin option for the role, or (4) control whether the user has access to the role by default after connecting to the database.

Figure 12-15   How to use SQL Developer to work with roles

How to grant and revoke system privileges

Figure 12-16 shows how to use SQL Developer to grant or revoke system privileges. Here, you can see the System Privileges tab of the dialog box that was displayed in figure 12-14. This tab shows that the user named John has only been granted one system privilege, the CREATE PROCEDURE privilege. At this point, you can grant additional system privileges by checking the Granted column, or you can allow the user to grant system privileges to other users by checking the Admin Option column.

Conversely, you can reverse these settings by removing the check mark from the appropriate column. For example, you can revoke the CREATE PROCEDURE role from John by removing the check mark from the Granted column for this role.

Finally, note that this dialog box displays a list of all system privileges. If you compare these system privileges with the system privileges that are shown in figure 12-5, you can see that figure 12-5 only presents a small subset of these privileges.

The dialog box for working with system privileges

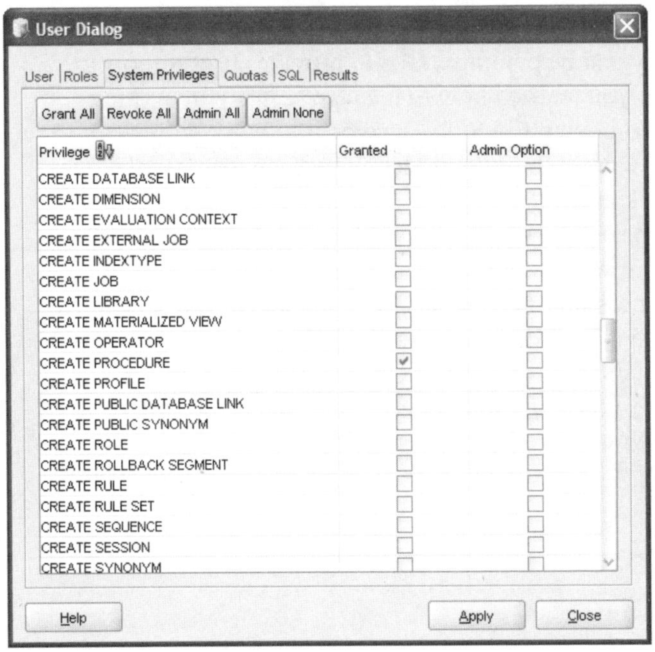

Description

- To work with the system privileges that are assigned to a user, right-click on the user, select the Edit User command, and click on the System Privileges tab in the resulting dialog box.

- You can use the System Privileges tab in the User Dialog box to (1) view the system privileges that are assigned to the user, (2) grant or revoke a system privilege, or (3) grant or revoke the admin option for the system privilege.

Figure 12-16   How to use SQL Developer to work with system privileges

Perspective

Although managing security can be complex, Oracle provides useful tools to simplify the job. In this chapter, you learned how to manage security by writing SQL statements, and you learned how to use SQL Developer to work with users and roles. Once you're familiar with both of these techniques, you can use the one that's easiest for the security task at hand.

Although SQL Developer makes it easy to work with security, it can also slow you down. For example, if you're working with a database that has hundreds of users for an application, you'll probably need to use SQL statements and PL/SQL scripts to help you manage these users. Since many scripts for performing common security-related tasks are available from the Internet, you may be able to download a script that does what you want. Otherwise, you can use the skills that you'll learn in the next chapter to write your own script.

Terms

tablespace
schema
role
synonym
system privilege
object privilege
private synonym
public synonym

Exercises

1. Write a script that creates a database role named payment_entry in the AP schema. This new role should have SELECT and UPDATE privileges for the Vendors table; SELECT and UPDATE privileges for the Invoices table; and SELECT, UPDATE, and INSERT privileges for the Invoice_Line_Items table. This role should also have the right to create a session.

2. Write a script that creates a user named Tom with a password of "temp" and assigns the payment_entry role to him. Next, use SQL*Plus to test whether the username and password are able to connect to the database. Then, use SQL*Plus to run a SELECT statement that selects the vendor_id column from all rows in the Vendors table.

3. Use SQL Developer to test whether the user and role that you created in exercises 1 and 2 work correctly. To start, create a new connection for the used named Tom. Then, write a SELECT statement to select all of the columns for all of the rows in the Vendors table, and use the Tom connection to run it. (It should succeed, though you may need to qualify the table name with the schema name.) Finally, write a DELETE statement that attempts to delete one of the rows in the Vendors table, and use the Tom connection to run it. (It should fail due to insufficient privileges.)

4. Run SELECT statements like those in figure 12-13 to view the user and role privileges that are available to Tom.

5. Write a script that grants the privilege of creating public synonyms to the payment_entry user. Then, use the AP connection to execute this script.

6. Write a script that creates public synonyms for each of the tables used by the payment_entry user. Then, use the Tom connection to execute this script. Finally, write and run some SELECT statements that test whether these public synonyms work correctly.

Section 4

The essential PL/SQL skills

This section presents the essential skills for using Oracle's procedure language, which is called PL/SQL. These are the skills that will take your SQL capabilities to the next level.

In chapter 13, you'll learn the basics of PL/SQL coding. In chapter 14, you'll learn how to use PL/SQL to help manage transactions and locking. In chapter 15, you'll learn how to use PL/SQL to create stored procedures and functions. And in chapter 16, you'll learn how to use PL/SQL to create triggers.

13

How to write PL/SQL code

In chapter 12, you saw a simple script that created a user and a table within that user's schema. Now, this chapter shows you how to code more complex scripts that include blocks of PL/SQL (Procedural Language/SQL) code. With the skills you'll learn in this chapter, you'll be able to code scripts that provide functionality similar to procedural programming languages like Java, C++, C#, and Visual Basic.

If you have experience with another procedural language, you shouldn't have any trouble with the skills presented in this chapter. However, you should know that the programming power of PL/SQL is limited when compared to other languages. That's because PL/SQL is designed specifically to work with Oracle databases rather than as a general-purpose programming language. For its intended use, however, PL/SQL is both powerful and flexible.

An introduction to PL/SQL

Before you learn the details for writing PL/SQL code, it's helpful to get an overview by looking at a block of PL/SQL code that's included within a script. In addition, it's helpful to preview the statements that are commonly used within scripts and within blocks of PL/SQL code.

An anonymous PL/SQL block in a script

As you learned earlier in this book, a *script* is a series of SQL statements that you can store in a file. In this chapter, you'll learn how to include PL/SQL in a script. *PL/SQL (Procedural Language/SQL)* is Oracle's extension to standard SQL that allows you to write procedural SQL code that works with an Oracle database. For example, you can use an IF statement to control the execution of a script based on a conditional expression, or you can use a loop to execute a statement multiple times based on the value of a conditional expression.

To include PL/SQL within a script, you can code a block of PL/SQL code as shown in figure 13-1. Since this block of PL/SQL code doesn't have a name, it is known as an *anonymous PL/SQL block*. In the next chapter, you'll learn how to store a named block of PL/SQL code within the database.

An anonymous PL/SQL block has three main sections. To start, if you want to declare variables, you can code the DECLARE keyword, followed by one or more statements that declare variables. Then, to code the body of the PL/SQL block, you can code the BEGIN keyword, followed by one or more executable statements that form the main body of the script. Finally, if you want to handle exceptions, you can code the EXCEPTION keyword, followed by one or more statements that handle exceptions. Although the PL/SQL block in this figure includes all three of these sections, the DECLARE and EXCEPTION parts are optional. Later in this chapter, you'll see examples of scripts that don't include the DECLARE or EXCEPTION parts of a PL/SQL block.

In this figure, the script begins by connecting to the database as the AP user. Then, it executes a command that allows SQL Developer to display output in its Output Script window. Finally, it uses an anonymous PL/SQL block to print a message to SQL Developer's Script Output window that indicates the total balance due for the vendor.

As you review this script, note that you must code a semicolon at the end of each SQL statement. Similarly, you must code a semicolon after the END IF keywords and after the END keyword at the end of the PL/SQL block. In contrast, you don't have to code a semicolon after the CONNECT command because it is a command, not a SQL statement. However, it's okay to code one, and I like to do that for the sake of consistency. Finally, to execute an anonymous PL/SQL block, you must code a front slash (/) after the END keyword for the block.

For now, don't worry if you don't understand the coding details for this anonymous PL/SQL script. Instead, focus on the general ideas. Later in this chapter, you'll learn the details that you need to write effective PL/SQL code.

The syntax for an anonymous PL/SQL block

```
DECLARE
  declaration_statement_1;
  [declaration_statement_2;]...
BEGIN
  body_statement_1;
  [body_statement_2;]...
EXCEPTION
  WHEN OTHERS THEN
    exception_handling_statement_1;
    [exception_handling_statement_2;]...
END;
/
```

A script that contains an anonymous PL/SQL block

```
CONNECT ap/ap;

SET SERVEROUTPUT ON;

-- Begin an anonymous PL/SQL block
DECLARE
  sum_balance_due_var NUMBER(9, 2);
BEGIN
  SELECT SUM(invoice_total - payment_total - credit_total)
  INTO sum_balance_due_var
  FROM invoices
  WHERE vendor_id = 95;

  IF sum_balance_due_var > 0 THEN
    DBMS_OUTPUT.PUT_LINE('Balance due: $' ||
                         ROUND(sum_balance_due_var, 2));
  ELSE
    DBMS_OUTPUT.PUT_LINE('Balance paid in full');
  END IF;

EXCEPTION
  WHEN OTHERS THEN
    DBMS_OUTPUT.PUT_LINE('An error occured in the script');
END;
/
-- End an anonymous PL/SQL block
```

The response from the system

```
Connected
anonymous block completed
Balance due: $171.01
```

Description

- A *script* is a series of SQL statements that you can store in a file.
- *PL/SQL* (*Procedural Language/SQL*) is Oracle's extension to standard SQL that allows you to write procedural code such as IF statements and loops.
- An *anonymous PL/SQL block* is a block of PL/SQL that's coded within a script.
- To execute a PL/SQL block, you must code a front slash (/) after the END keyword.

Figure 13-1   An anonymous PL/SQL block in a script

A summary of statements for working with PL/SQL and scripts

Figure 13-2 begins by summarizing the PL/SQL statements that are presented in this chapter. These statements can be used within PL/SQL blocks to add functionality that's similar to the functionality provided by procedural languages.

After the PL/SQL statements, this figure presents two Oracle commands that are commonly used within scripts that contain blocks of PL/SQL code. First, it presents the CONNECT command that's used to connect to a database. By now, you should understand how this command works. Second, it presents the SET SERVEROUTPUT ON command. This command enables printing to the SQL*Plus command line or to the Script Output window for recent versions of SQL Developer. In the next figure, you can see an example of how it works.

After the two Oracle commands, this figure presents three procedures that are available from the DBMS_OUTPUT package that's included with Oracle Database. If you're using an older version of SQL Developer such as version 1.1, you can use the ENABLE procedure to enable printing to SQL Developer's Script Output window. However, if you're using a recent version of SQL Developer such as version 1.5, you won't need to use the ENABLE procedure. Instead, you use the SET SERVEROUTPUT ON command as shown throughout this chapter. Either way, though, you use the PUT and PUT_LINE procedures to print data to the SQL*Plus command line or to SQL Developer's Script Output window.

PL/SQL statements for controlling the flow of execution

Keywords	Description
IF...ELSIF...ELSE	Controls the flow of execution based on a condition.
CASE...WHEN...ELSE	Controls the flow of execution based on a condition.
FOR...IN...LOOP	Repeats statements while a condition is true.
WHILE...LOOP	Repeats statements while a condition is true.
LOOP...EXIT WHEN	Repeats statements while a condition is true.
CURSOR...IS	Defines a result set that can be processed by a loop.
EXECUTE IMMEDIATE	Can be used to execute DDL statements within a script and to execute dynamic SQL statements.

Commands for working with scripts

Command	Description
CONNECT	Connects to the database as the specified user.
SET SERVEROUTPUT ON	Enables printing to SQL Developer's Script Output window or to the SQL*Plus command line.

Procedures for printing output to the screen

Procedure	Description
DBMS_OUTPUT.ENABLE()	Enables printing to SQL Developer's Script Output window for versions 1.2 and earlier.
DBMS_OUTPUT.PUT(string)	Prints the specified string without a line break.
DBMS_OUTPUT.PUT_LINE(string)	Prints the specified string followed by a line break.

Description

- The PL/SQL statements can be used within scripts to add functionality similar to that provided by procedural programming languages.
- The procedures available from the DBMS_OUTPUT package that's included with Oracle Database can be used to print output to the screen.

Figure 13-2   A summary of statements for working with PL/SQL and scripts

How to code the basic PL/SQL statements

Now that you have a general idea of how to write a block of PL/SQL code, you're ready to learn the details for working with PL/SQL.

How to print data to an output window

When you develop PL/SQL code, you often need to print data to an output window as shown in figure 13-3. For example, you may need to print the value of a variable to help you debug some code.

To start, this figure shows how to print data to the Script Output window that's available from Oracle SQL Developer. Here, the main SQL Developer window contains a script that begins by calling the SET SERVEROUTPUT ON command. This enables the buffer that's used to store the character data that's printed to the output window. Then, this script contains an anonymous PL/SQL block that uses the PUT_LINE procedure of the DBMS_OUTPUT package to print some character data to the Script Output window.

In the Script Output window, you can see the output that was displayed after I ran the script in the main window. To start, the first line in the Script Output window indicates that the CONNECT command in the script successfully connected as the AP user. Then, the second line indicates that the anonymous PL/SQL block executed successfully. Finally, the third line shows the message that was printed by the script, "Test SQL Developer". Note that all of the character data is printed after the anonymous PL/SQL block has finished executing. That's because the character data is stored in a buffer until the anonymous PL/SQL block finishes executing.

Although we recommend using SQL Developer to work with PL/SQL code, you can use a similar procedure to print data to the SQL*Plus command line if you need to. To do that, you begin by calling the SET SERVEROUTPUT ON command. Then, you can use the PUT_LINE method of the DBMS_OUTPUT package to print the data to the output window.

Note that some older versions of SQL Developer such as 1.1 and some early builds of 1.2 don't yet support the SET SERVEROUTPUT ON command. For some of these versions, you can enable printing to the Script Output window by calling the ENABLE procedure of the DBMS_OUTPUT package. However, you must call this procedure from within a PL/SQL block like this:

```
BEGIN
  DBMS_OUTPUT.ENABLE();
  DBMS_OUTPUT.PUT_LINE('Test SQL Developer');
END;
/
```

How to print data to SQL Developer's Script Output window

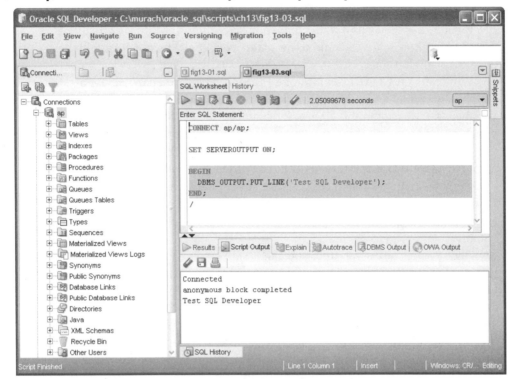

How to print data to the SQL*Plus command line

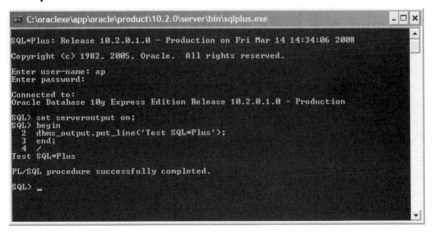

Description

- To print data to SQL Developer's Script Output window or the SQL*Plus command line, call the SET SERVEROUTPUT ON command. Then, use the PUT_LINE procedure of the DBMS_OUTPUT package to print data.

Figure 13-3   How to print data to an output window

How to declare and use variables

Figure 13-4 shows how to declare and use *variables*. More specifically, this figure shows how to declare and use a *scalar variable*, which is a variable that contains a single value.

Within the DECLARE section of a PL/SQL block, you can declare a variable by coding a statement that specifies a name and data type for the variable. In the script in this figure, for example, the PL/SQL block declares five variables. Of these variables, the first two statements use the %TYPE attribute to assign the same data type that's used for a column to the variable. For example, the first two variables are declared with the same data type as the invoice_total column of the invoices table. Then, the next three specify NUMBER as the data type. When specifying the data type for a variable, you can use any of the data types that you can use when you specify the data type for a column.

Once you declare a variable, you can assign a value to it. To assign a literal value or the result of an expression, you can code the assignment operator (:=) followed by the literal value of the expression. In the script in this figure, for example, the last statement in the DECLARE section uses the assignment operator to assign a value of 95 to the variable named vendor_id_var. In addition, the second statement in the BEGIN section uses the assignment operator to assign the result of a calculation to the variable named percent_difference.

If you want to assign a value that's returned by a SELECT statement to a variable, you can add an INTO clause to a SELECT statement. In the script in this figure, for example, the first statement in the BEGIN section uses the INTO clause to assign the three values that are returned by the SELECT statement to the corresponding three variables that are specified by the INTO clause. For this to work, the SELECT statement must return one value for each of the variables that are specified in the INTO clause. In addition, the data types for the columns must be compatible with the data types for the variables.

If you use the %TYPE attribute when you declare the variables, you can be sure that a variable will use the same data type as its column. However, using this attribute requires more typing and results in code that's more difficult to read. As a result, I have hard-coded the data type for most of the variables that are used in this chapter.

To review, the script in this figure uses five variables to calculate the percent difference between the minimum and maximum invoices for a particular vendor. To do that, this script uses the assignment operator to assign a value to two of the variables. In addition, it uses the INTO clause of a SELECT statement to assign values to the other three variables. Finally, a series of statements use the PUT_LINE procedure of the DBMS_OUT package to display the values of four of the variables. But first, it calls the SET SERVEROUTPUT ON command to enable the buffer that's used to store the data that's printed by the PUT_LINE procedure.

The syntax for declaring a variable

```
variable_name_1 DATA_TYPE;
```

The syntax for declaring a variable with the same data type as a column

```
variable_name_1 table_name.column_name%TYPE;
```

The syntax for setting a variable to a selected value

```
SELECT column_1[, column_2]...
INTO variable_name_1[, variable_name_2]...
```

The syntax for setting a variable to a literal value or the result of an expression

```
variable_name := literal_value_or_expression
```

A SQL script that uses variables

```
CONNECT ap/ap;

SET SERVEROUTPUT ON;

DECLARE
  max_invoice_total  invoices.invoice_total%TYPE;
  min_invoice_total  invoices.invoice_total%TYPE;
  percent_difference NUMBER;
  count_invoice_id   NUMBER;
  vendor_id_var      NUMBER := 95;
BEGIN
  SELECT MAX(invoice_total), MIN(invoice_total), COUNT(invoice_id)
  INTO max_invoice_total, min_invoice_total, count_invoice_id
  FROM invoices WHERE vendor_id = vendor_id_var;

  percent_difference := (max_invoice_total - min_invoice_total) /
                        min_invoice_total * 100;

  DBMS_OUTPUT.PUT_LINE('Maximum invoice: $' || max_invoice_total);
  DBMS_OUTPUT.PUT_LINE('Minimum invoice: $' || min_invoice_total);
  DBMS_OUTPUT.PUT_LINE('Percent difference: %' ||
                        ROUND(percent_difference, 2));
  DBMS_OUTPUT.PUT_LINE('Number of invoices: ' || count_invoice_id);
END;
/
```

The response from the system

```
Connected
anonymous block completed
Maximum invoice: $46.21
Minimum invoice: $16.33
Percent difference: %182.98
Number of invoices: 6
```

Description

- A *variable* is used to store data. A variable that contains a single value is called a *scalar variable*.

Figure 13-4   How to declare and use variables

How to code IF statements

Figure 13-5 shows how to use an IF statement to execute one or more statements based on a value that's returned by a *Boolean expression*. A Boolean expression is an expression that returns a true value or a false value.

The script in this figure uses an IF statement to test the value of a variable. This variable contains the oldest invoice due date in the Invoices table. If this due date is less than the current date, the Boolean expression evaluates to true, and the statement in the IF clause prints a message to the output window that indicates that outstanding invoices are overdue. If the value is equal to the current date, the statement in the ELSIF clause prints a message to the output window that indicates that outstanding invoices are due today. If neither of these conditions is true, the oldest due date must be greater than the current date. As a result, the script prints a message to the output window that indicates that no invoices are overdue.

In this figure, the IF statement only contains one ELSIF clause. However, you can add as many ELSIF clauses as you need. As a result, you can code dozens of these clauses if you need them. But if you don't need an ELSIF clause, you don't have to code one. For example, it's common to code an IF statement without an ELSIF clause like this:

```
IF first_invoice_due_date < SYSDATE() THEN
  DBMS_OUTPUT.PUT_LINE('Outstanding invoices overdue!');
ELSE
  DBMS_OUTPUT.PUT_LINE('No invoices are overdue.');
END IF;
```

Similarly, the ELSE clause is optional. As a result, it's common to code an IF statement like this:

```
IF first_invoice_due_date < SYSDATE() THEN
  DBMS_OUTPUT.PUT_LINE('Outstanding invoices overdue!');
END IF;
```

When you code IF statements, you can *nest* one IF statement within another For example, you can nest one IF statement within another like this:

```
IF first_invoice_due_date <= TRUNC(SYSDATE()) THEN
  DBMS_OUTPUT.PUT_LINE('Outstanding invoices are overdue!');
  IF first_invoice_due_date = TRUNC(SYSDATE()) THEN
    DBMS_OUTPUT.PUT_LINE('TODAY!');
  END IF;
END IF;
```

In this case, the outer IF statement will be executed when the oldest invoice due date is less than or equal to the current date. However, the nested IF statement will only be executed when the oldest invoice due date is equal to the current date. In other words, if the current date equals the oldest invoice due date, two lines will be printed to the output window. As you'll see later in this chapter, you can also nest an IF statement within other types of PL/SQL statements such as loops.

The syntax of the IF statement

```
IF boolean_expression THEN
  statement_1;
  [statement_2;]...
[ELSIF boolean_expression THEN
  statement_1;
  [statement_2;]...]...
[ELSE
  statement_1;
  [statement_2;]...]
END IF;
```

A script that uses an IF statement

```
CONNECT ap/ap;

SET SERVEROUTPUT ON;

DECLARE
  first_invoice_due_date DATE;
BEGIN
  SELECT MIN(invoice_due_date)
  INTO first_invoice_due_date
  FROM invoices
  WHERE invoice_total - payment_total - credit_total > 0;

  IF first_invoice_due_date < SYSDATE() THEN
    DBMS_OUTPUT.PUT_LINE('Outstanding invoices overdue!');
  ELSIF first_invoice_due_date = SYSDATE() THEN
    DBMS_OUTPUT.PUT_LINE('Outstanding invoices are due today!');
  ELSE
    DBMS_OUTPUT.PUT_LINE('No invoices are overdue.');
  END IF;
END;
/
```

The response from the system

```
Outstanding invoices overdue!
```

Description

- You can use an *IF statement* to execute one or more statements depending on one or more Boolean expressions. A *Boolean expression* is an expression that evaluates to true or false.

- You can *nest* an IF statement within another IF statement or within other PL/SQL statements such as the statements for coding loops.

Figure 13-5   How to code IF statements

How to code CASE statements

In chapter 8, you learned how to code a CASE expression within a SELECT statement. A CASE expression like that usually runs faster than a CASE statement that's coded within a PL/SQL script. As a result, if you can use a CASE expression to solve the task at hand, you should. However, there are times when you will need to use a CASE statement as shown in figure 13-6.

The script in this figure shows how to use a *Simple CASE statement* to execute one or more statements depending on a value that's returned by an expression. To do that, you begin by coding the CASE keyword followed by an expression that returns a value. In this script, the variable that's coded after the CASE statement returns an integer value that indicates the payment terms for an invoice.

After the CASE clause, you can code one or more WHEN clauses that contain the statement or statements that are executed for each of the values that may be returned. In this example, there are three WHEN clauses for the values of 1, 2, and 3. Each of these clauses prints an appropriate message to SQL Developer's Script Output window.

After the WHEN clauses, you can code an optional ELSE clause that's executed if the value that's returned doesn't match the values coded in any of the WHEN clauses. This works much like the ELSE clause that's available from the IF statement.

Although this figure doesn't show an example of it, you can also use a *Searched CASE statement* to execute one or more statements depending on one or more Boolean expressions. This works similarly to an IF statement. For example, you can use a Searched CASE statement to replace the IF statement in the previous figure like this:

```
CASE
  WHEN first_invoice_due_date < SYSDATE() THEN
    DBMS_OUTPUT.PUT_LINE('Outstanding invoices overdue!');
  WHEN first_invoice_due_date = SYSDATE() THEN
    DBMS_OUTPUT.PUT_LINE('Outstanding invoices are due today!');
  ELSE
    DBMS_OUTPUT.PUT_LINE('No invoices are overdue.');
END CASE;
```

Conversely, you can easily rewrite the Simple CASE statement shown in this figure as an IF statement.

So, when should you use an IF statement and when should you use a CASE statement? Although this is largely a matter of personal preference, you usually should try to use the statement that yields the code that's easiest to read and understand.

The syntax of the Simple CASE statement

```
CASE expression
  WHEN expression_value_1 THEN
    statement_1;
    [statement_2;]...
  [WHEN expression_value_2 THEN
    statement_1;
    [statement_2;]...]...
  [ELSE
    statement_1;
    [statement_2;]...]
END CASE;
```

A script that uses a Simple CASE statement

```
CONNECT ap/ap;

SET SERVEROUTPUT ON;

DECLARE
  terms_id_var NUMBER;
BEGIN
  SELECT terms_id INTO terms_id_var
  FROM invoices WHERE invoice_id = 4;

  CASE terms_id_var
    WHEN 1 THEN
      DBMS_OUTPUT.PUT_LINE('Net due 10 days');
    WHEN 2 THEN
      DBMS_OUTPUT.PUT_LINE('Net due 20 days');
    WHEN 3 THEN
      DBMS_OUTPUT.PUT_LINE('Net due 30 days');
    ELSE
      DBMS_OUTPUT.PUT_LINE('Net due more than 30 days');
  END CASE;
END;
/
```

The syntax of a Searched CASE expression

```
CASE
  WHEN boolean_expression THEN
    statement_1;
    [statement_2;]...
  [WHEN boolean_expression THEN
    statement_1;
    [statement_2;]...]...
  [ELSE
    statement_1;
    [statement_2;]...]
END CASE;
```

Description

- You can use a *Simple CASE statement* or a *Searched Case statement* to execute one or more statements depending on a value that's returned by an expression.

Figure 13-6   How to code CASE statements

How to code loops

Figure 13-7 shows how to use a *loop* to repeat a statement or a block of statements while a condition is true. This figure starts by showing how to use a *FOR loop* to continue executing while a *counter* is within the specified range. In the example, the code specifies a counter variable named i that will be increased by 1 each time through the loop, starting with a value of 1 and ending with a value of 3 (1…3). As a result, the statement within the loop is executed three times, once for each of the counter values (1, 2, and 3). The statement within the loop just prints the value of the counter variable to the output window.

The syntax for the FOR loop also shows that you can use the REVERSE keyword to execute a FOR loop in reverse order. For example, you could code the first line of the FOR loop in this figure like this:

```
FOR i IN REVERSE 1..3 LOOP
```

Then, the loop would yield counter values of 3, 2, and 1.

After the FOR loop, this figure shows how to use a *WHILE loop* to continue executing until a Boolean expression becomes true. In this example, the WHILE loop continues to execute while a counter variable named i is less than 4. To get this loop to work, you must first declare the counter variable in the DECLARE section. Then, you must assign a value to the counter before you begin the loop, and you must increment the counter within the body of the loop. In this example, the last statement in the loop adds a value of 1 to the counter variable.

Finally, this figure shows how to use a *simple LOOP* that ends when the Boolean expression in the EXIT WHEN clause is true. In the example, the last statement in the loop uses an EXIT WHEN statement to exit the loop when the counter variable named i is greater than or equal to 4. Here again, the counter variable must be declared in the DECLARE section. Alternately, this loop could achieve the same result by using an EXIT statement within an IF statement like this:

```
IF i >= 4 THEN
  EXIT;
END IF;
```

In the rare case that you need to jump to the beginning of a loop, you can use the CONTINUE or CONTINUE WHEN statements. These statements work like the EXIT and EXIT WHEN statements, except that they jump to the beginning of a loop instead of jumping to the end of a loop.

Please note that all three of the loops in this figure produce the same result. However, the FOR loop uses just three lines of code, the WHILE loops uses five lines of code, and the simple loop uses six lines of code. This shows that FOR loops are easier to use whenever you need to use a counter variable to loop through a range of values. However, there are times when a WHILE loop or a simple loop is more appropriate for the task at hand.

The syntax of the FOR loop

```
FOR counter_var IN [REVERSE] counter_start..counter_end LOOP
  statement_1;
  [statement_2;]...
END LOOP;
```

A FOR loop

```
FOR i IN 1..3 LOOP
  DBMS_OUTPUT.PUT_LINE('i: ' || i);
END LOOP;
```

The syntax for a WHILE loop

```
WHILE boolean_expression LOOP
  statement_1;
  [statement_2;]...
END LOOP;
```

A WHILE loop

```
i := 1;
WHILE i < 4 LOOP
  DBMS_OUTPUT.PUT_LINE('i: ' || i);
  i := i + 1;
END LOOP;
```

The syntax for a simple loop

```
LOOP
  statement_1;
  [statement_2;]...
  EXIT WHEN boolean_expression;
END LOOP;
```

A simple loop

```
i := 1;
LOOP
  DBMS_OUTPUT.PUT_LINE('i: ' || i);
  i := i + 1;
  EXIT WHEN i >= 4;
END LOOP;
```

The output for all three loops

```
i: 1
i: 2
i: 3
```

Description

- To execute a SQL statement repeatedly, you can use a *loop*. Oracle provides for three types of loops: a *FOR loop*, a *WHILE loop*, and a *simple loop*.
- You can use the EXIT and EXIT WHEN keywords to go to the end of a loop.
- You can use the CONTINUE and CONTINUE WHEN keywords to go to the beginning of the loop.

Figure 13-7   How to code loops

How to use a cursor

By default, SQL statements work with an entire result set rather than individual rows. However, there are times when you need to be able to work with the data in a result set one row at a time. To do that, you can use a *cursor* as described in figure 13-8.

The DECLARE section of the script in this figure begins by declaring a CURSOR named invoices_cursor that contains two columns from the invoices table and all of the rows that have a balance due. Then, this script declares a variable named invoice_row. This declaration uses the %ROWTYPE attribute to indicate that the invoice_row variable can store the same data types as a row in the invoices table.

After these two variables have been declared, the BEGIN section uses a FOR loop to loop through each row in the cursor. Here, the FOR loop uses the invoice_row variable as the counter variable, and it uses the IN keyword to specify that the loop should continue for each row in the cursor. Within the FOR loop, an IF statement is used to check if the invoice_total value of the current row is greater than 1000. If so, an UPDATE statement is used to add 10% of the invoice_total column to the credit_total column for the row. Then, it prints a message to the output window to show which rows have been updated.

Before you use a cursor to solve a particular problem, you should consider other solutions first. That's because standard database access is faster and uses fewer server resources than cursor-based access. For example, you can accomplish the same update as the script in this figure with this UPDATE statement:

```
UPDATE invoices
SET credit_total = credit_total + (invoice_total * .1)
WHERE invoice_total - payment_total - credit_total > 0
AND invoice_total > 1000
```

However, if you encounter a problem where it makes sense to use a cursor, the skills presented in this figure should put you on the road to solving the problem.

The syntax for declaring a cursor

```
CURSOR cursor_name IS select_statement;
```

The syntax for declaring a variable for a row

```
row_variable_name table_name%ROWTYPE;
```

The syntax for getting a column value from a row variable

```
row_variable_name.column_name
```

A script that uses a cursor

```
CONNECT ap/ap;

SET SERVEROUTPUT ON;

DECLARE
  CURSOR invoices_cursor IS
    SELECT invoice_id, invoice_total  FROM invoices
    WHERE invoice_total - payment_total - credit_total > 0;

  invoice_row invoices%ROWTYPE;
BEGIN
  FOR invoice_row IN invoices_cursor LOOP

    IF (invoice_row.invoice_total > 1000) THEN
      UPDATE invoices
      SET credit_total = credit_total + (invoice_total * .1)
      WHERE invoice_id = invoice_row.invoice_id;

      DBMS_OUTPUT.PUT_LINE('1 row updated where invoice_id = ' ||
                           invoice_row.invoice_id);
    END IF;

  END LOOP;
END;
/
```

The response from the system

```
1 row updated where invoice_id = 3
1 row updated where invoice_id = 6
1 row updated where invoice_id = 8
1 row updated where invoice_id = 19
1 row updated where invoice_id = 34
1 row updated where invoice_id = 81
1 row updated where invoice_id = 88
1 row updated where invoice_id = 113
```

Description

- You can use a *cursor* to process individual rows in a result set. To do that, you can loop through each row in the cursor and process one row at a time.

Figure 13-8   How to use a cursor

How to use collections

When you need to work with a set of related values, you can typically use a cursor as described in the previous figure. However, in some situations, you may need to use a collection as described in figure 13-9. A *collection* is a list of related values, and this figure describes all three types of collections that are provided by Oracle.

This first example shows how to use a *varray*. To start, you declare the type of data the varray can store. To do this, you code the TYPE keyword, followed by a name for the type, followed by the IS VARRAY keywords, followed by a set of parentheses. Within the parentheses, you code a number that indicates the number of items that the varray can store. After the parentheses, you code the OF keyword, followed by the data type for the items in the varray. In this figure, for example, the varray stores three items of the VARCHAR2(25) type. However, a varray can store most other Oracle data types as well.

After you declare the type of the varray, you can declare a variable of that type. In addition, you must initialize the variable by assigning initial values to each of the items in the varray. In this figure, for example, the statement creates a varray of the "names_array" type with a name of "names". Then, it initializes each value within the array by coding the assignment statement, followed by the varray type, followed by a set of parentheses that contains the list of values. In this figure, each statement is initialized to a NULL value. However, you can also initialize each item to a non-NULL value like this:

```
names names_array := names_array('John', 'Jane', 'Joel');
```

In that case, you don't need to code the assignment statements shown in this figure since values have already been assigned to the items in the list.

After the DECLARE section, the body of the script begins by setting the names for the three items in the names varray. To do that, it uses an integer value as an index to access each of the values that are stored in the names varray. Note that an index of 1 accesses the first item, an index of 2 accesses the second item, and so on.

After the values have been set, the script uses a FOR loop to get the values from the varray, and it prints these values to the output window. To do that, the loop declares a counter variable named i that counts from 1 to the total number of items in the varray. Here, the COUNT method of the collection returns the total number of items in the varray. Then, the counter variable is used to return the value for each of the items in the varray.

When you declare a varray, it has a fixed size. As a result, if you attempt to use an index to refer to an item outside the range of the varray, Oracle will raise an error. For example, Oracle will raise an error if you refer to a fourth element like this:

```
names(4) := 'Jack';
```

In contrast, when you declare a *nested table* as shown in the second example, you don't declare a size for the list. Instead, you code the TABLE keyword. Other than that, though, nested tables work similarly to varrays. If you want to increase the number of elements that are stored by the list, though, you

The syntax for declaring a varray

```
TYPE type_name     IS VARRAY(count) OF data_type;
coll_name          type_name := type_name(value1 [, value2]...);
```

The syntax for setting a value in a collection

```
coll_name(index) := value;
```

The syntax for getting a value from a collection

```
var_name := coll_name(index);
```

A script that uses a varray

```
DECLARE
  TYPE names_array     IS VARRAY(3) OF VARCHAR2(25);
  names                names_array := names_array(NULL, NULL, NULL);
BEGIN
  names(1) := 'John';
  names(2) := 'Jane';
  names(3) := 'Joel';

  FOR i IN 1..names.COUNT LOOP
    DBMS_OUTPUT.PUT_LINE('Name ' || i || ': ' || names(i));
  END LOOP;
END;
/
```

The response from the system

```
Name 1: John
Name 2: Jane
Name 3: Joel
```

The syntax for declaring a nested table

```
TYPE type_name    IS TABLE OF data_type;
coll_name         type_name := type_name(value1 [, value2]...);
```

A script that uses a nested table

```
DECLARE
  TYPE names_table     IS TABLE OF VARCHAR2(25);
  names                names_table := names_table(NULL, NULL, NULL);
BEGIN
  names(1) := 'John';
  names(2) := 'Jane';
  names(3) := 'Joel';

  FOR i IN 1..names.COUNT LOOP
    DBMS_OUTPUT.PUT_LINE('Name ' || i || ': ' || names(i));
  END LOOP;
END;
/
```

Description

- You can use a *collection* to store a list of related values.

- Oracle provides three types of collections: *varrays*, *nested tables*, and *associative arrays* (which were known as *index-by tables* prior to Oracle Database 10g).

Figure 13-9   How to use collections (part 1 of 2)

can call the EXTEND method and specify the number of elements that you want to add. If, for example, you want to add one item to the names collection presented in the second example, you can code the EXTEND method like this:

```
names.EXTEND(1);
```

Then, you can use the fourth index to set a value for the new item like this:

```
names(4) := 'Jack';
```

The third example shows how to use an *associative array*. Prior to Oracle 10g, associative arrays were known as *index-by tables*. Regardless of the name, this type of collection works similarly to nested tables. However, the index values for the collection don't have to be sequential, and they don't have to be integers. In addition, the size of the collection is increased automatically whenever that's necessary.

When you declare an associative array, you begin with a syntax that's similar to the syntax for declaring nested tables. Then, you code the INDEX BY keywords followed by the data type for the index. Here, you can specify the BINARY_INTEGER or PLS_INTEGER type for an integer index or the VARCHAR2 type for a string index.

After the DECLARE section, the body of the script uses non-sequential integers as the indexes for the items. Then, a FOR statement uses the FIRST and LAST methods of the collection to loop from the first index in the list to the last index in the list. In other words, it loops from 76 to 123. Within the body of the FOR loop, an IF statement uses the EXISTS method to check if a value exists for the specified index. If so, it prints the value for the item to the output window. This prevents an error that occurs if you attempt to access an item that doesn't exist in the list.

The fourth example shows how to use a SELECT statement to fill a collection with values. This example begins by declaring a nested table of the VARCHAR2(40) type and assigning this nested table to a variable named vendor_names. Then, the body of the script uses a SELECT statement with a BULK COLLECT clause to fill this variable with values that are selected from the vendor_name column of the Vendors table. In this example, the SELECT statement uses the ROWNUM pseudo column to return three rows. However, you can use the same technique to fill a variable with a large number of values.

Note that the syntax for using the BULK COLLECT clause is similar to the syntax for setting a variable to a single selected value. However, with a BULK COLLECT clause, the target variable must be defined as one of the collection types.

At this point, you may be wondering when you will need to use collections. To answer that question, you can refer to figure 16-10 of chapter 16. This figure shows how collections can be used to fix a common Oracle error.

The syntax for declaring an associative array

```
TYPE type_name     IS TABLE OF data_type [NOT NULL]
                   INDEX BY {PLS_INTEGER|BINARY_INTEGER|VARCHAR2(size)};
coll_name          type_name := type_name(value1 [, value2]...);
```

A script that uses an associative array

```
DECLARE
  TYPE names_table     IS TABLE OF VARCHAR2(25)
                       INDEX BY BINARY_INTEGER;
  names                names_table;
BEGIN
  names(76)  := 'John';
  names(100) := 'Jane';
  names(123) := 'Joel';

  FOR i IN names.FIRST..names.LAST LOOP
    IF names.EXISTS(i) THEN
      DBMS_OUTPUT.PUT_LINE('Name ' || i || ': ' || names(i));
    END IF;
  END LOOP;
END;
/
```

A script that uses a BULK COLLECT clause to fill a collection

```
DECLARE
  TYPE names_table     IS TABLE OF VARCHAR2(40);
  vendor_names         names_table;
BEGIN
  SELECT vendor_name
  BULK COLLECT INTO vendor_names
  FROM vendors
  WHERE rownum < 4
  ORDER BY vendor_id;

  FOR i IN 1..vendor_names.COUNT LOOP
    DBMS_OUTPUT.PUT_LINE('Vendor name ' || i || ': ' || vendor_names(i));
  END LOOP;
END;
/
```

The response from the system

```
Vendor name 1: US Postal Service
Vendor name 2: National Information Data Ctr
Vendor name 3: Register of Copyrights
```

Description

- Varrays have a fixed size that's declared at compile-time. The size of nested tables and associative arrays can be dynamically adjusted at runtime.

- You can use the methods of a collection (such as the COUNT, FIRST, LAST, and EXISTS methods) to work with a collection.

- You can use the BULK COLLECT clause of a SELECT statement to retrieve a list of values into a collection.

Figure 13-9   How to use collections (part 2 of 2)

How to handle exceptions

Figure 13-10 shows how to use the EXCEPTION section of a PL/SQL block to handle the exceptions that may occur in your PL/SQL code. This is often referred to as *exception handling* or *error handling*.

This figure begins by showing a script that doesn't handle exceptions. Here, the INSERT statement attempts to insert a duplicate value ("Cash") into a column (account_description) that has been defined with a unique key. This causes Oracle to raise an exception. Since this exception isn't handled, this causes the system to display an error message like the one that's shown.

Although error messages like this can be helpful to a developer when PL/SQL code is being developed, they aren't helpful to the end user of an application. As a result, you typically want to handle exceptions before you put your PL/SQL code into production. To do that, you can begin by looking up any errors that you discover during testing as described in the next figure. If, for example, you look up error number 00001, you'll see that it has a name of DUP_VAL_ON_INDEX. Then, you can use the EXCEPTION section of a PL/SQL block to display a more user-friendly message to the user. Or, you can use the EXCEPTION section to perform other error handling tasks such as writing information about the error to a log table or rolling back a transaction.

The second script in this figure handles two exceptions: (1) the DUP_VAL_ON_INDEX exception that's thrown by the first script, and (2) any other exceptions that may be thrown. To do that, this script includes an EXCEPTION section that has two WHEN clauses. Here, the first WHEN clause handles the DUP_VAL_ON_INDEX exception by printing a user-friendly message to the output window. Then, the second WHEN clause uses the OTHERS keyword to handle all other exceptions by printing two lines to the output window. Within this clause, the first statement prints a user-friendly message that indicates that an unexpected exception has occurred. Then, the second statement prints the error number and message that are returned by the built-in SQLERRM function. Since the second WHEN clause handles all exceptions, it must be coded last. Otherwise, you'll get an error when you attempt to run your script.

To test this script, you can change the values in the INSERT statement. If you run the statement as shown in this figure, the script will print the line shown in the first WHEN clause. If you enter 'xx' as the first value for the INSERT statement, the script will print the first line shown in the second WHEN clause. Then, it will print the string that's returned by the SQLERRM function. Together, these two lines will look something like this:

```
An unexpected exception occurred.
ORA-01722: invalid number
```

Finally, if you enter valid values, the script will print a message that indicates that 1 row was inserted.

A script that doesn't handle exceptions

```
CONNECT ap/ap;
INSERT INTO general_ledger_accounts VALUES (130, 'Cash');
```

The response from the system

```
SQL Error: ORA-00001: unique constraint (AP.GL_ACCOUNT_DESCRIPTION_UQ) violated
00001. 00000 -  "unique constraint (%s.%s) violated"
*Cause:    An UPDATE or INSERT statement attempted to insert a duplicate key.
           For Trusted Oracle configured in DBMS MAC mode, you may see
           this message if a duplicate entry exists at a different level.
*Action:   Either remove the unique restriction or do not insert the key.
```

The syntax of the EXCEPTION block

```
EXCEPTION
  WHEN most_specific_exception THEN
    statement_1;
    [statement_2;]...

  [WHEN less_specific_exception THEN
    statement_1;
    [statement_2;]...]...
```

A script that uses the EXCEPTION block to handle exceptions

```
CONNECT ap/ap;

SET SERVEROUTPUT ON;

BEGIN
  INSERT INTO general_ledger_accounts VALUES (130, 'Cash');

  DBMS_OUTPUT.PUT_LINE('1 row inserted.');
EXCEPTION
  WHEN DUP_VAL_ON_INDEX THEN
    DBMS_OUTPUT.PUT_LINE('You attempted to insert a duplicate value.');

  WHEN OTHERS THEN
    DBMS_OUTPUT.PUT_LINE('An unexpected exception occurred.');
    DBMS_OUTPUT.PUT_LINE(SQLERRM);
END;
/
```

The response from the system

```
You attempted to insert a duplicate value.
```

Description

- In a PL/SQL block, you can use the EXCEPTION block to handle exceptions. This is referred to as *exception handling* or *error handling*.

- Within a WHEN clause, you can specify the name of a specific exception to handle, or you can use the OTHERS keyword to handle all exceptions that haven't been handled by a previous WHEN clause.

- Within a WHEN clause, you can use the SQLERRM function to return a string that contains an error number and message for the error that was raised.

Figure 13-10   How to handle exceptions

A list of predefined exceptions

Figure 13-11 shows four of the *predefined exceptions* that are defined and raised by Oracle. These exceptions should give you an idea of the types of predefined exceptions that are provided by Oracle. For example, the first exception in this list shows the DUP_VAL_ON_INDEX exception that was described in the previous figure. Note that its ORA error number (00001) corresponds with the error number that's shown in the error message in the previous figure.

In all, Oracle provides over 20 predefined exceptions. For a complete list of these exceptions, you can search the Oracle Database PL/SQL Language Reference manual for "predefined PL/SQL exceptions".

In most cases, you can use the predefined exceptions to handle the exceptions that you encounter. In some cases, though, you may need to use *user-defined exceptions*, which are exceptions that have been defined by a DBA or another developer. If, for example, you're developing stored procedures or functions as described in the chapter 15, you may need to create your own user-defined exceptions. Since most application developers don't need to do that, though, that skill isn't covered in this book.

A list of commonly used exceptions

ORA Error	Exception	Description
00001	DUP_VAL_ON_INDEX	Occurs when a program attempts to store duplicate values in a column that has a unique constraint or index.
01403	NO_DATA_FOUND	Occurs when a SELECT INTO statement doesn't return any data.
01476	ZERO_DIVIDE	Occurs when a program attempts to divide a number by zero.
01722	INVALID_NUMBER	Occurs when a program fails to convert a string into a number. This is usually because the characters in the string do not form a valid number.
06502	VALUE_ERROR	Occurs when a program encounters an arithmetic, conversion, truncation, or size-constraint error.

Description

- Oracle provides *predefined exceptions* for exceptions that commonly occur.

- For a complete list of the predefined exceptions provided by Oracle, you can search the Oracle Database PL/SQL Language Reference manual for "predefined PL/SQL exceptions".

- In most cases, you can use the predefined exceptions provided by Oracle to handle exceptions. However, in some cases, you may need to use *user-defined exceptions*, which are exceptions that have been defined by a DBA or another developer.

- To learn more about user-defined exceptions, look up "user-defined exceptions" in the PL/SQL Reference manual.

Figure 13-11   A list of predefined exceptions

Other scripting and PL/SQL skills

The remaining topics of this chapter present some additional techniques you can use to work with the scripts and PL/SQL code that you write.

How to drop database objects without displaying errors

Frequently, you'll need to write scripts that create database objects. For example, the script that you used to create the AP schema creates all of the tables and sequences for the database. However, if you attempt to create an object that already exists, Oracle returns an error and the script doesn't execute correctly. For example, if you try to create the Vendors table and that table already exists, Oracle returns an error that indicates that the table can't be created because it already exists.

To solve this problem, you can code a DROP statement that drops the database object before you create it as shown by the first script in figure 13-12. Although that allows the script to successfully create the table, it also causes an error to be displayed if the database object doesn't exist. For example, if the table named Test1 doesn't exist, this script will display an error like the one that's shown.

To solve this problem, you can use an anonymous PL/SQL block to handle the error as shown by the second script in this figure. Here, the BEGIN section of the PL/SQL block uses the EXECUTE IMMEDIATE command to execute the DROP TABLE statement that drops the table named Test1. This is necessary because you can't execute a DDL statement such as a DROP TABLE statement within a PL/SQL block. Instead, you must use the EXECUTE IMMEDATE command to execute a string that contains the DDL command. Note that the EXECUTE IMMEDIATE command was introduced with Oracle 9i.

Then, the EXCEPTION section of the PL/SQL block handles this error by using the NULL statement to do nothing. This is known as *squelching* an error, and it prevents the error message from being displayed. Although squelching errors is generally considered a bad practice, it's helpful in this example since you want to prevent the error message from being displayed.

The syntax of the EXECUTE IMMEDIATE statement

```
EXECUTE IMMEDIATE 'sql_string'
```

A script that will display an error if the object doesn't already exist

```
CONNECT ap/ap;
DROP TABLE test1;
CREATE TABLE test1 (test_id NUMBER);
```

The response from the system

```
Connected

Error starting at line 2 in command:
DROP TABLE test1
Error report:
SQL Error: ORA-00942: table or view does not exist
00942. 00000 -  "table or view does not exist"
*Cause:
*Action:
CREATE TABLE succeeded.
```

A script that will execute correctly without displaying an error

```
CONNECT ap/ap;

BEGIN
  EXECUTE IMMEDIATE 'DROP TABLE test1';
EXCEPTION
  WHEN OTHERS THEN
    NULL;
END;
/

CREATE TABLE test1 (test_id NUMBER);
```

The response from the system

```
Connected
anonymous block completed
CREATE TABLE succeeded.
```

Description

- You can't execute DDL statements within a PL/SQL block. However, as of Oracle 9i, you can use the EXECUTE IMMEDIATE statement to execute a string that contains a DDL statement.

- You can use the NULL statement if a clause requires a statement but you don't want to execute any code.

Figure 13-12   How to drop database objects without displaying errors

How to use bind variables

Figure 13-13 begins by showing how to use a *bind variable*, which is a special type of variable that has several advantages over a regular variable. First, SQL statements that use bind variables usually run more efficiently than SQL statements that concatenate a regular variable. As a result, you should use bind variables whenever efficiency is a concern. For example, Oracle will be able to cache the SELECT statement shown in this figure and substitute the bind variable. This runs more efficiently than concatenating a regular variable to the end of the SELECT statement.

Second, a bind variable can be used in regular SQL statements that are executed outside of a PL/SQL block. In this figure, for example, the SELECT statement that uses the bind variable named invoice_id_value isn't coded within a PL/SQL block.

Third, a bind variable stays in scope for an entire script. More accurately, a bind variable stays in scope for the entire SQL Developer or SQL*Plus session. As a result, you can use a bind variable across all statements in a script. In this figure, for example, the bind variable named invoice_id_value is used in the first PL/SQL block, the SELECT statement that follows, and the second PL/SQL block.

To declare a bind variable, you code a statement that starts with the VARIABLE keyword. This works similarly to declaring a regular PL/SQL variable except that you must begin the statement with the VARIABLE keyword. In addition, you must code this statement outside of a PL/SQL block, which makes sense when you consider that the scope of a bind variable is larger than a single PL/SQL block.

After you declare a bind variable, you can reference it by prefacing it with a colon (:). In this figure, for example, all statements that use the bind variable named invoice_id_value preface it with a colon.

How to use substitution variables

If you want to prompt the user to enter a variable, you can code a substitution variable. A *substitution variable* causes SQL Developer or SQL*Plus to prompt the user who runs the script to enter a value that's substituted for the substitution variable. You code a substitution variable by prefacing the variable name with an ampersand (&). In this figure, for example, the statement in the first PL/SQL script uses a substitution variable named invoice_id to assign a value to the bind variable.

As a result, if you use SQL Developer to run this script, SQL Developer will display a dialog box that prompts the user to enter a value for the invoice_id variable, as shown in this figure. Then, this value is assigned to the bind variable. In this example, I entered a value of 1 for the substitution variable. However, I could have entered any valid invoice ID, and the script would have executed successfully.

A script that uses bind variables

```
CONNECT ap/ap;
SET SERVEROUTPUT ON;

-- Use the VARIABLE keyword to declare a bind variable
VARIABLE invoice_id_value NUMBER;

-- Use a PL/SQL block to set the value of a bind variable
-- to the value that's entered for a substitution variable
BEGIN
  :invoice_id_value := &invoice_id;
END;
/

-- Use a bind variable in a SELECT statement
SELECT invoice_id, invoice_number
FROM invoices
WHERE invoice_id = :invoice_id_value;

-- Use a bind variable in another PL/SQL block
BEGIN
  DBMS_OUTPUT.PUT_LINE('invoice_id_value: ' || :invoice_id_value);
END;
/
```

The dialog box that prompts for a substitution variable

The response from the system

```
Connected
anonymous block completed
INVOICE_ID              INVOICE_NUMBER
---------------------- -------------------------------------------------
1                       QP58872

1 rows selected

anonymous block completed
invoice_id_value: 1
```

Description

- A *bind variable* stays in scope for an entire script and can be used in SQL statements or in PL/SQL blocks. To code a bind variable, preface the variable name with a colon (:).
- A *substitution variable* causes SQL Developer to prompt the user who runs the script to enter a value for the substitution variable. To code a substitution variable, preface the variable name with an ampersand (&).

Figure 13-13   How to use bind variables and substitution variables

How to use dynamic SQL

So far, most of the scripts you've seen in this chapter have contained hard-coded SQL statements. In other words, the SQL statements don't change from one execution of the script to another. In contrast, when you use *dynamic SQL*, you define a SQL statement as a script executes. Then, you use the EXECUTE IMMEDIATE statement to execute the SQL that was dynamically generated by the script.

Figure 13-14 shows how you can use the EXECUTE IMMEDIATE statement to execute a dynamic SQL statement. To start, the script in this figure declares three variables. The first two variables are used to store the values of the invoice ID and the terms ID, and the third variable is used to store the dynamic SQL statement.

After the DECLARE section, the body of the script begins by using substitution variables to set the values for the invoice ID and terms ID variables. Then, it builds an UPDATE statement by concatenating these values with some string literals, and it assigns the UPDATE statement to the variable named dynamic_sql. Finally, this code uses the EXECUTE IMMEDIATE command to execute the UPDATE statement that's stored in the dynamic_sql variable.

The EXECUTE IMMEDIATE statement is part of the *Native Dynamic SQL* (*NDS*) feature that was introduced with Oracle 9i. Prior to Oracle 9i, you needed to use the DBMS_SQL package to work with dynamic SQL. In general, NDS provides many advantages over the DBMS_SQL package. In particular, it runs faster, has a more intuitive syntax, and provides features that aren't available from the DBMS_SQL package. As a result, if you're using Oracle 9i or later, you'll usually want to use NDS instead of the DBMS_SQL package.

Dynamic SQL that updates the terms ID for the specified invoice

```
CONNECT ap/ap;

DECLARE
  invoice_id_var NUMBER;
  terms_id_var NUMBER;
  dynamic_sql VARCHAR2(400);
BEGIN
  invoice_id_var := &invoice_id;
  terms_id_var := &terms_id;

  dynamic_sql := 'UPDATE invoices ' ||
                 'SET terms_id = ' || terms_id_var || ' ' ||
                 'WHERE invoice_id = ' || invoice_id_var;

  EXECUTE IMMEDIATE dynamic_sql;
END;
/
```

The first dialog box that prompts for a substitution variable

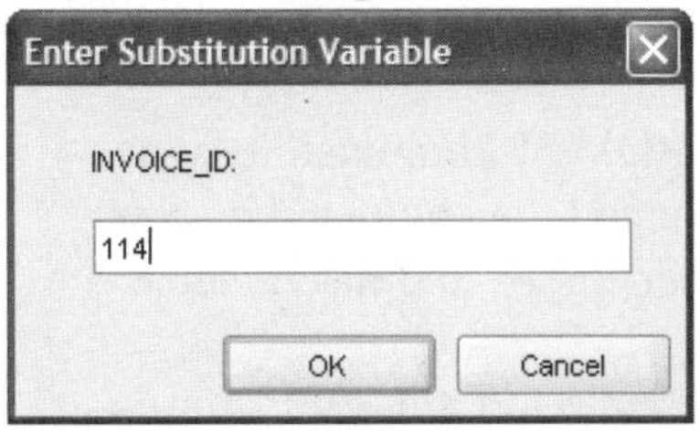

The second dialog box that prompts for a substitution variable

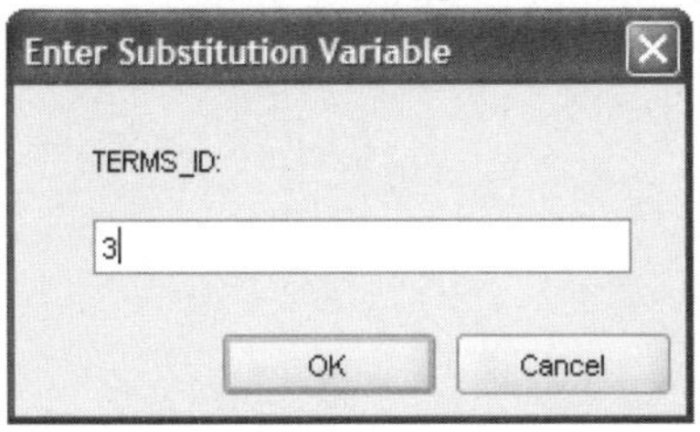

The contents of the variable named dynamic_sql at runtime

```
UPDATE invoices SET terms_id = 3 WHERE invoice_id = 114
```

Description

- You can use a PL/SQL block to build a string variable that contains a SQL statement. Then, you can use the EXECUTE IMMEDIATE statement to execute the statement contained in the string. This is known as *dynamic SQL*.

- The EXECUTE IMMEDIATE statement is part of *Native Dynamic SQL* (*NDS*), which was introduced with Oracle 9i. Prior to Oracle 9i, you needed to use the DBMS_SQL package to work with dynamic SQL.

Figure 13-14   How to use dynamic SQL

How to run a script from a command line

Figure 13-15 shows how you can use SQL*Plus to run SQL scripts from a command line. This provides a way to use a *DOS batch file* or a *Unix shell script* to run a SQL script, which in turn provides an easy way for an end user to execute a SQL script. On a Windows system, for example, a user can execute a batch file that executes a SQL script by double-clicking on the batch file.

This figure begins by showing a SQL script that creates a user named AR and creates a table named Customers within this user's schema. To start, this script uses a SPOOL command to write the output for the script to a log file named create_ar.log. If the script doesn't execute successfully this log file can be used to troubleshoot problems with the script.

After the SPOOL command, this script uses the PROMPT command to write a message to the log file and also to the command prompt. Then, it uses a second PROMPT command to write a blank line.

After the PROMPT commands, this script uses a PL/SQL block to drop the AR user and any objects that exist within this user's schema. Then, it creates the AR user and grants privileges to the AR user.

After creating the AR user, this script uses the PROMPT command to write another message and another blank line to the log file and the command prompt. Then, it connects as the AR user, creates the Customers table, and inserts three rows into this table.

After creating the Customers table, this script uses the SPOOL OFF command to finish writing to the log file. Then, it uses the PROMPT command to write another message and another blank line to the command prompt. Finally, this script uses the EXIT command to exit from SQL*Plus.

The code for the create_ar.sql script

```
SPOOL create_ar.log;

PROMPT Creating AR user...
PROMPT

CONNECT system/system;
BEGIN
  EXECUTE IMMEDIATE 'DROP USER ar CASCADE';
EXCEPTION
  WHEN OTHERS THEN
    NULL;
END;
/
CREATE USER ar IDENTIFIED BY ar DEFAULT TABLESPACE users;
GRANT ALL PRIVILEGES TO ar;

PROMPT Creating AR tables...
PROMPT

CONNECT ar/ar;
CREATE TABLE customers
(
  customer_id             NUMBER          NOT NULL,
  customer_first_name     VARCHAR2(50)    NOT NULL,
  customer_last_name      VARCHAR2(50)    NOT NULL,
  CONSTRAINT customers_pk
    PRIMARY KEY (customer_id)
);
INSERT INTO customers VALUES (1, 'Jack', 'Samson');
INSERT INTO customers VALUES (2, 'Joan', 'Redding');
INSERT INTO customers VALUES (3, 'Jim', 'Abbot');

SPOOL OFF;

PROMPT Check create_ar.log for details...
PROMPT

EXIT;
```

Figure 13-15   How to run a script from the command line (part 1 of 2)

Figure 13-15 continues by showing the code for the DOS batch file named create_ar.bat. To start, this batch file uses the @ECHO OFF command to prevent the commands that are executed by the batch file from being displayed (echoed) in the DOS window.

Then, this batch file uses the SQLPLUS command to use SQL*Plus to run the SQL script named create_ar, which is the SQL script shown in the previous figure. Here, the SQLPLUS command connects to the database as the user named system using a password of system. Note that this works because the create_ar.bat and create_ar.sql files are stored in the same directory. If these files weren't stored in the same directory, you would need to qualify the name of the SQL script with a complete path. Note also that you don't need to include the .sql extension for the file that stores the script.

After executing the SQL script, this batch file uses the ECHO command to print a blank line, print a message that the batch file has finished, and print another blank line to the DOS window.

Finally, this batch file uses the PAUSE command to display the 'Press any key to continue' message that's displayed at the end of the command prompt. Without this command, the DOS window would automatically close, and the user wouldn't be able to review the output that has been printed to the DOS window. Although it isn't critical to display this window, it lets the user review the messages that have been printed to the window by the SQL script and the DOS batch file. That way, the user can confirm that the script executed successfully. Or, if the output shows that the script encountered errors, the user can use this information to troubleshoot the problem.

The code for the create_ar.bat file

```
@ECHO off
:: Use SQL*Plus to run the create_ar.sql script
SQLPLUS system/system @create_ar

:: Display a message about the log file
ECHO.
ECHO The create_ar.bat file has finished running.
ECHO.

:: Display 'press any key to continue' message
PAUSE
```

The output that's displayed in the DOS window

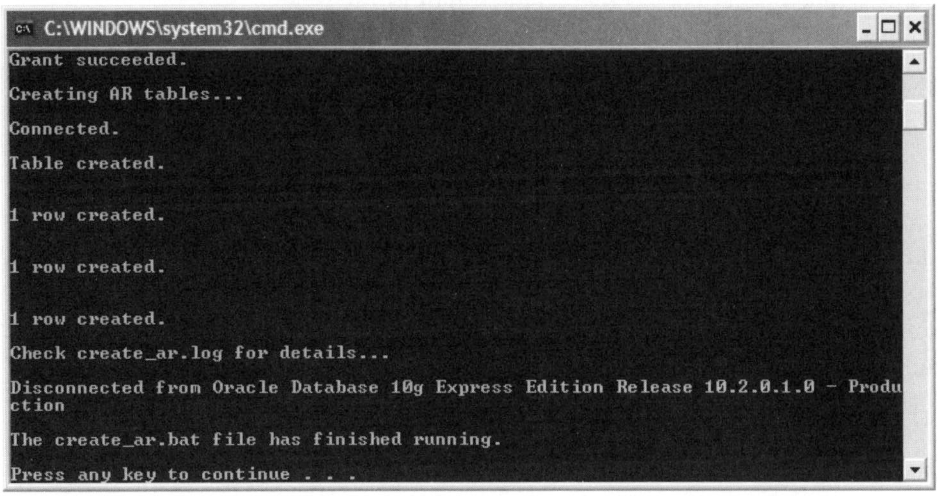

Description

- You can use the SQLPLUS command to execute SQL scripts from a command line. This provides a way to use a *DOS batch file* or a *Unix shell script* to run a SQL script.
- On a Windows system, you can execute a batch (*.bat) file by double-clicking on it after you find it in the Windows Explorer.

Figure 13-15   How to run a script from the command line (part 2 of 2)

Perspective

In this chapter, you learned how to use PL/SQL to write procedural code. You also learned how to use dynamic SQL to solve problems that can't be solved using any other technique. By using these techniques, you'll be able to code scripts that are more general, more useful, and less susceptible to failure.

In the next three chapters, you'll learn more about the use of PL/SQL code. In chapter 14, you'll learn how to manage transactions and locking. In chapter 15, you'll learn how to code stored procedures and functions, which are essentially named blocks of PL/SQL code that are stored within the database as objects. And in chapter 16, you'll learn how to code triggers. When you finish those chapters, you'll have a much better perspective on the use of PL/SQL.

Terms

script	collection
PL/SQL	varray
anonymous PL/SQL block	nested table
variable	associative array
scalar variable	index-by table
IF statement	exception handling
Boolean expression	error handling
nested statements	predefined exception
Simple CASE statement	user-defined exception
Searched CASE statement	squelching an error
loop	dynamic SQL
FOR loop	Native Dynamic SQL (NDS)
counter	bind variable
WHILE loop	substitution variable
simple loop	DOS batch file
cursor	UNIX shell script

Exercises

1. Write a script that declares and sets a variable that's equal to the count of all rows in the Invoices table that have a balance due that's greater than or equal to $5,000. Then, the script should display a message that looks like this:

```
3 invoices exceed $5,000.
```

2. Write a script that uses variables to get (1) the count of all of the invoices in the Invoices table that have a balance due and (2) the sum of the balances due for all of those invoices. If that total balance due is greater than or equal to $50,000, the script should display a message like this:

```
Number of unpaid invoices is 40.
Total balance due is $66,796.24.
```

Otherwise, the script should display this message:

```
Total balance due is less than $50,000.
```

3. Write a script that creates a cursor consisting of vendor_name, invoice_number, and balance_due for each invoice with a balance due that's greater than or equal to $5,000. The rows in this cursor should be sorted in descending sequence by balance due. Then, for each invoice, display the balance due, invoice number, and vendor name so it looks something like this:

```
$19,351.18    P-0608    Malloy Lithographing Inc
```

4. Enhance your solution to exercise 3 so it shows the invoice data in three groups based on the balance due amounts with these headings:

```
$20,000 or More
$10,000 to $20,000
$5,000 to $10,000
```

Each group should have a heading followed by the data for the invoices that fall into that group. Also, the groups should be separated by one blank line.

5. Enhance your solution to exercise 3 so it uses a substitution variable to set a bind variable that you use to determine what the minimum balance due should be for the invoices that the SELECT statement is going to retrieve. You should also use this bind variable to display a heading like this before the list of invoices:

```
Invoice amounts greater than or equal to $2,000
====================================================
```

where 2,000 is the value of the bind variable.

How to manage transactions and locking

If you've been working with Oracle on your own computer, you've been the only user of your database. In the real world, though, a database may be used by thousands of users at the same time. Then, what happens when two users try to update the same data at the same time? In this chapter, you'll learn how Oracle handles this situation. But first, you'll learn how to combine multiple SQL statements into a single logical unit of work known as a transaction.

How to work with transactions

A *transaction* is a group of SQL statements that you combine into a single logical unit of work. By combining SQL statements like this, you can prevent certain kinds of database errors.

How to commit and rollback transactions

Figure 14-1 starts by presenting a script that includes a PL/SQL block that contains three INSERT statements that are coded as a transaction. Here, the first INSERT statement adds a new invoice to the Invoices table. The next two INSERT statements add the line items for the invoice to the Invoice_Line_Items table. And the COMMIT statement *commits* the changes to the database, which makes the changes permanent.

On the other hand, if any of the INSERT statements causes an error, the execution of the script will jump into the EXCEPTION part of the PL/SQL block. Then, the first statement in the WHEN OTHERS THEN clause uses the ROLLBACK statement to undo, or *rollback*, all three INSERT statements.

To understand why this is necessary, suppose that you split the INSERT statements into three separate transactions by coding a COMMIT statement after each of the INSERT statements. Then, what will happen if the third INSERT statement fails? In that case, the Invoices and Invoice_Line_Items tables won't match. Specifically, the sum of the line_item_amt columns in the Invoice_Line_Items table won't be equal to the invoice_total column in the Invoices table. In other words, the data integrity won't be maintained.

Similarly, consider the example of a transfer between a checking and a savings account in a banking system. In that case, one update reduces the balance in the checking account and another update increases the balance in the savings account. Then, if one of these updates fails, the customer either gains or loses the amount of the transaction. But here again, treating the two updates as a single transaction solves this problem.

As you work with Oracle, remember that it doesn't automatically commit INSERT, UPDATE, and DELETE statements after you execute them as some database management systems do. As a result, you need to get into the habit of explicitly coding COMMIT and ROLLBACK statements when you write code that works with these statements.

A script that contains three INSERT statements that are coded as a transaction

```
CONNECT ap/ap;

SET SERVEROUTPUT ON;

BEGIN
  INSERT INTO invoices
  VALUES (115, 34, 'ZXA-080', '30-AUG-06',
          14092.59, 0, 0, 3, '30-SEP-06', NULL);

  INSERT INTO invoice_line_items
  VALUES (115, 1, 160, 4447.23, 'HW upgrade');

  INSERT INTO invoice_line_items
  VALUES (115, 2, 167, 9645.36, 'OS upgrade');

  COMMIT;
  DBMS_OUTPUT.PUT_LINE('The transaction was committed.');
EXCEPTION
  WHEN OTHERS THEN
    ROLLBACK;
    DBMS_OUTPUT.PUT_LINE('The transaction was rolled back.');
END;
/
```

When to use transactions

- When you code two or more INSERT, UPDATE, or DELETE statements that affect related data.
- When you move rows from one table to another table by using INSERT and DELETE statements.
- Whenever the failure of an INSERT, UPDATE, or DELETE statement would violate data integrity.

Description

- A *transaction* is one or more SQL statements that perform a logical unit of work.
- By default, Oracle doesn't *commit* the changes made by your INSERT, UPDATE, and DELETE statements until you explicitly commit them. To do that, you code a COMMIT statement after one or more SQL statements.
- If one or more SQL statements within a PL/SQL block encounters an error, you can code a ROLLBACK statement to *rollback* the changes.
- Oracle automatically executes a COMMIT statement after a DDL statement such as a CREATE TABLE statement or if the application exits successfully.
- Oracle automatically executes a ROLLBACK statement if the application crashes.

Figure 14-1   How to commit and roll back transactions

How to work with save points

The script in figure 14-2 shows how to use the SAVEPOINT statement to identify one or more *save points* within a transaction. Here, a SAVEPOINT statement is used to identify a save point before each of the three INSERT statements that are included in the script. As a result, the script includes three save points.

This script also shows how to use the ROLLBACK TO statement to rollback all or part of a transaction. Here, the three ROLLBACK TO statements rollback the transaction to each of the three save points. The first ROLLBACK TO statement rolls back to the point before the second line item was inserted. The second statement rolls back to the point before the first line item was inserted. And the third statement rolls back to the point before the invoice was inserted.

At this point, the script calls the COMMIT statement to commit any changes that have been made. However, the three ROLLBACK TO statements have rolled back all three INSERT statements, so this doesn't commit any changes to the database. To verify this, you can use a SELECT statement to view the rows in the Invoices and Invoice_Line_Items tables that have an invoice_id of 115.

In general, save points are used when a transaction contains so many statements that rolling back the entire transaction would be inefficient. In that case, an application can rollback to the last save point before an error occurred and continue from there. For most applications, though, you won't need to use save points.

A script that uses save points

```
SAVEPOINT before_invoice;

INSERT INTO invoices
VALUES (115, 34, 'ZXA-080', '30-AUG-08',
        14092.59, 0, 0, 3, '30-SEP-08', NULL);

SAVEPOINT before_line_item1;

INSERT INTO invoice_line_items
VALUES (115, 1, 160, 4447.23, 'HW upgrade');

SAVEPOINT before_line_item2;

INSERT INTO invoice_line_items
VALUES (115, 2, 167, 9645.36,'OS upgrade');

ROLLBACK TO SAVEPOINT before_line_item2;
ROLLBACK TO SAVEPOINT before_line_item1;
ROLLBACK TO SAVEPOINT before_invoice;

COMMIT;
```

The response from the system

```
SAVEPOINT before_invoice succeeded.
1 rows inserted
SAVEPOINT before_line_item1 succeeded.
1 rows inserted
SAVEPOINT before_line_item2 succeeded.
1 rows inserted
ROLLBACK TO succeeded.
ROLLBACK TO succeeded.
ROLLBACK TO succeeded.
COMMIT succeeded.
```

Description

- When you use *save points*, you can rollback a transaction to the beginning of the transaction or to a particular save point.
- You can use the SAVEPOINT statement to create a save point with the specified name.
- You can use the ROLLBACK TO statement to rollback a transaction to the specified save point.
- Save points are useful when a single transaction contains so many SQL statements that rolling back the entire transaction would be inefficient.

Figure 14-2   How to work with save points

How to work with concurrency and locking

When two or more users have access to the same database, it's possible for them to be working with the same data at the same time. This is called *concurrency*. Although concurrency isn't a problem when two users retrieve the same data at the same time, it can become a problem when one user updates data that other users are also viewing or updating. In the topics that follow, you'll learn how to prevent concurrency problems.

How concurrency and locking are related

Figure 14-3 presents two transactions that show how Oracle handles concurrency by default. To start, transaction A submits an UPDATE statement that adds a value of 100 to the value that's stored in the credit_total column of the invoice that has an invoice_id value of 6. Because transaction A hasn't yet committed this change to the database, it retains a *lock* on this row. This is known as *locking*.

At this point, if you run the SELECT statement in transaction B, the result set doesn't include the updated value in the credit_total column. In other words, the SELECT statement only reads changes that have been committed.

In addition, the UPDATE statement in transaction B won't be able to update the row due to the lock that transaction A has on the row. As a result, it will have to wait for transaction A to finish before it updates the row.

Once transaction A commits the change made by the UPDATE statement, the SELECT statement in transaction B will show the updated value in the credit_total column if you run it again. In addition, when transaction A commits the update, it releases its lock on the row. Then, the UPDATE statement in transaction B finishes executing if it has been waiting. Or, if you execute the UPDATE statement in transaction B again, it will execute immediately.

To experiment with concurrency, you can simulate multiple users by starting multiple instances of SQL Developer or SQL*Plus to execute SQL statements. For example, you can start two instances of SQL Developer and execute transaction A in the first instance and transaction B in the second instance. Then, you can use the Execute Statement (F9) command to run one statement at a time. This allows you to slow down the execution of each script. Otherwise, if you use the Run Script (F5) command, the script will run so quickly that you won't be able to get both scripts to access the same row at the same time.

This example shows that Oracle's default locking behavior prevents most concurrency problems. It also provides fast performance. However, it does allow a few concurrency problems that are described in figure 14-4. Although these concurrency problems are acceptable most of the time, you can prevent them by overriding Oracle's default locking behavior as shown in figure 14-5.

Two transactions that retrieve and then modify the data in the same row

Transaction A

```
UPDATE invoices SET credit_total = credit_total + 100 WHERE invoice_id = 6;

-- the SELECT statement in Transaction B won't show the updated data
-- the UPDATE statement in Transaction B will wait for A to finish

COMMIT;

-- the SELECT statement in Transaction B will show the updated data
-- the UPDATE statement in Transaction B will execute immediately
```

Transaction B

```
-- Use a second instance of SQL Developer or SQL*Plus
-- to execute these statements!
-- Otherwise, they won't work as described.

SELECT invoice_id, credit_total FROM invoices WHERE invoice_id = 6;

UPDATE invoices SET credit_total = credit_total + 200 WHERE invoice_id = 6;

COMMIT;
```

Description

- *Concurrency* is the ability of a system to support two or more transactions working with the same data at the same time.

- Oracle can automatically prevent some concurrency problems by using *locks*. A lock stops the execution of another transaction if it conflicts with a transaction that is already running.

- Concurrency is a problem only when the data is being modified. When two or more SELECT statements read the same data, the SELECT statements don't affect each other.

Figure 14-3   How concurrency and locking are related

The four concurrency problems that locks can prevent

Figure 14-4 describes the four most common concurrency problems. To start, a *lost update* is the problem that you've already learned about. It occurs when two transactions select the same row and then update the row based on the values originally selected. Since each transaction is unaware of the other, the later update overwrites the earlier update. For many applications, though, this type of problem rarely occurs, and it isn't serious when it does occur.

Like lost updates, the other three problems may not adversely affect a database. In fact, for many applications, these problems occur infrequently. Then, when they do occur, they can be corrected by resubmitting the SQL statement that experienced the problem. On some database systems, however, these problems can compromise data integrity so they need to be dealt with.

Although locks can prevent the problems listed in this figure, Oracle's default locking behavior only prevents dirty reads. If this level of locking isn't acceptable, though, you can change the default locking behavior by setting the transaction isolation level as shown in the next figure.

The four types of concurrency problems

Problem	Description
Lost updates	Occur when two transactions select the same row and then update the row based on the values originally selected. Since each transaction is unaware of the other, the later update overwrites the earlier update.
Dirty reads	Occur when a transaction selects data that hasn't been committed by another transaction. For example, transaction A changes a row. Transaction B then selects the changed row before transaction A commits the change. If transaction A then rolls back the change, transaction B has selected a row that doesn't exist in the database.
Nonrepeatable reads	Occur when two SELECT statements that try to get the same data get different values because another transaction has updated the data in the time between the two statements. For example, transaction A selects a row. Transaction B then updates the row. When transaction A selects the same row again, the data is different.
Phantom reads	Occur when you perform an update or delete on a set of rows at the same time that another transaction is performing an insert or delete that affects one or more rows in that same set of rows. For example, transaction A updates the payment total for each invoice that has a balance due, but transaction B inserts a new, unpaid, invoice while transaction A is still running. After transaction A finishes, there is still an invoice with a balance due.

Description

- In a large system with many users, you should expect for these kinds of problems to occur. In general, you don't need to take any action except to anticipate the problem. In many cases, if the SQL statement is resubmitted, the problem goes away.

- On some systems, if two transactions overwrite each other, the validity of the database is compromised and resubmitting one of the transactions won't eliminate the problem. If you're working on such a system, you must anticipate these concurrency problems and account for them in your code.

- If one of these problems could affect the data integrity of your system, you can change the default locking behavior by setting the transaction isolation level as shown in the next figure.

Figure 14-4   The four concurrency problems that locks can prevent

How to set the transaction isolation level

The simplest way to prevent concurrency problems is to change the default locking behavior as shown in figure 14-5. To change this behavior, you use the SET TRANSACTION ISOLATION LEVEL statement to set the *transaction isolation level* for the current session.

Note, however, that Oracle doesn't support the READ UNCOMMITTED or REPEATABLE READ transaction isolation levels. Also, it doesn't allow you to use the SNAPSHOT keyword to specify an isolation level. As a result, you must choose between the READ COMMITTED and SERIALIZABLE levels.

When you set the isolation level to SERIALIZABLE, each transaction is completely isolated from every other transaction. This prevents all four of the concurrency problems.

Since the SERIALIZABLE level eliminates all concurrency problems, you may think that this is always the best option. However, this option requires more overhead to manage all of the locks so the access time for each transaction is increased. For some systems, this may cause significant performance problems. As a result, you typically only want to use the SERIALIZABLE isolation level for situations in which the four concurrency problems aren't acceptable. In most situations, though, the default isolation level of READ COMMITTED is adequate.

In later versions of Oracle, the SERIALIZABLE isolation level may actually be using techniques that implement the newer SNAPSHOT isolation level that was developed during the mid-1990s. However, these two levels prevent the same concurrency problems. The difference between them is the mechanism that Oracle uses to prevent the concurrency problems. As a result, in most cases, the difference is transparent to the developer. In other words, to prevent all four concurrency problems described in this figure, you still set the transaction isolation level to SERIALIZABLE.

The concurrency problems prevented by each transaction isolation level

Isolation level	Dirty reads	Lost updates	Nonrepeatable reads	Phantom reads
READ UNCOMMITTED	Allows	Allows	Allows	Allows
READ COMMITTED	Prevents	Allows	Allows	Allows
REPEATABLE READ	Prevents	Prevents	Prevents	Allows
SERIALIZABLE	Prevents	Prevents	Prevents	Prevents
SNAPSHOT	Prevents	Prevents	Prevents	Prevents

The syntax of the SET TRANSACTION ISOLATION LEVEL statement

```
SET TRANSACTION ISOLATION LEVEL {READ COMMITTED|SERIALIZABLE}
```

A statement that sets the transaction isolation level to SERIALIZABLE

```
SET TRANSACTION ISOLATION LEVEL SERIALIZABLE;
```

A statement that sets the transaction isolation level to Oracle's default

```
SET TRANSACTION ISOLATION LEVEL READ COMMITTED;
```

Description

- The *transaction isolation level* controls the degree to which transactions are isolated from one another.
- At the more restrictive isolation levels, concurrency problems are reduced or eliminated. However, at the least restrictive levels, performance is enhanced.
- Oracle doesn't support the READ UNCOMMITTED or REPEATABLE READ transaction isolation levels. As a result, you must choose between the SERIALIZABLE level and the READ COMMITTED level (which is the default).
- In later versions of Oracle, the SERIALIZABLE isolation level may actually implement the newer SNAPSHOT isolation level that was developed during the mid 1990s. In most cases, the difference is transparent to the developer.

Figure 14-5   How to set the transaction isolation level

How to prevent deadlocks

A *deadlock* occurs when neither of two transactions can be committed because each has a lock on a resource needed by the other transaction. This is illustrated by the banking transactions in figure 14-6. Here, transaction A updates the savings account first and then the checking account, while transaction B updates the checking account first and then the savings account.

Now, suppose that the first statement in transaction A locks the savings account, and the first statement in transaction B locks the checking account. At that point, the deadlock occurs because transaction A needs the savings account and transaction B needs the checking account, but both are locked. Eventually, one of the transactions has to be rolled back so the other can proceed, and the loser is known as a *deadlock victim*.

To prevent deadlocks, you can use the four techniques that are presented in this figure. First, you shouldn't leave transactions open any longer than is necessary. That's because the longer a transaction remains open and uncommitted, the more likely it is that another transaction will need to work with that same resource.

So, when you're coding transactions, make sure to include the appropriate COMMIT and ROLLBACK statements. In addition, don't code statements that take a long time to execute within the INSERT, UPDATE, or DELETE statements that start a transaction and the COMMIT or ROLLBACK statements that finish a transaction.

Second, you shouldn't use a higher isolation level than you need. That's because the higher you set the isolation level, the more likely it is that two transactions will be unable to work with the same resource at the same time.

Third, you should schedule transactions that modify a large number of rows to run when no other transactions, or only a small number of other transactions, will be running. That way, it's less likely that the transactions will try to change the same rows at the same time.

Finally, you should consider how the SQL statements you write could cause a deadlock. To prevent the situation that's illustrated in this figure, for example, you should always update related accounts in the same sequence.

Don't allow transactions to remain open for very long

- Keep transactions short.
- Keep SELECT statements outside of the transaction except when absolutely necessary.
- Never code requests for user input during a transaction.

Use the lowest possible transaction isolation level

- The READ COMMITTED level, which is the default, is usually sufficient.
- Reserve the use of the SERIALIZABLE level for short transactions that make changes to data where integrity is vital.

Make large changes when you can be assured of nearly exclusive access

- If you need to change millions of rows in an active table, don't do so during hours of peak usage.
- If possible, give yourself exclusive access to the database before making large changes.

Consider locking when coding your transactions

- If you need to code two or more transactions that update the same resources, code the updates in the same order in each transaction.

UPDATE statements that illustrate deadlocking

Transaction A

```
UPDATE savings SET balance = balance - :transfer_amount;
UPDATE checking SET balance = balance + :transfer_amount;
COMMIT;
```

Transaction B (possible deadlock)

```
UPDATE checking SET balance = balance - :transfer_amount;
UPDATE savings SET balance = balance + :transfer_amount;
COMMIT;
```

Transaction B (prevents deadlocks)

```
UPDATE savings SET balance = balance + :transfer_amount;
UPDATE checking SET balance = balance - :transfer_amount;
COMMIT;
```

Description

- A *deadlock* occurs when neither of two transactions can be committed because each transaction has a lock on a resource needed by the other transaction.

Figure 14-6   How to prevent deadlocks

Perspective

In this chapter, you've learned what the application developer needs to know about transactions, concurrency, locking, and deadlocks. In particular, this chapter has tried to show you what an Oracle database does automatically and what you need to do as an application developer. In particular, you need to make sure that you commit or rollback each transaction that an application issues.

Terms

transaction
commit a transaction
rollback a transaction
save point
concurrency
locking
lost update
dirty read
nonrepeatable read
phantom read
transaction isolation level
deadlock
deadlock victim

Exercises

1. Write a set of three SQL statements coded as a transaction to reflect the following change: United Parcel Service has been purchased by Federal Express Corporation and the new company is named FedUP. Rename one of the vendors and delete the other after updating the vendor_id column in the Invoices table.

2. Write a set of two SQL statements coded as a transaction to delete the row with an invoice ID of 114 from the Invoices table. To do this, you must first delete all line items for that invoice from the Invoice_Line_Items table.

15

How to create stored procedures and functions

In chapter 13, you learned how to include anonymous blocks of PL/SQL code in a SQL script. In this chapter, you'll learn how to extend this functionality by creating named database objects that store blocks of PL/SQL code within a database. These objects can be executed by any database user who has appropriate privileges. As you'll see, these types of objects allow you to store procedural logic such as data validation in a central location. In addition, they provide a powerful way to control how users are allowed to access the database.

How to code stored procedures

A *stored procedure*, which can also be referred to as a *sproc* or just a *procedure*, is a database object that contains a block of PL/SQL code. You can use stored procedures to modify the data that's stored within a database. For example, you can use a stored procedure to execute an INSERT, UPDATE, or DELETE statement.

How to create and call a stored procedure

Figure 15-1 shows how to use the CREATE PROCEDURE statement to create a stored procedure. To start, you code the CREATE keyword, followed by the optional OR REPLACE keywords, followed by the PROCEDURE keyword, followed by the name of the procedure. In this figure, for example, the statement creates a procedure named update_invoices_credit_total. Since this statement includes the OR REPLACE keywords, it creates the procedure if it doesn't already exist, and it replaces the procedure if it does already exist.

Note that the name of this procedure clearly indicates that the procedure updates the credit_total column of the invoices table. Throughout this chapter, I will use a similar naming convention for the other procedures.

After the name of the procedure, you code a set of parentheses. Within the parentheses, you can code one or more *parameters* for the procedure. A parameter is typically used to pass a value to the stored procedure from a calling program. However, a parameter can also be used to pass a value back from the stored procedure to the calling program.

If a procedure accepts more than one parameter, you must use a comma to separate each parameter. When you declare a parameter, you code the name of the parameter followed by its data type. In this figure, for example, the procedure accepts two parameters. The first parameter is named invoice_number_param with a data type of VARCHAR2, and the second parameter is named credit_total_param with a data type of NUMBER.

After the parentheses, you code the IS keyword or the AS keyword, followed by the PL/SQL code to be executed. In general, this PL/SQL code works like the anonymous blocks of PL/SQL code that you learned how to code in chapter 13. However, if you need to declare variables, you don't use the DECLARE keyword to identify the DECLARE section. Instead, you just declare the variables immediately after the IS or AS keyword but before the BEGIN keyword. Although this isn't illustrated in this figure, it is shown in the next figure.

When you run the CREATE PROCEDURE statement, Oracle *compiles* the PL/SQL code for the procedure and stores the compiled code in the database. As part of this process, Oracle's compiler checks the syntax of the code within the procedure. If you've made a coding error, the system responds with an appropriate message and the procedure isn't created.

The syntax of the CREATE PROCEDURE statement

```
CREATE [OR REPLACE] PROCEDURE procedure_name
[(
    parameter_name_1 data_type
    [, parameter_name_2 data_type]...
)]
{IS | AS}
pl_sql_block
```

A script that creates a stored procedure that updates a table

```
CREATE OR REPLACE PROCEDURE update_invoices_credit_total
(
  invoice_number_param   VARCHAR2,
  credit_total_param     NUMBER
)
AS
BEGIN
  UPDATE invoices
  SET credit_total = credit_total_param
  WHERE invoice_number = invoice_number_param;

  COMMIT;
EXCEPTION
  WHEN OTHERS THEN
    ROLLBACK;
END;
/
```

Description

- You use the CREATE PROCEDURE statement to create a stored procedure. A *stored procedure* is an executable database object that contains a block of PL/SQL code. A stored procedure can also be called a *sproc* or a *procedure*.

- Stored procedures are *compiled* before they are stored in the database.

- You can use *parameters* to pass one or more values from the calling program to the stored procedure or from the procedure to the calling program. For more information on working with parameters, see figures 15-2 and 15-3.

- To declare a parameter within a stored procedure, you code the name of the parameter followed by its data type. If you declare two or more parameters, you separate the parameters with commas.

Figure 15-1   How to create and call a stored procedure (part 1 of 2)

You can execute, or *call*, a stored procedure by using the CALL statement. In part 2 of this figure, for example, the CALL statement calls the procedure that's created in part 1. This statement passes one value for each of the parameters that are defined by the procedure. Here, the first parameter is a VARCHAR2 literal that specifies the invoice number, and the second parameter is a NUMBER literal that identifies the new amount for the credit total.

When you use the CALL statement, you must pass parameters *by position*. In other words, you must code the parameters in the same order as they are coded in the CREATE PROCEDURE statement. This is the most common way to call stored procedures that have a short list of parameters.

If you are coding a script that calls a procedure, you don't code the CALL keyword. Instead, you just code the name of the procedure and its parameters. In this figure, for example, the first script performs the same task as the CALL statement.

When you call a procedure from a script, you can also pass parameters *by name*. To do that, you include the names of the parameters as defined in the CREATE PROCEDURE statement, followed by the association operator (=>), followed by the value that's passed. When you use this technique, you can list parameters in any order. This is illustrated by the second script in this figure. If a procedure has many parameters, passing parameters by name is often easier and less error-prone than passing parameters by position.

In chapter 12, you learned how to grant INSERT, UPDATE, and DELETE privileges to specific users. However, if you want to have more fine-grained control over the privileges that you grant to users, you can create stored procedures that perform all of the types of data manipulation that you want to allow within your database. Then, you can grant privileges to execute these stored procedures. For systems where security is critical, this can be an excellent way to prevent both accidental errors and malicious damage to your data.

A statement that calls a stored procedure

```
CALL update_invoices_credit_total('367447', 300);
```

A script that calls a stored procedure

```
BEGIN
  update_invoices_credit_total('367447', 300);
END;
/
```

A script that passes parameters by name

```
BEGIN
  update_invoices_credit_total(
    credit_total_param=>300,
    invoice_number_param=>'367447');
END;
/
```

Description

- You can use the CALL statement to *call a procedure*. When a procedure accepts parameters, you pass them to the procedure by coding them within the parentheses that follow the procedure name, and by separating each parameter with a comma.

- When you use a CALL statement to call a procedure, you pass parameters *by position*. This means that you list them in the same order as they appear in the CREATE PROCEDURE statement.

- When you use a script to call a procedure, you can pass parameters by position or *by name*. When you pass parameters by name, you code the name of each parameter, followed by the association operator (=>), followed by the value. In this case, the parameters don't have to be in the same order as they appear in the CREATE PROCEDURE statement.

Figure 15-1   How to create and call a stored procedure (part 2 of 2)

How to code input and output parameters

Figure 15-2 shows how to code input and output parameters for a stored procedure. Stored procedures provide for three different types of parameters: input parameters, output parameters, and input/output parameters.

An *input parameter* is passed to the stored procedure from the calling program. You can explicitly identify an input parameter by coding the IN keyword after the name of the parameter. In this figure, for example, the first two parameters are identified as input parameters. However, if you omit this keyword, the parameter is assumed to be an input parameter. In figure 15-1, for example, both parameters are input parameters.

Within a procedure, you can use input parameters like variables. However, you can't change the value of the parameter. In this figure, for example, the procedure uses the first parameter within an UPDATE statement to specify the invoice number for the invoice row to be updated. Then, it uses this parameter within a SELECT statement to get a count of the number of rows that have been updated.

An *output parameter* is returned to the calling program from the stored procedure. To code an output parameter, you must explicitly identify the parameter by coding the OUT keyword after the name of the parameter. In this figure, for example, the third parameter is an output parameter. If the UPDATE statement executes successfully, the SELECT statement stores the count of the rows that were updated in this parameter. Since the invoice number should be unique, this should store a value of 1 in the output parameter. On the other hand, if the UPDATE statement doesn't execute successfully, the SELECT statement in the EXCEPTION section of the procedure stores a value of 0 in the output parameter. Either way, the value of the output parameter is returned to the calling program when the procedure finishes.

To show how a calling program works, this figure includes a script that calls the procedure. Here, initial values are supplied for the two input parameters, and a variable named row_count is supplied for the output parameter. After the procedure executes, the value of the output parameter is stored in the variable named row_count. Then, the calling program can use this variable to check how many rows have been updated. In this figure, for example, the script prints the value of this variable to the console. However, it could also use an IF statement to check the value of the variable and perform an appropriate action.

An *input/output parameter* stores an initial value that's passed in from the calling program like an input parameter. However, the procedure can change this value and return it to a calling program like an output parameter. To identify an input/output parameter, you must code the IN OUT keywords after the name of the parameter. Although this can be useful in some situations, it can also be confusing. As a result, it often makes sense to avoid the use of input/output parameters.

The syntax for declaring input and output parameters

```
parameter_name_1 [IN|OUT|IN OUT] data_type
```

A stored procedure that uses input and output parameters

```
CREATE OR REPLACE PROCEDURE update_invoices_credit_total
(
    invoice_number_param IN  VARCHAR2,
    credit_total_param   IN  NUMBER,
    update_count         OUT INTEGER
)
AS
BEGIN
    UPDATE invoices
    SET credit_total = credit_total_param
    WHERE invoice_number = invoice_number_param;

    SELECT COUNT(*)
    INTO update_count
    FROM invoices
    WHERE invoice_number = invoice_number_param;

    COMMIT;
EXCEPTION
    WHEN OTHERS THEN
        SELECT 0 INTO update_count FROM dual;
        ROLLBACK;
END;
/
```

A script that calls the stored procedure and uses the output parameter

```
SET SERVEROUTPUT ON;
DECLARE
    row_count INTEGER;
BEGIN
    update_invoices_credit_total('367447', 200, row_count);
    DBMS_OUTPUT.PUT_LINE('row_count: ' || row_count);
END;
/
```

Description

- *Input parameters* accept values that are passed from the calling program. These values cannot be changed by the body of the stored procedure. By default, parameters are defined as input parameters. As a result, the IN keyword is optional for identifying input parameters.

- *Output parameters* store values that are passed back to the calling program. These values must be set by the body of the stored procedure. To identify an output parameter, you must code the OUT keyword. To use an output parameter, the calling program must declare a variable to store its value, and it must include this variable in the parameter list.

- *Input/output parameters* can store an initial value that's passed from the calling program. However, the body of the stored procedure can change this parameter. To identify an input/output parameter, you must code the IN OUT keywords.

Figure 15-2   How to code input and output parameters

How to code optional parameters

Figure 15-3 shows how to code an *optional parameter*. When you call a procedure that has optional parameters, you can omit any of its optional parameters. In this figure, for example, the second parameter is an optional parameter. As a result, when you call this procedure, you can omit the second parameter. In that case, the credit total for the specified invoice is set to a default value of 100. Or, you can pass both parameters. In that case, the credit total for the specified invoice is set to the value of the second parameter.

To start, it usually makes sense to code all optional parameters at the end of the parameter list. Then, you use the DEFAULT keyword to specify a default value for each of the parameters. In this figure, for example, the DEFAULT keyword specifies a default value of 100 for the second parameter.

The first CALL statement in this figure supplies both parameters. As a result, the credit total for the invoice is set to 200. However, the second CALL statement in this figure omits the second parameter. As a result, the credit total for the invoice is set to the default value of 100.

In this figure, it's easy to supply a default value for the optional parameter. However, you may sometimes need to write code that sets a value of a parameter depending on the values of the other parameters. In that case, you can set the default value for the optional parameter to NULL. Then, within the body of the procedure, you can write an IF statement that tests for the NULL value and executes the appropriate code. For an example of this technique, you can check the code in figure 15-5 that sets the default values for the terms_id and invoice_due_date columns.

The syntax for declaring an optional parameter

```
parameter_name_1 data_type [DEFAULT default_value]
```

A CREATE PROCEDURE statement that uses an optional parameter

```
CREATE OR REPLACE PROCEDURE update_invoices_credit_total
(
  invoice_number_param VARCHAR2,
  credit_total_param   NUMBER    DEFAULT 100
)
AS
BEGIN
  UPDATE invoices
  SET credit_total = credit_total_param
  WHERE invoice_number = invoice_number_param;

  COMMIT;
EXCEPTION
  WHEN OTHERS THEN
    ROLLBACK;
END;
/
```

A statement that calls the stored procedure

```
CALL update_invoices_credit_total('367447', 200);
```

Another statement that calls the stored procedure

```
CALL update_invoices_credit_total('367447');
```

Description

- *Optional parameters* are parameters that don't require that a value be passed from the calling program. To declare an optional parameter, you use the DEFAULT keyword to assign it a default value.

- It's a good programming practice to code your CREATE PROCEDURE statements so that they list required parameters first, followed by optional parameters.

Figure 15-3   How to code optional parameters

How to raise errors

Within a stored procedure, it's generally considered a good practice to prevent errors by checking the parameters before they're used to make sure they're valid. This is often referred to as *data validation*. Then, if the data isn't valid, you can execute code that makes it valid, or you can *raise an error*, which returns an error to the calling program.

Part 1 of figure 15-4 shows how to raise an error by raising one of the predefined exceptions that are available from Oracle. To do that, you code the RAISE statement followed by the name of the predefined exception. In this figure, for example, the IF statement checks whether the value of the second parameter is less than zero. If so, it raises the predefined VALUE_ERROR exception that's described in chapter 13.

If the calling program doesn't catch this exception, the system displays an error. In this figure, for example, the CALL statement passes a negative value to the second parameter, which causes the VALUE_ERROR exception to be raised. As a result, the system displays an error message that indicates that a value error has occurred.

However, if the calling program catches this exception, it can include code that handles the exception. In this figure, for example, the script that calls the procedure includes an EXCEPTION section that handles this exception by printing a message to the console that says, "A VALUE_ERROR occurred." If necessary, this message could be improved to be more user-friendly. In addition, the EXCEPTION section handles all other exceptions by printing a message to the console that says, "An unexpected error occurred." This shows how a calling program can handle each specific exception differently.

The syntax of the RAISE statement

```
RAISE exception_name
```

A stored procedure that raises a predefined exception

```
CREATE OR REPLACE PROCEDURE update_invoices_credit_total
(
  invoice_number_param VARCHAR2,
  credit_total_param   NUMBER
)
AS
BEGIN
  IF credit_total_param < 0 THEN
    RAISE VALUE_ERROR;
  END IF;

  UPDATE invoices
  SET credit_total = credit_total_param
  WHERE invoice_number = invoice_number_param;

  COMMIT;
END;
/
```

A statement that calls the procedure

```
CALL update_invoices_credit_total('367447', -100);
```

The response from the system

```
Error report:
SQL Error: ORA-06502: PL/SQL: numeric or value error
ORA-06512: at "AP.UPDATE_INVOICES_CREDIT_TOTAL", line 9
```

A script that calls the procedure

```
SET SERVEROUTPUT ON;

BEGIN
  update_invoices_credit_total('367447', -100);
EXCEPTION
  WHEN VALUE_ERROR THEN
    DBMS_OUTPUT.PUT_LINE('A VALUE_ERROR occurred.');
  WHEN OTHERS THEN
    DBMS_OUTPUT.PUT_LINE('An unknown exception occurred.');
END;
/
```

The response from the system

```
A VALUE_ERROR occurred.
```

Figure 15-4   How to raise errors (part 1 of 2)

Part 2 of figure 15-4 shows how to raise an error by raising an *application error*, which is an error that you create. To do that, you call the RAISE_APPLICATION_ERROR procedure that's available from Oracle. Within the parentheses for this procedure, the first parameter specifies the error number, and the second parameter specifies the error message. Here, the error number parameter must be between -20000 and -20999.

When you use the RAISE_APPLICATION_ERROR procedure, you can specify more helpful and user-friendly messages than the generic messages that are available from the predefined exceptions. In this figure, for example, the error message says, "Credit total may not be negative." At this point, the user or programmer of the calling application should be able to identify and fix the problem.

However, when you raise an application error, the calling program can't use specific exception handlers. Instead, the calling program must use the WHEN OTHERS THEN clause to catch all application errors. In most cases, that's acceptable. If it isn't, you need to define your own user-defined exceptions. For information about doing that, you can refer to the Oracle Database PL/SQL Language Reference.

The syntax of the RAISE_APPLICATION_ERROR procedure

```
RAISE_APPLICATION_ERROR(error_number, error_message);
```

A statement that raises an application error

```
RAISE_APPLICATION_ERROR(-20001, 'Credit total may not be negative.');
```

The response from the system if the error is not caught

```
Error report:
SQL Error: ORA-20001: Credit total may not be negative.
ORA-06512: at "AP.UPDATE_INVOICES_CREDIT_TOTAL", line 10
```

A script that catches an application error

```
BEGIN
  update_invoices_credit_total('367447', -100);
EXCEPTION
  WHEN VALUE_ERROR THEN
    DBMS_OUTPUT.PUT_LINE('A VALUE_ERROR occurred.');
  WHEN OTHERS THEN
    DBMS_OUTPUT.PUT_LINE('An unknown exception occurred.');
END;
/
```

The response from the system

```
An unknown exception occurred.
```

Description

- It's generally considered a good practice to validate the data within a stored procedure before using the data. This is referred to as *data validation*.

- The RAISE statement *raises* a predefined exception such as the exceptions described in chapter 13.

- The RAISE_APPLICATION_ERROR procedure raises an *application error* with the specified error number and message. When you use this statement, the error number parameter must be between -20000 and -20999.

- Raised errors are returned to the caller like errors that are raised by the database engine.

- You can use the WHEN clause to catch predefined exceptions.

- You can use the WHEN OTHERS THEN clause to catch application errors.

Figure 15-4   How to raise errors (part 2 of 2)

A stored procedure that inserts a row

Figure 15-5 presents a stored procedure that inserts new rows into the invoices table. This should give you a better idea of how you can use stored procedures.

This procedure uses nine parameters that correspond to nine of the columns in the invoices table. All of these parameters are input parameters, and each parameter is assigned the same data type as the matching column in the invoices table. As a result, if the calling program passes a value that can't be converted to the proper data type, an error will be raised when the procedure is called.

Note that none of these parameters corresponds with the invoice_id column. That's because the body of the procedure uses a sequence to provide a value for this column, which is usually what you want.

Note also that the last five parameters are optional parameters that have been assigned default values. Of these, the last three parameters have been assigned a default value of NULL.

After the AS keyword, the procedure begins by declaring four variables. Of these variables, the first three have data types that correspond with columns in the invoices table. However, the fourth one uses the INTEGER data type to store the number of days before the invoice is due.

Note that all of the variables have a suffix of "_var" while all of the parameters defined earlier have a suffix of "_param". This makes it easy to tell the difference between the parameters that are passed to the procedure from the calling program and the variables that are used within the procedure.

After the BEGIN keyword, a SELECT statement stores the next value in the sequence for the invoice_id column in a variable. To do that, this SELECT statement selects the value that's returned by the NEXTVAL pseudo column of the sequence into the variable named invoice_id_var.

After the SELECT statement, the procedure begins by using a simple IF statement to check the value of the parameter for the invoice_total column to see if it is less than zero. If so, the procedure uses the RAISE statement to raise the predefined VALUE_ERROR exception. This statement exits the stored procedure and returns the exception to the calling program. Although this figure only codes a single IF statement, it's common to code a series of IF statements like this one to provide more extensive data validation.

After the SELECT statement, an IF statement checks the optional parameter for the terms_id column to see if it contains a NULL value. If so, a SELECT statement sets the variable that corresponds to the parameter to an appropriate value. Here, for example, the variable for the terms_id column is set to the value that's stored in the default_terms_id column of the vendors table. Otherwise, this code sets the corresponding variable to the value of the parameter.

In other words, if the parameter contains a NULL value, some code is executed to set it to an appropriate value. Or, if the parameter contains a non-null value, the code uses that value.

A stored procedure that validates the data in a new invoice

```
CREATE OR REPLACE PROCEDURE insert_invoice
(
  vendor_id_param           invoices.vendor_id%TYPE,
  invoice_number_param      invoices.invoice_number%TYPE,
  invoice_date_param        invoices.invoice_date%TYPE,
  invoice_total_param       invoices.invoice_total%TYPE,
  payment_total_param       invoices.payment_total%TYPE DEFAULT 0,
  credit_total_param        invoices.credit_total%TYPE DEFAULT 0,
  terms_id_param            invoices.terms_id%TYPE DEFAULT NULL,
  invoice_due_date_param invoices.invoice_due_date%TYPE DEFAULT NULL,
  payment_date_param        invoices.payment_date%TYPE DEFAULT NULL
)
AS
  invoice_id_var            invoices.invoice_id%TYPE;
  terms_id_var              invoices.terms_id%TYPE;
  invoice_due_date_var      invoices.invoice_date%TYPE;
  terms_due_days_var        INTEGER;
BEGIN
  IF invoice_total_param < 0 THEN
    RAISE VALUE_ERROR;
  END IF;

  SELECT invoice_id_seq.NEXTVAL INTO invoice_id_var FROM dual;

  IF terms_id_param IS NULL THEN
    SELECT default_terms_id INTO terms_id_var
    FROM vendors WHERE vendor_id = vendor_id_param;
  ELSE
    terms_id_var := terms_id_param;
  END IF;

  IF invoice_due_date_param IS NULL THEN
    SELECT terms_due_days INTO terms_due_days_var
      FROM terms WHERE terms_id = terms_id_var;
    invoice_due_date_var := invoice_date_param + terms_due_days_var;
  ELSE
    invoice_due_date_var := invoice_due_date_param;
  END IF;

  INSERT INTO invoices
  VALUES (invoice_id_var,
          vendor_id_param, invoice_number_param, invoice_date_param,
          invoice_total_param, payment_total_param, credit_total_param,
          terms_id_var, invoice_due_date_var, payment_date_param);

END;
/
```

Figure 15-5   A stored procedure that inserts a row (part 1 of 2)

At this point, another IF statement checks the optional parameter for the invoice_due_date column. Since this works similarly to the previous IF statement, you shouldn't have much trouble understanding how it works. To start, it checks the parameter to see if it contains a NULL value. If so, a SELECT statement uses the value of the terms_id_var to get the number of days until the invoice is due from the terms table, and it stores this value in the variable named terms_due_days_var. Then, it calculates a due date for the invoice by adding the number of days until the invoice is due to the invoice date. Otherwise, this code sets the corresponding variable to the value that's stored in the parameter.

After the values have been set for the variables for the invoice_id, terms_id, and invoice_due_date columns, this procedure executes an INSERT statement. If this statement executes successfully, the row is inserted into the database. However, since the line items for the invoice haven't yet been inserted, this stored procedure does not use a COMMIT statement to commit changes to the database. As a result, the program that's calling this statement must issue the COMMIT statement. Typically, this would happen after the application program uses a similar stored procedure to insert the line items for the invoice. That way, the line items and the invoice are part of the same transaction.

In most cases, a stored procedure like this is called from an application program. However, to test a procedure before it's used by an application program, you can use CALL statements like the ones in this figure.

The first three CALL statements provide valid values that successfully insert a new row. Of these three statements, the first supplies all of the parameters for the procedure. The second supplies the first eight parameters, but not the ninth. And the third only supplies the first four parameters. This shows that the first four parameters are the only parameters that are required by the procedure. That's because the procedure will either use the default values coded after the parameter, or it will set a default value within the body of the procedure.

The fourth CALL statement provides a negative number for the invoice total parameter. As a result, this CALL statement will cause the stored procedure to raise the predefined VALUE_ERROR exception. Since the CALL statement doesn't handle this exception, this causes an error message to be displayed. However, if you call the stored procedure from a block of PL/SQL code or from an application, you can include code that handles the exception.

Three statements that call the stored procedure

```
CALL insert_invoice(34, 'ZXA-080', '30-AUG-08', 14092.59,
                    0, 0, 3, '30-SEP-08', NULL);

CALL insert_invoice(34, 'ZXA-080', '30-AUG-08', 14092.59,
                    0, 0, 3, '30-SEP-08');

CALL insert_invoice(34, 'ZXA-080', '30-AUG-08', 14092.59);
```

The response from the system for a successful insert

```
CALL insert_invoice(34, succeeded.
```

A statement that raises an error

```
CALL insert_invoice(34, 'ZXA-080', '30-AUG-08', -14092.59);
```

The response from the system when a validation error occurs

```
Error report:
SQL Error: ORA-06502: PL/SQL: numeric or value error
ORA-06512: at "AP.INSERT_INVOICE", line 20
```

Description

- If the data for each of the columns of the row is valid, the procedure executes an INSERT statement to insert the row. Otherwise, the database engine raises an error and exits the procedure.

- If an application program calls this procedure, it can handle any errors that are raised by the procedure or by the database engine.

- Since this procedure doesn't include a COMMIT statement, the application program that calls this procedure must commit the change to the database. Ideally, an application program would commit the invoice data to the database after the line items for the invoice have also been inserted.

Figure 15-5   A stored procedure that inserts a row (part 2 of 2)

A stored procedure that drops a table

Figure 15-6 presents a simple but useful stored procedure that drops a table. This shows that you can code a procedure to execute DDL statements such as the DROP TABLE statement.

To start, this procedure accepts a single parameter that specifies the name of the table. Then, it uses the EXECUTE IMMEDIATE statement to execute a string that contains the DROP TABLE keywords followed by the parameter that stores the name of the table. As a result, if a table with that name exists, it is dropped from the database.

However, if a table with that name doesn't exist within the database, the EXECUTE IMMEDIATE statement will cause an exception to be raised. Then, execution will jump into the EXCEPTION section, and the code in this section will handle the exception. This code handles all exceptions by using the NULL statement to do nothing, which suppresses any error messages. As a result, this procedure can be useful for database creation scripts that begin by dropping tables before creating tables with the same names such as the script that you used to create the tables for the AP user/schema.

A stored procedure that drops a table

```
CREATE OR REPLACE PROCEDURE drop_table
(
  table_name VARCHAR2
)
AS
BEGIN
  EXECUTE IMMEDIATE 'DROP TABLE ' || table_name;
EXCEPTION
  WHEN OTHERS THEN
    NULL;
END;
/
```

A statement that calls the stored procedure

```
CALL drop_table('test1');
```

The response from the system

```
CALL drop_table('test1') succeeded.
```

Description

- You can code a stored procedure to execute DDL statements such as the DROP TABLE statement.

Figure 15-6   A stored procedure that drops a table

How to drop a stored procedure

Figure 15-7 shows how to drop a stored procedure. To do that, you can code the DROP PROCEDURE keywords followed by the name of the procedure. In this figure, the first example uses the CREATE PROCEDURE statement to create a procedure named clear_invoices_credit_total. Then, the second example uses the DROP PROCEDURE statement to drop that procedure.

If you drop a table, sequence, or view used by a procedure, you should be sure to drop the procedure as well. If you don't, the procedure can still be called by any user or program that has been granted the appropriate privileges. Then, an error will occur because the table, sequence, or view that the procedure depends on no longer exists.

The syntax of the DROP PROCEDURE statement

```
DROP PROCEDURE procedure_name
```

A statement that creates a stored procedure

```
CREATE PROCEDURE clear_invoices_credit_total
(
   invoice_number_param   VARCHAR2
)
AS
BEGIN
  UPDATE invoices
  SET credit_total = 0
  WHERE invoice_number = invoice_number_param;

  COMMIT;
END;
/
```

A statement that drops a stored procedure

```
DROP PROCEDURE clear_invoices_credit_total
```

Description

- To drop a stored procedure from the database, use the DROP PROCEDURE statement.

Figure 15-7   How to drop a stored procedure

How to code user-defined functions

In chapter 8, you learned about some built-in functions that are provided by Oracle. Now, you'll learn how to create your own functions. These functions are referred to as *user-defined functions (UDFs)*, *stored functions*, or just *functions*.

In many ways, the code for creating a function works similarly to the code for creating a stored procedure. However, there are two primary differences between stored procedures and functions. First, a function always returns a value or a table. Second, a function can't make changes to the database such as executing an INSERT, UPDATE, or DELETE statement.

How to create and call a function

Figure 15-8 shows how to create a *scalar function*, which is a function that returns a single value. That's the type of function that you'll learn to create in this chapter.

To start, you code the CREATE FUNCTION statement, followed by the name of the function. If you want to automatically drop any existing function that has the same name, you can include the optional OR REPLACE keywords. In this figure, the example shows how to create a function named get_vendor_id.

After the name of the function, you code a set of parentheses. Within the parentheses, you code the parameters for the function. In this figure, for example, the function only contains a single parameter of the VARCHAR2 type that's named vendor_name_param. Since this works similarly to declaring parameters for a stored procedure, you shouldn't have much trouble understanding how this works. The main difference is that it rarely makes sense to use output parameters for a function. As a result, functions almost always use input parameters as shown by the examples in this chapter.

After the parentheses, you code the RETURN keyword, followed by the data type that's returned by the function. In this figure, the example returns a value of the NUMBER type.

After the declaration of the return type, you code the IS or AS keyword to signal that you are about to begin coding the PL/SQL code for the function. In this figure, the PL/SQL code begins by declaring a variable of the NUMBER type named vendor_id_var.

After the BEGIN keyword, this function uses a SELECT statement to get the vendor ID value that corresponds with the vendor name parameter and to store this value in the vendor ID variable. Then, it uses the RETURN statement to return this value to the calling program.

To call a user-defined function, you can use it in an expression as if it's one of Oracle's built-in functions. Then, the value that's returned by the function is substituted for the function. In this figure, the last example shows how to use the get_vendor_id function within a SELECT statement to return the vendor ID value for the vendor with the name of "IBM".

The syntax for creating a function

```
CREATE [OR REPLACE] FUNCTION function_name
[(
    parameter_name_1 data_type
    [, parameter_name_2 data_type]...
)]
RETURN data_type
{IS | AS}
pl_sql_block
```

A function that returns the vendor ID that matches a vendor's name

```
CREATE OR REPLACE FUNCTION get_vendor_id
(
    vendor_name_param VARCHAR2
)
RETURN NUMBER
AS
  vendor_id_var NUMBER;
BEGIN
  SELECT vendor_id
  INTO vendor_id_var
  FROM vendors
  WHERE vendor_name = vendor_name_param;

  RETURN vendor_id_var;
END;
/
```

A SELECT statement that uses the function

```
SELECT invoice_number, invoice_total
FROM invoices
WHERE vendor_id = get_vendor_id('IBM')
```

The response from the system

INVOICE_NUMBER	INVOICE_TOTAL
1 QP58872	116.54
2 Q545443	1083.58

Description

- A *user-defined function* (*UDF*), which can also be called a *stored function* or just a *function*, is an executable database object that contains a block of PL/SQL code.

- A *scalar-valued function* returns a single value of any data type.

- A function can accept input parameters that work like the input parameters for a stored procedure.

- A function always returns a value. You use the RETURN keyword to specify the value that's returned by the function.

- A function can't make changes to the database such as executing an INSERT, UPDATE, or DELETE statement.

Figure 15-8   How to create and call a function

If you find yourself repeatedly coding the same expression within a SQL statement, you may want to create a scalar-valued function for the expression. Then, you can use that function in place of the expression, which can save you coding time and make your code easier to maintain. When you start work on a new database, for example, you may want to create a set of useful UDFs.

A function that calculates balance due

Figure 15-9 shows a function that calculates the balance due for an invoice. To do that, this function accepts a parameter that contains an invoice ID value. Then, the body of the function calculates the balance due, stores the result of the calculation in a variable named balance_due_var, and uses the RETURN statement to return that value.

The SELECT statement in this figure uses this function to return the balance due for the specified invoice ID value. Note that calling the function like this:

```
get_balance_due(invoice_id) AS balance_due
```

has the same effect as performing a calculation like this:

```
invoice_total - payment_total - credit_total AS balance_due
```

However, there are two advantages to using the function. First, as you can see, the code is shorter, which makes it easier to type. Second, the code for calculating the balance due is stored in a single location. As a result, if the formula for calculating the balance due later changes, you only need to change it in one location.

A function that calculates balance due

```
CREATE OR REPLACE FUNCTION get_balance_due
(
    invoice_id_param NUMBER
)
RETURN NUMBER
AS
  balance_due_var NUMBER;
BEGIN
  SELECT invoice_total - payment_total - credit_total AS balance_due
  INTO balance_due_var
  FROM invoices
  WHERE invoice_id = invoice_id_param;

  RETURN balance_due_var;
END;
/
```

A statement that calls the function

```
SELECT vendor_id, invoice_number,
       get_balance_due(invoice_id) AS balance_due
FROM invoices
WHERE vendor_id = 37;
```

The response from the system

	VENDOR_ID	INVOICE_NUMBER	BALANCE_DUE
1	37	547479217	116
2	37	547480102	224
3	37	547481328	224

Description

- This function accepts a single parameter that specifies the ID for an invoice, and it returns the balance due for that invoice.

Figure 15-9   A function that calculates balance due

How to drop a function

Figure 15-10 shows how to drop a user-defined function. To do that, you code the DROP FUNCTION keyword followed by the name of the procedure. This is illustrated by the third example in this figure.

To start, though, the first example presents another function named get_sum_balance_due. This function uses the aggregate SUM function described in chapter 5 to return the sum of the total balance due for the specified vendor. What's interesting here is that this function calls the get_balance_due function presented in the previous figure. In other words, this function "depends" on the get_balance_due function.

Then, the second example shows a SELECT statement that uses the get_sum_balance_due function. This statement gets the total balance due for the vendor with an ID of 37.

Like stored procedures, functions depend on underlying database objects such as tables, sequences, and views as well as other procedures or functions. Then, if you drop a database object that a function depends on, the function won't work properly. As a result, you should avoid dropping any database objects that depend on other database objects. For example, you shouldn't use the DROP FUNCTION object to drop the get_balance_due function since the get_sum_balance_due function depends on it.

The syntax of the DROP FUNCTION statement

```
DROP FUNCTION function_name
```

A statement that creates a function

```
CREATE FUNCTION get_sum_balance_due
(
    vendor_id_param NUMBER
)
RETURN NUMBER
AS
  sum_balance_due_var NUMBER;
BEGIN
  SELECT SUM(get_balance_due(invoice_id)) AS sum_balance_due
  INTO sum_balance_due_var
  FROM invoices
  WHERE vendor_id = vendor_id_param;

  RETURN sum_balance_due_var;
END;
/
```

A statement that calls the function

```
SELECT vendor_id, invoice_number,
       get_balance_due(invoice_id) AS balance_due,
       get_sum_balance_due(vendor_id) AS sum_balance_due
FROM invoices
WHERE vendor_id = 37;
```

The response from the system

	VENDOR_ID	INVOICE_NUMBER	BALANCE_DUE	SUM_BALANCE_DUE
1	37	547479217	116	564
2	37	547480102	224	564
3	37	547481328	224	564

A statement that drops a function

```
DROP FUNCTION get_sum_balance_due;
```

Description

- To delete a user-defined function from the database, use the DROP FUNCTION statement.

Notes about the function in this figure

- The function in this figure uses the get_balance_due function that's presented in the previous figure. As a result, if you drop the get_balance_due function, the function in this figure won't work.

Figure 15-10   How to drop a function

How to work with packages

A *package* is a container that organizes and groups related stored procedures and user-defined functions. In chapter 13, for example, you learned how to use the built-in package named DBMS_OUTPUT to print data to the output window. Now, you'll learn how to store your own procedures and functions within a package.

The Oracle documentation occasionally uses the term *subprogram* as a generic term that can refer to a procedure or a function. This makes sense if you recognize that procedures and functions are essentially small programs.

How to create a package

Figure 15-11 shows how to create a package. To start, you use the CREATE PACKAGE statement to create the *specification* for the package. A package specification lists the names and parameters for all of the procedures and functions that are contained within the package. In addition, it specifies the return types for its functions. In this figure, for instance, the first example specifies that the package named murach contains one procedure and one function. It specifies two parameters for the procedure. It specifies one parameter for the function. And it specifies the return type for the function.

Once you've created the specification for a package, you can use the CREATE PACKAGE BODY statement to create the *body* for the package. A package body contains the code for its procedures and functions. Within the body, the names, parameters, and return types must match the names, parameters, and return types in the specification. In this figure, you can see that the package specification matches the package body. However, if the specification doesn't match the body, an error is displayed when Oracle attempts to compile the package.

The syntax for defining the specification for a package

```
CREATE [OR REPLACE] PACKAGE package_name {IS | AS}
  prodedure_or_function_specification_1;
  [prodedure_or_function_specification_2;]...
END [package_name];
/
```

Code that defines the specification for a package named murach

```
CREATE OR REPLACE PACKAGE murach AS

  PROCEDURE update_invoices_credit_total
  (invoice_number_param VARCHAR2, credit_total_param NUMBER);

  FUNCTION get_vendor_id
  (vendor_name_param VARCHAR2)
  RETURN NUMBER;

END murach;
/
```

The syntax for defining the body for a package

```
CREATE [OR REPLACE] PACKAGE BODY package_name {IS | AS}
  prodedure_or_function_body_1;
  [prodedure_or_function_body_2;]...
END [package_name];
/
```

Code that defines the body for a package named murach

```
CREATE OR REPLACE PACKAGE BODY murach AS

  PROCEDURE update_invoices_credit_total
  (
    invoice_number_param  VARCHAR2,
    credit_total_param    NUMBER
  )
  AS
  BEGIN
    UPDATE invoices
    SET credit_total = credit_total_param
    WHERE invoice_number = invoice_number_param;

    COMMIT;
  EXCEPTION
    WHEN OTHERS THEN
      ROLLBACK;
  END;
```

Figure 15-11   How to create and drop packages (part 1 of 2)

In general, you can use the techniques you learned earlier in this chapter to call a procedure or function that's stored in package. However, you must preface the name of the procedure or function with the name of the package. In part 2 of this figure, for example, the CALL statement calls the procedure that's stored in the murach package, and the SELECT statement uses the function that's stored in the murach package. Note that storing this procedure and function in a package prevents a naming conflict with a procedure and function of the same name that aren't stored in a package.

In this figure, the package contains just one short procedure and one short function. In practice, though, a package might include dozens of procedures and functions and some of them might be far more complex than the ones in this chapter. A more realistic package might also include global variables that can be shared between procedures and functions.

How to drop a package

As you would expect, you use the DROP PACKAGE statement to drop a package. When you use this statement, the specification and the body for the package are dropped. In this figure, for example, the first DROP statement drops the specification and the body for the package named murach.

In some cases, though, you may only want to drop the body for the package. That way, other procedures or functions that reference the package specification can still be compiled. In that case, you can use the DROP PACKAGE BODY statement to drop only the body of the package.

Advantages of packages

Although you don't need to store your procedures and functions within a package, there are several advantages to using a package. First, packages help you organize your code so all related code is stored in the same package. This has the added benefit of avoiding naming conflicts with other procedures or functions. Second, packages provide some enhanced functionality. For example, if you declare a variable outside of a procedure or function, that variable is available within the package for the entire session. Third, packages generally provide improved performance since they are loaded into memory when they are first used. Last, package specifications reduce unnecessary recompiling of dependent procedures and functions in other packages.

Code that defines the body for a package named murach (continued)

```
FUNCTION get_vendor_id
(vendor_name_param VARCHAR2)
RETURN NUMBER
AS
  vendor_id_var NUMBER;
BEGIN
  SELECT vendor_id
  INTO vendor_id_var
  FROM vendors
  WHERE vendor_name = vendor_name_param;

  RETURN vendor_id_var;
END;

END murach;
/
```

A statement that calls a procedure that's stored in a package

```
CALL murach.update_invoices_credit_total('367447', 200);
```

A SELECT statement that calls a function that's stored in a package

```
SELECT invoice_number, invoice_total
FROM invoices
WHERE vendor_id = murach.get_vendor_id('IBM');
```

The response from the system

INVOICE_NUMBER	INVOICE_TOTAL
1 QP58872	116.54
2 Q545443	1083.58

A statement that drops the specification and body for a package

```
DROP PACKAGE murach;
```

A statement that drops only the body for a package

```
DROP PACKAGE BODY murach;
```

Description

- A *package* is a container that allows you to organize and group related stored procedures and user-defined functions.
- The *specification* of a package lists the names and parameters for its procedures and functions. In addition, it specifies the return types for its functions.
- The *body* of a package contains the code for its procedures and functions. Within the body, the names, parameters, and return types must match the names, parameters, and return types in the specification.

Figure 15-11   How to create and drop packages (part 2 of 2)

How to use SQL Developer

To develop effective stored procedures and functions, you must understand the SQL and PL/SQL statements that are presented earlier in this chapter. However, once you understand these statements, SQL Developer provides some tools that can help you compile, edit, and drop the procedures, functions, and packages that you create. In addition, SQL Developer provides an excellent tool for debugging stored procedures and functions.

How to view and drop procedures, functions, and packages

Figure 15-12 shows how to use SQL Developer to view and drop procedures, functions, and packages. To start, you can view the procedures, functions, and packages for a database by connecting to the database and expanding the appropriate folder. In this figure, for example, I have expanded the Packages, Procedures, and Functions folders so you can see all of the procedures, functions, and packages that were presented in this chapter. Note that the package named MURACH provides separate objects for the specification and the body. Note also that you can view the parameters for a procedure or function by clicking on the plus sign (+) to the left of its name.

Once you've displayed one of these database objects, you can drop them by right-clicking on the object and selecting the Drop command. Then, you can use the resulting dialog box to confirm the drop.

If you want to view the code for a procedure or function, you can do that by clicking on its name. Then, the code for the procedure or function will be displayed in the main window. In this figure, for example, I clicked on the procedure named update_invoices_credit_total to display it in the main window. At this point, you can view the code for this procedure.

In addition, you can view other information about the procedure by clicking on one of the other tabs. For example, you can click on the Grants tab to view the roles and users that have been granted privileges on the object. You can click on the Dependencies tab to view the database objects that this object depends on. You can click on the References tab to view the database objects that refer to this object. And you can click on the Details tab to view other details about this object such as the date that the object was created. Before you drop an object, you might want to check the References tab to make sure that other objects don't reference (depend on) this object.

Although this figure shows how to view a procedure or function, you can't edit the procedure or function until you click on the Edit button in the toolbar. In this figure, for example, I have positioned the mouse cursor over the Edit button and am about to click on it. If you click on this button, it will display the procedure in an Edit window like the one shown in the next figure.

A procedure after it has been viewed in SQL Developer

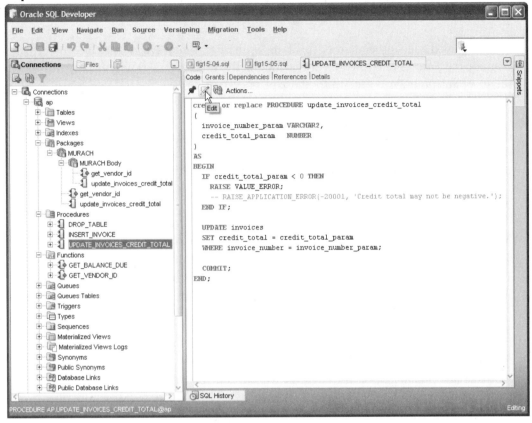

Description

- To view the procedures, functions, and packages for a database, you can use SQL Developer to connect to the database. Then, you can expand the appropriate folder.

- To drop a procedure, function, or package, right-click on the object and select the Drop command. Then, use the resulting dialog box to confirm the drop.

- To view the parameters for a procedure or function, expand it by clicking on the plus sign (+) to the left of its name.

- To view the code for a procedure or function, click on its name. Then, the code for the procedure or function will be displayed in the main window.

- To view other information about a procedure or a function, click on its name to display it in the main window. Then, click on one of the other tabs (Grants, Dependencies, References, or Details) to get more information.

- To edit a stored procedure or function, click on its name to display it in the main window. Then, click on the Edit button in the toolbar.

Figure 15-12   How to view and drop procedures, functions, and packages

How to edit and compile procedures and functions

When you run a procedure or function for the first time, Oracle tries to compile the procedure. However, if the compiler detects errors, it will display them. At this point, you need to fix these errors. Then, to compile the procedure or function again, you can use the techniques in figure 15-13.

When you compile a procedure or function that has errors, the compiler will often display error messages that can help you identify the cause of the compilation error. In this figure, for example, the Compiler – Log window shows an error message that clearly indicates that the SET keyword is missing from the UPDATE statement. In addition, the Edit window has underlined the section of code that caused the error.

As a result, you can fix this problem by using the Edit window to enter the SET keyword in the appropriate place. Once you're done editing the code, you can click on the Compile button to recompile the code. If necessary, you can repeat this process until you get the code to compile cleanly. Then, you can test the code by calling it from a script.

Note that there are two ways to compile a stored procedure or a function. On one hand, you can compile a stored procedure or a function at any time by right-clicking on it and selecting the Compile command. On the other hand, if the stored procedure or function is open in an Edit window, you can compile it by clicking on the Compile button in the toolbar that's displayed at the top of the screen.

How to grant and revoke privileges

In chapter 12, you learned how to code scripts that grant and revoke privileges to database objects. Now, this figure shows an easy way to use SQL Developer to grant or revoke privileges to your procedures, functions, and packages. For example, you can grant privileges to a procedure, function, or package by right-clicking on its name and selecting the Grant command. Then, you can use the resulting dialog box to specify the role or the user and the privileges to be granted.

A procedure after it has been displayed in the Edit window

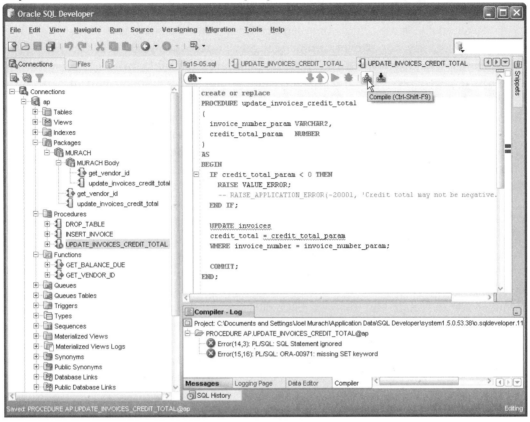

How to compile

- To compile a procedure, function, or package, right-click on its name and select the Compile command.

- Once you display a procedure or function in the Edit window, you can edit the code that's stored in the database. In addition, you can use the Compile button in the toolbar to compile the code.

- If the edited code contains errors when you compile it, SQL Developer will display the compile-time errors in a Compiler – Log tab at the bottom of the main window.

How to grant or revoke privileges

- To grant privileges for a procedure, function, or package, right-click on its name and select the Grant command. Then, use the resulting dialog box to specify the user or role and the privileges to be granted.

- To revoke privileges for a procedure, function, or package, right-click on its name and select the Revoke command. Then, use the resulting dialog box to specify the user or role and the privileges to be revoked.

Figure 15-13   How to compile procedures and functions

How to debug procedures and functions

After you've successfully compiled a procedure or a function, it still might not work properly. For example, you might get an error when you call it. Or, it may return unanticipated results. These types of problems are known as *bugs*. When you encounter bugs, you typically want to find them and remove them. This is known as *debugging*. Fortunately, SQL Developer provides a tool known as a *debugger* than can help you find and remove bugs from your program.

Figure 15-14 shows how to use SQL Developer's debugger. To start, you can display the procedure or function that you want to debug in the Edit window. Then, you can create a *breakpoint* by clicking in the margin to the left of a statement. This statement will be marked by a red dot in the margin, and the execution of the procedure or function will be stopped when it reaches this breakpoint. In this figure, for example, I set a breakpoint on the first statement in the body of the procedure.

Once you've set a breakpoint before the section of code that you suspect contains the bug, you can click on the Compile for Debug button in the Edit window and then on the Debug button. Then, you can use the Debug PL/SQL dialog box to specify the values for the input parameters that you want to use for debugging. To do that, you code the values in the assignment statements that come after the BEGIN keyword in this dialog box. In this figure, for example, I assigned a string value of '367447' to the first parameter, and I assigned a numeric value of -100 to the second parameter. I picked the -100 value because I want to check the IF statement to make sure that it's working properly.

A breakpoint in the SQL Developer window

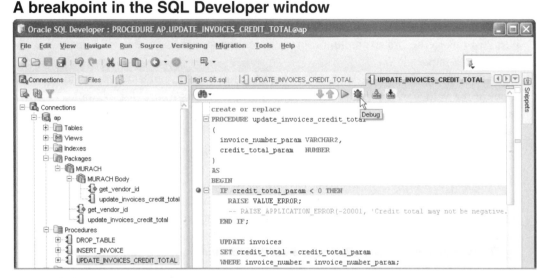

The dialog box for specifying input parameters

Description

- To set a *breakpoint*, display the procedure or function in the Edit window. Then, click in the margin to the left of the line of code where you want to set the breakpoint. After that, a red dot will mark the breakpoint.

- To begin debugging, click the Compile for Debug button in the Edit window. Then, click the Debug button to display the Debug PL/SQL dialog box. Here, you can use the assignment statements that are after the BEGIN keyword to set the input parameters.

Figure 15-14   How to debug procedures and functions (part 1 of 2)

After you specify the values for the input parameters and click OK, program execution will start, but it will stop at the first breakpoint that it encounters. In part 2 of this figure, for example, program execution stopped at the breakpoint that was set in part 1.

At any point during the debugging session, you can use the Data window to monitor the values of the variables that are in scope. In this figure, for example, the only variables that are in scope are the two parameters. However, if other variables were in scope, their values would be displayed in this window too. Often, you can determine the cause of a bug by viewing the values of these variables.

You can also use the Smart Data window to monitor values that are selected automatically by SQL Developer. In this figure, for example, the Smart Data window will only display the value of the parameter named credit_total_param because that parameter is close to the execution point.

To execute the next statement in a procedure or function, you can click on one of the Step buttons that are available from the Debugging – Log window. In this figure, for example, the mouse cursor is positioned over the Step Over button. If you experiment with these buttons, you'll see that they work a little differently if your procedure or function calls another procedure or function. But if your procedure or function doesn't call other procedures or functions, both the Step Over and Step Into buttons execute the next statement in your procedure or function.

In this figure, when I clicked on the Step Over button, program execution moved to the RAISE statement. That's because I assigned a value of -100 to the parameter named credit_total_param.

If you want to continue execution of the program without stepping through it, you can click on the Resume button in the Debugging – Log window toolbar. Then, execution will continue until it reaches another break point or until the program finishes executing.

When a program contains multiple breakpoints, you can use the Breakpoints window view all of the breakpoints. In addition, you can use this window to work with these breakpoints. For example, you can right-click in this window and select the Disable All command to temporarily disable all breakpoints for the application.

If you want to stop debugging, you can click on the Terminate button in the Debugging – Log window toolbar. This immediately ends the debugging session. If your debugging session goes well, you can click on this button whenever you think you've discovered the cause of a bug and are ready to fix it.

A breakpoint in the SQL Developer window

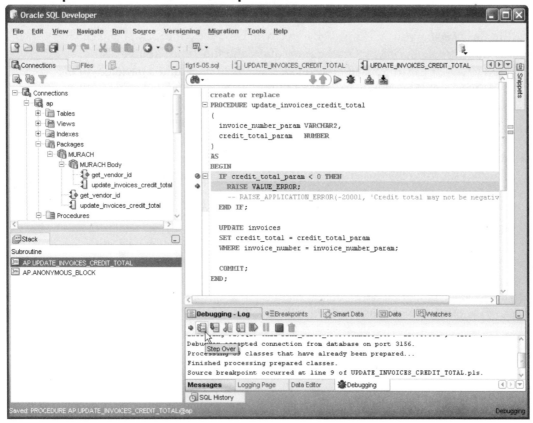

Description

- To step through the code one statement at a time starting at a breakpoint, click on the Debugging – Log tab. Then, click on the Step Over, Step Into, or Step Out button.

- The Step Over button steps over any called procedures or functions. The Step Into button steps into called procedures and functions. The Step Out button skips the rest of a called procedure or function and returns to the calling procedure or function.

- To view the values of the variables at each step in the execution of a procedure or function, click on the Smart Data or Data tab.

- To resume execution until the next breakpoint or the end of the procedure or function, click on the Resume button. To end debugging, click on the Terminate button.

- To view the breakpoints for a procedure or function, click on the Breakpoints tab. To remove a breakpoint, click on the red marker in the Edit window or right-click on the breakpoint in the Breakpoints tab and select the Delete command.

Figure 15-14   How to debug procedures and functions (part 2 of 2)

Perspective

In this chapter, you've learned how to create two types of executable database objects that are supported by Oracle: procedures and functions. You've also learned how to organize related procedures and functions within a package. In the next chapter, you'll learn how to create a third type of executable database object known as a trigger.

The focus of this chapter has been on the skills that application developers typically need for working with procedures and functions. However, you should know that there's a lot more to coding procedures and functions than what this chapter has shown. With this chapter as background, though, you should be able to learn whatever else you need on your own.

For instance, although this chapter has shown you how to create a function that returns a scalar value, you can also create a function that returns a result set. This type of function can be useful because it behaves like a view but can accept parameters that change the result set. Chances are that you may never need to create a function like this. But if you do, you can find more information by searching for "Oracle table functions" on the Internet. In addition, the downloadable files for this chapter include a simple example of a table function.

Terms

stored procedure	raising an error
sproc	application error
procedure	user-defined function (UDF)
parameter	stored function
compiling a procedure	scalar function
calling a procedure	package
passing parameters by position	subprogram
passing parameters by name	package specification
input parameter	package body
output parameter	bug
input/output parameter	debug
optional parameter	debugger
data validation	breakpoint

Exercises

1. Create a stored procedure named insert_glaccount that lets a user add a new row to the General_Ledger_Accounts table in the AP schema. This procedure should have two parameters, one for each of the two columns in this table. Then, code a CALL statement that tests the procedure. (Note that this table doesn't allow duplicate account descriptions.)

2. Code a script that calls the procedure that you created in exercise 1 and passes the parameters by name. This procedure should provide exception handling that displays this message if the INSERT statement fails because the account number or account description is already in the table (a DUP_VAL_ON_INDEX error):

    `A DUP_VAL_ON_INDEX error occurred.`

    It should provide this message if any other type of error occurs:

    `An unknown exception occurred.`

3. Code a function named test_glaccounts_description that accepts one parameter that tests whether an account description is already in the General_Ledger_Accounts table. This function should return a value of 1 if the account description is in the table or zero if it isn't. (Note: If a SELECT statement doesn't return any data, it throws a NO_DATA_FOUND exception that your function can handle.)

4. Code a script that calls the function that you created in exercise 1. This script should display this message if the account description is in the table:

    `Account description is already in use.`

    It should provide this message if any other type of error occurs:

    `Account description is available.`

5. Modify the stored procedure that you created in exercise 1 and save it as insert_glaccount_with_test. This procedure should use the function that you created in step 3 to test whether the account description is going to be okay before it issues the INSERT statement. If the account description is a duplicate, this procedure should raise an application error with -20002 as the error number and an error message of

    `Duplicate account description`

6. Modify the script that you created in step 2 so it uses the procedure of exercise 5. This script should use the SQLERRM function to display the error number and message for the application error if the account description is already in use.

16

How to create triggers

Now that you've learned how to work with stored procedures and user-defined functions, you're ready to learn about another type of executable database object: a trigger. Triggers provide a powerful way to control the SQL statements that modify the data in your database. Since you can program virtually any logic within the code for a trigger, you can use triggers to enforce data consistency with a flexibility that isn't available from other database features such as constraints. In addition, you can use triggers to log changes to the database, provide for updateable views, and implement business rules.

How to work with triggers

A *trigger* is a named block of PL/SQL code that is executed, or *fired*, automatically when a particular type of SQL statement is executed. Most of the time, a trigger is fired when an INSERT, UPDATE, or DELETE statement is executed on a table or view. However, it's also possible to create a trigger that's fired when a DDL statement such as a CREATE, ALTER, or DROP statement is executed.

How to create a BEFORE trigger for a table

Figure 16-1 presents the syntax for a CREATE TRIGGER statement that creates a trigger that fires when INSERT, UPDATE, or DELETE statements are executed on a table. To start, you code the CREATE keyword, followed by the optional OR REPLACE keywords, followed by the TRIGGER keyword, followed by the name of the trigger. In the example in this figure, the statement creates a trigger named vendors_before_update_state. Since this statement includes the OR REPLACE keywords, it creates the trigger if it doesn't already exist, and it replaces the trigger if it does already exist.

Note that the name of this trigger indicates that this trigger is associated with the Vendors table and that it is fired before an update of the vendor_state column. Throughout this chapter, I will use a similar naming convention for the other triggers.

After the name of the trigger, you code the BEFORE or AFTER keyword that indicates when the trigger is fired. Then, you code a list of statement types that cause the trigger to fire, separating each statement type with the OR keyword. For an UPDATE statement, you can use the optional OF keyword to specify a list of columns that limits when the trigger is fired. If you specify multiple columns, you separate the columns with commas. Finally, you code an ON clause that identifies the name of the table. In the example in this figure, the first statement creates a trigger that's executed before any INSERT statements on the Vendors table and before any UPDATE statements that update the vendor_state column of the Vendors table.

After the ON clause, you can optionally specify the FOR EACH ROW clause to indicate that the trigger is a *row-level trigger* that will fire for each row that's modified. If you don't code this clause, the trigger is a *statement-level trigger* that's only executed once for each statement.

If you specify a FOR EACH ROW clause, you can optionally specify a WHEN clause to control when the trigger is fired. To code a WHEN clause, you code the WHEN keyword followed by a set of parentheses. Within the parentheses, you can code a condition that evaluates to True or False.

Within a WHEN clause, you can code a *correlation identifier* to work with the new values in the row that's being inserted or updated. Or, you can use a correlation identifier to work with the old values in the row that's being updated or deleted. By default, the correlation identifiers are named NEW and OLD. In this figure, for example, the NEW identifier is used to get the value for the vendor_state column of the new row.

The syntax of the CREATE TRIGGER statement for a table

```
CREATE [OR REPLACE] TRIGGER trigger_name
{BEFORE|AFTER}
{DELETE|INSERT|UPDATE [OF col_name1 [, col_name2]...]}
[OR {DELETE|INSERT|UPDATE [OF col_name1 [, col_name2]...]}]...
ON table_name
[FOR EACH ROW
[WHEN (trigger_condition)]]
pl_sql_block
```

A CREATE TRIGGER statement that corrects mixed-case state names

```
CREATE OR REPLACE TRIGGER vendors_before_update_state
BEFORE INSERT OR UPDATE OF vendor_state
ON vendors
FOR EACH ROW
WHEN (NEW.vendor_state != UPPER(NEW.vendor_state))
BEGIN
  :NEW.vendor_state := UPPER(:NEW.vendor_state);
END;
/
```

An UPDATE statement that fires the trigger

```
UPDATE vendors
SET vendor_state = 'wi'
WHERE vendor_id = 1;
```

A SELECT statement that shows the new row

```
SELECT vendor_name, vendor_state
FROM vendors
WHERE vendor_id = 1;
```

The result set

	VENDOR_NAME	VENDOR_STATE
1	US Postal Service	WI

Description

- A *trigger* is a named block of PL/SQL code that executes, or *fires*, in response to an event.

- You can fire a trigger before or after an INSERT, UPDATE, or DELETE statement is executed on a table.

- If you don't specify a FOR EACH ROW clause, the trigger is a *statement-level trigger* that fires once for each statement.

- If you specify a FOR EACH ROW clause, the trigger is a *row-level trigger* that fires once for each row that's modified. For a row-level trigger, you can use the OLD and NEW *correlation identifiers* to work with the values for the columns that are stored in the old row and the new row.

Figure 16-1   How to create a BEFORE trigger for a table

When you use the NEW and OLD identifiers, you'll get a NULL value if you use the NEW identifier for a row that's about to be deleted since this row doesn't have any new values. Conversely, you'll get a NULL value if you use the OLD identifier for a row that's about to be inserted since this row doesn't have any old values. Finally, note that you don't need to preface the NEW and OLD identifier with a colon (:) when they're used within the WHEN clause. However, you do need to preface these keyword with a colon when they're not used within the WHEN clause. This syntax is similar to the syntax for working with a bind variable, and it indicates that the NEW and OLD identifiers are a special type of variable that's similar to a bind variable.

The body for this trigger is a PL/SQL block that contains a single statement. This statement, updates the vendor_state column so that state codes are always stored with uppercase letters. To accomplish this, this statement uses the UPPER function to convert the new value for the vendor_state column to uppercase.

How to use a trigger to enforce data consistency

Triggers are commonly used to enforce data consistency. For example, the sum of line item amounts in the Invoice_Line_Items table should always be equal to the corresponding invoice total amount in the Invoices table. However, you can't enforce this constraint on the Invoices table or the Invoice_Line_Items table. To do that, you need to use a trigger like the one in figure 16-2.

To understand how this trigger works, consider how an invoice is entered into the database. First, you must insert the invoice into the Invoices table. If you tried to insert the line items first, you'd violate referential integrity since the value for the invoice_id column hasn't been inserted into the database yet. Once the invoice has been inserted, you can insert the first line item into the Invoice_Line_Items table. However, you can't constrain the value for the line item amount because the constraint would have to be based on the value in the Invoices table. In addition, even if you could implement such a constraint, you would only want to do so once the last line item was inserted. Then, you'd want to be sure that the sum of the line item amounts equaled the invoice total.

The trigger shown here enforces this rule by firing after an UPDATE statement attempts to update the invoice_total column in the Invoices table. When the trigger fires, it tries to verify that the sum of the line items is equal to the invoice total. If this isn't true, the trigger raises an error. Then, the application that issued the UPDATE statement can handle the exception.

Although this example isn't entirely realistic, you can use triggers like this to enforce business rules or to verify data consistency. Since you can program a trigger to accommodate most situations, triggers are more flexible than constraints.

A trigger that validates line item amounts when updating the invoice total

```
CREATE OR REPLACE TRIGGER invoices_before_update_total
BEFORE UPDATE OF invoice_total
ON invoices
FOR EACH ROW
DECLARE
  sum_line_item_amount NUMBER;
BEGIN
  SELECT SUM(line_item_amt)
  INTO sum_line_item_amount
  FROM invoice_line_items
  WHERE invoice_id = :new.invoice_id;

  IF sum_line_item_amount != :new.invoice_total THEN
    RAISE_APPLICATION_ERROR(-20001,
      'Line item total must match invoice total.');
  END IF;
END;
/
```

An UPDATE statement that fires the trigger

```
UPDATE invoices
SET invoice_total = 600
WHERE invoice_id = 100;
```

The response from the system

```
ORA-20001: Line item total must match invoice total.
```

Description

- Triggers can be used to enforce rules for data consistency that can't be enforced by constraints.

Figure 16-2   How to use a trigger to enforce data consistency

How to use a trigger to work with a sequence

When you create a sequence that generates a value for column in a table, you typically want to use that value every time you insert a new row. To illustrate, let's assume that you have defined a sequence named invoice_id_seq that generates a unique value for the invoice_id column of the Invoices table. In that case, you want to use this sequence every time you insert a new row in the Invoices table.

To do this automatically, you can use a trigger like the one in figure 16-3. Here, the trigger is executed before a row is inserted into the Invoices table. However, this trigger is only executed if the value of the invoice_id column in the new row is a NULL value. As a result, if the new row already contains a value for the invoice_id column, the trigger isn't executed.

Within the body of this statement, a single SELECT statement uses the NEXTVAL pseudo column of the sequence named invoice_id_seq to select the next value of the sequence into the invoice_id column of the new row that's being inserted. As a result, an INSERT statement on the Invoices table doesn't need to specify a value for the invoice_id column since this value is set automatically by the trigger.

As you review this code, note that the WHEN clause is necessary because other programs might issue INSERT statements that call the NEXTVAL pseudo column of the sequence. In that case, the WHEN clause prevents the NEXTVAL pseudo column from being called twice before the row is inserted. For example, the trigger shown in figure 16-5 issues an INSERT statement that calls the NEXTVAL pseudo column. As a result, if you didn't include the WHEN clause in this trigger, these two triggers would cause a gap in the numbering sequence.

A trigger that sets the next primary key value for a row

```
CREATE OR REPLACE TRIGGER invoices_before_insert
BEFORE INSERT ON invoices
FOR EACH ROW
WHEN (NEW.invoice_id IS NULL)
BEGIN
  SELECT invoice_id_seq.NEXTVAL
  INTO :new.invoice_id
  FROM dual;
END;
/
```

An INSERT statement that fires the trigger

```
INSERT INTO invoices
(vendor_id, invoice_number, invoice_date, invoice_total, terms_id,
invoice_due_date)
VALUES
(34, 'ZXA-080', '30-AUG-08', 14092.59, 3, '30-SEP-08');
```

A SELECT statement that retrieves the row that was inserted

```
SELECT * FROM invoices WHERE invoice_number = 'ZXA-080';
```

The result set

INVOICE_ID	VENDOR_ID	INVOICE_NUMBER	INVOICE_DATE	INVOICE_TOTAL	PAYMENT_TOTAL
134	34	ZXA-080	30-AUG-08	14092.59	0

Description

- You can use a trigger to set a value in a new row that's about to be inserted with a value that's generated by a sequence.

Figure 16-3   How to use a trigger to work with a sequence

How to create an AFTER trigger for a table

Triggers are commonly used to store information about events that occur in a database so these events can be reviewed later. In particular, AFTER triggers are used to store information about a statement after it executes. Figure 16-4 shows how this works.

To start, this figure shows a CREATE TABLE statement that creates a table named Invoices_Audit. This table contains five columns that store information about the action that occurred on the Invoices table. Of these columns, the first three store values from the Invoices table, and the last two store information about the action that caused the statement to execute.

After the CREATE TABLE statement, this figure shows a CREATE TRIGGER statement that creates a trigger that executes after an INSERT, UPDATE, or DELETE statement is executed on the Invoices table. The body of this trigger uses an IF statement with the INSERTING, UPDATING, and DELETING *trigger predicates* to check the type of the event that caused the trigger to fire. Then, the trigger executes an appropriate INSERT statement depending on whether data in the table has been inserted, updated, or deleted. If, for example, data has been inserted into the table, the first INSERT statement in the trigger is executed. This inserts the new values for the vendor_id, invoice_number, and invoice_total columns into the Invoices_Audit table. In addition, it inserts a string value of "Inserted" to indicate that the row has been inserted, and it uses the SYSDATE function to insert the date of the action.

Note that the first INSERT statement inserts the new values for the row that's being inserted since there aren't any old values for this row. However, the second and third INSERT statements insert the old values for the row that's being updated or deleted since there are old values for these rows.

Although the example that's presented in this figure has been simplified, it presents all of the skills that you need for creating more complex audit tables. For example, if you're having a problem updating rows in a database, you can create an audit table and a trigger to store whatever data you want to store about each update. Then, the next time the update problem occurs, you can review the data in the audit table to identify the cause of the problem.

A statement that creates an audit table for actions on the invoices table

```
CREATE TABLE invoices_audit
(
  vendor_id           NUMBER          NOT NULL,
  invoice_number      VARCHAR2(50)    NOT NULL,
  invoice_total       NUMBER          NOT NULL,
  action_type         VARCHAR2(50)    NOT NULL,
  action_date         DATE            NOT NULL
);
```

An AFTER trigger that inserts rows into the audit table

```
CREATE OR REPLACE TRIGGER invoices_after_dml
AFTER INSERT OR UPDATE OR DELETE
ON invoices
FOR EACH ROW
BEGIN
  IF INSERTING THEN
    INSERT INTO invoices_audit VALUES
    (:new.vendor_id, :new.invoice_number, :new.invoice_total,
     'INSERTED', SYSDATE);
  ELSIF UPDATING THEN
    INSERT INTO invoices_audit VALUES
    (:old.vendor_id, :old.invoice_number, :old.invoice_total,
     'UPDATED', SYSDATE);
  ELSIF DELETING THEN
    INSERT INTO invoices_audit VALUES
    (:old.vendor_id, :old.invoice_number, :old.invoice_total,
     'DELETED', SYSDATE);
  END IF;
END;
/
```

An INSERT statement that causes the trigger to fire

```
INSERT INTO invoices VALUES
(115, 34, 'ZXA-080', '30-AUG-08', 14092.59, 0, 0, 3, '30-SEP-08', NULL);
```

A DELETE statement that causes the trigger to fire

```
DELETE FROM invoices WHERE invoice_number = 'ZXA-080';
```

A SELECT statement that retrieves the rows in the audit table

```
SELECT * FROM invoices_deleted;
```

The result set

	VENDOR_ID	INVOICE_NUMBER	INVOICE_TOTAL	ACTION_TYPE	ACTION_DATE
1	34	ZXA-080	14092.59	INSERTED	13-OCT-08
2	34	ZXA-080	14092.59	DELETED	13-OCT-08

Description

- You can use an AFTER trigger to insert rows into an audit table.
- If a trigger works for multiple types of DML statements, you can use the INSERTING, UPDATING, and DELETING *trigger predicates* to check the type of DML statement that caused the trigger to fire.

Figure 16-4   How to create an AFTER trigger for a table

How to use an INSTEAD OF trigger for a view

In chapter 11, you learned how to create updateable views, and you learned that there are some limitations to updating data in updateable views. Now, you'll learn how you can use an INSTEAD OF trigger to get around many of those limitations. To do that, you can code an INSTEAD OF trigger that executes an INSERT, UPDATE, or DELETE statement on the underlying table or tables that the view is based on instead of attempting to insert, update, or delete data through the view.

Figure 16-5 shows the syntax for using an INSTEAD OF trigger on a view. If you compare this syntax with the syntax for using a BEFORE or AFTER trigger on a table, you'll see that they're similar. As a result, you shouldn't have much trouble understanding this syntax.

The INSTEAD OF trigger in this figure allows you to insert rows into the view named IBM_Invoices that was presented in figure 11-6. This view selects invoices from the Invoices table for the vendor named IBM, which has a vendor ID of 34. Since some of the columns that are required for an INSERT statement aren't included in the view, you can't insert data through this view unless you create a trigger like the one in this figure.

This trigger accommodates the missing columns by calculating their values based on three logical assumptions. First, the invoice ID can be retrieved from a sequence. Second, the vendor ID can be assumed to be 34 because that's part of the definition of the view. Third, the terms ID for the invoice can be assumed to be 3 since this is the default terms ID for this vendor. Fourth, the due date for the invoice can be calculated based on the invoice date and the terms that correspond with the terms ID value. In this case, the invoice must be paid within 30 days of the invoice date. In addition, this trigger uses the NEW identifier to retrieve the values from the new row that the INSERT statement is attempting to insert.

Since an INSTEAD OF trigger is executed instead of the SQL statement that caused it to fire, the SQL statement won't execute unless you code it as part of the trigger. That's why the only statement in the body of this trigger is an INSERT statement that inserts the new row into the underlying Invoices table.

If a stored procedure is available that does what you want it to do, you can call that procedure from a trigger. For instance, you can use the stored procedure named insert_invoice in figure 15-5 of the last chapter instead of the INSERT statement shown in this figure. To do that, you call the insert_invoice procedure from the trigger like this:

```
insert_invoice(34, :new.invoice_number, :new.invoice_date,
               :new.invoice_total);
```

This approach has two advantages. First, it makes your code easier to maintain by allowing you to store all logic for inserting an invoice in one location. Second, it makes your code more flexible since the procedure looks up the terms ID and calculates the due date based on that value.

The syntax of the CREATE TRIGGER statement for a view

```
CREATE [OR REPLACE] TRIGGER trigger_name
INSTEAD OF
{DELETE|INSERT|UPDATE [OF col_name1 [, ] col_name2...]}
[OR {DELETE|INSERT|UPDATE [OF col_name1 [, ] col_name2...]}]...
ON view_name
[FOR EACH ROW
[WHEN (trigger_condition)]]
pl_sql_block
```

A statement that creates a view

```
CREATE OR REPLACE VIEW ibm_invoices AS
  SELECT invoice_number, invoice_date, invoice_total
  FROM invoices
  WHERE vendor_id = 34;
```

An INSTEAD OF INSERT trigger for a view

```
CREATE OR REPLACE TRIGGER ibm_invoices_instead_of_insert
INSTEAD OF INSERT
ON ibm_invoices
BEGIN
  INSERT INTO invoices VALUES
  (invoice_id_seq.NEXTVAL, 34, :new.invoice_number, :new.invoice_date,
   :new.invoice_total, 0, 0, 3, :new.invoice_date + 30, NULL);
END;
/
```

An INSERT statement that succeeds due to the trigger

```
INSERT INTO ibm_invoices VALUES ('ZXA-080', '30-AUG-08', 14092.59);
```

A SELECT statement that retrieves the rows from the view

```
SELECT * FROM ibm_invoices;
```

The result set

	INVOICE_NUMBER	INVOICE_DATE	INVOICE_TOTAL
1	ZXA-080	30-AUG-06	14092.59
2	QP58872	25-FEB-08	116.54
3	Q545443	14-MAR-08	1083.58

Description

- You can use an INSTEAD OF trigger to make views updatable by executing INSERT, UPDATE, or DELETE statements on the underlying table or tables of the view instead of attempting to insert, update, or delete data through the view.

Figure 16-5   How to use an INSTEAD OF trigger for a view

How to use a trigger to work with DDL statements

So far, you've learned how to use a trigger to work with DML statements such as INSERT, UPDATE, and DELETE statements. However, you can also use a trigger to work with DDL statements such as CREATE, ALTER, and DROP statements as shown in figure 16-6.

When you code a trigger that works with DDL statements, the trigger can respond to the DDL events shown in this figure. For example, to fire the trigger for most DDL events, you can code the DDL keyword. Or, you can code the keyword for a more specific DDL event such as the CREATE event or the DROP event. If you code more than one DDL event, you must separate the different events with the OR keyword.

Within the ON clause, you can specify that you only want the trigger to fire for a specific schema by coding the name of the schema, followed by a dot operator, followed by the SCHEMA keyword. Or, you can code the SCHEMA keyword without explicitly specifying the name of the schema. In that case, the trigger fires for DDL events on the same schema that contains the trigger. On the other hand, if you want the trigger to fire for all schemas on the current database server, you can code the DATABASE keyword instead of the SCHEMA keyword.

In the example in this figure, the trigger fires before a CREATE or DROP statement is executed on the AP schema. Then, the body of the trigger raises an application error, which prevents the CREATE or DROP statement from executing. In this example, the trigger prevents the CREATE TABLE statement from executing. But it will also prevent any other CREATE statements such as a CREATE VIEW statement from executing.

Fortunately, though, this trigger doesn't prevent a user with the appropriate privileges from dropping the trigger later. Otherwise, it would be possible to accidentally create a trigger that would prevent you from making any changes to the database objects in your database.

How to use a trigger to work with database events

If necessary, you can use a trigger to respond to database events such as when the database starts up or shuts down or when a user logs on or off. To do that, you can use a syntax that's similar to the syntax in this figure. However, you use the DATABASE keyword, and you specify database events such as the STARTUP, SHUTDOWN, LOGON, and LOGOFF events. Since these types of triggers are typically coded by DBAs, they aren't presented in this book. For more information about them, you can search the Internet.

The syntax of the CREATE TRIGGER statement for a DDL statement

```
CREATE [OR REPLACE] TRIGGER trigger_name
{BEFORE|AFTER} ddl_event [OR ddl_event]...
ON {[schema_name.]SCHEMA|DATABASE}
pl_sql_block
```

DDL events

DDL event	Description
CREATE	Fired when an object is created.
ALTER	Fired when an object is altered.
DROP	Fired when an object is dropped.
GRANT	Fired when a GRANT statement is issued.
REVOKE	Fired when a REVOKE statement is issued.
DDL	Fired when most DDL statements are issued.

A trigger that works with DDL statements

```
CREATE OR REPLACE TRIGGER ap_before_create_drop
BEFORE CREATE OR DROP ON ap.SCHEMA
BEGIN
  RAISE_APPLICATION_ERROR(-20001,
    'You cannot create or drop an object in the AP schema');
END;
/
```

A CREATE TABLE statement that fires the trigger

```
CREATE TABLE ap.test1 (test_id NUMBER);
```

The response from the system

```
ORA-20001: You cannot create or drop an object in the AP schema
```

Description

- In the ON clause, you can use the SCHEMA keyword to fire the trigger when DDL events occur on the specified schema. If you don't explicitly specify the schema, the statement will use the schema that contains the trigger.

- In the ON clause, you can use the DATABASE keyword to fire the trigger when DDL events occur on any schema on the current server.

Figure 16-6   How to use a trigger to work with DDL statements

How to enable, disable, rename, or drop a trigger

If the tables that you're working with contain triggers, you may want to temporarily disable them before you perform certain functions. For example, you may want to disable the triggers for one or more tables before inserting a large number of rows into the table or tables. This can help the INSERT statements run faster and it lets you insert data that isn't allowed by the triggers. Then, when you're done, you can enable the triggers that were disabled.

Figure 16-7 shows how to code the SQL statements that enable and disable triggers. In addition, it shows how to code the SQL statements that rename or drop a trigger.

To enable or disable a specific trigger, you code the ALTER TRIGGER keywords, followed by the name of the trigger, followed by the ENABLE or DISABLE keywords. In this figure, the first example disables the trigger that was created in the previous figure so objects can be created and dropped within the AP schema. Then, it creates and drops a table. Finally, it enables the trigger so objects can't be created and dropped within the AP schema.

To enable or disable all triggers for a table, you code the ALTER TRIGGER keywords, followed by the name of the table, followed by the ENABLE or DISABLE keywords, followed by the ALL TRIGGERS keywords. In this figure, the second example disables all triggers for the Invoices table. Then, it enables all of the triggers for the Invoices table.

To rename a trigger, you code the ALTER TRIGGER keywords, followed by the old name of the trigger, followed by the RENAME TO keywords, followed by the new name for the trigger. In this figure, the third example renames the trigger that was created in figure 16-2.

To drop a trigger, you code the DROP TRIGGER keywords followed by the name of the trigger. In this figure, the fourth example uses the DROP TRIGGER statement to drop the trigger that was created in the previous figure.

If you drop a table, sequence, or view used by a trigger, you should be sure to drop or disable the trigger as well. If you don't, the trigger can still be fired by a database user. Then, an error will occur because the table, sequence, or view that the trigger depends on no longer exists.

Statements that disable and enable a trigger

```
ALTER TRIGGER ap_before_create DISABLE;
CREATE TABLE test1 (test_id NUMBER);
DROP TABLE test1;
ALTER TRIGGER ap_before_create ENABLE;
```

Statements that disable and enable all triggers for a table

```
ALTER TABLE invoices DISABLE ALL TRIGGERS;
ALTER TABLE invoices ENABLE ALL TRIGGERS;
```

A statement that renames a trigger

```
ALTER TRIGGER invoices_before_update_total
RENAME TO invoices_before_update_inv_tot;
```

A statement that drops a trigger

```
DROP TRIGGER ap_before_create;
```

Description

- To enable or disable a specific trigger, use the ALTER TRIGGER statement with the ENABLE or DISABLE keywords.

- To enable or disable all triggers for a table, use the ALTER TRIGGER statement with the ENABLE or DISABLE keywords and the ALL TRIGGERS keywords.

- To rename a trigger, use the ALTER TRIGGER statement with the RENAME TO keywords.

- To drop a trigger, use the DROP TRIGGER statement.

Figure 16-7   How to enable, disable, rename, or drop a trigger

Other skills for working with triggers

Oracle Database 11g introduced a new type of trigger known as a compound trigger. This type of trigger provides an easy way to solve a well-known Oracle error that was difficult to solve with the old trigger types.

How to code a compound trigger

A *compound trigger* can contain blocks of PL/SQL code that are executed (1) before the triggering statement is executed, (2) before the row is modified, (3) after the row is modified, or (4) after the triggering statement has finished executing. In addition, a compound trigger can share variables between these blocks of code.

In figure 16-8, for example, the body of the trigger begins by declaring a variable that stores an integer value. Then, it uses the BEFORE STATEMENT, BEFORE EACH ROW, AFTER EACH ROW, and AFTER STATEMENT blocks to display the value of this variable. This shows that all four blocks can access the value that's stored in the variable. In addition, it shows how to code all four blocks for a compound trigger. Note, however, that it's common to code a compound trigger that only has two blocks.

When you declare a compound trigger, you use the FOR keyword instead of the BEFORE or AFTER keywords to identify the DML event that causes the trigger to fire. This makes sense because a compound trigger can execute both BEFORE *and* AFTER a DML statement. In addition, you use the COMPOUND TRIGGER keywords to identify the beginning of the trigger. Then, within each BEFORE or AFTER block you use the IS keyword to identify the beginning of the PL/SQL block, and you use the corresponding END clause to end each block.

Note that the statements that print data to the output window are coded within the trigger. However, the SET SERVEROUTPUT ON command that enables the buffer for these statements is called before the UPDATE statement that fires the trigger. This is necessary because the SET SERVEROUTPUT ON command isn't a valid PL/SQL statement. Instead, this command works with external tools such as SQL*Plus and SQL Developer.

A compound trigger

```
CREATE OR REPLACE TRIGGER invoices_compound_update
FOR UPDATE OF invoice_total, credit_total
ON invoices
COMPOUND TRIGGER
  test_value NUMBER := 1;

  BEFORE STATEMENT IS
  BEGIN
    DBMS_OUTPUT.PUT_LINE('before statement: ' || test_value);
  END BEFORE STATEMENT;

  BEFORE EACH ROW IS
  BEGIN
    DBMS_OUTPUT.PUT_LINE('before row: ' || test_value);
  END BEFORE EACH ROW;

  AFTER EACH ROW IS
  BEGIN
    DBMS_OUTPUT.PUT_LINE('after row: ' || test_value);
  END AFTER EACH ROW;

  AFTER STATEMENT IS
  BEGIN
    DBMS_OUTPUT.PUT_LINE('after statement: ' || test_value);
  END AFTER STATEMENT;
END;
/
```

A script that fires the trigger

```
SET SERVEROUTPUT ON;

UPDATE invoices
SET credit_total = 0
WHERE invoice_id = 100;
```

The response from the system

```
before statement: 1
before row: 1
after row: 1
after statement: 1
```

Description

- A *compound trigger* can contain blocks of code that are executed (1) before the triggering statement is executed, (2) before the row is modified, (3) after the row is modified, or (4) after the triggering statement has finished executing.
- Within the body of a compound trigger, you can declare variables that are shared between the blocks within the body of the trigger.
- You use the FOR keyword to identify the DML event that fires the compound trigger.
- You use the COMPOUND TRIGGER keywords to identify the start of the body for the trigger.
- Compound triggers were introduced with Oracle Database 11g.

Figure 16-8   How to code a compound trigger

A trigger that causes the mutating-table error

If you code a row-level trigger that issues a SELECT statement against the same table that the trigger is defined on, the trigger will compile cleanly. However, when you execute a statement that fires the trigger, you'll get an error that is known as the *mutating-table error.* This error includes a message that indicates that the table is mutating and that the trigger might not be able to "see" the changes. As a result, the trigger fails to execute properly.

To understand this error more thoroughly, let's assume that you have a business rule that says that the credit total for an invoice should never be greater than the maximum invoice total for a vendor. Unfortunately, this business rule is too complex to implement with a constraint. At first glance, though, it seems like you should be able to implement this business rule by coding a trigger like the one shown in figure 16-9.

Here, the declaration for the trigger indicates that the trigger executes before an UPDATE statement is executed against each row of the Invoices table. Then, the body of the trigger declares a variable and uses a SELECT statement to store the maximum invoice total for the vendor in the variable. Finally, this trigger uses an IF statement to check if the new credit total is greater than the maximum invoice total that's stored in the variable. If so, the trigger raises an appropriate application error, which prevents the UPDATE statement from executing.

When you run this CREATE TRIGGER statement, it compiles cleanly. However, when you issue an UPDATE statement like the one in this figure, Oracle returns the mutating-table error because the trigger is attempting to read data from the table at the same time that the UPDATE statement is attempting to update the table.

At this point, you may wonder why this trigger causes the mutating-table error while the trigger presented in figure 16-2 does not. If you compare these triggers, you'll see that they're both row-level triggers based on the Invoices table and that they both use a SELECT statement within the body of the trigger. However, the trigger in figure 16-2 selects data from the Invoice_Line_Items table. As a result, it doesn't cause the mutating-table error.

If your trigger doesn't need to use the NEW or OLD identifiers, you can solve the mutating-table error by removing the FOR EACH ROW clause from the trigger. In that case, the row-level trigger will be converted to a statement-level trigger, and the mutating-table error won't occur. Unfortunately, the trigger shown in this figure needs to use the NEW identifier to check the new credit total for the row.

A trigger that causes the mutating-table error

```
CREATE OR REPLACE TRIGGER invoices_before_update_total_2
BEFORE UPDATE OF invoice_total, credit_total
ON invoices
FOR EACH ROW
DECLARE
  max_invoice_total NUMBER;
BEGIN
  SELECT MAX(invoice_total)
  INTO max_invoice_total
  FROM invoices
  WHERE invoice_id = :new.invoice_id;

  IF (:new.credit_total > max_invoice_total) THEN
    RAISE_APPLICATION_ERROR(-20001,
    'invoice_credit value may not exceed the maximum invoice_total value.');
  END IF;
END;
/
```

A statement that fires the trigger

```
UPDATE invoices
SET credit_total = 0
WHERE invoice_id = 100;
```

The response from the system

```
ORA-04091: table AP.INVOICES is mutating, trigger/function may not see it
```

Description

- The *mutating-table error* is raised when a trigger attempts to execute a SELECT statement on the same table that the trigger is defined on.

Figure 16-9   A trigger that causes the mutating-table error

How to solve the mutating-table problem

Figure 16-10 shows how to use compound triggers to solve the mutating-table problem. This trigger works because it uses a statement-level trigger to execute the SELECT statement that retrieves the data before the triggering statement is executed, and it stores this data in variables. Then, it uses a row-level trigger to process each row using the data that has been stored the variables. As a result, the row-level trigger never attempts to retrieve data from the table while it is mutating.

Since compound triggers were introduced with Oracle Database 11g, this solution will only work with Oracle 11g or later. As a result, if you're using an earlier version of Oracle, you will have to use an older workaround that involves coding a statement-level trigger, a row-level trigger, and a package that stores the variables that are used by these triggers. Fortunately, this workaround is well-documented, and you should be able to find plenty of information about it by searching the web.

The trigger shown in this figure is a compound trigger that's fired when the invoice_total or credit_total column of the Invoice table is updated. This trigger begins by declaring some variables that store data about the maximum invoice total for each vendor. In particular, the first two statements declare nested tables that store the vendor IDs and maximum invoice totals for each vendor. Then, the third statement declares an index-by table. This table is later used to store the maximum invoice totals for each vendor and to index these values by vendor ID. Finally, the next three statements assign these three collections to variables named vendor_ids, max_invoice_totals, and ids_totals.

After this trigger declares these variables, it executes the code in the BEFORE STATEMENT block. This block begins by declaring two NUMBER variables, one to store the vendor ID and one to store the maximum invoice total. Then, this code uses a SELECT statement to select the vendor IDs and the maximum invoice totals into their corresponding variables. To accomplish this task, this SELECT statement uses the BULK COLLECT keywords. In addition, it uses a GROUP BY clause to create a summary query. As a result, this SELECT statement will only return one row for each vendor.

After the SELECT statement, a FOR loop stores the vendor IDs and maximum invoice totals in the variable named ids_totals. Within the loop, the first two statements use the counter variable for the loop to return the values for the vendor ID and the maximum invoice total. Finally, the last statement in the loop stores the maximum invoice total in the id_totals variable, and it uses the vendor ID value as the index.

After the BEFORE STATEMENT block, the code in the BEFORE EACH ROW block begins by declaring a NUMBER variable to store the maximum invoice total that's retrieved from the indexed table. Then, it uses the new vendor ID value to retrieve the maximum invoice total for the vendor. Finally, it uses an IF statement to check if the new credit total value is greater than the maximum invoice total value. If so, this trigger raises an application error.

A compound trigger that solves the mutating-table problem

```
CREATE OR REPLACE TRIGGER invoices_before_update_total_2
FOR UPDATE OF invoice_total, credit_total
ON invoices
COMPOUND TRIGGER
  TYPE vendor_ids_table          IS TABLE OF NUMBER;
  TYPE max_invoice_totals_table  IS TABLE OF NUMBER;
  TYPE ids_totals_table          IS TABLE OF NUMBER
                                 INDEX BY BINARY_INTEGER;

  vendor_ids                     vendor_ids_table;
  max_invoice_totals             max_invoice_totals_table;
  ids_totals                     ids_totals_table;

  BEFORE STATEMENT IS
    vendor_id NUMBER;
    max_invoice_total NUMBER;
  BEGIN
    SELECT vendor_id, MAX(invoice_total)
    BULK COLLECT INTO vendor_ids, max_invoice_totals
    FROM invoices
    GROUP BY vendor_id;

    FOR i IN 1..vendor_ids.COUNT() LOOP
      vendor_id := vendor_ids(i);
      max_invoice_total:= max_invoice_totals(i);
      ids_totals(vendor_id) := max_invoice_total;
    END LOOP;
  END BEFORE STATEMENT;

  BEFORE EACH ROW IS
    max_invoice_total NUMBER;
  BEGIN
    max_invoice_total := ids_totals(:new.vendor_id);
    IF :new.credit_total > max_invoice_total THEN
      RAISE_APPLICATION_ERROR(-20001,
        'invoice_credit value may not exceed the maximum
        invoice_total value for a vendor.');
    END IF;
  END BEFORE EACH ROW;

END;
/
```

A statement that fires the trigger

```
UPDATE invoices
SET credit_total = 1000
WHERE invoice_id = 100;
```

The response from the system

```
ORA-20001: invoice_credit value may not exceed the maximum invoice_total
value for a vendor.
```

Description

- With Oracle 11g, you can use compound triggers to solve the mutating-table error.

Figure 16-10   How to solve the mutating-table problem

How to use SQL Developer

To be able to develop effective triggers, you must understand the SQL and PL/SQL statements that are presented earlier in this chapter. However, once you understand these statements, SQL Developer provides some tools that can help you work with the triggers that you create.

How to view, rename, or drop a trigger

Figure 16-11 shows how to use SQL Developer to view, rename, and drop triggers. To start, you can view the triggers for a database by connecting to the database and expanding the appropriate folder. In this figure, I have expanded the Triggers folders so you can see all of the triggers that were presented in this chapter. If you take a moment to review these triggers, you can see that the naming convention that I've used throughout this chapter causes all triggers for a database object to be displayed next to each other. This makes it easy to see that there are five triggers defined on the Invoices table.

Note that triggers can be stored in packages just as procedure and functions are stored in packages. As a result, if you want to view a trigger that's stored in a package, you must begin by expanding the package that contains the trigger.

Once you've displayed a trigger, you can rename it or drop it by right-clicking on it and selecting the appropriate command. Then, you can use the resulting dialog box to provide a new name for the trigger or to confirm the drop.

If you want to view the code for a trigger, you can do that by clicking on its name. Then, the code for the trigger will be displayed in the main window. In this figure, for example, I clicked on the trigger named invoices_after_dml to display it in the main window.

To view other information about the trigger, click on one of the other tabs. For example, you can click on the Dependencies tab to view the database objects that this trigger depends on. Or, you can click on the Details tab to view other details about the trigger such as the date that the trigger was created.

Although this figure shows how to view a trigger, you can't edit the trigger until you click on the Edit button in the toolbar. In this figure, I have positioned the mouse cursor over the Edit button and am about to click on it. When you click on this button, SQL Developer will display the trigger in an Edit window like the one shown in the next figure.

How to enable or disable a trigger

To enable or disable a trigger, right-click on its name in the Connections window and select the appropriate command. Then, you can use the resulting dialog box to confirm the action.

A trigger after it has been viewed in SQL Developer

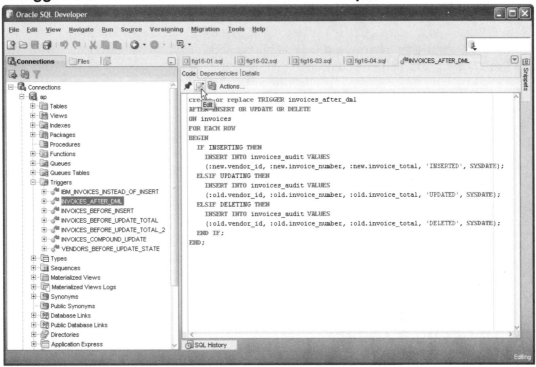

Description

- To view the triggers for a database, you can use SQL Developer to connect to the database. Then, you can expand the appropriate folder.

- To drop a trigger, right-click on the trigger and select the Drop Trigger command. Then, use the resulting dialog box to confirm the drop.

- To view the code for a trigger, click on its name. When you do, the code for the trigger will be displayed in the main window.

- To view other information about a trigger, click on its name to display it in the main window. Then, click on one of the other tabs (Dependencies or Details) to get more information.

- To edit a trigger, click on its name to display it in the main window. Then, click on the Edit button in the toolbar.

Figure 16-11   How to view, rename, and drop triggers

How to edit a trigger

When you execute a CREATE TRIGGER statement, Oracle automatically compiles the trigger. However, if the compiler detects errors, it will display these errors. At this point, you need to find the causes of the errors and fix them. To help you do that, you can open the trigger in an Edit window and compile the trigger again.

When you compile a trigger that has errors, the compiler displays error messages that can help you identify the causes of the errors. In figure 16-12, for example, the Compiler – Log window shows an error message that indicates that the problem occurred when the compiler reached the first INSERT statement. If you look at this statement closely, you'll notice that the first IF statement should use the INSERTING predicate instead of the INSERT keyword.

As a result, you can fix this problem by using the Edit window to edit the code. When you're done, you can click on the Compile button to recompile the code. If necessary, you can repeat the process until you get the code to compile cleanly. Then, you can test the code by executing a statement that causes the trigger to fire.

How to debug a trigger

Unfortunately, SQL Developer 1.5 doesn't provide the same debugger for triggers that it does for stored procedures and functions. As a result, you may need to use the time-tested technique of using the PUT_LINE procedure of the DBMS_OUTPUT package to display the values of variables and other debugging information.

A trigger after it has been displayed in the Edit window

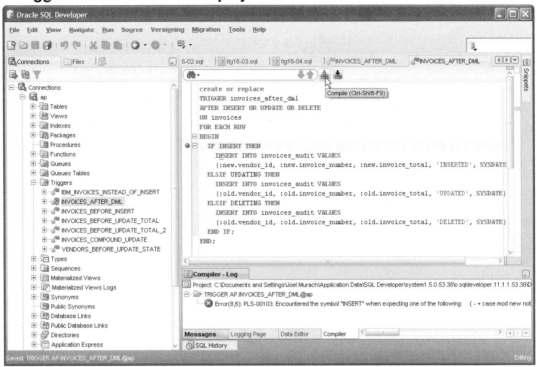

Description

- To display a trigger in the Edit window, right-click on its name and select the Edit command. Or, after you display a trigger in the main window, click on the Edit button.

- When a trigger is in the Edit window, you can edit the code that's stored in the database. To compile the trigger, you can click the Compile button in the toolbar.

- If the edited code contains errors when you compile it, SQL Developer will display the compile-time errors in a Compiler – Log tab at the bottom of the main window.

- SQL Developer 1.5 doesn't provide a debugger for triggers. To debug a trigger, you can use the DBMS_OUTPUT.PUT_LINE statement to print the values of variables and other debugging information to the output window.

Figure 16-12 How to edit a trigger

Perspective

In this chapter, you learned how to use triggers to perform tasks that would be difficult or impossible to perform with other Oracle features like constraints. At this point, then, you should be able to create and use triggers that enforce data consistency, implement business rules, log changes to the database, and provide for updateable views.

Although this is more than the typical application developer needs to know, this gives you the perspective that you need when you encounter the triggers that have been created by others. This also provides the background that you need for learning more about triggers on your own.

Terms

trigger
fire a trigger
statement-level trigger
row-level trigger
correlation identifier
trigger predicate
compound triggers
mutating-table error

Exercises

1. Create a trigger named invoices_before_update_payment for the Invoices table that raises an application error whenever the payment total plus the credit total becomes larger than the invoice total in a row. Then, test this trigger with an appropriate UPDATE statement. (Note that you could code a check constraint to accomplish the same task.)

2. Create a trigger named invoices_after_update_payment for the Invoices table that displays the vendor name, invoice number, and payment total in the output window whenever the payment total is increased. Then, test this trigger with an appropriate UPDATE statement. (A trigger like this could be modified so it stores the data in an audit table.)

3. Use the script for figure 11-4 of chapter 11 to create an updateable view named balance_due_view. Then, create and test an INSTEAD OF trigger named invoices_instead_of_insert that lets the user update the columns in the view by directly updating the Invoices table. Within this trigger, you can call the stored procedure named insert_invoice that's created by the script for figure 15-5 of chapter 15.

Section 5

Advanced data types

This section presents some SQL skills for working with the data types that weren't presented in chapter 8. In chapter 17, you'll learn how to work with the TIMESTAMP and INTERVAL data types that were introduced with Oracle 9i. These data types make it easier to work with time zones and time intervals.

In chapter 18, you'll learn how to work with the large object data types that were introduced with Oracle 8. These data types let you to store virtually any type of text or binary data within a database such as the data that's stored in text, XML, Word, PDF, image, sound, and video files.

17

How to work with timestamps and intervals

In chapter 8, you learned how to work with the most common temporal data type, the DATE type. Now, this chapter expands on that coverage by showing how to work with the TIMESTAMP and INTERVAL data types that were introduced with Oracle 9i. Although the DATE type is adequate for working with most date/time values, the new data types make it easier to work with time zones and time intervals.

An introduction to time zones

When client applications from multiple time zones access the same database, you need to handle the different time zones when you store a time in the database. Prior to Oracle 9i, Oracle only provided the DATE type for storing times, and this data type doesn't support time zones. As a result, the client application needed to handle the time zone by converting the local time zone to the database time zone.

With Oracle 9i, however, Oracle provides features for working with time zones. Before you learn how to use them, though, this chapter introduces you to some terms and concepts for working with time zones, and it shows you how to change the default date format and the default time zone.

Database time zone vs. session time zone

Figure 17-1 introduces some concepts for working a *time zone*, which is an *offset* from the time in Greenwich, England. That time zone is known as *Greenwich Mean Time* (*GMT*) or *Coordinated Universal Time* (*UTC*).

When you use Oracle to work with time zones, you can specify a time zone by coding an offset from GMT. To specify a time zone offset, you can code values like the ones at the top of this figure. For example, the first offset is one hour ahead of GMT, and the second offset is one hour behind GMT.

You can also specify a time zone by coding its name or abbreviated name. To look up time zones from around the world, you can code a SELECT statement like the first one in this figure. Here, the result set shows that Pacific Standard Time has a name of US/Pacific or US/Pacific-New and many possible abbreviations. Of these abbreviations, PST and PDT are the most common.

When you use Oracle to work with time zones, the *session time zone* is the time zone for the current session. For example, when start SQL Developer, you start a session. Conversely, when you exit SQL Developer, you end a session. If you want to view the time zone offset for a session, you can use the SESSIONTIMEZONE function. For example, when I ran the second SELECT statement in this figure, this function returned an offset of -7:00 because I am in California, which has an offset of -7:00 or -8:00, depending on whether it is daylight savings. In this case, it is summer, so this function returns an offset of -7:00. This shows that Oracle automatically adjusts for daylight savings time.

When you use Oracle to work with time zones, the *database time zone* is the time zone for the current database. Typically, the database time zone is set correctly when you install Oracle. However, if the database time zone isn't set correctly you can use the ALTER DATABASE command to change it. To view the database time zone, you can use the DBTIMEZONE function. For example, when I ran the third SELECT statement in this figure, this function returned an offset of +00:00. This offset indicates that the database is using the same time zone as the operating system for the database server.

Time zone offsets

```
+01:00
-01:00
+02:00
-02:00
```

How to view time zone names

```
SELECT * FROM v$timezone_names
```

The result set

	TZNAME		TZABBREV
1363	US/Michigan		EDT
1364	US/Mountain		LMT
1365	US/Mountain		MST
1366	US/Mountain		MWT
1367	US/Mountain		MDT
1368	US/Pacific		LMT
1369	US/Pacific		PST
1370	US/Pacific		PWT
1371	US/Pacific		PDT
1372	US/Pacific-New		LMT
1373	US/Pacific-New		PST
1374	US/Pacific-New		PWT
1375	US/Pacific-New		PDT
1376	US/Samoa		LMT
1377	US/Samoa		SAMT

How to view the default session time zone

```
SELECT SESSIONTIMEZONE FROM dual
```

The result set

```
-07:00
```

How to view the default database time zone

```
SELECT DBTIMEZONE FROM dual
```

The result set

```
+00:00
```

Description

- A *time zone* is an *offset* from the time in Greenwich, England. The time zone in Greenwich England is known as *Greenwich Mean Time* (*GMT*) or *Coordinated Universal Time* (*UTC*).
- A time zone can be stored as an offset or as a region name or abbreviation.
- The *session time zone* is the time zone for the current session.
- The *database time zone* is the time zone for the current database.

Figure 17-1   An introduction to time zones

How to change the default date format

By default, Oracle uses the DD-MON-RR format for date/time values. However, to make it easier to work with date/time values that are in other formats, you can use the ALTER SESSION statement to change the default date format for the current session. If, for example, you are working with dates that include time values, it makes sense to change the default date/time format so it includes time values as shown in figure 17-2.

Here, the first example changes the default date format so it includes HH:MM and AM or PM in the time portion of a date/time value. Then, the second example uses this format to insert a DATE value. Since the string literal for the DATE value that's supplied by this INSERT statement uses the newly set date/time format, you don't have to use the TO_DATE function to convert this string literal to a DATE value. Finally, the third example shows that the newly set date/time format is used by the result set to display the date/time values.

How to change the default time zone

The rest of the statements in this figure show how to use the ALTER SESSION statement to change the time zone for the session. Here, the first two statements in the fourth example use keywords to change the time zone for the session. The first statement sets the time zone to the time zone that's used by the operating system, and the second statement sets the time zone to the time zone that's used by the database. Most of the time, these two time zones are the same.

The last three statements in this figure use offsets and time zone names to set the time zone to the Mountain Time Zone in the United States. Here, the offset is -06:00 because that's the offset for this time zone during daylight savings time. However, during the winter months, the offset is -07:00.

Session settings vs. database settings

When you change settings for the session, the settings are temporary and only apply to the current session. As a result, if you want to reset all settings to their default values, you can do that by ending the session and starting a new one. To do that with SQL Developer or SQL*Plus, you can exit the program and restart it.

If you want to permanently change the date format or time zone settings, you can use the ALTER DATABASE statement instead of the ALTER SESSION statement. Since the ALTER DATABASE statement works much like the ALTER SESSION statement, you shouldn't have any trouble using it. Of course, to do this, you must log on as a user that has the appropriate privileges to alter the database.

A statement that changes the date format for the session

```
ALTER SESSION SET NLS_DATE_FORMAT = 'DD-MON-RR HH:MI AM'
```

An INSERT statement after the date format has been changed

```
INSERT INTO date_sample VALUES (7, '02-MAR-08 09:02 AM')
```

A SELECT statement after the data format has been changed

```
SELECT * FROM date_sample
```

The result set

	DATE_ID	START_DATE
1	1	01-MAR-79 12:00 AM
2	2	28-FEB-99 12:00 AM
3	3	31-OCT-03 12:00 AM
4	4	28-FEB-05 10:00 AM
5	5	28-FEB-06 01:58 PM
6	6	01-MAR-06 09:02 AM
7	7	02-MAR-08 09:02 AM

Statements that use keywords to change the time zone for the session

```
ALTER SESSION SET TIME_ZONE = LOCAL
ALTER SESSION SET TIME_ZONE = DBTIMEZONE
```

Statements that change the time zone for the session

```
ALTER SESSION SET TIME_ZONE = -06:00
ALTER SESSION SET TIME_ZONE = 'MST'
ALTER SESSION SET TIME_ZONE = 'US/Mountain'
```

Description

- You can use the ALTER SESSION statement to change the default date format or time zone for the current session.

- If you change any settings for the session, you can reset all settings by ending the session and starting a new one.

- You can use the ALTER DATABASE statement to permanently change the date format or time zone.

Figure 17-2   How to set the default date format and time zone

How to use functions to work with time zones

In chapter 8, you learned how to work with the SYSDATE and CURRENT_DATE functions. Now, figure 17-3 reviews the use of these functions and shows how to use some of the functions for working with time zones.

To start, note that the SYSDATE and CURRENT_DATE functions usually return the same DATE value. However, if the time zone has been changed for the session, the CURRENT_DATE function will adjust the DATE value accordingly.

As you learned earlier, you can use the DBTIMEZONE function to return an offset for the database time zone relative to the operating system time zone. Similarly, you can use the SESSIONTIMEZONE function to return an offset for the session time zone relative to the UTC time zone.

In addition, you can use the TZ_OFFSET function to return a time zone offset for the specified time zone. When you use this function, you can specify the name of the time zone or the abbreviation for the time zone. Note that this function automatically adjusts for daylight savings time. This causes the results shown in this figure to be different during the winter months.

Finally, you can use the NEW_TIME function to convert a DATE value from one time zone to another. In this figure, for instance, the last three examples show how to convert the current date from Pacific Standard Time (PST) to Mountain Standard Time (MST), Central Standard Time (CST), and Eastern Standard Time (EST).

Some common functions for working with time zones

Function	Description
SYSDATE	Returns the current local date and time based on the operating system's clock.
CURRENT_DATE	Returns the local date and time adjusted for the current session time zone.
DBTIMEZONE	Returns the time zone offset for the database.
SESSIONTIMEZONE	Returns the time zone offset for the session.
TZ_OFFSET(time_zone)	Returns the offset in hours for the specified time zone.
NEW_TIME(date, zone1, zone2)	Converts the specified date from the first specified time zone to the second time zone.

Examples that use functions to work with time zones

Example	Result
SYSDATE	19-AUG-08 04:20 PM
CURRENT_DATE	19-AUG-08 04:20 PM
DBTIMEZONE	+00:00
SESSIONTIMEZONE	'America/Los_Angeles'
TZ_OFFSET('AMERICA/LOS_ANGELES')	-07:00
TZ_OFFSET('PST')	-07:00
TZ_OFFSET('MST')	-06:00
TZ_OFFSET('CST')	-05:00
TZ_OFFSET('EST')	-04:00
NEW_TIME(CURRENT_DATE,'PST','MST')	19-AUG-08 05:20 PM
NEW_TIME(CURRENT_DATE,'PST','CST')	19-AUG-08 06:20 PM
NEW_TIME(CURRENT_DATE,'PST','EST')	19-AUG-08 07:20 PM

Figure 17-3   How to use functions to work with time zones

How to work with timestamps

Now that you understand how time zones work, you're ready to learn how to work with the TIMESTAMP types that were introduced with Oracle 9i. These data types provide two advantages over the DATE type. First, they make it easier to work with time zones. Second, they allow you to store fractional seconds.

An introduction to the TIMESTAMP types

Figure 17-4 lists the three TIMESTAMP types. Here, the TIMESTAMP type works much like the DATE type, except that it allows you to store fractional seconds. When you specify a TIMESTAMP type, you can specify a value of 0 to 9 to set the fractional second precision, which is the number of decimal places that Oracle uses for fractional seconds. Or, if you don't specify the fractional second precision, Oracle will use a default value of 6.

The TIMESTAMP WITH LOCAL TIME ZONE type works much like the TIMESTAMP type. However, when a date/time value is stored in a column of this data type, Oracle automatically converts the date/time value from the session time zone to the database time zone. Conversely, when a date/time value is retrieved from a column of this type, Oracle automatically converts the date/time value from the database time zone to the session time zone. Since Oracle automatically handles these conversions, this data type makes it easy to work with time zones.

The TIMESTAMP WITH TIME ZONE type works like the TIMESTAMP type, except that it actually stores a time zone name, abbreviation, or offset in the database. That's why it requires more storage space than the other two TIMESTAMP types.

The TIMESTAMP types

Type	Bytes	Description
TIMESTAMP[(fsp)]	7 to 11	An extension of DATE. Stores year, month, day, hour, minute, second, and (optionally) the fractional part of a second where the fractional second precision (fsp) is the number of decimal places used to store the fractional second. This type does not have a time zone.
TIMESTAMP [(fsp)] WITH LOCAL TIME ZONE	7 to 11	Works like TIMESTAMP except that the time zone is set to the database time zone when it is stored in the database, and it's set to the session time zone when the data is retrieved.
TIMESTAMP [(fsp)] WITH TIME ZONE	13	Works like TIMESTAMP except that it includes either a time zone name, abbreviation, or offset.

Description

- The default value for fractional second precision is 6.
- All precision parameters for fractional seconds accept values of 0 to 9.

Figure 17-4   The TIMESTAMP types

How to work with the TIMESTAMP type

Figure 17-5 shows how to work with the TIMESTAMP type. To start, the first example shows how to create a table named Downloads that stores data of the TIMESTAMP type. Here, the first column in the table contains a NUMBER value that uniquely identifies each download. Then, the second column in the table contains a TIMESTAMP value that stores the exact time of the download.

The second example shows a script that inserts three rows into the table. Here, the first INSERT statement specifies a literal value for a timestamp by coding the TIMESTAMP keyword followed by a timestamp value enclosed in single quotes. Note that this INSERT statement uses the default format to specify the TIMESTAMP literal. Note also that this format is different than the default format that's used to display a TIMESTAMP value.

The second INSERT statement also uses the TIMESTAMP keyword to specify a literal value for a timestamp. In contrast, the third INSERT statement uses the CURRENT_TIMESTAMP function to return a TIMESTAMP WITH TIME ZONE value for the current time. However, this value is automatically converted to a TIMESTAMP value before it's inserted into the table. Finally, the COMMIT statement commits the changes to the database.

The third example shows a SELECT statement that retrieves all data from the table. The result set that's returned by this SELECT statement shows that the fractional seconds are rounded to the precision that's specified by the CREATE TABLE statement. For example, the second INSERT statement contains seven digits for the fraction second portion of the TIMESTAMP value. However, the CREATE TABLE statement specifies a precision of six digits. As a result, these seven digits are rounded to six digits before they are stored in the database.

Note that the CURRENT_TIMESTAMP function in this figure only returns three digits for the fractional seconds of the TIMESTAMP value. As a result, this value doesn't need to be rounded before it's stored in the database. However, on some systems, the CURRENT_TIMESTAMP function may return more digits for the fractional seconds. In that case, this value will be rounded to the specified precision before it's stored in the database.

A table that uses the TIMESTAMP type

```
CREATE TABLE downloads
(
  download_id         NUMBER         PRIMARY KEY,
  download_timestamp  TIMESTAMP(6)
);
```

A script that inserts three TIMESTAMP values into a table

```
INSERT INTO downloads
VALUES (1, TIMESTAMP '2008-08-15 16:20:47.123456');

INSERT INTO downloads
VALUES (2, TIMESTAMP '2008-08-15 16:20:47.1234567');

INSERT INTO downloads
VALUES (3, CURRENT_TIMESTAMP(6));

COMMIT;
```

A statement that retrieves the TIMESTAMP values

```
SELECT * FROM downloads;
```

The result set

	DOWNLOAD_ID	DOWNLOAD_TIMESTAMP
1	1	15-AUG-08 04.20.47.123456000 PM
2	2	15-AUG-08 04.20.47.123457000 PM
3	3	19-AUG-08 04.20.53.265000000 PM

The default format for specifying a TIMESTAMP literal

```
TIMESTAMP 'YYYY-MM-DD HH24:MI:SS.FF9'
```

The default format for returned TIMESTAMP values

```
DD-MON-RR HH.MI.SS.FF9 AM
```

Description

- To specify a literal value for a timestamp, code the TIMESTAMP keyword followed by a literal value enclosed in single quotes as shown above.

- If the fractional seconds are longer than the precision for the TIMESTAMP, they will be rounded to the nearest fractional second.

- The CURRENT_TIMESTAMP function returns a TIMESTAMP WITH TIME ZONE value for the current data and time in the session time zone (see figure 17-9).

Figure 17-5   How to work with the TIMESTAMP type

How to work with the **TIMESTAMP WITH LOCAL TIME ZONE** type

Figure 17-6 shows how to work with the TIMESTAMP WITH LOCAL TIME ZONE type. The main difference between this and working with the TIMESTAMP type is that Oracle automatically adjusts the time zone so it's transparent to the users of the database.

When a user inserts data, the database converts the session time zone to the database time zone. In addition, if a user specifies a time zone name or offset in a TIMESTAMP literal, Oracle automatically converts the timestamp to the database time zone before it stores its value. In this figure, for example, the first INSERT statement specifies the PST time zone, the second specifies the EST time zone, and the third specifies an offset of -7:00, which is the offset for the PST time zone during daylight savings time. Then, the fourth INSERT statement uses the CURRENT_TIMESTAMP function to insert a timestamp for the current session.

Conversely, when a user retrieves data from the database, the database converts the database time zone to the session time zone. In this figure, for example, the result set shows a time of 4:20 for all of the rows for the PST time zone and a time of 1:20 for the EST time zone. This makes it easy to see that the EST time zone is three hours earlier than the PST time zone.

A table that uses the TIMESTAMP WITH LOCAL TIME ZONE type

```
CREATE TABLE downloads_ltz
(
  download_id         NUMBER                              PRIMARY KEY,
  download_timestamp  TIMESTAMP WITH LOCAL TIME ZONE
);
```

A script that inserts four TIMESTAMP WITH LOCAL TIME ZONE values

```
INSERT INTO downloads_ltz
VALUES (1, TIMESTAMP '2008-08-15 16:20:47.123456 PST');

INSERT INTO downloads_ltz
VALUES (2, TIMESTAMP '2008-08-15 16:20:47.123456 EST');

INSERT INTO downloads_ltz
VALUES (3, TIMESTAMP '2008-08-15 16:20:47.123456 -7:00');

INSERT INTO downloads_ltz
VALUES (4, CURRENT_TIMESTAMP);

COMMIT;
```

A statement that retrieves the TIMESTAMP values

```
SELECT * FROM downloads_ltz;
```

The result set

	DOWNLOAD_ID	DOWNLOAD_TIMESTAMP
1	1	15-AUG-08 04.20.47.123456000 PM
2	2	15-AUG-08 01.20.47.123456000 PM
3	3	15-AUG-08 04.20.47.123456000 PM
4	4	19-AUG-08 04.20.57.828000000 PM

Description

- When a user inserts data, the database converts the session time zone to the database time zone.
- When a user retrieves data from the database, the database converts the database time zone to the session time zone.

Figure 17-6   How to work with the TIMESTAMP WITH LOCAL TIME ZONE type

How to work with the TIMESTAMP WITH TIME ZONE type

Figure 17-7 shows how to work with the TIMESTAMP WITH TIME ZONE type. Unlike the previous two TIMESTAMP types, the TIMESTAMP WITH TIME ZONE type actually stores the time zone in the database.

When you store data for this type, the time zone name or offset that you specify is stored in the database. In this figure, for example, the first three INSERT statements all specify Pacific Standard Time. The first INSERT statement uses a full name, the second uses an abbreviation, and the third uses an offset of -7:00, which is the same as the PST time zone during daylight savings. Then, the fourth INSERT statement uses an abbreviation for Easter Standard Time, and the fifth INSERT statement uses the CURRENT_TIMESTAMP function to insert a timestamp for the current session.

If you don't specify a time zone, an offset for the session time zone is stored in the database. In this figure, for example, the session time zone is Pacific Standard Time, and it is daylight savings time. As a result, if you don't specify a time zone, an offset of -7:00 is stored in the database.

When you retrieve data from this type, the result set includes the time zone. If you specify a name or abbreviation for a time zone, the name or abbreviation is returned. However, UTC is used for all time zone abbreviations except for the current database time zone. That's why the fourth row in the result set returns the time as UTC instead of EST. Note also that UTC doesn't account for daylight savings time. As a result, there's a four hour difference between the first row and the third row instead of a three hour difference. Later in this chapter, you'll learn how to format the data that's retrieved so it takes daylight savings into account.

A table that uses the TIMESTAMP WITH TIME ZONE type

```
CREATE TABLE downloads_tz
(
  download_id          NUMBER                      PRIMARY KEY,
  download_timestamp   TIMESTAMP WITH TIME ZONE
);
```

A script that inserts four TIMESTAMP WITH TIME ZONE values

```
INSERT INTO downloads_tz
VALUES (1, TIMESTAMP '2008-08-15 16:20:47.123456789 PST');

INSERT INTO downloads_tz
VALUES (2, TIMESTAMP '2008-08-15 16:20:47.123456 US/Pacific');

INSERT INTO downloads_tz
VALUES (3, TIMESTAMP '2008-08-15 16:20:47.123456 -7:00');

INSERT INTO downloads_tz
VALUES (4, TIMESTAMP '2008-08-15 16:20:47.123456 EST');

INSERT INTO downloads_tz
VALUES (5, CURRENT_TIMESTAMP);

COMMIT;
```

A statement that retrieves the TIMESTAMP values

```
SELECT * FROM downloads_tz;
```

The result set

	DOWNLOAD_ID	DOWNLOAD_TIMESTAMP
1	1	15-AUG-08 04.20.47.123457000 PM PST
2	2	15-AUG-08 04.20.47.123456000 PM US/PACIFIC
3	3	15-AUG-08 04.20.47.123456000 PM -07:00
4	4	15-AUG-08 08.20.47.123456000 PM UTC
5	5	19-AUG-08 04.21.04.312000000 PM -07:00

Description

- This data type works the same as the TIMESTAMP type, but it includes a time zone after the fractional seconds.
- UTC is used for all time zone abbreviations except for the current database time zone.

Figure 17-7   How to work with the TIMESTAMP WITH TIME ZONE type

Common format elements for timestamps

Figure 17-8 summarizes the most common format elements for timestamps and provides some examples that show how to use format elements to specify fractional seconds and time zones. If you study these examples, you shouldn't have much trouble understanding how they work.

Common format elements for timestamps

Element	Description
FF[1-9]	Fractional seconds.
TZH	Time zone hour offset.
TZM	Time zone minutes offset.
TZR	Time zone region.
TZD	Time zone with daylight savings.

Time formats that use fractional seconds and time zones

Format	Example
HH:MI:SS.FF AM	04:20:36.123456 PM
HH:MI:SS.FF3 AM	04:20:36.123 PM
HH:MI:SS.FF9 AM TZH:TZM	04:20:36.123456000 PM -07:00
HH:MI:SS.FF9 AM TZR	04:20:36.123456789 PM PST
HH:MI:SS.FF9 AM TZD	04:20:36.123456789 PM PDT

Description

- For more information about date/time format elements, look up "Datetime Format Elements" in the Oracle Database SQL Language Reference.

Figure 17-8   Common format elements for timestamps

How to use functions to work with timestamps

Part 1 of figure 17-9 shows some of the common functions for working with timestamps. To start, you can use the first three functions to return a TIMESTAMP or TIMESTAMP WITH TIME ZONE value. When you use these functions, you can the fractional second precision parameter to control the maximum number of fractional seconds that are returned by the function. Or, if you omit this parameter, the default is 6. However, the maximum number of fractional seconds may be limited by the system clock on the computer that's hosting the database. On my system, for example, these functions only return 3 fractional seconds.

The first four examples in this figure show how to use the functions that return a timestamp for the current time. Here, the SYSTIMESTAMP function returns a timestamp with a time zone offset. The CURRENT_TIMESTAMP function returns a timestamp with a time zone name. The LOCALTIMESTAMP function returns a timestamp that doesn't include the time zone portion of the timestamp. And the second SYSTIMESTAMP function specifies a fractional second precision of 2 so the fractional seconds for this timestamp are rounded to 2 decimal places.

The last three examples show how to use the FROM_TZ and SYS_EXTRACT_UTC functions. Here, the FROM_TZ function converts the current timestamp from the PST time zone to the EST time zone. Note that this function returns the newly converted timestamp with the UTC time zone. Then, the two SYS_EXTRACT_UTC functions convert two different timestamps to the UTC time zone.

Although it isn't shown in this figure, you can also use the EXTRACT function to extract a year, month, day, hour, minute, or second from a DATE or TIMESTAMP value. To do that, you use the YEAR, MONTH, DAY, HOUR, MINUTE, and SECOND keywords to specify the part of the data that you want to extract. For example, if you want to extract the year from the TIMESTAMP values stored in the Downloads table that was created in figure 17-5, you can use a statement like this:

```
SELECT EXTRACT(YEAR FROM download_timestamp) AS download_year
FROM downloads;
```

You can also use the TIMEZONE_HOUR, TIMEZONE_MINUTE, TIMEZONE_REGION, and TIMEZONE_ABBR keywords to extract the time zone offset, region name, or region abbreviation. For example, if you want to extract the hour offset for a time zone, you can use a statement like this:

```
SELECT EXTRACT(TIMEZONE_HOUR FROM download_timestamp) AS tz_hour
FROM downloads_tz;
```

However, this only works if the value has been stored as a TIMESTAMP WITH TIME ZONE value. That's why this statement selects data from the Downloads_TZ table that was created in figure 17-7.

Common functions for working with timestamps

Function	Description
SYSTIMESTAMP([fsp])	Returns a TIMESTAMP WITH TIME ZONE value for the current date and time in the database time zone.
CURRENT_TIMESTAMP([fsp])	Returns a TIMESTAMP WITH TIME ZONE value for the current date and time in the session time zone.
LOCALTIMESTAMP([fsp])	Returns a TIMESTAMP value for the current date and time in the session time zone.
FROM_TZ(timestamp, time_zone)	Converts a TIMESTAMP value and a time zone to a TIMESTAMP WITH TIME ZONE value.
SYS_EXTRACT_UTC(timestamp)	Extracts the UTC time from a TIMESTAMP value with a time zone offset or time zone region name.
TO_TIMESTAMP(expr[, fmt])	Converts the result of an expression to a value of the TIMESTAMP type.
TO_TIMESTAMP_TZ(expr[, fmt])	Converts the result of an expression to a value of the TIMESTAMP WITH TIME ZONE type.

Examples that use functions to work with timestamps

Example	Result
SYSTIMESTAMP	19-AUG-08 04.20.16.906000000 PM -07:00
CURRENT_TIMESTAMP	19-AUG-08 04.20.16.906000000 PM PST
LOCALTIMESTAMP	19-AUG-08 04.20.16.906000000 PM
SYSTIMESTAMP(2)	19-AUG-08 04.20.16.910000000 PM -07:00
FROM_TZ(LOCALTIMESTAMP, 'EST')	19-AUG-08 08.20.16.906000000 PM UTC
SYS_EXTRACT_UTC(SYSTIMESTAMP)	19-AUG-08 11.20.16.906000000 PM
SYS_EXTRACT_UTC(CURRENT_TIMESTAMP)	19-AUG-08 11.20.16.906000000 PM

Description

- If you omit the fractional second precision (fsp) parameter, the default is 6.
- You can also use the EXTRACT function to extract a year, month, day, hour, minute, second, or time zone from a DATE or TIMESTAMP value.
- These examples assume that current date and time is August 19 2008 at 04:20:16.906000000 PM Pacific Standard Time with daylight savings.
- The maximum number of fractional seconds that's returned by the TIMESTAMP functions is determined by the system on which the database resides. On many systems, the TIMESTAMP functions returns only 3 fractional seconds.

Figure 17-9   How to use functions to work with timestamps (part 1 of 2)

Part 2 of figure 17-9 presents some more examples that show how to use the functions presented in part 1. These examples show that you can test these functions within a SELECT statement that selects data from the Dual table.

The first example shows how to use the TO_TIMESTAMP function to convert a string literal for a timestamp to a TIMESTAMP value. To do that with one parameter, you can specify the TIMESTAMP value in the default format as shown in the first statement. Or, you can use a second parameter to specify the format of the timestamp as shown in the second statement. Either way, the value that's returned is the same.

The second example shows how to use the TO_TIMESTAMP_TZ function to convert a string literal for a timestamp to a TIMESTAMP WITH TIME ZONE value. This works much like the TO_TIMESTAMP function except that you can specify a time zone for this function.

The third example shows how to use the TO_CHAR function to format the TIMESTAMP WITH TIME ZONE value that's returned by the CURRENT_TIMESTAMP function. Note that this function formats the timestamp so it displays 9 digits for the fractional seconds. In addition, it uses the TZR format to display the PST abbreviation for the time zone region.

The fourth example shows how to use the TO_CHAR function to format the TIMESTAMP WITH TIME ZONE values that were stored in the Downloads_TZ table that was created in figure 17-7. Since this format uses the TZD format element to format the time zone values for daylight savings time, this table uses the PDT abbreviation for Pacific Standard Time instead of PST, and it uses the EDT abbreviation for Eastern Standard Time instead of EST. In addition, it doesn't return a time zone for the third and fifth rows, which have values that use time zone offsets instead of time zone names.

At first, you may find these examples to be a little confusing. However, with a little experimentation and practice, you should be able to use these functions to get the timestamps in your database to work the way you want them to work.

How to convert a string to a TIMESTAMP value

```
SELECT TO_TIMESTAMP('15-AUG-08 4:20:47.123456 PM')
FROM dual;

SELECT TO_TIMESTAMP('2008-08-15 4:20:47.123456 PM',
                    'YYYY-MM-DD HH:MI:SS.FF6 AM')
FROM dual;
```

Result set

TO_TIMESTAMP('2008-08-154:20:47.123456PM','YYYY-MM-DDHH:MI:SS.FF6AM')
1 15-AUG-08 04.20.47.123456000 PM

How to convert a string to a TIMESTAMP WITH TIME ZONE value

```
SELECT TO_TIMESTAMP_TZ('15-AUG-08 4:20:47.123456 PM PST')
FROM dual;

SELECT TO_TIMESTAMP_TZ('2008-08-15 16:20:47.123 PST',
                       'YYYY-MM-DD HH24:MI:SS.FF6 TZR')
FROM dual;
```

Result set

TO_TIMESTAMP_TZ('2008-08-1516:20:47.123456PST','YYYY-MM-DDHH24:MI:SS.FF6TZR')
1 15-AUG-08 04.20.47.123456000 PM PST

A SELECT statement that formats a timestamp

```
SELECT TO_CHAR(CURRENT_TIMESTAMP, 'DD-MON-RR HH:MI:SS.FF9 AM TZR')
  AS time_zone_test
FROM dual;
```

Result set

TIME_ZONE_TEST
1 19-AUG-08 04:22:47.734000000 PM PST

Another SELECT statement that formats a timestamp

```
SELECT TO_CHAR(transaction_timestamp, 'DD-MON-RR HH:MI:SS.FF AM TZD')
  AS download_timestamp
FROM timestamp_tz_sample;
```

Result set

DOWNLOAD_TIMESTAMP
1 15-AUG-08 04:20:47.123457 PM PDT
2 15-AUG-08 04:20:47.123456 PM PDT
3 15-AUG-08 04:20:47.123456 PM
4 15-AUG-08 04:20:47.123456 PM EDT
5 19-AUG-08 04:21:04.312000 PM

Figure 17-9   How to use functions to work with timestamps (part 2 of 2)

How to work with intervals

The INTERVAL types were introduced with Oracle Database 9i. These data types make it easier to work with time intervals like 2 days, 2 hours, and 12 minutes. Before these data types were introduced, it was common to use the NUMBER type to store intervals of time.

An introduction to the INTERVAL types

Figure 17-10 lists the three INTERVAL types. Here, the INTERVAL YEAR TO MONTH type stores a time interval in years and months. For example, you can store an interval of 1 year and 3 months. When you use this type, you can specify a value from 0 to 9 for year precision, which is the number of digits that Oracle uses to store the years. By default, this value is set to 2, which allows you to store a maximum of 99 years.

The INTERVAL DAY TO SECOND type stores a time interval in days, hours, minutes and seconds. When you use this type, you can specify a value from 0 to 9 for the day precision, which is the maximum number of digits that Oracle uses to store the days. By default, this value is set to 2, which allows you to store a maximum of 99 days. In addition, you can specify fractional second precision. This works the same as fractional seconds for the TIMESTAMP types.

The INTERVAL types

Type	Bytes	Description
INTERVAL YEAR [(yp)] TO MONTH	5	Stores a time interval in years and months. Year precision (yp) is the number of digits in the year, and the default is 2.
INTERVAL DAY [(dp)] TO SECOND [(fsp)]	11	Stores a time interval in days, hours, minutes and seconds. Day precision (dp) is the maximum number of digits in the day, and the default is 2. Fractional second precision (fsp) is the maximum number of digits for fractional seconds, and the default is 6.

INTERVAL YEAR TO MONTH units

YEAR
MONTH

INTERVAL DAY TO SECOND units

DAY
HOUR
MINUTE
SECOND

Description

- You can use the INTERVAL types to store intervals of time in years, months, days, hours, minutes, seconds, and fractional seconds.
- All precision parameters accept values of 0 to 9.

Figure 17-10   The INTERVAL types

How to work with the INTERVAL YEAR TO MONTH type

Figure 17-11 shows how to work with the INTERVAL YEAR TO MONTH type. To start, the first example shows how to create a table named Interval_YM_Sample that stores data of this type. Here, the first column in the table specifies a NUMBER value that uniquely identifies each row. Then, the second column in the table specifies an INTERVAL YEAR TO MONTH value with a year precision of 3. As a result, you can store a value with a maximum of 999 years or a minimum of -999 years.

The second example shows a script that inserts six rows into the table. Here, the first INSERT statement specifies a year by coding the INTERVAL keyword, followed by a literal value for the year enclosed in single quotes, followed by the YEAR keyword. The second statement specifies a literal value for a month by coding the INTERVAL keyword, followed by a literal value for the month, followed by the MONTH keyword. The third statement works like the second one, except that it specifies a month value that's greater than 12 to show how Oracle handles this situation. The fourth statement specifies a year and a month by coding the INTERVAL keyword, followed by a literal value for the year and month, followed by the YEAR TO MONTH keywords. The fifth statement works like the fourth one, except that it specifies a negative value. Finally, the sixth statement specifies a year with a precision of 3 by coding the precision after the YEAR keyword for the literal value. Note that this works because the table allows a year precision of 3.

The third example shows a SELECT statement that retrieves all data from the table. The result set that's returned by this SELECT statement shows that a value of 0 is added to the month portion of year values that don't include month values. Similarly, it shows that a value of 0 is added to the year portion of month values that don't include a year. In addition, it shows that month values that are greater than 12 are converted into an equivalent year and month value. That's why the values for the third and fourth rows are the same. Finally, it shows that a minus sign is used to display negative interval values.

A table that uses the INTERVAL YEAR TO MONTH type

```
CREATE TABLE interval_ym_sample
(
  interval_id              NUMBER                      PRIMARY KEY,
  interval_value           INTERVAL YEAR(3) TO MONTH
);
```

A script that inserts INTERVAL values

```
INSERT INTO interval_ym_sample
VALUES (1, INTERVAL '1' YEAR);

INSERT INTO interval_ym_sample
VALUES (2, INTERVAL '3' MONTH);

INSERT INTO interval_ym_sample
VALUES (3, INTERVAL '15' MONTH);

INSERT INTO interval_ym_sample
VALUES (4, INTERVAL '1-3' YEAR TO MONTH);

INSERT INTO interval_ym_sample
VALUES (5, INTERVAL '-1-3' YEAR TO MONTH);

INSERT INTO interval_ym_sample
VALUES (6, INTERVAL '100' YEAR(3));

COMMIT;
```

A statement that retrieves INTERVAL values

```
SELECT * FROM interval_ym_sample
```

The result set

INTERVAL_ID	INTERVAL_VALUE
1	1 1-0
2	2 0-3
3	3 1-3
4	4 1-3
5	5 -1-3
6	6 100-0

Description

- To specify a literal value for an interval, code the INTERVAL keyword followed by a literal value enclosed in single quotes followed by the YEAR, MONTH, or YEAR TO MONTH keywords that correspond with the literal value.

Figure 17-11   How to work with the INTERVAL YEAR TO MONTH type

How to work with the INTERVAL DAY TO SECOND type

Figure 17-12 shows how to work with the INTERVAL DAY TO SECOND type. This is much like working with the INTERVAL YEAR TO MONTH type as in the previous figure. The main difference is that you can use four keywords (DAY, HOUR, MINUTE, and SECOND) to work with the four components of the INTERVAL DAY TO SECOND type. You can also use fractional seconds when you're working with the second component.

A table that uses the INTERVAL DAY TO SECOND type

```
CREATE TABLE interval_ds_sample
(
  interval_id              NUMBER                          PRIMARY KEY,
  interval_value           INTERVAL DAY(3) TO SECOND(2)
);
```

A script that inserts INTERVAL values

```
INSERT INTO interval_ds_sample
VALUES (1, INTERVAL '1' DAY);

INSERT INTO interval_ds_sample
VALUES (2, INTERVAL '4' HOUR);

INSERT INTO interval_ds_sample
VALUES (3, INTERVAL '20' MINUTE);

INSERT INTO interval_ds_sample
VALUES (4, INTERVAL '31' SECOND);

INSERT INTO interval_ds_sample
VALUES (5, INTERVAL '31.45' SECOND);

INSERT INTO interval_ds_sample
VALUES (6, INTERVAL '1 4:20:31.45' DAY TO SECOND);

INSERT INTO interval_ds_sample
VALUES (7, INTERVAL '-1 4:20:31.45' DAY TO SECOND);

INSERT INTO interval_ds_sample
VALUES (8, INTERVAL '100 4:20:31.45' DAY(3) TO SECOND);

COMMIT;
```

A statement that retrieves INTERVAL values

```
SELECT * FROM interval_ds_sample
```

The result set

INTERVAL_ID	INTERVAL_VALUE
1	1 1 0:0:0.0
2	2 0 4:0:0.0
3	3 0 0:20:0.0
4	4 0 0:0:31.0
5	5 0 0:0:31.450000000
6	6 1 4:20:31.450000000
7	7 -1 4:20:31.450000000
8	8 100 4:20:31.450000000

Figure 17-12   How to work with the INTERVAL DAY TO SECOND type

How to use functions to work with intervals

Figure 17-13 shows some of the common functions for working with intervals. For instance, you can use the first two functions to convert numbers to INTERVAL values. And you can use the last two functions to convert strings to INTERVAL values.

The first four examples in the table show how you can use the NUMTOYMINTERVAL function to convert a number to an INTERVAL YEAR TO MONTH value. Within these statements, you can use the YEAR or MONTH keywords to specify the conversion unit. For example, the first two functions convert numbers to a year values, and the next two functions convert numbers to month values. Because the INTERVAL YEAR TO MONTH type doesn't have a component that can store the decimal portion of a month, the decimal part of the number in the fourth function is truncated.

The next six examples show how to use the NUMTODSINTERVAL function to convert a number to an INTERVAL DAY TO SECOND value. As you can see, this function works much like the NUMTOYMINTERVAL function.

The last four examples in the table show how to use the TO_YMINTERVAL and TO_DSINTERVAL functions. Here, the TO_YMINTERVAL functions use two valid string literal formats for the same YEAR TO MONTH interval, but the first format specifies some leading zeros that aren't necessary. Then, the two TO_DSINTERVAL functions show two valid string literal formats for the same DAY TO SECOND interval, but the first format specifies some leading zeros that aren't necessary. Either way, the results of the functions are the same.

The final example in this figure shows how you can use these functions within a SELECT statement. Here, the only column that's returned by the SELECT statement uses the NUMTODSINTERVAL function to return an INTERVAL DAY TO SECOND value for the number of days that's calculated by subtracting the invoice date from the payment date in a table of invoices. This should give you some how idea of how the INTERVAL data types and functions can make it easier for you to work with intervals in your own applications.

Common functions for working with intervals

Function	Description
NUMTOYMINTERVAL(n, 'ym_unit')	Converts a number to an INTERVAL YEAR TO MONTH value. The second argument must be YEAR or MONTH.
NUMTODSINTERVAL(n, 'ds_unit')	Converts a number to an INTERVAL DAY TO SECOND value. The second argument must be DAY, HOUR, MINUTE, or SECOND.
TO_YMINTERVAL('ym_literal')	Converts a string that contains a valid INTERVAL YEAR TO MONTH literal to the data type.
TO_DSINTERVAL('ds_literal')	Converts a string that contains a valid INTERVAL DAY TO SECOND literal to the data type.

Examples that use functions to work with intervals

Example	Result
NUMTOYMINTERVAL(2,'YEAR')	2-0
NUMTOYMINTERVAL(1.25,'YEAR')	1-3
NUMTOYMINTERVAL(2,'MONTH')	0-2
NUMTOYMINTERVAL(1.25,'MONTH')	0-1
NUMTODSINTERVAL(30,'DAY')	30 0:0:0.0
NUMTODSINTERVAL(30,'HOUR')	1 6:0:0.0
NUMTODSINTERVAL(30,'MINUTE')	0 0:30:0.0
NUMTODSINTERVAL(30,'SECOND')	0 0:0:30.0
NUMTODSINTERVAL(90,'SECOND')	0 0:1:30.0
NUMTODSINTERVAL(30.123,'SECOND')	0 0:0:30.123000000
TO_YMINTERVAL('01-03')	1-3
TO_YMINTERVAL('1-3')	1-3
TO_DSINTERVAL('1 06:00:00.00')	1 6:0:0.0
TO_DSINTERVAL('1 6:0:0')	1 6:0:0.0

A SELECT statement that retrieves an interval

```
SELECT NUMTODSINTERVAL(payment_date - invoice_date, 'DAY')
       AS payment_interval
FROM invoices
WHERE payment_date IS NOT NULL
```

Result set

PAYMENT_INTERVAL
1 46 0:0:0.0
2 61 0:0:0.0
3 26 0:0:0.0

Figure 17-13   How to use functions to work with intervals

Perspective

In this chapter, you learned how you can use the TIMESTAMP and INTER-VAL data types to make it easier for you to work with time zones and intervals. Although this can be a little confusing as you read about all of the variations, you shouldn't have much trouble applying what you've learned whenever you develop applications that require these features.

Terms

time zone
offset
Greenwich Mean Time (GMT)
Coordinated Universal Time (UTC)
database time zone
session time zone

Exercises

1. Create a table named Timestamp_Values in the EX schema that contains four columns: timestamp_id as a NUMBER data type; timestamp_value as a TIMESTAMP(6) data type; timestamp_wltz_value as a TIMESTAMP WITH LOCAL TIME ZONE data type; and timestamp_wtz_value as a TIMESTAMP WITH TIME ZONE data type. Next, insert a row into this table with 1 for the id column, LOCALTIMESTAMP(3) for the second column, and CURRENT_TIMESTAMP(3) for the last two columns. Finally, write a SELECT statement that selects this data and review the data that's returned.

2. First, change the date format for the current session so it shows the time in 24-hour format. Second, write a SELECT statement that retrieves the four columns of the one row in the Timestamp_Values table that you created in exercise 1. Third, change the time zone for the session to MST. Fourth, insert a row just like the one you inserted in exercise 1 but with an id of 2. Fifth, run the SELECT statement again to review the differences in the two rows.

3. Keep the date format for the current session as described in exercise 2. Then, write a SELECT statement that retrieves four columns from the Timestamp_Values table of exercises 1 and 2: (1) timestamp_id, (2) timestamp_value, and (3) timestamp_value after it has been converted to Central Standard Time (CST) with cst_time as the column name.

4. Keep the date format for the current session as described in exercise 2. Then, write a SELECT statement that retrieves the invoice_number and invoice_date columns from the Invoices table in the AP schema, followed by a column named days_old that uses an interval function to retrieve the number of days, hours, and seconds that have elapsed between the invoice date and the current date. Sort the rows by the days_old value and only retrieve rows when the days_old value is greater than 30.

18

How to work with large objects

In chapter 8, you were introduced to the large object data types that can be used to store images, sound, video, and large amounts of text in an Oracle database. In this chapter, you'll review these data types, and you'll learn how to use them.

An introduction to large objects

Oracle's *large object (LOB)* data types can store large amounts of character or binary data. These data types can be used to store data that's in just about any type of file including text, XML, Word, PDF, image, sound, and video files.

The LOB types

Figure 18-1 presents the four LOB types that were introduced with Oracle Database 8. The *CLOB* (*Character Large Object*) and *NCLOB* (*National Character Large Object*) types can store character data. These data types are commonly used to store large text and XML files. The primary difference between these types is that the CLOB type uses 1 byte per character to store characters in the ASCII character set while the NCLOB type uses 2 or 3 bytes per character to store characters in the Unicode character set.

The *BLOB* (*Binary Large Object*) type can store data in binary format. It can be used to store binary files such as PDF files, and it can be used to store image, sound, and video files.

The *BFILE* (*Binary File*) type stores a pointer to a binary file that's stored outside of the database. These binary files can be stored anywhere that's accessible through the host computer's file system.

This figure also presents the old RAW, LONG, and LONG RAW data types for storing large objects that were used prior to Oracle Database 8. These data types are provided primarily for backward compatibility. Fortunately, it's easy to migrate to the new types if you want to do that as shown in figure 18-6.

APIs for working with LOBs

In most cases, LOBs are used by client-side applications. For example, a client-side application may want to get an image from a database and display it. Conversely, a client-side application may want to upload an image from a user's hard drive and store it in the database.

To allow communication between a client-side application and the database, Oracle provides APIs for working with LOBs. Figure 18-1 lists some of the most commonly used APIs provided by Oracle. For example, it's common to use Java or a .NET language such as Visual Basic or C# to work with LOBs. In addition, Oracle provides an API for using PL/SQL to work with LOBs. Since PL/SQL doesn't provide any capabilities for viewing images or playing music, it's mainly used to perform server-side processing that can be called by a client-side application via a stored procedure or function.

In this chapter, you'll learn how to use the Java API to store and retrieve a LOB from a database table. In addition, you'll be introduced to the PL/SQL API that you can use to perform server-side processing on LOBs.

The new data types for large objects

Type	Description
CLOB	Character large object. Stores up to 8 terabytes of character data inside the database.
NCLOB	National character large object. Stores up to 8 terabytes of national character data inside the database.
BLOB	Binary large object. Stores up to 8 terabytes of binary data inside the database.
BFILE	Binary file. Stores a pointer to a large binary file stored outside the database in the file system of the host computer.

The old data types for large objects

Type	Description
RAW(size)	Stores up to 2000 bytes of binary data that is not intended to be converted by Oracle when moving data between different systems.
LONG	Stores up to 2 gigabytes of character data.
LONG RAW	Stores up to 2 gigabytes of row binary data that is not intended to be converted.

Some of the APIs for working with large objects

- Java
- .NET Framework
- C++
- COBOL
- PL/SQL

Description

- The *large object* (*LOB*) data types can store large amounts of binary and character data.
- The CLOB, NCLOB, and BLOB types are sometimes referred to as *internal LOB types*, and the BFILE type is sometimes referred to as an *external LOB type*.
- The four new LOB types were introduced with Oracle Database 8.
- Oracle provides APIs for many programming languages that you can use to work with LOB types.

Figure 18-1   The LOB types

How to use SQL to work with large objects

If you want to work with LOBs, you need to store them in the database, and you need to retrieve them from the database. As you might expect, you can use the basic SQL statements to accomplish these tasks.

How to work with CLOBs

Figure 18-2 shows how to work with CLOBs. To start, the first example shows how to create a table named Product_Reviews that stores data of the CLOB type. Here, the first column in the table contains a NUMBER value that uniquely identifies each row. Then, the second column in the table contains a CLOB value.

The second example shows a script that inserts three rows into the table. Here, the first INSERT statement uses the TO_CLOB function to convert a string literal to a CLOB value. This accomplishes two tasks: (1) it initializes a *LOB locator* that points to a CLOB value and (2) it inserts the characters in the string literal into the CLOB value. In contrast, the second INSERT statement uses the EMPTY_CLOB function to initialize a LOB locator that points to a CLOB value, but it doesn't fill the CLOB value with any data. Then, the third INSERT statement stores a NULL value, which doesn't initialize a LOB locator. Finally, the COMMIT statement commits the changes to the database.

The third example shows a SELECT statement that retrieves data from the table. To start, this statement retrieves both of the columns of the table. Then, it creates a third column by using the LENGTH function to return the number of characters in the CLOB value that's stored in the database.

The result set that's returned by the SELECT statement shows how SQL Developer displays a CLOB value. To start, it displays "(CLOB)" to indicate that the column contains a LOB locator that has been initialized. Then, it displays any characters that have been stored in the CLOB. However, if the LOB locator hasn't been initialized, the result set displays a NULL value.

Of course, if you're using another tool such as SQL*Plus, the display may be different. For example, by default, SQL*Plus only displays the first 80 characters of a CLOB value.

How to work with NCLOBs

Once you understand how to work with CLOBs, you should be able to apply most of those skills to NCLOBs. For example, to convert figure 18-2 so it works with NCLOBs, you just specify the NCLOB type in the table definition and use the TO_NCLOB function in the first INSERT statement. The rest of the code works the same.

A statement that creates a table that can store CLOBs

```
CREATE TABLE product_reviews
(
  product_id      NUMBER      PRIMARY KEY,
  product_review  CLOB
);
```

A script that inserts three rows into the table

```
INSERT INTO product_reviews VALUES
(1, TO_CLOB('Imagine this is a long string of characters.'));

INSERT INTO product_reviews VALUES
(2, EMPTY_CLOB());

INSERT INTO product_reviews VALUES
(3, NULL);

COMMIT;
```

A statement that displays the values in the table

```
SELECT product_id, product_review,
       LENGTH(product_review) AS clob_length
FROM product_reviews;
```

The result set

	PRODUCT_ID	PRODUCT_REVIEW		CHAR_COUNT
1	1	(CLOB) Imagine this is a long string of characters.		44
2	2	(CLOB)		0
3	3	(null)		(null)

Description

- When you create a table, you can use the CLOB or NCLOB data types just as you would use any other data type.
- You can use the TO_CLOB and TO_NCLOB functions to convert a string to the CLOB or NCLOB types.
- You can use the EMPTY_CLOB function to return a *LOB locator* for an empty CLOB or NCLOB.
- You can use the LENGTH function to return the number of characters that are stored in a CLOB or NCLOB.

Figure 18-2   How to work with CLOBs

How to work with BLOBs

Figure 18-3 shows how to work with BLOBs. If you understand how to work with CLOBs as described in the previous figure, you shouldn't have much trouble working with BLOBs since many of the same skills apply. The main difference is that you use the TO_BLOB and EMPTY_BLOB functions instead of the TO_CLOB and EMPTY_CLOB functions. In addition, when applied to a BLOB, the LENGTH method returns the number of bytes instead of the number of characters.

Since binary data consists of ones and zeros, it's hard to code a meaningful string literal for a BLOB. In this figure, I coded 32 hexadecimal digits for a total of 16 bytes. Since a hexadecimal digit represents four bits (binary digits), two hexadecimal digits represent eight bits, which is one byte. As a result, the number of bytes for a hexadecimal string literal will always be the number of hexadecimal digits divided by two. Later in this chapter, you'll learn how to store binary data for a JPG image in the database by reading the binary data for the JPG image from a file and storing it in the database.

Since it isn't easy to present binary data in a form that's meaningful to humans, SQL Developer has limited capabilities for displaying a BLOB. Although it can display "(BLOB)" to indicate that the column contains a LOB locator that has been initialized, it can't display the binary data.

For the sake of comparison, if you try to use SQL*Plus to display a BLOB, it will display a message that says:

```
SP2-0678: Column or attribute type can not be displayed by SQL*Plus
```

A statement that creates a table that can store BLOBs

```
CREATE TABLE product_images
(
  product_id    NUMBER     PRIMARY KEY,
  product_image BLOB
);
```

A script that inserts three rows into the table

```
INSERT INTO product_images VALUES
(1, TO_BLOB('0123456789ABCDEF0123456789ABCDEF'));

INSERT INTO product_images VALUES
(2, EMPTY_BLOB());

INSERT INTO product_images VALUES
(3, NULL);

COMMIT;
```

A statement that displays the values in the table

```
SELECT product_id, product_image,
       LENGTH(product_image) AS byte_count
FROM product_images;
```

The result set

	PRODUCT_ID	PRODUCT_IMAGE	BYTE_COUNT
1	1	(BLOB)	16
2	2	(BLOB)	0
3	3	(null)	(null)

Description

- When you create a table, you can specify the BLOB type just as you would specify any other data type.
- You can use the TO_BLOB function to convert a string literal that contains a series of hexadecimal values to a BLOB value.
- You can use the EMPTY_BLOB function to return a LOB locator for an empty BLOB.
- You can use the LENGTH function to return the number of bytes that are stored in a BLOB.

Figure 18-3   How to work with BLOBs

How to work with BFILEs

Figure 18-4 shows how to work with the BFILEs. Like a BLOB, a BFILE stores binary data. Unlike a BLOB, a BFILE stores a reference to a file that's stored outside the database. That's why the BFILE type is sometimes referred to as an *external LOB type* while the BLOB and CLOB types are sometimes referred to as the *internal LOB types*.

To work with a BFILE, you start by defining a table that includes a BFILE column. In this figure, the first example creates a table named Product_Images_2 that stores data of the BFILE type. Here, the second column in the table contains a BFILE value. This works like the BLOB example shown in the previous figure except that the binary file is stored outside of the database.

Before you can work with a BFILE value, you need to use the CREATE DIRECTORY statement to store a reference to a directory in the database. This directory can be any directory that's available to the file system of the host computer. In this figure, the second example creates a directory named images_dir that refers to a directory named ch18files that's stored on the same drive as the database server. However, this directory could be stored on any network drive that's available to the computer that's running the database server.

Note that this example uses front slashes to separate the directory entries. That's because front slashes work for both Windows and Unix while backslashes only work on Windows.

Once you've created a directory for the files that store the binary data, you can use the BFILENAME function to return a LOB locator for the specified directory and filename. In this figure, the third example begins by using the BFILENAME function within an INSERT statement to insert a LOB locator for a binary file named "8601_cover.jpg" that's stored in the directory that was created in the previous example. Then, the second INSERT statement uses the same technique to insert a LOB locator for a binary file named "jr01_cover.jpg". Next, the third INSERT statement inserts a NULL value. Finally, the COMMIT statement commits these changes to the database.

The fourth example uses a SELECT statement to view the values that are stored in the Product_Images_2 table. Here, SQL Developer displays "(BFILE)" for BFILE column in the first two rows to indicate that a LOB locator has been stored in these rows. However, it displays "(null)" for the BFILE column of the third row to indicate that a NULL value has been stored in this row.

If necessary, you can use the DROP DIRECTORY statement to drop a reference to a directory from the database. If, for example, the directory that contains your binary files is moved, you can drop the reference to this directory from the database. Then, you can create a new reference with the same name as the old reference that refers to the new directory.

If, for example, the ch18files directory is moved to a network drive, you can drop the directory named product_dir from the database. Then, you can create a new directory named product_dir that refers to the new location for the ch18files directory. That way, you won't have to change any of your existing code that uses the directory named product_dir.

A statement that creates a table that can store BFILEs

```
CREATE TABLE product_images_2
(
  product_id      NUMBER      PRIMARY KEY,
  product_image   BFILE
);
```

A statement that identifies a directory that stores binary files

```
CREATE DIRECTORY product_dir AS 'C:/murach/oracle_sql/java/ch18files';
```

A script that inserts three rows into the table

```
INSERT INTO product_images_2 VALUES
(1, BFILENAME('product_dir', '8601_cover.jpg'));

INSERT INTO product_images_2 VALUES
(2, BFILENAME('product_dir', 'jr01_cover.jpg'));

INSERT INTO product_images_2 VALUES
(3, NULL);

COMMIT;
```

A statement that displays the values in the table

```
SELECT product_id, product_image
FROM product_images_2;
```

The result set

	PRODUCT_ID	PRODUCT_IMAGE
1	1	(BFILE)
2	2	(BFILE)
3	3	(null)

A statement that drops a directory

```
DROP DIRECTORY product_dir;
```

Description

- You can use the CREATE DIRECTORY statement to store a reference to a directory in the database.
- You can use the DROP DIRECTORY statement to drop a reference to a directory from the database.
- You can use BFILENAME function to return a LOB locator for the specified directory and filename.

Figure 18-4   How to work with BFILEs

How to specify LOB storage options

So far, the examples presented in this chapter have used the default options for storing LOB values. However, when you create a table that stores LOBs, you can often improve the performance of LOB operations by specifying the storage options shown in figure 18-5.

To code the storage options for a LOB, you code one LOB clause for each LOB column in a table. In this figure, the CREATE TABLE statement contains a single LOB clause for the BLOB column named product_image. However, if a table contains multiple LOB columns, you can specify one LOB clause for each column. Or, if you want to use the same settings for multiple LOB columns, you can code the LOB keyword, followed by a set of parentheses. Then, within the parentheses, you can code multiple column names, separated by commas.

You may also be able to improve performance by using the TABLESPACE option to specify a separate tablespace for storing LOB values instead of the tablespace that's used for storing the rest of the data in the table. In this figure, for example, the table is stored in the tablespace named users. However, the LOB values for the table are stored in the tablespace named users_lobs. Before you attempt to create a separate tablespace to store LOB values, though, you may want to consult your DBA to make sure that a separate tablespace will result in improved performance.

Since LOBs are usually large, you can often improve performance by reading and writing large amounts of data at a time. To accomplish this, you can use the CHUNK option to set the *chunk size*, which is how many bytes can be read at a time. By default, the chunk size is set to the same size as the *block size*, which is set when the tablespace is created. However, you often want to set the chunk size so it's a larger multiple of the block size. That way, Oracle can read multiple blocks at a time. Since block size is often set to 8KB (8192 bytes), you can usually set the chunk size to a larger multiple of 8KB such as 16KB (16384 bytes) or 32KB (32768 bytes).

By default, the ENABLE STORAGE IN ROW option stores the LOB value in the row if it is less than 4KB (4096 bytes) and stores the LOB value out of the row if the LOB value is greater than 4KB. In general, this option works well if all of your LOB values are either less than or greater than 4KB. However, if your LOB values are of a wide range of sizes, you may want to use the DIS-ABLE option to store all of the LOB values outside the row. This improves the performance for SELECT and UPDATE statements on non-LOB columns.

By default, the NOCACHE option prevents LOB blocks from being cached. However, if the same LOB data is accessed frequently, you may be able to improve performance by using the CACHE option to cache reads and writes or the CACHE READS option to only cache reads.

When you use the NOCACHE or CACHE READS options, you can specify the LOGGING and NOLOGGING options. For most operations, you want to use the LOGGING option. However, if you're loading a large amount of data into the database, you may be able to improve performance by using the NOLOGGING option. To do that, you can use the ALTER TABLE statement to modify the table so the LOB column uses the NOCACHE and NOLOGGING options.

The syntax for the LOB clause of a CREATE TABLE statement

```
LOB (lob_column_name1[, lob_column_name2])
STORE AS lob_segment_name
(
  [TABLESPACE users]
  [CHUNK chunk_size]
  [{ENABLE|DISABLE} STORAGE IN ROW]
  [{NOCACHE|CACHE [READS]} [{LOGGING|NOLOGGING}]]
  [PCTVERSION percentage_threshold]
)
```

A CREATE TABLE statement that specifies LOB storage details

```
CREATE TABLE product_images
(
  product_id      NUMBER      PRIMARY KEY,
  product_image   BLOB
)
TABLESPACE users
LOB (product_image)
STORE AS product_image_lob_seg
(
  TABLESPACE users_lobs
  CHUNK 32768
  DISABLE STORAGE IN ROW
  CACHE READS LOGGING
  PCTVERSION 20
);
```

Description

- You can code one STORE AS clause for each LOB column in a table, and you must specify at least one of the storage options for each STORE AS clause. You can also code a STORE AS clause that applies to more than one column.

- The TABLESPACE option specifies the tablespace for storing the LOB values for a column.

- The CHUNK option controls how many bytes can be read at a time. By default, the CHUNK option is set to the same size as a block. The *chunk size* must be set to a multiple of the *block size*, which is often set to 8KB (8192 bytes).

- The ENABLE STORAGE IN ROW option stores the LOB value in the row if it is less than 4KB (4096 bytes) and stores a pointer to a file if the LOB value is greater than 4KB. The DISABLE STORAGE IN ROW option prevents LOB values from being stored in the row.

- The CACHE and NOCACHE options control how LOB blocks are cached. By default, the NOCACHE option is used. When you specify the NOCACHE and CACHE READS options, you can specify the LOGGING and NOLOGGING options.

- The PCTVERSION option is used when a LOB value is changed. It controls the percentage of LOB blocks that can contain old LOB data for undo operations before the old LOB blocks can be reused by Oracle. By default, this option is set to 10 percent.

Figure 18-5 How to specify LOB storage details

The PCTVERSION option is used when a LOB value is changed. It controls the percentage of LOB blocks that contain old LOB data that can be used for undo operations. By default, this option is set to 10 percent. However, if the updates of your LOB values are frequent and large, you may be able to improve performance by increasing this value. Conversely, if the updates to your LOB values are infrequent and small, you may be able to decrease the value for this option. For example, if access to your LOBs is read-only, you can set this value to 0 since there will never be any old LOB data.

How to migrate to the new LOB types

The new LOB types that I've just described provide a richer set of features for working with large objects than the old LOB types. As a result, you typically want to use the new LOB types whenever possible. Fortunately, if you're working with old tables that use the old LOB types, it's easy to migrate those old LOB types to the new LOB types.

To do that, you can use the ALTER TABLE statement as shown in figure 18-6. Here, the first example creates a table that includes a column that uses the old LONG RAW type to store binary data. Then, the second example stores two rows of data in this table. Finally, the third example uses the ALTER TABLE statement to convert the LONG RAW type to the new BLOB type.

Similarly, if a table contains character data of the old LONG type, you can convert it to the CLOB type by substituting the LONG data type for the LONG RAW data type. In either case, though, you'll want to thoroughly test the conversion to make sure it works correctly before you implement it on a production database.

A statement that creates a table that uses the old LONG RAW data type

```
CREATE TABLE product_images_3
(
  product_id      NUMBER        PRIMARY KEY,
  product_image  LONG RAW
);
```

A script that inserts two rows

```
INSERT INTO product_images_3 VALUES
(1, '1010101010101010101010101010101010');

INSERT INTO product_images_3 VALUES
(2, '1010101010101010101010101010101010');

COMMIT;
```

A statement that migrates data from the LONG RAW type to the BLOB type

```
ALTER TABLE product_images_3 MODIFY (product_image BLOB);
```

Description

- You can use an ALTER TABLE statement to convert the old LONG RAW type to the BLOB type.
- You can use an ALTER TABLE statement to convert the old LONG type to the CLOB type.

Figure 18-6   How to migrate to the new LOB types

How to use Java to work with large objects

Since it's common to use Java to work with Oracle LOBs, this topic presents a simple application that uses the Java API to work with large objects. This application consists of three Java classes. By studying this application, you can learn how to read a binary file for an image and write it to a BLOB column in a database table. You can also learn how to read a BLOB from a database table and write it to a file.

If you have some Java programming experience, you shouldn't have much trouble understanding this code. If you don't have Java experience, that's okay too. In that case, you can focus on how this code uses the Java API to execute the SQL statements against an Oracle database. Then, if you want to learn more about using Java to work with a database, we recommend *Murach's Java SE 6* and *Murach's Java Servlets and JSP*.

Before you attempt to execute the code in this topic, you need to add a JAR file that contains the Oracle JDBC driver to your classpath. That way, Java will be able to find the files for the driver. The easiest way to do that is to copy the JAR file that contains the drivers into the JDK's jre/lib/ext directory. This is explained in more detail in figure 1-19 of chapter 1.

In this topic, the code works with a BLOB. However, a similar technique can be used for working with a CLOB, NCLOB, or BFILE. Whatever LOB type you use, the Java API lets you execute the SQL statements described earlier.

The main method for the sample application

The BLOBTestApp class presented in figure 18-7 contains the main method for the application presented in this topic. This method begins by declaring three variables that are used by the rest of the statements in this method. Here, the first statement declares a string named productsDir that points to the ch18files directory. The second statement declares a string variable named filePath that will be used to store the complete path to the file. And the third statement declares an integer variable named byteCount that will be used to store the count of the bytes that are written or read by each operation.

After declaring these three variables, the main method uses the writeImage method of the ProductDB class to write three images to the database. Here, each group of statements begins with a statement that sets the value of the filePath variable by concatenating the productsDir variable with the name of the file to write to the database. Then, the second statement passes a product ID value and the filePath value to the writeImage method of the ProductDB class. Finally, the third statement prints the byteCount variable that's returned by this method to the console. Note that all three of these statements work because they point to JPG files that exist within the ch18files directory.

After writing three images to the database, the main method continues by using the readImage method of the ProductDB class to read one image from the

A Java class that reads and writes Oracle LOBs

```java
public class BLOBTestApp
{
    public static void main(String args[])
    {
        String productsDir =
            "C:/murach/oracle_sql/java/ch18files/";
        String filePath = "";
        int byteCount = 0;

        // Read 3 images from file and write to database
        filePath = productsDir + "8601_cover.jpg";
        byteCount = ProductDB.writeImage(1, filePath);
        System.out.println(byteCount + " bytes written to the database.");

        filePath = productsDir + "pf01_cover.jpg";
        byteCount = ProductDB.writeImage(2, filePath);
        System.out.println(byteCount + " bytes written to the database.");

        filePath = productsDir + "jr01_cover.jpg";
        byteCount = ProductDB.writeImage(3, filePath);
        System.out.println(byteCount + " bytes written to the database.");

        // Read 1 image from database and write to file
        filePath = productsDir + "8601_temp.jpg";
        byteCount = ProductDB.readImage(1, filePath);
        System.out.println(byteCount + " bytes read from the database.");
    }
}
```

The result

```
C:\WINDOWS\system32\cmd.exe                                    _ □ ×
13573 bytes written to the database.
23579 bytes written to the database.
18157 bytes written to the database.
13573 bytes read from the database.
Press any key to continue . . .
```

Description

- In this example, the code works with a BLOB. However, a similar technique could be used for working with a CLOB, NCLOB, or BFILE.

Figure 18-7   The BlobTestApp class

database. Specifically, this method reads the product image for the product with a product ID of 1, and it writes this product to a file named "8601_temp.jpg". Note that this statement works whether or not this file exists. If the file doesn't exist, it is created. Otherwise, it is overwritten. To verify this, you can use a graphics program such as Paint to open this file and view it.

After the class in this figure, you can see the data that is printed to the console by the main method. The first three lines show that three images with different byte counts were written to the database. The fourth line shows that one image was read from the database. The byte counts, of course, are returned by the writeImage and readImage methods that are stored in the ProductDB class, which is presented next.

How to write an image to a table

The ProductDB class in figure 18-7 begins by importing all Java JDBC and IO classes necessary for working with LOBs. In addition, it imports two Oracle JDBC classes that yield better performance than the Java JDBC classes. These classes are stored in the same JAR file that contains the Oracle JDBC driver. As a result, you need to add this JAR file to your classpath as described in figure 1-19 of chapter 1.

This code shows that there are two sets of JDBC classes that you can use when using Java to work with an Oracle database. In addition, it shows that you can mix and match these classes as you see fit.

The ProductDB class contains a static writeImage method that you can use to read an image from a file and write it to a column in a table. This method accepts two parameters. The first parameter specifies the ID that uniquely identifies the product. The second parameter specifies the complete path to the file.

Within the body of the writeImage method, the first three statements declare the Connection, PreparedStatement, and OracleResultSet objects that are used by the rest of the method. Here, the static getConnection method of the DBUtil class returns a Connection object. To see how this method works, you can view the code for the DBUtil class that's presented in figure 18-9.

After the first three statements, the code in the try block sets up an input stream for the file path specified by the second parameter. Then, it uses the Java API to execute an INSERT statement that stores a LOB locator for a BLOB value in the database.

After inserting a new row, this code uses the Java API to execute a SELECT statement that retrieves a LOB locator for the newly inserted BLOB and stores it in the variable named productImageBLOB. Note that this SELECT statement must include a FOR UPDATE clause. This clause indicates that the BLOB is being retrieved for an update, and it causes the BLOB value to be locked until you commit or roll back the update. As a result, it's critical that your code either commits or rolls back the update.

After getting a reference to the BLOB, this code sets up the output stream to the database. To do that, it calls the setBinaryStream method from the variable named productImageBLOB and it passes an argument of 0 to begin writing at the

The ProductDB class

```
// import all necessary Java JDBC and IO classes
import java.sql.*;
import java.io.*;

// import two Oracle JDBC classes for better performance!
import oracle.sql.BLOB;
import oracle.jdbc.OracleResultSet;

public class ProductDB
{
    public static int writeImage(int product_id, String file_path)
    {
        Connection connection = DBUtil.getConnection();
        PreparedStatement ps = null;
        OracleResultSet rs = null;
        try
        {
            // set up the input stream from file
            File inputFile = new File(file_path);
            FileInputStream fileInputStream = new FileInputStream(inputFile);

            // initialize the BLOB in the database
            String sql =
                "INSERT INTO product_images (product_id, product_image) " +
                "   VALUES(?, EMPTY_BLOB())";
            ps = connection.prepareStatement(sql);
            ps.setInt(1, product_id);
            ps.executeUpdate();

            // get a reference to the BLOB
            sql =
                "SELECT product_image " +
                "FROM product_images " +
                "WHERE product_id = ? " +
                "FOR UPDATE";
            ps = connection.prepareStatement(sql);
            ps.setInt(1, product_id);
            rs = (OracleResultSet) ps.executeQuery();
            rs.next();
            BLOB productImageBLOB = rs.getBLOB("product_image");

            // set up the output stream to the database
            OutputStream outputStream = productImageBLOB.setBinaryStream(0);

            // set up the buffer
            int chunkSize = productImageBLOB.getChunkSize();
            byte[] byteBuffer = new byte[chunkSize];
```

Figure 18-8   The ProductDB class (part 1 of 3)

first byte of the column. After setting up the output stream, this code sets up the buffer that's used to temporarily store the bytes as they're transferred from the input stream to the output stream. Note that the getChunkSize method is called from the BLOB object to return the chunk size to use when reading and writing the BLOB value.

After setting up the buffer, the try block uses a while loop to read from the input stream (the specified file) and write to the output stream (the specified column in the database). When this loop finishes, the code closes the input and output streams, commits the change, and returns the total number of bytes that were written to the database. If this loop completes successfully, the number of bytes that were written will be the same as the number of bytes that were read.

After the try block, the catch block catches any exceptions that might have occurred and handles them. To do that, this catch block prints the exception to the console, rolls back any changes, and returns a value of 0.

After the catch block, the finally block frees the resources that are used by the writeImage method. To do that, this block uses three static methods that are available from the DBUtil class shown in figure 18-9 to close the ResultSet, PreparedStatement, and Connection objects.

The ProductDB class

```java
            // read input and write output
            int byteCount = 0;
            int bytesRead = 0;
            while ((bytesRead = fileInputStream.read(byteBuffer)) != -1)
            {
                outputStream.write(byteBuffer, 0, bytesRead);
                byteCount += bytesRead;
            }

            // close the input and output streams
            fileInputStream.close();
            outputStream.close();

            // commit the change!
            connection.commit();

            return byteCount;
        }
        catch (Exception e)
        {
            e.printStackTrace();
            DBUtil.rollback(connection);
            return 0;
        }
        finally
        {
            DBUtil.closeResultSet(rs);
            DBUtil.closePreparedStatement(ps);
            DBUtil.closeConnection(connection);
        }
    }
```

Figure 18-8   The ProductDB class (part 2 of 3)

How to read an image from a table

Besides the static writeImage method, the ProductDB class also contains a static readImage method that you can use to read an image from a column in the database and write it to a file. For the most part, this works like the writeImage method in reverse. However, since the readImage method doesn't update the database, you don't need to obtain a lock on the LOB value. As a result, you don't need to add the FOR UPDATE clause to the SELECT statement. In addition, you don't need to commit or roll back any changes to the database.

The ProductDB class

```
public static int readImage(int product_id, String filename)
{
    Connection connection = DBUtil.getConnection();
    PreparedStatement ps = null;
    OracleResultSet rs = null;
    try
    {
        // set up output stream to file
        File outputFile = new File(filename);
        FileOutputStream outputStream  = new FileOutputStream(outputFile);

        // set up input steam from database
        String sql =
            "SELECT product_image " +
            "FROM    product_images " +
            "WHERE   product_id = ?";
        ps = connection.prepareStatement(sql);
        ps.setInt(1, product_id);
        rs = (OracleResultSet) ps.executeQuery();
        rs.next();
        BLOB productImageBLOB = rs.getBLOB("product_image");
        InputStream inputStream = productImageBLOB.getBinaryStream();

        // set up the buffer
        int chunkSize = productImageBLOB.getChunkSize();
        byte[] binaryBuffer = new byte[chunkSize];

        // read input and write output
        int byteCount = 0;
        int bytesRead = 0;
        while ((bytesRead = inputStream.read(binaryBuffer)) != -1)
        {
            outputStream.write(binaryBuffer, 0, bytesRead);
            byteCount += bytesRead;
        }

        // close the input and output streams
        outputStream.close();
        inputStream.close();

        return byteCount;
    }
    catch (Exception e)
    {
        e.printStackTrace();
        return 0;
    }
    finally
    {
        DBUtil.closeResultSet(rs);
        DBUtil.closePreparedStatement(ps);
        DBUtil.closeConnection(connection);
    }
}
}
```

Figure 18-8   The ProductDB class (part 3 of 3)

A utility class for working with databases

The DBUtil class presented in figure 18-9 contains static methods that are used by the ProductDB class. To start, the getConnection method returns a Connection object for the EX user. To do that, the first block of code uses the forName method of the Class class to load the Oracle JDBC driver. This block of code is needed if you're using Oracle 10g because its database driver uses JDBC 3.0 (which is part of JDK 1.5). If you're using Oracle 11g, though, you will usually want to omit this block of code because the 11g driver supports JDBC 4.0 (which is part of JDK 1.6), and JDBC 4.0 can automatically find the driver.

After the driver has been loaded, the second block creates and returns a Connection object. To do that, the first statement specifies a database URL that uses the thin driver to connect to the Express Edition (XE) of Oracle that's running on port 1521 on the same computer as the Java application. Then, the second and third statements specify the username and password for the EX user. The fourth statement uses the getConnection method of the DriverManager class to return a Connection object. And the fifth statement returns the Connection object to the calling method.

After the getConnection method, the DBUtil class provides a rollback method. This method accepts a Connection object as a parameter. Then, the body of the method checks to make sure the Connection object is not null. In that case, it calls the rollback method of the Connection object to rollback any changes. In addition, this method handles the exception that may be thrown by the rollback method by printing the stack trace to the console. This exception handling makes it easier for other classes like the ProductDB class to rollback changes.

The DBUtil class

```java
import java.sql.*;

public class DBUtil
{
    public static Connection getConnection()
    {
        // Load the database driver
        // NOTE: This block is necessary for Oracle 10g (JDBC 3.0),
        // but not for Oracle 11g (JDBC 4.0)
        try
        {
            Class.forName("oracle.jdbc.OracleDriver");
        }
        catch(ClassNotFoundException e)
        {
            e.printStackTrace();
            return null;
        }

        // Return a connection to the database
        try
        {
            String dbUrl = "jdbc:oracle:thin:@localhost:1521:XE";
            String username = "ex";
            String password = "ex";
            Connection connection = DriverManager.getConnection(
                dbUrl, username, password);
            return connection;
        }
        catch(SQLException e)
        {
            e.printStackTrace();
            return null;
        }
    }

    public static void rollback(Connection c)
    {
        try
        {
            if (c != null)
                c.rollback();
        }
        catch(SQLException e)
        {
            e.printStackTrace();
        }
    }
}
```

Figure 18-9   The DBUtil class (part 1 of 2)

This class also contains the closeConnection, closePreparedStatement, and closeResultSet methods. Like the rollback method, the exception handling that's implemented by these methods makes it easier for other classes such as the ProductDB class to close JDBC objects. If, for example, you look at the finally clause in both the readImage and writeImage methods of the ProductDB class, you can see that the methods of the DBUtil class are used to close the Connection, PreparedStatement, and ResultSet objects. In addition, the methods of the DBUtil class let you store the exception handling code for closing JDBC objects in a single location.

The DBUtil class   **Part 2**

```
public static void closeConnection(Connection c)
{
    try
    {
        if (c != null)
            c.close();
    }
    catch(SQLException e)
    {
        e.printStackTrace();
    }
}

public static void closePreparedStatement(PreparedStatement ps)
{
    try
    {
        if (ps != null)
            ps.close();
    }
    catch(SQLException e)
    {
        e.printStackTrace();
    }
}

public static void closeResultSet(ResultSet rs)
{
    try
    {
        if (rs != null)
            rs.close();
    }
    catch(SQLException e)
    {
        e.printStackTrace();
    }
}
}
```

Figure 18-9   The DBUtil class (part 2 of 2)

How to use PL/SQL to work with large objects

Since PL/SQL runs on the server, it only provides limited capabilities for viewing or interacting with LOB types. However, the DBMS_LOB package provided by Oracle makes it possible to use PL/SQL to perform a wide range of server-side processing on the LOB types.

The methods of the DBMS_LOB package

Figure 18-10 shows the most commonly used *methods* of the DBMS_LOB package. Technically, the methods of the DBMS_LOB package are actually stored procedures or functions. However, to make it easier to refer to these procedures and functions, they are often referred to as methods.

Although this figure doesn't present the operational details for using these methods, it does give you a general idea of what types of operations are available from this package. For a complete list of methods that are available from this package and for the operational details on how to use them, you can search the Internet for the *Oracle Database PL/SQL Packages and Types Reference*.

In this figure, you can use the first group of methods to work with the CLOB, NCLOB, BLOB, and BFILE types. Of course, not all of these methods are available for all types, but most of these methods work where you would expect them to work. For example, you can use the OPEN and CLOSE methods to open and close all types of LOBs, and you can use the ISOPEN method to check if a LOB is already open before you attempt to open it.

Once you have a LOB open, you can use the rest of the methods in this group to work with the LOBs. For example, you can use the APPEND method to append one LOB to another LOB of the same type. Or, you can use the READ method to read from one LOB, and you can use the WRITE method to write to another LOB of the same type. Or, you can use the CONVERTTOBLOB function to convert a CLOB value to a BLOB value. Or, you can use the last three methods in this group to create and work with a temporary LOB that's used within a block of PL/SQL code.

You can use the second group of methods to work with BFILE types. For example, you can use the FILEEXISTS method to check if the binary file for a BFILE exists. Or, you can use the FILEISOPEN method to check if the binary file for a BFILE is open. Or, you can use the FILECLOSEALL method to close all binary files that are open. Or, you can use the last two methods to load data from a BFILE to a BLOB or CLOB value.

General methods for working with LOBs

Method name	Description
OPEN	Opens a LOB.
CLOSE	Closes a LOB.
ISOPEN	Checks if a LOB is open.
APPEND	Appends one LOB to another.
COPY	Copies all or part of one LOB to another.
ERASE	Erases part of a LOB.
COMPARE	Compares all or part of a LOB.
INSTR	Checks if a string pattern exists in a LOB.
SUBSTR	Reads a string from a LOB.
TRIM	Trims the LOB to the specified size.
READ	Reads data into a buffer.
WRITE	Writes the buffer to a LOB.
WRITEAPPEND	Appends the buffer to a LOB.
GETCHUNKSIZE	Gets the chunk size of the LOB.
GETLENGTH	Gets the length of the LOB.
CONVERTTOBLOB	Converts a CLOB to a BLOB.
CONVERTTOCLOB	Converts a BLOB to a CLOB.
CREATETEMPORARY	Creates a temporary LOB.
FREETEMPORARY	Frees the resources used by a temporary LOB.
ISTEMPORARY	Checks if a LOB is temporary.

Methods for working with BFILEs

Method name	Description
FILEEXISTS	Checks if a BFILE exists.
FILEISOPEN	Checks if a BFILE is open.
FILECLOSEALL	Closes all open BFILEs.
FILEGETNAME	Gets the directory and filename for a BFILE.
LOADBLOBFROMFILE	Loads data from a BFILE to a BLOB.
LOADCLOBFROMFILE	Loads data from a BFILE to a CLOB or NCLOB.

Figure 18-10   The methods of the DBMS_LOB package

An example that uses the DBMS_LOB package

Figure 18-11 begins by showing a stored procedure that uses the DBMS_LOB package to compare two BLOB values. Then, it shows a script that calls this stored procedure and prints a message to the output window. This example is intended only to give you a general idea of how you can write PL/SQL code that uses the DBMS_LOB package to work with LOBs.

To start, the stored procedure named compare_blobs defines three parameters. Here, the first two parameters are IN OUT parameters for the two BLOB values to compare. When specifying a parameter for a LOB type, the parameter must be an IN OUT parameter since Oracle needs to both read and write data from these parameters.

If you don't plan on modifying the LOB parameter, you may be able to improve performance by including the optional NOCOPY hint for these types of parameters. This hint tells the PL/SQL compiler to use a reference to the variable instead of incurring the overhead of making a copy of the variable. Finally, the third parameter is an OUT parameter of the NUMBER type that's used to indicate whether the two BLOB values are the same.

After the parameters have been declared, the procedure declares and initializes three variables. Here, the first two variables specify a value of 1 for the offsets for the two BLOB values. This causes the comparison of the BLOB values to start at the beginning of each of the BLOB values. Note that Oracle uses an offset of 1 to indicate the beginning of a LOB while some other APIs such as Java use an offset of 0.

After the variables have been declared, the body of the stored procedure uses the COMPARE method of the DBMS_LOB package to compare both of the BLOB values that were passed in as parameters. This method returns a value of 0 if the two LOB values are the same. Otherwise, it returns a value of -1. Finally, the body of the stored procedure handles any exceptions by printing an error message to the output window.

The script that calls the compare_blobs procedure begins by declaring two variables to store the two BLOB values and a third variable to store the value that's returned by the procedure. Within the body of the script, the two SELECT statements read the BLOB values into the two BLOB variables for the products with IDs of 1 and 2. In this case, the BLOB values are images that are stored in the Product_Images table. Then, the script calls the compare_blobs procedure, which stores the returned value in the variable named compare_result. Finally, an IF statement checks whether this variable is equal to 0. If so, it prints a message to the output window that indicates that the two images are equal. Otherwise, it prints a message to the output window that indicates that the two images are not equal.

A stored procedure that compares BLOBs

```
CONNECT ex/ex;

CREATE OR REPLACE PROCEDURE compare_blobs
(
  blob1              IN OUT NOCOPY  BLOB,
  blob2              IN OUT NOCOPY  BLOB,
  compare_result  OUT              NUMBER
)
AS
  blob1_offset NUMBER := 1;
  blob2_offset NUMBER := 1;
  buffer_size NUMBER := 32768;
BEGIN
  compare_result := DBMS_LOB.COMPARE(blob1, blob2, buffer_size,
                                     blob1_offset, blob2_offset);

EXCEPTION
  WHEN OTHERS THEN
    DBMS_OUTPUT.PUT_LINE(SQLERRM);
END;
/
```

A script that uses the stored procedure

```
SET SERVEROUTPUT ON;

DECLARE
  image1          BLOB;
  image2          BLOB;
  compare_result  NUMBER;
BEGIN
  SELECT product_image
  INTO image1
  FROM product_images
  WHERE product_id = 1;

  SELECT product_image
  INTO image2
  FROM product_images
  WHERE product_id = 2;

  compare_blobs(image1, image2, compare_result);

  IF compare_result = 0 THEN
    DBMS_OUTPUT.PUT_LINE('The two images are the same');
  ELSE
    DBMS_OUTPUT.PUT_LINE('The two images are NOT the same');
  END IF;
EXCEPTION
  WHEN OTHERS THEN
    DBMS_OUTPUT.PUT_LINE(SQLERRM);
END;
/
```

Figure 18-11   An example that uses the DBMS_LOB package

Perspective

In this chapter, you learned how to write LOB types to a database table and how to read LOB types from a database type. In addition, you saw an example of how to use the Java API to work with LOBs on the client, and you saw an example of how to use PL/SQL to work with LOBs on the server. At this point, you have the core concepts and skills for working with LOBs.

Now, if you want to use PL/SQL to do more LOB processing on the server, you should be able to do more research on your own. In particular, you may want to learn more about the methods of the DBMS_LOB package. Keep in mind, though, that most LOB processing is done on the client with one of the APIs that Oracle provides for working with LOBs. As a result, you usually don't need to use the DBMS_LOB package to do processing on the server.

Terms

large object (LOB)
character large object (CLOB)
national character large object (NCLOB)
binary large object (BLOB)
internal LOB type
external LOB type
LOB locator
chunk size
block size
methods of a package

Exercises

1. Create a table named Scripts in the EX schema that will contain SQL scripts as BFILE data types. The first column should be a number that represents the script ID. The second column should be the BFILE value that points to the script.

2. Create a directory reference that points to the directory that contains the SQL scripts for chapter 18 (c:\murach\oracle_sql\scripts\ch18). Then, code two INSERT statements that insert the first two scripts in that directory into the table that you created in exercise 1.

3. Code a SELECT statement that gets the script IDs and BFILE values for each row in the Scripts table that you created in exercise 1.

Appendix A

How to install the software and source code for this book

Before you begin reading this book, we recommend that you install three products: (1) the Oracle Database Express Edition, (2) Oracle SQL Developer, and (3) the PDF files for the Oracle's SQL and PL/SQL documentation. All three of these products are available for free from the Oracle web site, and you can download and install them on your computer as described in this appendix.

After you install these products, we recommend that you download the source files for this book that are available from the Murach web site (www.murach.com). Then, we recommend that you run the setup_database.sql script that creates the users and tables that are used throughout this book.

When you've installed all of the products described in this appendix, you're ready to gain valuable hands-on experience by doing the exercises that are presented at the end of each chapter. To start, chapter 2 shows how to use Oracle SQL Developer to run the SQL statements against the Oracle Database. Then, as you progress through the rest of the book, you can use SQL Developer to open the SQL statements that are installed on your computer and run them against the database tables that are installed on your computer.

How to install the software from oracle.com

This topic shows how to install three software products that are available for free from the Oracle web site. As you read this topic, please keep in mind that it only covers the versions of Oracle software that are current as this book goes to press. In particular, the current version of the Express Edition of the Oracle Database is version 10g. However, version 11g of the Express Edition will probably be released in late 2008.

How to install the Oracle Database Express Edition

Oracle Database Express Edition (Oracle Database XE) is an entry-level, small-footprint database that's free to download and easy to use. Since it is designed to run on most modern computers, the Express Edition is ideal for developers who want to install it on their own computer so they can learn how to work with the Oracle Database. That's why this book assumes that you have installed the Express Edition of the Oracle Database on your computer as shown in figure A-1.

When you install the Oracle Database on your computer, you will need to specify a password for the system and sys accounts. When you do, *make sure to remember the password that you enter.* If security isn't a concern for you as you're learning, *we recommend using "system" as the password.* That way, it will be easy to remember the password. In addition, the password will match the password that's specified by the scripts that create the users and tables for this book as described in figure A-5.

All of the SQL statements presented in this book have been tested against the 10g and 11g versions of the Oracle Database. As a result, you can use the skills presented in this book to work with either version of the database. So when the Express Edition of version of 11g is released, you can install and use that version instead of 10g.

The URL for the Oracle Database

```
http://www.oracle.com/technology/software/products/database/index.html
```

The Install Wizard for the Express Edition of the Oracle Database

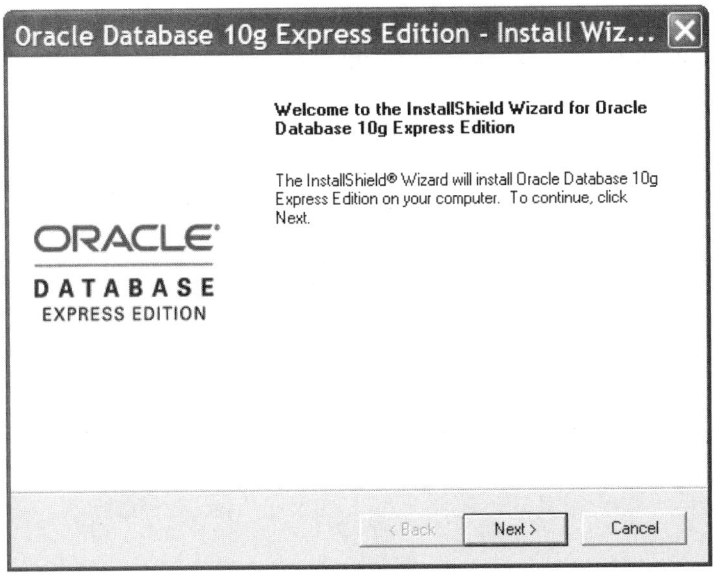

How to download and install the Express Edition of the Oracle Database

1. Find the download page for the Express Edition of the Oracle Database. This page is currently available at the URL shown above. If necessary, you can search the Internet for "Oracle 10g Express Edition download" or "Oracle 11g Express Edition download."

2. Follow the instructions provided on that web page to download the setup file to your hard drive.

3. Find the setup file on your hard drive and run it.

4. Respond to the resulting Install Wizard dialog boxes. When these dialog boxes ask you to specify a password for the system and sys accounts, *make sure to remember the password that you enter.* If security isn't a concern for you as you're learning, *we recommend using "system" as the password.*

5. When you finish the Install Wizard dialog boxes, the Database Login screen for the Oracle Database will be displayed by default. To make sure the database has been installed correctly, use the password you entered in step 4 to log in to the database as the system user.

Notes on the Express Edition for 11g

*   Since the Express Edition of Oracle Database 11g hasn't been released as of the print date for this book, this figure shows how to install Oracle Database 10g. However, when the Express Edition of Oracle Database 11g becomes available, you should be able to use a similar procedure to install it.

Figure A-1   How to install the Oracle Database Express Edition

How to install Oracle SQL Developer

In the past, it was common for developers to use a command-line tool known as SQL*Plus to work with Oracle databases. Although you can still use SQL*Plus, Oracle has recently created a free graphical tool known as Oracle SQL Developer that makes it easier to work with Oracle databases. Since SQL Developer is an ideal tool for learning how to work with Oracle, we recommend that you download and install it as described in figure A-2. Then, you can learn how to use it in chapter 2, and you can use it to work with the SQL statements that are presented throughout this book.

Unlike many software programs, SQL Developer doesn't require an install program. Instead, you install it by downloading a zip file and unzipping that file onto your hard drive. Then, you can run SQL Developer by running the exe file for the program. To make that easier, you can create a shortcut to this file and add it to your Start menu or desktop.

Although this figure assumes that you're using Microsoft Windows as your operating system, the Oracle web site provides documentation for installing SQL Developer on most modern operating systems. For example, you can get more information about installing SQL Developer on Linux or Macintosh OS X from the Oracle web site.

The URL for Oracle SQL Developer

```
http://www.oracle.com/technology/software/products/sql/index.html
```

The SQL Developer files after they have been downloaded and unzipped

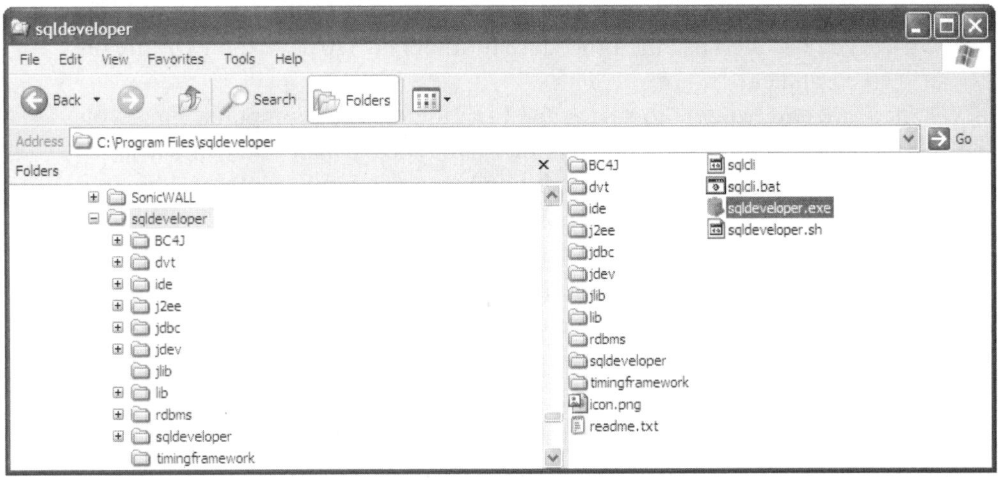

How to download and install Oracle SQL Developer

1. Find the download page for SQL Developer. This page is currently available at the URL shown above. If necessary, you can search the Internet for "Oracle SQL Developer download."

2. Follow the instructions provided on that web page to download SQL Developer. Since SQL Developer only works with certain versions of Java, we recommend that you download the version that includes the JDK whenever possible.

3. Install SQL Developer by unzipping it. On a Windows system, we recommend unzipping it into the C:\Program Files directory as shown above.

4. Once you have unzipped the zip file for SQL Developer, you can start SQL Developer by executing the sqldeveloper.exe file. To do that on a Windows system, you can use the Windows Explorer to double-click on the sqldeveloper.exe file. If you followed our recommendation in step 3, this file should be in the C:\Program Files\sqldeveloper directory as shown above.

Notes

- To make it easy to start SQL Developer, you may want to manually create a shortcut to the sqldeveloper.exe file and add it to your Start menu or desktop. Once you do that, you can start SQL Developer just like you start your other programs.

Figure A-2   How to install Oracle SQL Developer

How to install the SQL documentation

If you want to view the SQL documentation for Oracle Database, you can view it in a web browser just by navigating to the correct URL on the Oracle web site. Then, you can view this documentation as HTML pages or a PDF file. However, you can also use the procedure in figure A-3 to save the PDF file on your own computer.

There are two benefits to saving the PDF file on your computer. First, you can browse or search this documentation more quickly than you can when you're using an Internet connection. Second, you can browse or search this documentation even if you aren't connected to the Internet.

The name of the SQL documentation may vary depending on the version of Oracle that you're using. For Oracle 10g, the name of this manual is the *SQL Reference*. For Oracle 11g, the name of this manual is the *SQL Language Reference*.

How to install the PL/SQL documentation

If you want to view or install the PL/SQL documentation, you can use a procedure like the one for installing the SQL documentation. However, to find the PL/SQL documentation, you may need to click on the "Application Development" link.

Like the SQL manual, the name of the PL/SQL manual may vary depending on the version of Oracle. For Oracle 10g, the name of this manual is the *PL/SQL User's Guide and Reference*. For Oracle 11g, the name of this manual is the *PL/SQL Language Reference*.

The URL for the Oracle Database documentation

```
http://www.oracle.com/technology/documentation/index.html
```

How to download and install the SQL documentation

1. Find the download page for the Oracle Database documentation that you want to download. For example, the documentation for Oracle Database 11g Release 1 is currently available from this URL:

```
http://www.oracle.com/pls/db111/homepage
```

2. Click on the PDF link for the *SQL Reference* (10g) or *SQL Language Reference* (11g) to open the document (it may take you a while to find this link because the page has many options). Then, use the File→Save As command to save the document on your computer. This command opens the Save a Copy dialog box. There, you can save the manual in whatever directory you want and with whatever name you want.

3. To view the documentation after you have saved it to your computer, open the PDF file in the Adobe Reader. On most Windows systems, you can do that by using the Windows Explorer to double-click on the PDF file.

How to download and install the PL/SQL documentation

- Follow the same steps for downloading the *SQL User's Guide and Reference* (10g) or *SQL Language Reference* (11g). However, before step 2, you may need to click on the "Application Development" link or folder to display the page that contains the link to the PDF file.

Note

- To make it easy to start these PDF files, you can create a shortcut for the file and add it to your Start menu or desktop. Then, you can start the PDF file just like you start your other programs.

- To install the Adobe Reader, you can visit Adobe's web site (www.adobe.com) and follow the directions there for installing the Adobe Reader.

Figure A-3   How to install the Oracle Database SQL and PL/SQL manuals

How to install the software from murach.com

Once you have installed the Oracle software products, we recommend that you install the source files for this book. In addition, we recommend that you create the users and tables that are used by the examples in this book.

How to install the source files for this book

Figure A-4 shows how to install the source files for this book. These source files include SQL scripts that contain the SQL code for all of the examples in this book. These files also include SQL scripts that you can use to create the tables and users that are used by the examples in this book.

The source files for this book are contained in a self-extracting zip file (an exe file) that you can download from www.murach.com. When you download and execute this zip file, it will unzip the SQL script files for the book into the C:\murach\oracle_sql directory. Within this directory, the scripts directory contains the SQL code that's presented in this book.

The default installation directory for the source files

```
C:\murach\oracle_sql
```

How to download and install these files

1. Go to www.murach.com, and go to the page for *Murach's Oracle SQL and PL/SQL*.
2. Click the link for "FREE download of the book examples."
3. Select the "All book files" link and respond to the resulting pages and dialog boxes. This will download a setup file named osql_allfiles.exe onto your hard drive.
4. Use the Windows Explorer to find the setup file on your hard drive.
5. Double-click this file and respond to the dialog boxes that follow. If you accept the defaults, this installs the files into the directory shown above.

The source files that get installed into the oracle_sql subdirectories

Directory	Description
db_setup	The batch files and scripts that are used to create the database tables and users for the examples in this book.
scripts	The scripts for all of the examples presented in this book.

Description

*   All of the source files described in this book are in a self-extracting zip file (an exe file) that can be downloaded from www.murach.com.

Figure A-4   How to install the source files for this book

How to create the tables and users for this book

Before you can run the SQL statements presented in this book, you need to create the appropriate tables and users on the database server. The easiest way to do that is to run the setup_database.bat file described in figure A-5. When you run this file, it executes a script named setup_database.sql that creates the three users listed in this figure along with all of the appropriate tables for each user.

Keep in mind that the setup_database.bat file will work correctly only if you have specified "system" as the password for the system user when you installed Oracle Database. If that's not the case, you can edit the setup_database.bat file to replace system with the correct password before you run this file. Or, you can enter the correct username and password at the prompt that's displayed after the invalid username/password message is displayed.

Similarly, the setup_database.bat file will work correctly only if your computer is able to find the correct version of the SQL*Plus application. Most of the time, your computer will be able to automatically find this application. However, if your computer can't find the correct version of the SQL*Plus application, you can edit the setup_database.bat file and supply a complete path to the SQL*Plus application as shown in this figure. Here, the path points to the version of SQL*Plus that comes with the Express Edition of Oracle Database 10g, but you can use a similar path to point to the version of SQL*Plus that comes with other editions and versions of the Oracle Database.

How to restore the tables and users

As you work with the examples in this book, you may make changes to the users or tables that you don't intend to make. In that case, you may want to restore the users and tables to their original state so your results will match the results shown in this book. To do that, you can run the setup_database.bat file a second time. This will drop the three users described in this figure and all tables available to those users, and it will recreate these three users and all tables available to those users.

The directory that contains the setup_database.bat file

```
C:\murach\oracle_sql\db_setup
```

The users that are created

User	Description
AP	The user that corresponds with the AP (Accounts Payable) schema. This is the primary schema that's used in this book.
OM	The user that corresponds with the OM (Order Management) schema. This schema is used in some of the examples in this book.
EX	The user that corresponds with the EX (Examples) schema. This schema contains several tables that are used for short examples.

How to create the tables and users for this book

1. Use the Windows Explorer to find the setup_database.bat file in the directory shown above.
2. Double-click this file to run it. This should display a DOS window that indicates the status of the task.
3. When the bat file finishes, press any key to continue.
4. To check to see whether all the tables and users were installed correctly, open the setup_database.log file that's in the directory shown above.

How to restore the tables and users for this book

- Run the procedure for creating the tables and users again. This will drop all of the tables and users before creating them again.

How to modify the setup_database.bat file to specify the complete path for the SQL*Plus directory (not usually necessary)

```
C:\oraclexe\app\oracle\product\10.2.0\server\BIN\sqlplus
```

Description

- For the setup_database.bat file to work, it must specify the correct password for the system user. This password is set to "system" in the bat file, but you can open this bat file in a text editor and edit the password if necessary. Or, you can enter the correct username and password after an invalid username/password prompt is displayed.
- For the setup_database.bat file to work, the database server must be running. By default, the database server is automatically started when your start your system. If it isn't running on your system, you can start it as described in chapter 2.

Figure A-5   How to create and restore the tables and users for this book

Appendix B

How to install the Standard or Enterprise Edition of Oracle Database

Before you begin reading this book, we recommend that you install the Express Edition of the Oracle Database as described in appendix A. We recommend this edition of Oracle because it is ideal for developers who want to install Oracle Database on their own computers so they can learn how to work with it.

However, if you have a compelling reason to install the Standard Edition or the Enterprise Edition of the Oracle database, you can use this appendix to install one of those editions. Fortunately, if you join the Oracle Technology Network (OTN), you can download these editions of the database for evaluation purposes for free. Unfortunately, these editions take longer to download and install and require more system resources than the Express Edition.

In addition, the Standard and Enterprise Editions are designed to be accessed from across a network. As a result, they may require some additional configuration before they will work properly for standalone use on your computer. This appendix shows how to configure these editions for standalone use on Windows XP. However, for other operating systems, you may need to search the Internet to find out how to configure your system properly.

Finally, when you use the Standard or Enterprise Edition, you need to use a different procedure for creating a connection for SQL Developer than the procedure that's described in chapter 2. That's why this appendix finishes by describing how to create a connection between SQL Developer and these editions of the Oracle Database.

How to install the Standard or Enterprise Edition of Oracle Database

You can use the procedure shown in figure B-1 to install Oracle Database Standard Edition or Oracle Database Enterprise Edition. As mentioned earlier, if you join the *Oracle Technology Network* (*OTN*), you can download these editions for free for evaluation purposes. Joining the OTN is also free and only takes a few minutes.

Before you run the setup file for the database, you should consider how you intend to use the database. If you want to run the database on your computer and also access it from a client that's running on your computer, you may need to install a network adapter. With Windows XP, for example, you must install the Microsoft Loopback Adapter as described in the next figure before you continue with step 4 in this figure. On the other hand, if you want to run the database on one computer and access it from a client that's running on another computer, you might not need to install a network adapter. In that case, you can skip the next figure.

When you install Oracle Database, you will need to specify a password for the system and sys accounts. When you do, *make sure to remember the password that you enter.* If security isn't a concern for you as you're learning, *we recommend using "system" as the password.* That way, it will be easy to remember the password. In addition, the password will match the password that's specified by the scripts that create the users and tables for this book as described in figure A-5 of appendix A.

The URL for the download page for Oracle Database

`http://www.oracle.com/technology/software/products/database/index.html`

The Oracle Database Installation dialog box

How to download and install Oracle Database

1. Find the download page for the Standard Edition or Enterprise Edition of Oracle Database. This page is currently available at the URL shown above.

2. Follow the instructions provided on that web page to download the setup file to your hard drive. If you aren't already a member of the Oracle Technology Network (OTN), you may need to join the OTN.

3. If you are installing Oracle Database on a computer that isn't connected to a network, you need to install the Microsoft Loopback adapter as described in figure B-2 before you continue.

4. Find the setup file on your hard drive and run it.

5. Respond to the resulting Oracle Universal Installer dialog boxes.
   - When you specify the base location, don't use spaces in the directory name.
   - When these dialog boxes ask you to specify a password for the system and sys accounts, *make sure to remember the password that you enter.* If security isn't a concern for you as you're learning, *we recommend using "system" as the password.*

Description

- The Standard and Enterprise Editions take longer to download and install than the Express Edition. In addition, they require more system resources. As a result, we recommend using the Express Edition whenever possible.

Figure B-1   How to install the Standard or Enterprise Edition of Oracle Database

How to configure Windows XP for standalone use

Figure B-2 shows how to configure Windows XP so you can run the database on your computer and access it from a client that's also running on your computer. To make that possible, you must install the Microsoft Loopback Adapter. Although the procedure for installing this adapter is long, it only takes a few minutes to complete if everything goes smoothly. Of course, if you encounter problems, it can be time-consuming to troubleshoot the problem.

Note that the steps in part 3 of this figure are optional for some systems. As a result, I recommend that you attempt to use SQL Developer to connect to the database after you restart the computer as described in step 19 of this procedure. To do that, you can use the procedure shown in the next figure. Then, if you're able to connect successfully, you can skip the steps in part 3 of this figure. In addition, if you need to complete the steps in part 3 of this figure, you may want to enlist the help of your network administrator as these steps could affect your access to other network resources.

How to install the Microsoft Loopback Adapter on Windows XP (part 1)

Install the Loopback Adapter

1. Open the Windows Control Panel and switch to Classic View.
2. Double-click on the Add Hardware icon to start the Add Hardware wizard.
3. In the Welcome window, click the Next button.
4. In the "Is the hardware connected?" window, select the "Yes, I have already connected the hardware" option, and click the Next button.
5. In the "The following hardware is already installed on your computer" window, go to the list of installed hardware, select the "Add a new hardware device" option, and click the Next button.
6. In the "The wizard can help you install other hardware" window, select the "Install the hardware that I manually select from a list" option, and click the Next button.
7. From the list of hardware types, select the type of hardware you are installing, select the "Network adapters" option, and click the Next button.
8. In the Select Network Adapter window, make the following selections:
   - Manufacturer: Microsoft.
   - Network Adapter: Microsoft Loopback Adapter.
9. Click the Next button.
10. In the "The wizard is ready to install your hardware" window, click the Next button.
11. In the Completing the Add Hardware Wizard window, click the Finish button.

Figure B-2   How to install the Microsoft Loopback Adapter (part 1 of 3)

How to install the Microsoft Loopback Adapter on Windows XP (part 2)

Configure the Loopback Adapter

12. Open the Windows Control Panel and switch to Classic View.

13. Double-click on the Network Connections icon. This displays the Network Connections window.

14. Right-click the connection that was just created (usually named "Local Area Connection 2"), and choose the Properties command.

15. On the General tab, select the Internet Protocol (TCP/IP) item, and click the Properties button.

16. In the Properties dialog box, click "Use the following IP address" and specify an IP address and subnet mask as shown here:

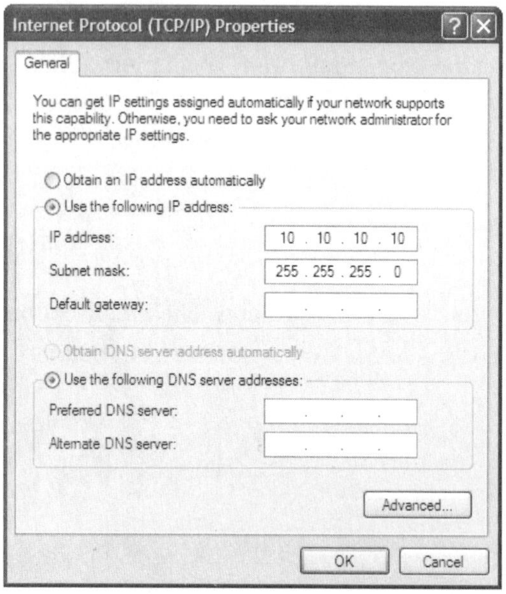

17. Click the OK button to accept the new settings.

18. Close the Network Connections window.

19. Restart the computer.

20. Start Oracle SQL Developer and attempt to create a connection to the database as described in figure B-3. If you are able to create a connection, you can skip the rest of this procedure.

Figure B-2   How to install the Microsoft Loopback Adapter (part 2 of 3)

How to install the Microsoft Loopback Adapter on Windows XP (part 3)

Check the network configuration (not always necessary)

21. Open the Windows Control Panel and switch to Classic View.

22. Double-click on the System icon to display the System Properties dialog box. Then, select the Computer Name tab. In the "Full computer name" label, make a note of the host name and the domain name. For example, the full computer name may be something like joel.murach.com. In that case, the host name is joel and the domain name is murach.com.

23. If necessary, you may be able to use the Change button to change these settings. However, you may want to contact your network administrator before you make any changes as that may affect your access to network resources.

Edit the hosts file (not always necessary)

24. Open the C:\WINDOWS\system32\drivers\etc\hosts file in a text editor.

25. Add a line after the localhost line that specifies the IP address for the Loopback Adapter and the name and domain name for the computer using this syntax:

    ```
    IP_address    host_name.domain_name    host_name
    ```

    For example:

    ```
    10.10.10.10    joel.murach.com    joel
    ```

26. Save your changes to the text file.

Figure B-2   How to install the Microsoft Loopback Adapter (part 3 of 3)

How to connect SQL Developer to the Standard or Enterprise Edition

Figure B-3 shows how to use SQL Developer to connect to the Standard or Enterprise Edition of the Oracle database. This procedure is similar to the procedure shown in figure 2-4 of chapter 2. However, instead of using a Basic connection type, you typically need to select the TNS connection type. Then, you must select the appropriate network alias, which is usually ORCL.

The SQL Developer dialog box for creating a database connection

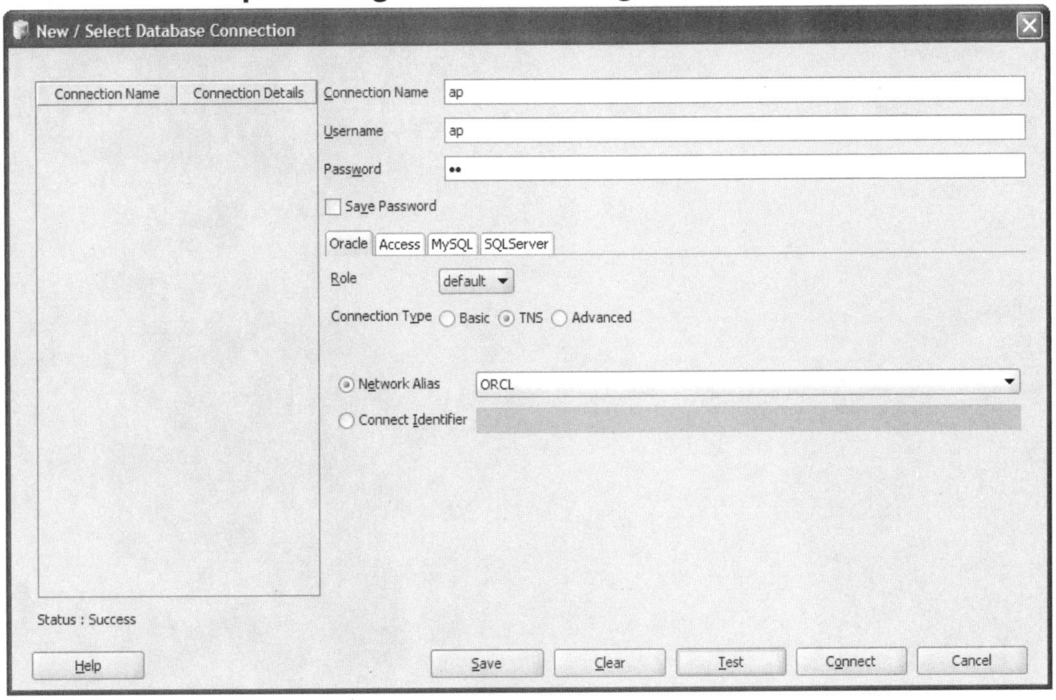

How to create a database connection

1. Start Oracle SQL Developer.
2. Right-click on the Connections node in the Connections window and select the New Connection command to display the dialog box for creating database connections.
3. Enter a connection name, username, and password for the connection.
4. Select the TNS connection type from the Connection Type list.
5. Select the network alias for the database from the Network Alias list.
6. Click the Test button to test the connection. If the connection works, a success message is displayed above the Help button.
7. Click the Save button to save the connection. When you do, the connection will be added to the dialog box and to the Connections window.

Description

*   With the Standard or Enterprise Edition of the Oracle database, the procedure for creating a database connection with SQL Developer is a little different than the procedure shown in figure 2-4 of chapter 2.

Figure B-3   How to connect SQL Developer to the Standard or Enterprise Edition

Index

ROLLBACK statement, 214, 215, 448-451
ROLLUP operator, 172, 173
 in GROUP BY clause, 272, 273
ROUND function, 92, 93, 256, 257
 with date format, 260, 261
Row, 10, 11
ROW_NUMBER function, 274, 275
Rowid data type, 230, 231
ROWID pseudo column, 230, 231
Row-level trigger, 504, 505
ROWNUM pseudo column, 98, 99
Rows
 duplicate, 96, 97
 limiting, 98, 99
RPAD function, 248-251
RR format element, 244, 245
RTRIM function, 248-251
Run Script button, 70, 71

S

Save point, 450, 451
Save SQL statements, 68, 69
SAVEPOINT statement, 450, 451
Scalar aggregate, 164, 165
Scalar function, 92, 93, 482, 483
Scalar variable, 416, 417
Scalar-valued function, 482, 483
Scale (NUMBER type), 234, 235
Scan (table), 298
Schema, 124, 125, 370, 371
 creating for this book, 212, 213
SCHEMA keyword (with trigger), 513, 514
Scientific notation, 234
Script, 332, 333, 410-413
 creating roles, 392-395
 creating users, 392-395
 running from a command line, 440, 441
Script Output tab, 70, 71
Search
 by date value, 264, 265
 by time value, 266, 267
 for null, 110, 111
Search condition, 80-82
 compound, 102, 103, 170, 171
 subquery, 180, 181
Searched CASE statement, 420, 421
Second normal form (2NF), 300, 301, 304, 305
Security
 managing, 370-403
 with SQL Developer, 398-403

SELECT clause 24, 25, 80, 81, 84-99
 with subquery, 198, 199
SELECT privilege, 374, 375, 379
SELECT statement, 21, 24, 25, 80-83
 CASE expression 268, 269
 COALESCE function, 271
 examples, 82
 floating-point numbers, 259
 GROUP BY clause, 165
 HAVING clause, 165
 NVL function, 271
 NVL2 function, 271
 subquery, 180, 181
 SUBSTR function, 253
 TRUNC function, 264, 265
Self-join, 128, 129
SEQUEL, (Structured English Query Language), 16, 17
Sequence, 22, 23, 328, 329
 altering, 330, 331
 dropping, 330, 331
 with SQL Developer, 344, 345
SERIALIZABLE keyword, 456, 457, 459
Server, 4, 5
 application, 8, 9
 database, 48, 49
 software, 6, 7
 web, 8, 9
Service
 database, 48, 49
 web, 8, 9
Session settings, 534, 535
Session time zone, 532, 533
SESSIONTIMEZONE function, 532, 533, 536, 537
Set (result), 24, 25
SET clause (UPDATE), 222, 223
SET NULL keyword (ON DELETE clause), 316, 317
Set operators, 154, 155
SET ROLE statement, 400, 401
SET SERVEROUTPUT ON command, 412-415, 518, 519
SET TRANSACTION ISOLATION LEVEL statement, 456, 457
Set up sample tables, 600, 601
SIGN function, 257
Simple CASE statement, 420, 421
Simple loop, 422, 423
Single quotes
 for string literal, 88, 89
 in alias, 86, 87
 to create literal value, 88, 89
 within string literal, 88, 89